T0355677

EMPIRE OF DOGS

Studies of the Weatherhead East Asian Institute, Columbia University

The Weatherhead East Asian Institute is Columbia University's center for research, publication, and teaching on modern and contemporary East Asia regions. The Studies of the Weatherhead East Asian Institute were inaugurated in 1962 to bring to a wider public the results of significant new research on modern and contemporary East Asia.

EMPIRE OF
DOGS

*Canines, Japan,
and the Making of the
Modern Imperial World*

AARON HERALD SKABELUND

CORNELL UNIVERSITY PRESS

Ithaca & London

Cornell University Press gratefully acknowledges support from the College of Home, Family, and Social Sciences at Brigham Young University, which assisted in the publication of this book.

Cornell University Press also expresses appreciation to the Warner Fund at the University Seminars at Columbia University for help in publication. The ideas presented in this book have benefitted from discussion in the University Seminar on Modern Japan.

First published 2011 by Cornell University Press
First paperback printing 2019

Printed in the United States of America

Library of Congress Cataloging-in-Publication Data

Skabelund, Aaron Herald.
    Empire of dogs : canines, Japan, and the making of the modern imperial world / Aaron Herald Skabelund.
        p. cm. — (Studies of the Weatherhead East Asian Institute, Columbia University)
    Includes bibliographical references and index.
    ISBN 978-0-8014-5025-9 (cloth : alk. paper)
    ISBN 978-1-5017-3588-2 (pbk. : alk. paper)
    1. Dogs—Japan—History—19th century.   2. Dogs—Japan—History—20th century. 3. Imperialism—Social aspects—Japan—History—19th century.   4. Imperialism—Social aspects—Japan—History—20th century.   I. Title.   II. Series: Studies of the Weatherhead East Asian Institute, Columbia University.
    SF422.6.J3S56   2011
    636.700952—dc22   2011013631

For my family

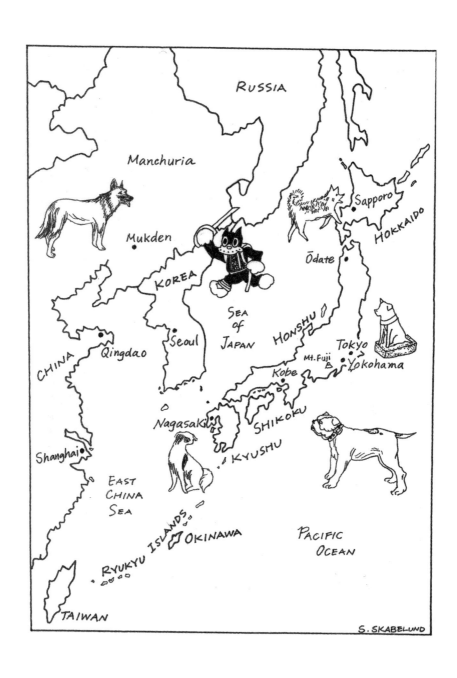

RUSSIA

Manchuria

Sapporo

HOKKAIDO

Mukden

Ōdate

KOREA

Sea
of
JAPAN

HONSHU

Tokyo

Seoul

Mt. Fuji

Yokohama

CHINA

Qingdao

Kobe

Nagasaki

SHIKOKU

Shanghai

KYUSHU

EAST
CHINA
SEA

RYUKYU ISLANDS

OKINAWA

PACIFIC
OCEAN

TAIWAN

S. SKABELUND

CONTENTS

List of Illustrations   *ix*

Acknowledgments   *xi*

Introduction: Canine Imperialism   *1*

1. The Native Dog and the Colonial Dog   *18*

2. Civilizing Canines; or, Domesticating and
   Destroying Dogs   *53*

3. Fascism's Furry Friends: The "Loyal Dog"
   Hachikō and the Creation of the "Japanese" Dog   *87*

4. Dogs of War: Mobilizing All Creatures
   Great and Small   *130*

5. A Dog's World: The Commodification
   of Contemporary Dog Keeping   *171*

Notes   *199*

Bibliography   *233*

Index   *253*

ILLUSTRATIONS

Black and White Images

1. Woodblock print of an English soldier and his dog, 1860   *32*
2. Sadahide print of Westerners accompanied by their dog in Yokohama, 1862   *33*
3. Sadahide print of foreign trader inspecting merchandise in Yokohama, 1862   *33*
4. *A Clown on a Journey* by Bigot, August 1887   *36*
5. *Canis Familiaris Japonicus*, 1842   *38*
6. "Unenlightened person," "half-enlightened person," and "enlightened person" with his hound, 1870   *58*
7. Edwin Dun, his dog, another American adviser to the Kaitakushi, and fourteen of their Japanese students, undated   *64*
8. Painting of Ainu chieftain and dog, 1790   *68*
9. Page from "Heaving a Foreigner over a Cliff for Fun, Kobe, 24 August 1897"   *74*
10. Next page from "Heaving a Foreigner over a Cliff for Fun"   *75*
11. *Massacre des Innocents* by Bigot, 1888   *78*
12. Cartoon by Honda Kinkichirō, 1880   *80*
13. Statue of Saigō Takamori and his dog in Ueno Park, Tokyo, 2003   *83*
14. Photograph of the "Loyal Dog" Hachikō, undated   *88*
15. Saitō Hirokichi, November 1931   *94*
16. Holiday greeting card from the Imperial Hotel, Tokyo, December 1933   *96*
17. The "Loyal Dog" Hachikō and Jirō, preserved by taxidermy in the National Science Museum, Tokyo, 2002   *100*
18. Cartoon by Maekawa Senpan, 1935   *110*

19. Dedication ceremony of Hachikō's statue outside of Shibuya Station, 21 April 1934   *111*
20. Early 1940s painting of grade-school girl and her "Japanese" dog   *120*
21. Textbook illustration of Momotarō and his vassal dog, 1933   *122*
22. Farewell ceremony for Hachikō's statue, 12 October 1944   *125*
23. Teachers, students, and shepherd dog in Manchuria, early 1940s   *137*
24. Military dogs on patrol with Japanese soldiers in China, 1938   *140*
25. Soeda Juichi, president of the Bank of Taiwan, with an English springer spaniel in Taipei, 1901   *142*
26. Pages from the national language primer for first-year students, 1933   *145*
27. Kongō and Nachi leading Imperial Army charge, 1939   *150*
28. Dogs marching in air defense preparedness parade, June 1941   *156*
29. Military dog exhibition, 1934   *158*
30. Girl in the Asakusa neighborhood collecting funds for army dogs, 1938   *159*
31. Teshima Tamie and her family with shepherd dog Aren Homare, August 1938   *160*
32. Statues of Japanese soldiers and army dogs at the Museum of Japanese Occupation of Manchuria in Changchun, 2007   *170*
33. Memorial to the Sakhalin huskies lost at the South Pole, 2003   *181*
34. Advertisement for Jintan health products, 1958   *183*

Color Images   *following page 144*

1. An American couple and their dog, 1860
2. "Dog Map of the World," 1933
3. Painting of Miako, June 1854
4. Painting of Shimoda, June 1854
5. Lithograph entitled *Kiken bijin* (Elite beauty), 1888
6. Norakuro launching an attack of the Regiment of Fierce Dogs, 1938
7. Cover of the monthly boys' magazine *Shōnen kurabu*, April 1944
8. Army Dog Memorial Statue on the premises of Yasukuni Shrine, 2002
9. Painting and poem from *Chūken Hachikō monogatari*, 1934
10. Advertisement for a Matsushita Electronic air-cleaning appliance, 2006

ACKNOWLEDGMENTS

Many people suppose that I wrote a book about dogs because I am a dog lover. My family kept two dogs, an English pointer Belle (1965–1979) and a German short-haired pointer Christy (1976–1978), when I was a child, but many years delivering newspapers added some ambiguity to my fondness for canines. I never thought I would write a book about dogs. Perhaps, though, I should have realized that canines were my fate. After all, I had been born in the year of the dog.

You are probably not persuaded by an explanation that is based on the Chinese zodiac. Even more important, invoking astrologic destiny would fail to recognize many generous individuals who helped make this book a reality. I am intellectually indebted foremost to Gregory Pflugfelder of Columbia University. From this book's inception through its many gestations, Greg has been a model mentor—pushing me to think big while paying attention to detail, critiquing drafts at various stages, and even welcoming my family to his mother's home and pool in northern California.

The Department of East Asian Languages and Cultures at Columbia was a wonderful place to study. Along with Greg, Carol Gluck and Henry D. Smith II offered their abiding support for this book from the beginning. In addition to this trinity, Richard Bulliet of Columbia University and Brett Walker of Montana State University offered useful suggestions. Also at Columbia, Paul Anderer, William Leach, David Lurie, Gregory Mann, Anupama Rao, and Marcia Wright provided invaluable assistance and concrete advice. I was blessed with superb colleagues at Columbia in the departments of History and East Asian Languages and Cultures, including Nicole Cohen, Tim Davis, Dennis Frost, Eric Han, Reto Hofmann, Lisa Hosokawa, Mark Jones, Joy Kim, Konrad Lawson, Ethan Mark, Laura Nietzl, Scott O'Bryan, Lee Pennington, Julie Rousseau, Kenneth Ruoff, Jordan Sand, Jack Stoneman, Lori Watt, Leila R. Wice, and Takashi Yoshida, whom I thank for their ongoing intellectual camaraderie. Special thanks go to Ian Miller, now at Harvard University, who from my first visit to Columbia has always been a superb *senpai* (senior colleague).

This book benefited immensely from the more than three years I spent in Japan between 2002 and 2006. I am thankful to Yoshida Yutaka of Hitotsubashi University for furnishing institutional affiliation during my initial research in Tokyo, and Matsuura Masataka of Hokkaido University for repeatedly securing funding that allowed me to complete my research and writing while based in Sapporo. For several years, Tsukamoto Manabu of the National Museum of Japanese History in Chiba served as an unofficial sponsor of, and inspiration for, my work. His colleague, Shinohara Toru, now the director general of the Lake Biwa Museum, was generous with his time. In the Faculty of Law at Hokkaido University, I am particularly indebted to Makabe Jun, who carefully read and checked the first two chapters, as well as Michael Burtscher, Naomi Hyunjoo Chi, Endō Ken, Furuya Jun, Kawashima Shin, Komori Teruo, Matsuo Motonori, Miyamoto Tarō, Satō Tatsu, Takada Naoko, Watari Tadasu, Michael Wood, and Yamaguchi Jirō. In the Faculty of Letters, Inoue Katsuo, Shirakizawa Asahiko, and Asai Ryōsuke lent invaluable guidance.

I am grateful to former colleagues at Nissho Electronics, especially Fukuda Takashi, Mizuno Masahiro, Michitaka Sachihiko, and the Moros (Toshio and Toshiko), for providing my family and me with a means to survive while studying in New York, even after I had left the company for Columbia, and a free place to stay at the Nissho dormitory in Koganei while in Tokyo.

During the course of my research, many people at numerous libraries, museums, and archives helped me, and I am able to thank only a few by name. Ria Koopmans-de-Bruijin and Mihoko Miki of the C. V. Starr East Asian Library at Columbia University aided me in the earliest stages. Archival materials housed by dog-fancying and animal-protection organizations proved essential to my work. I appreciate the cooperation of Barbara Kolk of the American Kennel Club, Kellie Snow of the (English) Kennel Club, Uki Terukuni of the Society for the Preservation of Japanese Dogs, Nakamoto Norio of the Japan Shepherd Association, Saitō Takeshi of the Nippon Police Dog Association, Aida Yasuhiko of the Japanese Society for the Prevention of Cruelty to Animals, and Takada Susumu of the Japan Kennel Club. I received kind assistance from New York book collector Don J. Cohn, Mori Shigeo of the East Japan Railway Company, Honma Zen'ei of Kōdansha Publishers, Mochimaru Yoriko and Nakagawa Shigeo of the Tokyo Zoological Park Society, Iwasaki Seiji and Obara Iwai of the National Science Museum, and Ono Masako of the Okinawa Prefectural Historiographical Institute. The talented staff members at the following libraries, archives, and museums made this project a pleasure: the Butler and Lehman libraries at Columbia University, the Hitotsubashi University Library, the Resource Collection for Northern Studies at Hokkaido University and the Hokkaido University Library, the Waseda University Library, the Historiographical Institute at the University of Tokyo, the Nippon Veterinary and Life Science University Library, the National Diet Library, the Tokyo Metropolitan libraries, the International Library of Children's Literature, the National Institute for Educational Policy of Japan Library, the Hokkaido Prefectural Archives, the

Tokyo Shoseki Archive, the Kaikō Archive and Yūshūkan Military and War Memorial Museum at Yasukuni Shrine, the Shochiku Ōtani Library, the Film Center of the National Museum of Modern Art, the Yokohama Archives of History, the National Showa-Memorial Museum, the Sanrizuka Museum of the Imperial Household Ranch, the Edwin Dun Memorial Museum, and the Pet Cemetery of the Jindaiji Temple. Physically tracking down all the material that now fills several filing cabinets in my office—and in the process interacting with so many wonderful people—was truly a pleasure.

From start to finish, this book has been a collaborative endeavor. Many individuals went out of their way to send me source material and leads, translate passages from German, Korean, and Chinese and check my feeble renderings of French, critique my written work, and help my research move along. Though I am surely leaving out many such benefactors, thanks go to Joseph Allen, Jacquie Atkins, Chiu Li-chen, Emi Chizuko, Sharon Domier, Holger Frank, Robert J. Gordon, Dan Hiatt, David Howell, Anthony Jenkins, Kataoka Miwako, Elizabeth Kenney, Ann Kim, Christine Kim, Li Da, John Mertz, Manuel Metzner, Setsu Murdock, Ōshima Reiko, Jaeoh Park, Boria Sax, Shimizu Isao, Shinoda Mariko, Lance van Sittert, Grant and Paul Skabelund, Uchikoshi Ayako, and Watabe Kōji. Four individuals were particularly generous in sharing their many years' worth of research: Hiroshi Sakamoto, Chiba Yū, Hayashi Masaharu, and Tanabe Yasuichi. In Tokyo, Sawabe Shōzō and Hiraiwa Yukiko kindly met with me to talk about their families' involvement with dogs.

Past teachers Peter Duus and the late Jeffrey Mass at Stanford University; J. Michael Allen, Van C. Gessel, and Lee Farnsworth at Brigham Young University; and Mr. (Glenn V.) Bird of Springville High School inspired and prepared me to become a historian. Peter Duus, in particular, supported this book from afar, tracking down, with the help of Alexander Bay, political cartoons that featured dogs from his rich collection.

Parts of this book were presented as papers at the following institutions and conferences: Columbia University; Hokkaido University; Seton Hall University; Utah Valley State College; the Western Association of Asian Studies annual meeting (2002); the Association of Asian Studies annual conference (2003); the "Animals in History: Studying the Not So Human Past" conference at the University of Cologne; the "Crime, Law, and Order in the Japanese Empire, 1895–1945" conference at the Netherlands Institute of War Documentation; the Asian Studies Conference Japan (2007); the Social and Cultural History of Children and Youth Conference (2007); the Considering Animals Conference at the University of Tasmania; and the Animals and Gender Conference at Uppsala University. I thank many individuals, including Paul Barclay, Barbara Brooks, Jonathan Burt, Thomas DuBois, Kathleen Kete, Hans Martin Krämer, Susan Pearson, Harriet Ritvo, Nigel Rothfels, and Conrad Totman, who provided useful feedback in response to those presentations. I am particularly indebted to Susan McHugh, whom I first met in Cologne and who kindly read and critiqued the entire manuscript in early 2009.

Since 2006 I have had the privilege of teaching and continuing my research and writing in the Department of History at Brigham Young University. Sincere thanks go to the members of the department's writing group, who not once but twice read different iterations of the introduction. In particular, I appreciate Kirk Larsen and Rebecca de Schweinitz, who went the second mile to critique several other chapters. Within and beyond the department, Kendall Brown, Jay Buckley, Cory Crawford, Leslie Hadfield, Arnold Green, Andrew Johns, Gail King, David McClure, Michael McKay, Scott Miller, Neil L. York, and Katherine White have been generous with their time and advice.

Opportunities to publish parts of my research helped to push this book forward. Earlier versions of this material have been published as "Can the Subaltern Bark? Imperialism, Civilization, and Canine Cultures in Nineteenth-Century Japan," in *JAPANimals: History and Culture in Japan's Animal Life*, ed. Gregory M. Pflugfelder and Brett L. Walker (Ann Arbor: Center for Japanese Studies, University of Michigan, 2005), 194–243; "Breeding Racism: The Imperial Battlefields of the 'German' Shepherd," *Society and Animals* 16, no. 4 (Winter 2008): 354–71; "Fascism's Furry Friends: Dogs, National Identity, and Racial Purity in 1930s Japan," in *The Culture of Japanese Fascism*, ed. Alan Tansman (Durham: Duke University Press, 2009), 155–82; "Rassismus züchten: Das imperiale Schlachtfeld des 'Deutschen' Schäferhunds" [Breeding racism: The imperial battlefields of the "German" shepherd], in *Tierische Geschichte: Die Beziehung von Mensch und Tier in der Kultur der Moderne* [Animal history: Human-animal relations in the culture of modernity], ed. Dorothee Brantz and Christof Mauch (Paderborn, DEU: Ferdinand Schöningh, 2009), 58–78. Other material is forthcoming as "The Teacher's Pet: Mobilizing Dogs and Children for War," in *Society, Animals, and Gender*, ed. Måns Andersson (Uppsala, SWE: Uppsala University Press). I am thankful to these editors and to anonymous manuscript readers for their thoughtful suggestions.

Research and writing were made possible through generous financial support from a number of institutions and individuals. I thank Boyd Smith of Palo Alto for generously providing "seed" money to begin my graduate work in New York, and to an anonymous individual who gave our struggling family an unexpected gift on our first Christmas at Columbia, an envelope containing a handful of very large bills in my department folder in the filing cabinet on the second floor of Kent Hall. The East Asian Languages and Cultures Department and Weatherhead East Asian Institute at Columbia University awarded me several fellowships. The Center of Historical Studies and McKeldin Library at the University of Maryland provided me with a Twentieth-Century Japan Research Award to conduct research in the Gordon W. Prange Collection. A Fulbright-Hays Doctoral Dissertation Research Abroad Fellowship from the U.S. Department of Education and a National Security Education Program David L. Boren Graduate Fellowship from the U.S. Department of Defense funded my field research in Japan. A two-year graduate research fellowship at the Faculty of Law at Hokkaido University and a postdoctoral fellowship from the Japanese Society for the Promotion of Science allowed me to complete my research and writing. Since

2006, funding from the Department of History, the College of Family, Home, and Social Sciences, and the David M. Kennedy Center for International Studies at Brigham Young University has enabled me to continue my research and writing, as well as underwriting the publication of this book. In addition, a subvention from University Seminars at Columbia University and a research grant from the College of Home, Family, and Social Sciences at Brigham Young University helped to defray the expense of including the illustrations herein.

An earlier, shorter version of this book was translated into Japanese and published in late 2009 as *Inu no teikoku: Bakumatsu Nippon kara gendai made* [Empire of dogs: Bakumatsu Nippon to the present] by Iwanami Shoten. The process of publishing the book first in Japanese contributed immensely to its development. I am thankful to my translator, Motohashi Tetsuya, and at Iwanami my editor, Yamada Mari, as well as Itō Rika, Odano Kōmei, and Yamakoshi Kazuko.

Carol Gluck arranged to have the manuscript published in Columbia University's Studies of the Weatherhead East Asian Institute monograph series. Daniel Rivero and his predecessor, Madge Huntington, at the Weatherhead East Asian Institute arranged for two anonymous reviews of the manuscript. I am grateful to both and to Roger Haydon and his superb team at Cornell University Press, whose guidance I have benefited from during the final stages of this project. A third anonymous reviewer helped me to better highlight some the manuscript's key arguments.

Finally, I appreciate Skabelund kin throughout the United States and the Todate family in Hokkaido for providing all kinds of encouragement, and most immediately to my sons Alistor and Mauri for the soccer games, swim meets, bike rides, skiing, and other satisfying "distractions," to Sora and Botan for nightly walks in Lions Park, and especially to my talented companion Seiko, who drew the map and lent her support in innumerable other ways.

Asian personal names in this book appear surname (family name) first followed by personal name except in the cases of Asian Americans or Asian scholars based in the United States who publish in English. I use the family name alone in subsequent references (e.g., Saitō for Saitō Hirokichi). I have included the appropriate diacritical marks for Japanese and Korean words and names, except for common words and place-names such as Tokyo and Hokkaido. All translations of Japanese and French are mine, unless otherwise noted.

EMPIRE OF DOGS

INTRODUCTION

CANINE IMPERIALISM

On the morning of 21 May 1925, a dog known as Hachikō walked with his master to a Tokyo railway station just as they had done each weekday morning for over a year since he had been adopted as a two-month-old puppy. That day his master, felled by a lethal stroke while at work, did not return. For the next decade, Hachikō frequented the environs of the station. In 1932, thanks to the efforts of an enterprising promoter of indigenous Japanese dogs, a national daily newspaper prominently featured a story about Hachikō, claiming that his presence at the station represented a vain wait for the return of his master. The article and subsequent media coverage led to a huge celebration of Hachikō's purported loyalty. Two years later, while the dog was still very much alive, education officials included a story about him in an official primary school textbook, which became required reading for students throughout the Japanese empire. That same year, in 1934, a coalition of dog enthusiasts, government officials, and local businessmen unveiled a life-size statue of Hachikō just outside the station, near where one still stands today. The dog, who became known as the "Loyal Dog" (Chūken) Hachikō, is famous to this day within and beyond Japan.

Many dog fans and people knowledgeable about Japan are likely familiar with this story. In many ways, it is not a unique tale. History is replete with stories of dogs who have been celebrated for their apparent fidelity. Such tales can provide a window on the history and cultural milieu that gave birth to these dogs and their stories. The story of Hachikō is revealing because he contributed, albeit unwittingly, to Japanese nationalism and imperial fascism in the 1930s. His story is but one example of how dogs, both real and some completely imagined, teamed with humans to construct imperialism in the nineteenth and twentieth centuries and how, in turn, imperialism shaped the world of dog breeding and dog keeping as we know it today. More specifically, Hachikō, as an actual dog and as a canine symbol, illustrates an extraordinary transformation of indigenous dogs in Japan that paralleled the country's dramatic shift from an object of Western imperialism during the second half of the nineteenth century to that of an imperial power by the 1930s. For several decades after Western imperial powers forced unequal

treaties on Japan in the 1850s, the country endured a period of semicolonization and was in danger of its sovereignty being even further compromised, like
its neighbor China, or being outright colonized, as was the case for much of the
rest of Asia and Africa. Instead, Japanese leaders embarked on a revolutionary
program of institutional change, industrial development, and military strengthening that enabled their country to avoid a national disaster. Fearful that its Asian
neighbors, especially Korea and China, would completely fall under the control
of the Western powers, and ambitious for parity with them, Japan consolidated
its borders and launched several minor imperialistic forays, before engaging in
two full-blown wars that netted two colonies by the early twentieth century. In
just over a generation, Japan had emerged from strategic isolation to become
a major regional geopolitical force. This dramatic metamorphosis transformed
dogs too. Most significantly, it rendered indigenous canines, disparaged by many
Westerners and even some Japanese as vicious and cowardly creatures in the
nineteenth century, into nationalized icons—like Hachikō—venerated for their
supposed loyalty, purity of breed, bravery, and valued as prized household pets
by the 1930s. In a word, Hachikō both shaped and reflected Imperial Japan.

Over the past several decades, a number of historians have begun to explore
the role of nonhuman animals in imperialism, whether used consciously in campaigns of military conquest and colonial rule or through the often unintended
consequences of "ecological imperialism."[1] Largely ignored, although just as important, was the metaphorical manipulation of beasts in imperializing and colonizing projects.[2] One of the less-noticed historical links between imperialism and
animals is a dynamic that I call "canine imperialism." In the broadest sense, this
dynamic was a configuration of relationships between colonizers and colonized,
between dogs who accompanied the colonizer from the metropole (their home
countries) and canines who lived in colonized and colonizable regions, and between different cultural modes of human interaction with dogs. More precisely,
by canine imperialism I refer both to the actions of individual dogs who accompanied Westerners and later Japanese to and in the imperial world, as well as to
a particular set of dog-keeping practices and specific breeds that materialized
chiefly in Britain and by the late nineteenth century took hold in continental
Europe and North America, thereafter spreading across the globe concurrently
with imperialism.

Canine imperialism changed both dogs and human-canine relations, although
change came at varying degrees and speeds in different geographic contexts and
some elements remained relatively constant over time. Until the advent of canine
imperialism, breeds—homogenous groups that exhibit defined physical characteristics within a species and are principally developed and maintained through
human intervention—were largely undefined and unstable. Breeding, which before the nineteenth century was not nearly as technologically sophisticated and sci-
entifically informed as it later would become, was concerned mainly with function
rather than physical appearance. Furthermore, breeders were involved only with
a relatively small portion of the canine population. As historian Keith Thomas

has written of seventeenth-century England, "Dogs differed in status because their owners did."[3] Some canines were kept as working dogs by people of lower status. The vast majority of dogs, though, interacted even less formally with people, roaming and scavenging in small packs within and along the edges of towns and cities. Similar patterns of human-canine relations existed in early modern Japan and nearly every society at the time. Millions of dogs in certain areas of the world, particularly in parts of Latin America, Asia, and Africa, still live this way.

In the context of seventeenth- and eighteenth-century Japan, historian Tsukamoto Manabu has identified what he calls a "feudal mode of dog ownership."[4] As in early modern Britain, dog ownership depended on social status, and human social divisions were applied to certain kinds of dogs. Political elites entrusted certain dogs to their followers in return for pledges of loyalty and severely restricted dog ownership by people of lower status. Wealthy commoners, who had the influence to acquire and the means to feed a dog, were sometimes able to avoid such regulations and employed dogs as guards. The vast majority of canines, who wandered the streets and outlying areas, had almost no status, but were periodically culled to be used as food for hawks kept by the ruling warrior status group. In many ways, dogs served to support the feudal hierarchy, but because of the difficulty of preventing them from moving and reproducing across social hierarchies, they could just as easily undermine the actual and symbolic power of this feudal mode of dog ownership.[5]

By the middle of the nineteenth century, what we might call a "modern mode of dog ownership" had emerged and become firmly established in Britain and was spreading to the imperial world. In contrast with past practices and those of much of the rest of the world, this new form of dog keeping defined dogs by breed, an attribute determined by physical appearance rather than function. Dog ownership became even more pervasive as middle classes expanded and came to emulate the dog-keeping practices of their social superiors. This meant treating dogs with greater attachment and, somewhat contradictorily, treating them as commodities to be bought and sold—and sometimes disposed of. By the end of the nineteenth century, many of today's breeds had been codified, and the now prevalent ways of relating to canines—such as the strict management of the movement and reproduction of certain dogs in order to preserve so-called purity of blood and breed, the display and sale of these purebred dogs as merchandise and prized pets, and the disdain for and often elimination of "mongrel" canines who roamed the streets—were routine in Britain and increasingly in other western European countries and the United States as well. These practices not only differed from the past but also from practices at that time in much of the imperial world, where dog breeds were defined by function if at all, few dogs were treated as prized pets or trusted companions, and many dogs wandered the streets and outskirts of cities and towns. As Western (and later Japanese) imperialism extended throughout the world, these new canines and practices spread along with it and aided imperial expansion and domination. In short, dogs and imperialism were inextricably intertwined and mutually sustaining.

In addition to imperialism, global commerce and warfare contributed to the cultural diffusion of certain dogs and the spread of breed codification and dog-keeping practices. Capitalist commercial networks, which often operated in conjunction with imperialism and on a similar scale, carried canines throughout the world as never before from the nineteenth century onward. The total wars of the twentieth century mobilized, manipulated, and moved dog-breeding practices and dog breeds in unprecedented ways and to unfamiliar places. By the mid-twentieth century, thanks primarily to these three global factors—imperialism, capitalism, and war—certain Western breeds and modes of dog keeping had solidified their cultural hegemony in many countries. These processes, and the manner in which dogs were practically and symbolically deployed in them, depended on time and place. Japan's experience is but one example of this global phenomenon. In some contexts, the actual and figurative uses of canines may have been less or more important than in Japan, and may have played out in different ways. Yet, dogs and dog-keeping practices crossed virtually every political border from the nineteenth century to the present. Indeed, canine imperialism, having literally circled the globe, continues to influence many societies to this day.

Japan, Land of the Dogs

Although a history of human-canine relations is global and transnational in its scope, this inquiry focuses primarily on Japan from the mid-nineteenth century onward. The dynamics of canine imperialism—both material and metaphorical—may be found most distinctly in many, albeit not absolutely all, colonial projects during the age of New Imperialism, which is to say the nineteenth and early twentieth centuries. Each empire and colonized area possesses its own history and local peculiarities, and it is necessary to be culturally specific when speaking about imperialism—or, to be more accurate, imperialisms. Furthermore, in some imperial contexts, different nonhuman animals may have figured larger than dogs. Nevertheless, the model of canine imperialism proposed here has applications nearly everywhere, if only in that dogs are everywhere and that imperialists, both Western and Japanese, had similar notions of the value of certain dogs breeds and ways of dog keeping wherever they went.

But why Japan? After all, Japan was one of only a few areas of the world that successfully avoided becoming fully colonized by the Western powers, and it was the only non-Western country to become a full-fledged imperial power in the twentieth century.[6] In many ways, its modern history is an anomaly. But because of its rapid and distinctive shift from an object to a subject of imperialism, Japan offers multiple angles to examine the different sides of canine imperialism, and its history illustrates patterns observable in varying inflections elsewhere. By the late nineteenth century, European and American imperial and colonial dominion extended nearly everywhere—including Japan, in the form of political ideologies, international power, and notions of Western progress—and opinions about dog keeping and dog breeding were part of its cultural hegemony. Even though

Westerners did not turn Japan into a colony, the country's territorial sovereignty was violated under the treaty-port system that took shape in the 1850s and that survived nearly until the end of the century. Foreigners never directly dictated policy within Japan in the second half of the nineteenth century, yet Europeans and Americans—as diplomats, businessmen, government advisers, and privileged residents in treaty ports—exerted great political, social, and cultural influence on the country. The primary goal of the Japanese government's foreign and domestic policies for a half-century, and the principal reason that it hired foreign advisers, was to escape semicolonial status and regain full sovereignty by persuading the Western powers to revise unequal diplomatic treaties they had imposed on the country. To that end, Japanese leaders of the Meiji period (1868–1912) embarked on a policy of Westernization under the twin slogans of "civilization and enlightenment" (*bunmei kaika*) and "rich country, strong army" (*fukoku kyōhei*), which were already making an indelible impact on daily life in the archipelago as early as the 1870s.

Even as its own autonomy remained compromised, Japan began to encroach upon the sovereignty of its weaker Asian neighbors and quickly became an imperial power with colonies of its own. The process was fast and imitative, although it built on earlier instances of expansion into peripheral islands. Within a few decades of the country's loss of full sovereignty in the early 1850s, the Meiji government consolidated its imperial domination of these outlying islands and came to emulate Western powers by threatening surrounding states using military, diplomatic, and economic means. Japanese leaders were motivated by an economic appetite for raw materials and markets and by a strategic ambition to bolster the nation's security against further encroachment by Western countries, yet they were also driven by nationalist desires for parity with those same Western powers. As the pairing of the official slogans "civilization and enlightenment" and "rich country, strong army" suggests, a colonial empire, won through military might and economic self-sufficiency, was the ultimate proof of civilization in the nineteenth- and early twentieth-century imperial world. Almost immediately after overthrowing the Tokugawa shogunate in 1868, the Meiji regime accelerated the colonization of Ezo in the north, which it renamed Hokkaido in 1869, and formally incorporated the Ryukyu Islands in the south, which it renamed Okinawa in 1879. Beginning with its acquisition of the island of Taiwan after defeating Qing China in 1895, Japan gradually built an expansive maritime and continental empire that came to rival that of the Western imperial powers and ultimately led to confrontation with them during the Asia-Pacific War from 1931 to 1945. In 1952 Japan emerged from a devastating defeat and a seven-year occupation by the United States as a poor and weak country. Nevertheless, within a few decades it had once again become a leading economic power, a position that it still holds.

As the story of Hachikō highlights, Japan's tremendous geopolitical and economic rise from the mid-nineteenth century was mirrored by a transformation of its canine population. As in other imperial contexts, indigenous canines were disparaged by Western observers as well as by many Japanese during the decades of semicolonization, and in many cases they were physically eliminated. During those same years, purebred Western breeds achieved tremendous popularity and widespread acceptance in Japan, surpassing what other imperial areas experienced. Perhaps because Japan was able to avoid becoming a de jure colony like India or the extended semicolonial humiliation of China, its people were able to adapt certain Western cultural forms, such as dog keeping, on their own terms, and surely such adaptability helped Japan escape the fate of almost all of the non-Western world. And, in turn, such adaptations helped Japan meet the threat of Western imperialism. As Japan became a major imperial power in its own right during the early twentieth century, its once ridiculed indigenous dogs were nationalized and recognized as legitimate codified breeds in the 1930s. Thus, Japan's complex relationship with imperialism, in both dovetailing with and diverging from the experiences of other societies, makes it a fascinating lens through which to examine the actual and metaphorical roles of canines in the modern world.

Why Dogs?

Just as we must ask why Japan, we also must ask why dogs? One of the reasons, as zoologist James Serpell has written, is that no animal, with the possible exception of apes, comes as close to people in affective and symbolic terms, nor does any make a stronger claim to be treated as human.[7] The dynamics and the degree of the relationship between *Homo sapiens* and *Canis familiaris* vary according to time and place, but, in general, domestic dogs, thanks to their longstanding and close ecological connection with people, occupy a distinctive and liminal space between human culture and the rest of the animal world. Dogs have long performed valuable roles for humans as guards, herders, hunters, and pet companions. In the last century and a half the specialized tasks that canines fulfill for people, such as guiding the blind, have multiplied even further. Such labor often requires a high level of intelligence and even some degree of judgment. It is perhaps not surprising given these relationships that many people regard dogs as quasi-human.

Indeed, canines are boundary crossers and boundary blurrers. Perhaps more than any other animal, dogs pass between domestication and wildness, and within and beyond the control of people. This physical mobility creates symbolic ambiguity, positioning canines between culture and nature. This condition underscores how domesticity/wildness as well as culture/nature are overlapping rather than exclusive categories. Because of the attachment of dogs to humans and vice versa in many societies, dogs are one of the few types of nonhuman animal allowed to move freely in and out of human dwellings and, though in an increasingly more restricted fashion, to wander inside and outside of human communities. Close canine contact with people has the potential of fluctuating between two extremes: from a trusted companion, who might even share a master's bed, to a hungry predator or roaming vagabond, who may bite or attack people or scavenge for food from human sources, even if that source might be a human corpse.

Dogs are not just physically mobile; they may also be the most physically malleable animal. Over the course of thousands of years and with greater precision, control, and speed, especially during the last two centuries, breeders have created more corporal variation among dogs than among any other species; think of the St. Bernard and the Chihuahua, both members of the *Canidae* family. Such fantastic physical plasticity lends itself to a metaphorical malleability used to differentiate among breeds, rank individuals within breeds, and project other human values onto both breeds and individual dogs.

Another reason why dogs warrant historical attention is their role as brokers in human interactions. Dogs traverse environmental boundaries and have long crisscrossed international and domestic political and cultural borders, as well as various divisions and demarcations of culture. Their relative smallness, docility, fecundity, and low cost have made them comparatively easy to transport and widely available. Canines, as assistants to people in gaining and maintaining power, often serve as intermediaries between opposing human groups both at home and in foreign lands. Since ancient times, people have given dogs as gifts and barter, and the diffusion of canines as merchandise across national borders increased dramatically during the last two centuries of imperialism and globalization. In short, dogs are pervasive and conspicuous in the formation and maintenance of human systems of political power and socioeconomic status.

Together, intimacy, mobility, and the variability of human/canine interactions contribute to the immense symbolic pliability of dogs. Canine behavior, as in a dog following a keeper's command, can be interpreted in completely opposite ways, as either venerable loyalty or shameful servility.[8] As creatures of metaphor, dogs oscillate between high-status animals and low-status people. They are said simultaneously to possess admirable traits (such as bravery) that make them akin to humans and despicable attributes (such as filth) that render them unalterably inferior—or in the minds of some, like "Other" humans.

In actual and in symbolic terms, dog keeping and certain social, and especially imperial, relationships are analogous. Asymmetrical power relationships of master and subject provide the logic for the interaction of dog keeper and pet, just as they link the colonizer and colonized government officials and populace, teacher and student, rich and poor, parent and child. The chief concern of the masters in each of these hierarchical structures is, like that of a dog keeper, that their subjects, as unpredictable as they might be, will prove loyal and useful. Conversely, masters' primary fear is that dependable underlings might rise against them. This dynamic explains, in part, why rabies was, and remains, so frightening to human sensibilities: the trusted canine companion lethally biting its own master invokes ominous fears. It also helps illuminate modern authorities' tendency to revile street dogs, wild dogs, and feral dogs (once-tame canines who have reverted to the wild); it is all too easy to regard such canines as domesticated dogs who have become degenerate and, while still relying on humans for sustenance through scavenging, have ungratefully turned their backs on their benefactors and joined other canines such as wolves in their hostility toward people. They therefore have been trusted neither by "civilized" people nor by the "better" canine classes. The unstable power relations inherent both in dog keeping and in human social hierarchies provide at least one of the reasons why dogs appear as a ubiquitous trope in imperial discourses.

The Vocabulary of Canine Imperialism

The language of empire bred the vocabulary of the modern canine world. As in the imperial realm, ideas of *race, civilization*, and *loyalty* became increasingly pervasive and persuasive in the world of dogs. These ideas were also intertwined with other notions that have defined the recent past, such as *nationality, class*, and *gender*. Although these expressions were translated and transformed as they crossed national, cultural, and linguistic borders, the essential ideas they represented remained fairly consistent, even as their emphases shifted in different spatial and temporal contexts.

Race, the categorization of human beings into groups according to distinctive physical characteristics transmitted by descent, and racism, the application of these assumptions into practices designed to control, exclude, or eliminate other "racial" groups, permeated the nineteenth-century imperial world. In the West, people had been constructing hierarchies based on evolving notions of race since at least the eighteenth century. By the end of the nineteenth century, many people considered race to be a central part of individual and group identity, and used science, including concepts derived from animal husbandry, to sanction unequal political and social relations in the imperial world. Though now largely mutually exclusive in their linguistic deployment, race, breed, and blood acted once as synonyms and were often used interchangeably to refer to both humans and other animals. People routinely spoke of races of dogs, savage breeds of people, and pure-blooded humans. From the late nineteenth century, the science of animal breeding was influenced by and, in turn, helped to shape social Darwinist thought and eugenic ideas, and contributed to heightened national anxieties about preserving and improving the "racial hygiene" of both humans and beasts.

The most fundamental manipulation of canines and other domesticated animals (and for that matter, humans) in the modern era is part and parcel of what became their core identity: whether an individual (dog or person) is of mixed or pure blood and, if the latter, what is their breed (or race). Canines deemed to be purebred—that is, an animal whose ancestors were supposed to have conformed to breeding standards established later, and who corresponded in physical appearance and health to prescribed criteria—were imagined as possessing purity of blood. Dogs, and people, who did not adhere to these often arbitrary and sometimes shifting racial breeding standards were disparaged as mongrels of mixed (or half) breed, blood, or caste. The ability to mold the bodies of animals rapidly and radically through strict control over reproduction, the elimination of certain offspring, and the recording of bloodlines in pedigrees bolstered these illusions. Anthropologist John Borneman has observed that "breed, like race, is confused with and often considered a matter of genetics and biology, and not culture, and since biology is considered the ultimate arbiter of phenomenological disputes, the naturalness of this social order is never questioned."[9] It is precisely for this reason that people commonly take for granted that a dog is of this or that breed, or of mixed breed. But just as the creation of animal breeds and human races is interrelated and interwoven, they are both contingent, constantly changing, culturally constructed categories that are inextricably interconnected to state formation, class structures, and national identities.[10]

The concept of "civilization" came to dominate Western thinking during the eighteenth and nineteenth centuries. The perspective of history that it presented was linear, developmental, and progressive. Languages, plant and animal species, human nations and races, and classes of people within particular societies were all said to pass at unequal speeds through a series of stages, which were often referred to, in ascending order of approval, as savagery, barbarism, and civilization. Like dogs and dog keeping, civilizationist discourses spread across the globe with imperialism. Many people in the nineteenth and early twentieth century used the prevailing rhetoric to justify imperialism and colonialism as civilizing projects, even as they employed such idioms to differentiate between the human and nonhuman world, and among humans and animals. In general, humans and other animals who hailed from the metropole were regarded as civilized, while those from imperialized areas were deemed savage. The degree to which a human or canine was civilized depended on race/breed and nationality, and was often influenced by other categories such as class and gender (usually of the human rather than the dog) within a common race/breed or national group. Although earlier notions of civilization were increasingly challenged in the twentieth century, successive conceptual outlooks such as "modernity" and "development" have not completely abandoned some of civilizationist ideology's underlying assumptions.

Like race and civilization, loyalty, that is to say, a sense of duty or devoted attachment to something or someone, became tightly linked to national identity and gained widespread currency in many nation-states in the nineteenth century. This is how loyalty evolved in Japan. For a millennium, Japanese and other East Asians influenced by Confucian thought venerated filial piety and devotion to social and political superiors. Such loyalties were familial and personal, but far from absolute, as highlighted by times of instability, such as Japan's Warring States period (1467–1568), when samurai vassals regularly betrayed their overlords as soon as an opportunity presented itself. During the subsequent Tokugawa period (1600–1868), political elites in Japan increasingly valorized the idea of individual fidelity in order to bolster feudal ties between lords and vassals and keep dominion over peasants and other commoners, all with the aim of maintaining the political status quo even as economic changes were severely undermining the social structure. Over time, loyalty gradually became impersonal and organizational, attached to regional domain rather than to a leader.[11] Only from the mid-nineteenth century, however, would loyalty be nationalized, which is to say, directed almost exclusively to the nation and expected collectively of all national subjects or citizens. With the rise of the nation-state, government and private spokespersons came to invoke loyalty and patriotism as a means of enhancing civil morality, heightening nationalistic solidarity with the emperor at the apex, and strengthening ideological, political, and social controls among the country's populace.

In order to mobilize imperial subjects for economic growth, empire, and war—and fend off Western imperialism—Japanese leaders encouraged national and ethnic allegiance to gain and maintain control over the masses. Sometimes such notions were projected onto nonhuman animals. In the case of dogs, many enthusiasts came to claim that certain canines, whether individually or of an entire breed, were endowed with exceptional characteristics, such as loyalty and bravery. Such declarations were much more strident and frequent when they were being made about a breed that supposedly embodied the particular virtues of a national race. In such cases, the stakes that particular dogs were man's—or at least a nation's—best friend seem to have been particularly high.

Loyalty, civilization, and race are closely related, though they may not appear to be at first glance. A semantic examination helps to parse how these concepts are linked. To *civilize* means to bring out of a primitive or uneducated state of nature, to make more *cultured* and *well-bred*, and more *human(e)*, to use more recent parlance. To become civilized, a subject must be teachable, pliable, and willing to adhere to order, training, and discipline. The word *culture*, too, has a history related to animal husbandry, or the development, improvement, and raising of certain animals.

Another synonym of the verb "to civilize" is to *domesticate*, which now usually refers to the process of taming nonhuman creatures through measures such as modifying their growth or traits by regulating their food, protecting them from enemies, and selectively breeding them so the animal species becomes dependent on humans for their survival. In former times, the notion of domestication could refer to similar efforts to shape the conduct and character of other humans. It is a derivative of *domestic*, which is defined as "pertaining to the home, household, or family." The term can refer to a tamed domestic animal or more frequently a household *domestic* servant, who is almost always of a different race or lower class than the master of the home. Both domestic servants and domesticated animals, especially pets, are subject to, dependent on, and required to be loyal to the master. To be included as a "member" of the family, both animal and servant are expected to attain and maintain civilized behavior, which in the nineteenth century was considered by some to be the exclusive domain of pure-blooded races or breeds. In the past, *domestication* might be used interchangeably with *civilization* to denote the process of subjugating other humans.

In addition to domestication, the verb *civilize* came in some contexts to be equated in meaning with *colonize*, to settle or people regions that colonizers claim to be uninhabited by other humans or, at least in their eyes, devoid of civilized beings. Some nineteenth-century colonizers asserted that nothing useful could be done with certain races whose inferiority was so profound and permanent that they were incapable of being civilized. For colonizers, the taming or domestication of such savages was not worth the trouble.

Each of these terms—*civilize, domesticate, colonize*—implies a process of subjection for the purpose of creating hierarchical relationships, which are contingent on fear, manipulation, dependency, or loyalty, and often some combination of the four. To be "uncivilized" or "mongrel" suggests that a person or other animal is savage, barbaric, or closer to nature, whether because of race, nationality, class, or gender, or through racial, physical, or moral degeneration. Until fairly recently, loyalty was often conceived as a quality attainable only by people or other animals who were civilized, cultured, and pure-blooded, while the savage, the barbarian, or the half-breed mongrel was thought to lack the ability or the will to be obedient to commitments or obligations. In sum, civilization, race, and loyalty dogged one another in their semantic operations and had become a familiar part of imperial rhetoric by the late nineteenth century.

In the Japanese archipelago, as elsewhere, people often spoke about dogs and people with this imperial vocabulary. In medieval and early modern times, the characterization of canines as faithful, cultured, and well-bred was usually restricted to certain categories of dogs, often large hounds, who were retained by people of high status, such as warriors. With the advent of the modern nation-state, however, people began to create and identify certain dog breeds with the nation and to claim that these breeds symbolically embodied the desiderata of civilization, race, and loyalty.

Whose Empire?

It is essential to remember that there were multiple canine imperialisms, or to put it another way, not just one empire of dogs, but various empires of dogs. This book deals in detail with the Japanese imperialist experience. At the same time, it seeks to shed light on other different forms of imperialism, including imperialism as it manifested itself in the West. The latter, of course, is not a uniform phenomenon but is divisible according to its many national practitioners, such as British imperialism, American imperialism, and French imperialism. Historically, imperialism has also differed according to where and when it was applied. Japanese imperialism, which stretched across geographic and cultural spaces from Micronesia to Manchuria, from the Bonin Islands to Burma, and over a time period lasting from the nineteenth century (and earlier) to 1945, was not monolithic in its application, nor were local responses to foreign rule and influence identical across time and space. Likewise, imperial dominion can take various forms to create, for example, classic, semicolonial, internal, wartime, neocolonial, economic, and cultural imperialism. Human-canine interactions, moreover, differed over time and among societies. The exact ways in which imperialists deployed dogs—both real and imagined—depended on these and other factors.

A consideration of nonhuman animals complicates matters even further. As a result of domestication, we are accustomed to thinking people have colonized canines by making them underlings largely submissive to their will. But it may well be that dogs have done some colonizing of their own. As science journalist

Michael Pollan has suggested, although the term "domesticated species" insinuates that people are in charge, domestication is not necessarily "something we do to other species." It may instead be "something certain plants and animals have done to us, a clever evolutionary strategy for advancing their own interests."[12] Biologists Raymond and Lorna Coppinger and popular science writer Stephen Budiansky, who are all unabashed dog lovers, go so far as to call canines "biological freeloaders" and manipulative "social parasites." They note, as Budiansky puts it, that while the dog is a "brilliant evolutionary success," its wild ancestor, the wolf, is practically extinct.[13] Dogs, they assert, have taken advantage of human sentimentality to thrive and create a relationship that canines cannot live without and many humans think they cannot live without. Unlike almost all other domesticated animals except perhaps cats, the very fact that human civilization would survive almost without a hitch if dogs abruptly disappeared, but dogs would most certainly not if humans suddenly went extinct, may indicate that our relationship is more the making of and to the practical benefit of canines. From this perspective, canine imperialism, too, arguably constitutes an empire of and by dogs.

But labeling dogs as colonizers probably goes too far. Dogs may walk people rather than the other way around, yet when it comes to imperialism, which is a far more complicated phenomenon, displacing agency and responsibility from humans to dogs seems not only illogical but immoral. It is more accurate to argue that, like, or perhaps even more than, some other animal and plant species that have adapted to humans, many (but not all) canines have forged what can be a mutually beneficial relationship with people. Consequently, imperialism must be seen as an empire of, and by, humans and dogs acting together, though not as equal partners.

Humans and dogs have not just acted together, they have evolved together. As with certain other species, certainly changes in human and dogs took place over hundreds of thousands of years and the evolution of each was influenced by their interaction with the other.[14] But domestication—ours and theirs—and evolution were not just processes that took place deep in the past. They are ongoing and codependent. The impact on dogs in the last century and a half through intensive breeding practices and training regimes, which have selected and bred for certain appearances and deportment, have rapidly and drastically reshaped the bodies and behaviors of dogs. In turn, human behaviors, if not bodies, have also been influenced by these recent interactions. Though it by no means reveals all the ways, both for good and ill, that people and canines have interacted, the history of imperialism since the mid-nineteenth century is a fundamental part of the story of our two species' recent relationship.

Such assertions once again do not make canines primarily or even equally responsible for imperialism, but they do acknowledge their contribution to the process of expansion. Notions of national identity, hierarchy, race, civilization, and loyalty were intertwined with dog-keeping practices and theories and were exported to and developed in the imperial world, all of which reinforced the application of these same concepts to human societies, especially in intercultural encounters lacking geopolitical parity. Dogs were not merely objects of these practices and theories. Their individual and collective actions and behavior, which were influenced by intensive breeding and training regimes but not entirely controlled by humans, bolstered (and sometimes undermined) actual practices and rhetoric used to gain and maintain imperial dominion.

In this sense, the contribution of dogs to imperialism extends beyond that of other "creatures of empire," to use Virginia DeJohn Anderson's felicitous term for the livestock that was bred in seventeenth-century British colonies in New England, Virginia, and Maryland. Anderson argues that livestock "occupied land in advance of English settlers, forcing native peoples who stood in their way either to fend off the animals as best they could or else to move on."[15] Furthermore, Anderson makes the important assertion that "animals not only produced changes in the land but also in the hearts and minds and behavior of the peoples who dealt with them," and that the "animals were never wholly under human control."[16] Anderson's analysis is useful for thinking about "dogs of empire." Like cattle, canines acted as an "advance guard" to expansion and as "agents of empire." Unlike livestock, they produced few changes to the land, and because their flesh did not have the economic value of beef, finding open land for them to graze on was not a motive for expansion. Another difference is also significant: there was neither a concerted nor even a conscious effort on the part of the English colonists to use livestock as "creatures of empire." The process was in many ways largely unintended. By contrast, imperializers often consciously, albeit inconsistently, employed dogs physically and often metaphorically to further their aims of expansion and domination of other peoples.

Dogs are not cattle. Indeed, they are unlike any other domesticated creature in their abilities and relationship with humans. Because many of the canines who accompanied colonizers around the world were highly trained as military, police, and guard dogs to perform in ways that would bolster imperial rule, and because dogs are highly intelligent and physically and emotionally much more connected to their keepers than other animals, they could, and at times did, act as deliberate agents of empire, when, and sometimes even when not, following human commands. At the same time, the symbolic power of dogs, which was linked always in some way to their concrete actions, was significantly more pliable and powerful than that of other creatures of empire.

Can the Subaltern Bark?

A provocative essay by the critical theorist Gayatri Chakravorty Spivak—"Can the Subaltern Speak?"—is extremely useful in thinking about the relationship of history, culture, and animals.[17] In this celebrated piece, Spivak asks whether it is possible to hear the voice of the subaltern, meaning those with the least access to power among the colonized, such as women and the poor. The subaltern has almost never left documents, nor do they appear often in historical sources, which are dominated by the voices of colonizing and colonized elites, so that they seem inaudible if not voiceless. Rephrasing Spivak's question so as to ask "Can the Subaltern Bark?" is not meant to offend anyone; rather the rewording can be illuminating in several ways.

First, recasting Spivak's query highlights the tremendous transformation of certain dogs in the imperial world from the nineteenth century to the present, especially in Japan but in other colonial contexts as well. This change transformed previously denigrated indigenous dogs into celebrated national symbols like Hachikō. That remarkable metamorphosis forms the backbone of this historical narrative.

The second consideration is epistemological. Why, until fairly recently, have researchers in the social sciences and the humanities—the etymology of the term, "humanities," is of course significant—directed their attention almost entirely to human affairs, relegating the study of the nonhuman world to the natural sciences? Why has it long been thought that only people have history and culture? What if nonhumans do too? Is it possible for historians to hear the bark of the dog of yesteryear, and what might be learned about the past—and present—through this attempt?

In the last couple of decades or so an increasing number of scholars have begun to probe the age-old record of human-animal relations. The subject exhibits such vibrancy that some participants and observers have declared it a new area of study or subfield, calling for further work in "animal studies" or "animal history." Although the interest in nonhuman animals is laudable, the staking out of new territory—to use a canine or imperial metaphor—is beset by obstacles. Although a dog barking makes a sound whether a human hears it or not, there are, as historian Erica Fudge has pointed out, enormously complex problems in writing an authentic history of animals.[18] While some owners may think otherwise, scientists have yet to discover a dog, or any other animal, who can talk on an equal basis with people. Canines—as well as some other animals—do, though, seem to communicate just fine among themselves and actively communicate with humans through what, in the case of dogs, psychologist Stanley Coren has called "doggish" and "doggerel."[19] Unfortunately, such communication is of little use to historians. Our subject is the past, and thus most canine historical subjects have long since been silenced by death. Even if they were still around, conducting oral history interviews with them would quickly remind of us our mutual inability to make ourselves fully understood and to fully understand them.[20]

Does this mean that, in the end, the subaltern cannot bark, or that at least there is no way to hear that bark? No, because in fact the subaltern can bark and we can hear the echoes of that barking at least in the case of certain dogs of yesteryear. Here lies the third reason why rephrasing Spivak's question is instructive. It is imperative to remember that the difficulties of attempting to recover the history of animals are similar to those faced in trying to retrieve the largely silent and invisible past of certain subaltern peoples.[21] Just as historians should not give up trying to recover the voices and experiences of such people, we should not be resigned to the idea that animals have never been able to and will never be able to "speak," even if that may seem like a logical conclusion. Is it perhaps only possible to write a history of human representations of human-animal interactions rather than human-animal history informed by sources from both sides of the relationship? That is essentially what a number of historians have concluded. Harriet Ritvo, for example, in her pioneering book *The Animal Estate: The English and Other Creatures in the Victorian Age* argues that animals cannot contest how they are used metaphorically, just as they are largely unable to resist how they are used materially. She contends that the actual "biological nature [of animals] and the practical purposes to which their owners dedicated them turned out to be *not* very restrictive of human understanding or interpretation." In other words, Victorian English and other people could rhetorically deploy animals however they pleased, because, unlike other humans who might offer alternative interpretations and evidence, animals "never talk back."[22]

While recognizing the immense difficulties of writing a history informed by the perspective of animals and their seeming inability to contest how they are represented, at least two modern technologies allow some animals who have lived in the last century or so to make themselves heard, however faintly. These technologies, photography—both still and motion picture—and taxidermy, produce visual sources that allow animals to contribute to and constrain human discourses about them. Hilda Keane and Jonathan Burt have argued that images of animals increased the literal and metaphorical visibility of animals and led to a shift in the status of animals in some societies.[23] Images of actual, physical animals do more, though, than simply contribute to a more humane treatment of animals. Rather, film and taxidermic animals help shape the possibilities of human discourse about them, especially about individual celebrity animals, whose fame is in part the creation of those same modern technologies.

The resulting source materials—photographic images and stuffed bodies that provide physical, concrete evidence of animals—impose certain constraints on the human discussions that otherwise can freely restructure and recreate animals with almost no regard for reality. Although the vocal utterances and actions of animals are extremely difficult to comprehend and are wide open to interpretation, the corporal presence of animals, whether recorded on film or stuffed, makes animals less than completely malleable to human manipulation. Such images and objects are produced primarily by humans, yet more than other sources, they enable animals to play a more direct, more collaborative role in their creation. Textual representations, along with conventional visual media, such as painting and statuary, can easily represent animals in ways that are but a figment of the human imagination, almost entirely divorced from their purported subjects' reality. Texts therefore do not offer the animal depicted the potential to exercise a say in shaping how the image is interpreted. In contrast, motion picture and still photography as well as taxidermy do so, albeit in a limited way. Even though photographic images are often perceived vernacularly as offering a view of what "actually" happened, and taxidermy, as Donna Haraway has observed, is sometimes regarded as a "servant of the 'real,'" photographers can undoubtedly manipulate images of animals on film in a variety of ways and taxidermists can reshape stuffed animals.[24] Yet, compared with other sources, photographic representations and taxidermic creations are far more dependent on the actual physical existence of real animals. As a result, they enable animals to go beyond being merely passive objects of discourse, serving in effect as active coproducers in shaping human discussions about them.

This book, which draws from an array of eclectic sources—from transcripts of radio broadcasts to public statuary, from songs to scientific treatises, from woodblock prints to interviews (with humans... not dogs)—relies heavily on visual evidence. It takes cultural artifacts, such as photographs and taxidermic objects, as seriously as it does written sources. The images included are not mere decorative and distracting illustrations; rather, they are carefully analyzed because they operate as key evidence in support of the book's arguments. Many of the figures demonstrate how animals through their photographically "captured" and taxidermically "preserved" bodies contributed to rhetorical reconstructions and material recreations of themselves and their actions. Photographed and stuffed bodies of animals allow them, in effect, to talk back, showing how they can still influence human discussions about the reality that both of us share.

Dogs—Both Real and Imagined

Listening to—by looking at—canines and other sentient creatures provides a way to rethink cultures, whether they are human or otherwise. A consideration of nonhuman animals can expose how humans, and especially those with power and wealth, deploy other creatures to define, regulate, and enforce political and social boundaries between themselves and other members of their own species. People often define what it means to be human in relation to the nonhuman, so that animals have served as apt metaphors with which to assert the humanity and civilized nature of one's own group and the animality and barbaric character of "Others." Because canines have lived everywhere, among all groups of people, they have provided a powerful (if generally unnoticed) way to regulate human society, particularly in the imperial world, where notions of social, racial, and Darwinian species hierarchy became central to the ideological mechanisms of imperial control. Nonhuman species became a useful symbolic tool for achieving imperializing national states' ends and the objectives of various groups that set out to determine an identity for themselves and, perhaps even more importantly, for "Others." My invocation of Spivak's famous query is meant to highlight precisely these parallels between colonial and canine discourses.

Many years ago the anthropologist Claude Lévi-Strauss observed that animals are good not only to eat but also to think with.[25] True indeed, but just as it is important to comprehend why we are choosing to eat (or not to eat) the flesh of sentient beings and the processes by which animal protein has arrived on our plates, it is essential to remember that animals are not just metaphors and symbols. A symbolic animal is only a symbol if it relates in a symbolic way to the real world, so actual dogs mattered and still matter. The practical deployment of dogs as hunters, guards, and pets, after all, has had tangible consequences. Although some of the dogs who appear in this book are completely fictional, and even if some of the actions of those canines who actually existed may have been completely fabricated by humans, most of the descriptions of dogs and their deeds recorded here are not based on disembodied fantasy. Rather, like other animal symbols, canine metaphors acquired their figurative power from the reality of individual dogs and specific dog breeds who interact with humans in specific ways. We cannot just view animals as mirrors or metaphors. To leave the matter there allows the symbolic significance of their existence to overshadow their tangible interactions with people. Although it is difficult to transcend the realm of representation and reconstruct the past in such a way that we can hear the actual woof or yap of past dogs, in this book I attempt to highlight the concrete uses of dogs, to talk about actual dogs, and to show how their actions were related to their metaphorical deployment in discussions about nation, race, class, and gender in the imperial and postcolonial world.

Dogs can bark, in fact they do so with some frequency, but they and other animals have rarely been listened to or taken seriously, at least by us humans. Although we may have drastically manipulated the physical appearance and behavior of canines, and we often interpret their actions and utterances according to human whims, the control that people exercise over other animal species is hardly absolute. For that reason, as well as for others, humans are far from being the only historical and cultural actors of consequence. A multitude of characters fill and shape our world, and listening for the bark of dogs may allow us to attune our ears more closely to these creatures' existence.

1

THE NATIVE DOG AND
THE COLONIAL DOG

The dog of the East has degenerated below the standard of the true savage; for, in his questionable position, like the half-civilized Indian, he retains none of the virtues of his original state, and acquires all the vices of artificial society. "In the East," says a distinguished traveler, "the dog loses all his good qualities; he is no longer the faithful animal, attached to his master, and ready to defend him even at the expense of his life; on the contrary, he is cruel and blood-thirsty—a gloomy egotist, cut off from all human intercourse, but not the less a slave."

—*Harper's New Monthly Magazine*, 1855

Over two decades after an unnamed *Harper's* writer asserted that, like American Indians, Asian canines were vicious, cutthroat, and decadent, the prolific British travel writer Isabella Bird (1831–1904) expressed a similar loathing for the dogs she encountered while journeying in northern Japan in 1878. The "primitive Japanese dog—a cream-coloured wolfish-looking animal, the size of a collie, very noisy and aggressive, but as cowardly as bullies are—," she complained, "was in great force in Fujihara, and the barking, growling, and quarrelling of these useless curs continued at intervals until daylight; and when they were not quarrelling, they were howling."[1] This may sound like a matter-of-fact account—especially to anyone whose sleep has been disrupted much of the night by barking dogs—but the repetition of words such as "barking, growling, quarrelling, howling" and particularly the use of terms like "primitive, wolfish, aggressive, cowardly, curs" were typical of the language of canine imperialism—the rhetoric of civilization and scientific racism—widely deployed by Westerners to describe indigenous dogs during the age of New Imperialism.

Like the *Harper's* writer and Bird, Western visitors to colonized and colonizable regions such as the Japanese archipelago repeatedly denigrated such canines in the harshest terms. Tellingly, regardless of where they were, Westerners often referred collectively to these animals as "native dogs" or "pariah dogs," consciously grouping them with canines who roamed cities and towns elsewhere in Asia, Africa, and the Middle East. Self-described British adventurer George Fleming's description of a group of indigenous dogs who barked at him "savagely" on the outskirts of a Chinese city was typical:

> It is somewhat curious to find this breed of the *Canis familiaris* so widely diffused over the world...abounding in every corner of China that one chances to put foot in. Closely allied to the Pariah dog of India, the savage pest of Cairo and Egypt generally, those of Syria, and those snarling droves which we have been so often obliged to pelt off with stones by moonlight, in the narrow streets of Stamboul [Istanbul]—the Pariah dog of North China is, like them, allowed to breed and to infest the towns and villages free from disturbance, to congregate on the plains or in the fields during the day, or to kennel in the graveyards; while at night they prowl about the streets like our scavengers at home, sweeping off the quantities of filth and trash that strew the thoroughfares.[2]

These dogs, who made up the vast majority of canines in mid-nineteenth-century Japan and many other areas, were semiferal animals who formed small groups and claimed particular urban neighborhoods and villages as their territory. Such dogs, who survive by scavenging human waste, still inhabit the peripheries in many places where humans dwell, especially in parts of Asia, Africa, and Latin America. The biologists Raymond and Lorna Coppinger call such canines "village dogs."[3] I prefer to call them street dogs, because they live(d) in and on the outskirts of both urban centers and rural areas. Unlike the canines who accompanied Westerners to Japan and elsewhere in the colonial world, local street dogs did not belong to anyone in particular, although some people in a neighborhood might take a liking to a certain dog and treat it kindly. Westerners were much less likely to do so. Almost without exception, they despised native street dogs, and their letters, travelogues, and memoirs are sprinkled with derogatory references to them and explicit comparisons linking these "uncivilized curs" with the peoples who inhabited the imperial realm.

When Europeans and Americans embarked on projects of empire building and colonial rule in the decades before and after Bird's visit to Japan, they were often accompanied by large, purebred, and powerful dogs. Just as colonized and colonizable areas and their inhabitants came to be associated with indigenous street dogs, Westerners came to be identified with their canines, whom I call "colonial dogs." Even among those Westerners who did not bring along a dog, an imagined, mutual affinity apparently drew human and beast together. This was the case for William Elliot Griffis (1843–1912) and an "American dog," at least according to the former. We shall, unfortunately, never know what the dog thought. In early 1871, Griffis, a recent graduate of Rutgers College in New Brunswick, New Jersey, arrived in the rural Japanese city of Fukui to teach at an academy sponsored by the former feudal domain of Echizen. He was soon joined—as he recalled in *The Mikado's Empire* (1876), one of the first serious Western books about Japan's history and society—by the "black dog, with but one eye." Griffis speculated that the animal, whose name he does not record, had mistakenly wandered away from the safety of the foreign settlement in Yokohama and followed a domain party on its journey to Echizen. On meeting this human compatriot, the dog, Griffis surmised, "apparently fully understood, as I could tell from the language of his tail, that I was one of his own country creatures, concentrating all his affection in his remaining orb."[4] The dog and Griffis were evidently not the only ones to make a connection between Westerners and foreign dogs. According to Griffis, before their initial meeting, the animal happened to "pass some farmers, who, reversing the proverb 'Love me, love my dog,' and hating foreigners, whom they believed to be descendants of these brutes…struck the poor creature in the eye with a grass-hook, and made him a Cyclops from that moment."[5] Although the sad fate of the "American dog" was not typical for a "colonial dog," Griffis' description of his canine companion was emblematic of the language Westerners employed to talk about their own dogs. As highlighted by Griffis' depiction of the dog signaling its affection via its tail and lone eye, Europeans and Americans depicted their dogs as warmhearted, reliable, and respected partners.

The rhetorical pairing of the colonial dog with the native dog is central to my analysis. Both colonizers and the colonized viewed the two sets of dogs as distinct and subjected them to explicit and implicit comparison. Individuals on both sides of the imperial divide portrayed the colonial dog as possessing attributes worthy of imperial power. Usually, they claimed that it was civilized, thoroughly domesticated but powerful, and they esteemed it as purebred. On the other hand, colonizers and many of the colonized described the native dog as primitive, aggressive but cowardly, and wolfish or of mixed, wild, or no breed. Such expressions were not merely idle talk. Often, though not always, when people talked about colonial and native dogs, they were revealing their attitudes about colonial and native peoples.

To be sure, such terms as the "colonial dog" and "native dog," like the phrase "canine imperialism," are anachronistic. Although both colonizers and the colonized viewed specific dogs and dog-keeping practices as representative of imperial power, rarely did they see them as worthy of note or analysis. The colonial dog was not a marked category but was taken for granted as the standard of the ideal canine, especially by colonizers. To the *Harper's* "distinguished traveler," the colonial dog was the implicit benchmark, the dog endowed with the "good qualities" of faithfulness, bravery, and attachment to his master, which the dog of the East had supposedly lost. Westerners, like the *Harper's* author, Bird, and Fleming talked far more often and explicitly about the characteristics of the native dog and the local human communities that interacted with it. The term "native dog," too, is problematic, with its baggage of colonial arrogance and anthropological conceit, but it is less anachronistic than other terms, such as "indigenous" or "local" dog. It coexisted and was synonymous with other derogatory labels for the dogs of the periphery, such as "pariah" and "kaffir," which were used also to designate—and denigrate—human populations, and whose connections with the colonial apparatus are obvious indeed. "Pariah," originally used to label members of a very extensive low caste in southern India, quickly became a term of aspersion for any person or animal of a degraded or despised class. Apart from its original usage, it was most often deployed toward dogs, as illustrated by the British adventurer Fleming's observations, not only on the Indian Subcontinent but throughout the colonial world, including Japan, China, the Middle East, as well as in other "backward" areas such as eastern Europe. Similarly, Europeans employed "kaffir," a derogatory term for black Africans, to mark other animal and plant objects, especially dogs, throughout that continent. In short, the "Otherness" and explicit inferiority of the native, whether human or canine, was a central theme of colonial discourses, whereas the cultural peculiarities of the colonizers went for the most part unremarked.

Perhaps because of the pervasive and commonplace presence of dogs, humans have often deployed them metaphorically, and frequently their statements about and actual interaction with canines reveal preoccupations and prejudices entirely unrelated to the canine world. This pattern is evident, among other places, in the *Harper's* passage, the description of street dogs by Bird and Fleming, and the treatment of the "American dog" by Griffis and (allegedly) by the local farmers, all of whom projected their respective political and cultural biases onto these animals. To paraphrase historian Kathleen Kete, when people spoke of dogs, they spoke about their times, and of themselves and others.[6] A historical consideration of human associations with and discussion of dogs, therefore, sheds light on relations between people and canines, but it also opens new perspectives on relations among humans in the past and present. This book's focus on dogs reveals something about the human that histories that are primarily concerned with people do not.

"A Dog Map of the World"

In her influential books about English attitudes toward animals in the nineteenth century, Harriet Ritvo has explored the complex interconnections of dog symbolism, dog breeding, and Victorian nationalism. While suggestive, her analysis of the English relationship with dogs and, for that matter, with all domestic animals is largely limited to the British Isles and pays scant attention to England's vast global empire.[7] Ritvo persuasively argues that the intense enthusiasm for the breeding and keeping of dogs in Britain was primarily fueled by domestic class anxieties. This is true, but empire mattered too. The imperial world and its human and canine population served as an additional foil to domestic class concerns in discussions about "pure-blooded" pedigreed dog breeding and civilized modes of dog keeping. Just as they brought the animals of empire home for display in zoos and as hunting trophies, English Victorians took to the imperium their enthusiasm for pets and particularly for the keeping of purebred dogs, and that process, in turn, influenced discussions about dogs in the metropole. Likewise, continental European powers and the United States transplanted these practices to their respective colonies, and that shaped the discourse of dog enthusiasts in the metropole. As a result, by the late nineteenth century, an imaginary canine geography had come into being, mirroring the imperial map of the human world. Because the culture of dog keeping and enthusiasm for dog breeding flourished over the same span of time that Western colonialism covered the planet, there was no part of the world that escaped the imposition of this canine cartography.

As in other societies, the inhabitants of the British Isles had closely interacted with canines from the beginning of recorded history, but as elsewhere, the keeping of dogs for companionship and amusement was almost completely isolated to those of the highest social rank. In early modern Britain the lower classes used canines as working dogs—for labor such as pulling, herding, and hunting—and regarded those animals with little sentimentality. By contrast, the upper classes, and most prominently, royalty and nobility, lavished affection on nonworking pets such as hounds and lapdogs, and, as a result, these dogs came to enjoy considerable status, thanks to the exalted position of their owners.[8]

Although the nineteenth-century British middle-class enthusiasm for dogs did not necessarily represent a complete departure from the past or from other societies, it radically changed the character of dog keeping in Britain and, eventually, the world over. The urban professional and business classes yearned to associate with their established social betters, the rural upper-class, and to differentiate themselves from their lower-class fellow city dwellers. As Ritvo observes, the urban middle class desired a "stable, hierarchical society, where rank was secure and individual merit, rather than just inherited position, appreciated."[9] The dog fancy provided one avenue to fashion such a society and changed dog keeping in at least three ways that were related to both unease about class and arrogance regarding British imperial exploits. First, the keeping of dogs primarily as pets, a practice borrowed from the upper echelons of society, spread throughout the middle classes in the early nineteenth century.[10] Adopting practices such as the acquisition of expensive dogs and pampering them with a variety of new products not only allowed the upwardly mobile classes to emulate the supposed sophistication of their social superiors but also enabled them to dissociate themselves from the urban masses. Such dog-keeping mores, in their minds, also distinguished themselves from the colonized in Britain's vast imperial realm, because, as they claimed, only the British were civilized enough to fully domesticate, carefully breed, and keep such fine dogs.

Second, the invention and codification of an array of new dog breeds, especially during the second half of the century, was a sharp departure from the past. Breeders redefined a canine population that since at least Tudor times (1485–1603) had been vaguely defined by function into an array of newly defined breeds based strictly on physical appearance that were supposedly pure-blooded and possessed ancient pedigrees. In doing so, they often attempted to link their animals to the lapdogs and hounds long treasured by the upper classes and separate them from the vulgar "mongrels" kept by the working classes.[11] But domestic dogs and class concerns were not their only point of reference, as illustrated by the words of an English sportsman on safari in Africa in the late nineteenth century. In typical fashion, he described his pack of hunting dogs for an audience back home: "dogs of high and low degree, from the pure-bred English greyhound to the Kaffir cur."[12] Indigenous canines—the Kaffir cur—in the imperial realm were equivalent to the mongrels at home, and both were the object of derision in sharp contrast to pure-blooded British breeds.

A final innovation of the nineteenth-century dog fancy was shows that put model specimens of the newly codified breeds on display. One other purpose of these shows, which proliferated from the mid-nineteenth century, was to improve various breeds of dogs by encouraging "proper" breeding practices.[13] In short, pure-blooded dogs should maintain their purity by only being bred with other dogs of the some breed to prevent being compromised by the blood of other breeds and so-called mongrels. These goals implicitly were linked to both class and empire. Organizers only allowed a select few foreign dogs—almost all of whom were lapdogs—to participate in the shows, while excluding the vast majority of dogs from the imperial world along with other domestic "curs" or "mongrels" associated with the lower classes. In this way, the modern dog fancy replicated and bolstered human hierarchal orders of domestic class structures in Britain and other Western countries and the racialized power inequalities of their colonial holdings.

Two organizational principles structured the imaginary geography of canine imperialism by the late nineteenth century. One was the identification of certain dog breeds with particular nation-states, as Ritvo has insightfully discussed in the case of the English bulldog. The other was a hierarchy, enforced by dog shows and breeding standards, that valued breeds that originated in colonial metropoles far more than canines associated with those regions that were objects of imperialist ambition. Such institutions as the (English) Kennel Club and the American Kennel Club (AKC) played an important role in codifying these principles through their practices of breed listing. An apt illustration is found in the "Dog Map of the World," a nineteen-by-thirty-inch diagram published in London in 1933, which highlights the snug relationship of dogs, nation-states, and empires.[14] On its surface, the map shows breeds recognized by the American Kennel Club, but in a larger sense it illustrates the nationalization of dogs and their positioning within imperial power structures. At the center lies a map of the world, a two-dimensional representation of the globe's surface. Precise political boundaries are delineated only for the European Continent, the United States, and Canada. The borders of countries in the Middle East and parts of Asia are shown, but haphazardly. For Africa, South America, and various other regions, political borders are nonexistent. Numbers placed within the borders of each country correspond with particular dog breeds that are pictured in two rows of squares that form a border around the map. (See color plate 2.)

The majority of breeds recognized by the English Kennel Club and the AKC originated in Britain, followed by several western European countries and the United States. Such a distribution adheres to the conceit expressed by an English commentator in 1854 that there was "no civilized land where the canine race is more the companion of man than in Great Britain or any nation which has so many valuable varieties of it."[15]

Of the approximately seventy breeds recognized by the AKC in 1933, thirty-eight hailed from the British Isles; another dozen or so originated in Germany, France, and the Low Countries; and three came from the United States. A strong association between canine breeds and nation-states had emerged by the late nineteenth century.[16] The "nationality" of many breeds is evident simply from their names: English Fox Hound and English Setter, as well as German Shepherd, Norwegian Elkhound, Irish Wolfhound, Yankee Terrier, and French Poodle. But nowhere was this connection stronger than in Britain, where the bulldog came, preeminently, to embody Britishness and empire. Once a dog associated with the working classes and used for the sport of bull baiting, the breed was elevated by Britain's middle classes during the nineteenth century into a symbol of British national and imperial might. As early as the eighteenth century, Scottish philosopher David Hume (1711–76) had claimed that the dog's courage made it peculiarly English, and nineteenth-century breed manuals consistently declared that it was England's national dog.[17]

In addition to becoming nationalized, dogs were placed within an imperial hierarchy that esteemed Western breeds more than those of colonial areas. This was in part the result of the emergence of dog fancying as an organized social enterprise, first in Britain and then in continental Europe and the United States. Dog enthusiasts, not surprisingly, recognized dog breeds that had been created primarily within the borders of their own nation-states, though they often sought to conceal their recent invention by claiming ancient roots. The first British dog shows in the mid-nineteenth century in fact lumped together dogs from outside the West in a "Foreign Dog" category without consideration for breed or function.[18] The same bias was apparent in the breed-recognition system of Western kennel clubs, of which the 1933 "Dog Map of the World" provides a visual representation. The most striking difference was quantitative, in that few dogs were recognized as purebred outside of the colonial metropoles. The AKC, for example, recognized none in Africa or Latin America, except for the Mexican Chihuahua, and only a handful in the Middle East and Asia.

There were also at least two qualitative differences between Western dogs and those whom the map identified with the periphery. First, dogs associated with many colonial areas (or with postcolonial states in Latin America and Australia) were not domesticated breeds at all, but wild canines. Featured on the 1933 "Dog Map of the World," for example, were the Wild Dog of East Africa, the Cape Jackal, the South American Wolf, and the Australian Dingo. The absence of a representative domesticated dog in these areas reflected a perception that the geographical regions in question, and their peoples, remained uncivilized and savage. In only one case was an undomesticated canine placed within the boundaries of a "civilized" nation-state: the Timber Wolf, which on the map roams the northern edge of the border between the United States and Canada. The animal's positioning reflected its own shrinking geographic range in North America, since it had once populated much of the continent before being driven to the brink of extinction. It functioned here not as a symbol of the American or Canadian nation-states, but rather of a continent and its Native American peoples that had been subdued by civilization.

Second, the few recognized dog breeds associated with colonial areas were generally of two types. One type was the lapdog. These small canines, also known as "toy dogs," included the Chinese Pekingese. Westerners in both metropole and the colonies described lapdogs as effeminate and exotic, and it is probably not a coincidence that these particular breeds were chosen to represent regions that were also viewed in the same terms. It seems that the characteristic gendering of Orientalism—the representation of Middle, Near, and Far Eastern societies in a stereotyped and exoticized fashion by Westerners—applied even to the world of dogs. The other recognized dog breeds linked with the colonies, although hypermasculinized rather than feminized, were several large dog breeds whose identity became strongly associated with military service and hunting, what the historian John M. MacKenzie has called "the most perfect expression of global dominance… [that] required all the most virile attributes of the imperial male."[19] The Afghan Hound and the Rhodesian Ridgehound (Ridgeback), for example, were adopted by the British for military use and for safari hunting throughout their vast colonial empire. They served as the canine parallel to the Gurkha people of Nepal, whose ethnic identity became inseparable from military service after the English designated them to serve as soldiers in British colonial armies.

The "Dog Map of the World" visually captures how Western imperialism created not only a human empire, but also an empire of dogs. In this realm, dogs originating from the major Western imperial powers dominated this imagined world. Domestic class anxieties and imperial conceit within and between metropole and empire combined to influence the relationship between people and dogs during the nineteenth century. In metropoles such as Britain, more people began to keep dogs, breeders developed an array of new types of dogs, and these breeds were closely identified with the nation and venerated in contrast to mongrels who roamed the streets at home and abroad in imperial lands. Fanciers came to recognize a few dogs from the imperial realm, which they regarded as representative of certain characteristics that they identified with these areas. One of the first of these was the Japanese Spaniel.

Canine Japonisme

The Japanese Spaniel, or *chin*, which was associated with the country on the 1933 "Dog Map of the World" and by Westerners more generally with Japan from the mid-nineteenth century, had a long and complicated history of representation. Japanese had intensively bred this import from China for centuries, so that by the middle of the Tokugawa period (1600–1868) the breed had become a toy dog primarily kept by well-to-do women of the samurai and merchant classes, who raised it indoors alongside the cat. In fact, Japanese did not consider the *chin* to be a dog at all; rather, as the British Japanologist Basil Hall Chamberlain (1850–1935) later observed, they spoke of "'dogs *and* pugs' (*inu ya chin*), as if the latter formed a distinct species."[20] Nevertheless, many nineteenth- and early twentieth-century Westerners, including Chamberlain, came to identify the *chin* as the official representative canine of Japan.

The Tokugawa shogunate contributed to this view. On 24 March 1854, it presented U.S. Commodore Matthew C. Perry (1794–1858) with four *chin* lapdogs along with rice, dried fish, and a variety of other gifts. This exchange took place during Perry's second visit to the Japanese archipelago in less than a year and was part of his mission that successfully forced the shogunate to establish diplomatic ties with the West after over two centuries of strategic isolation. The gift of the *chin*, which Westerners dubbed the Japanese spaniel, recommenced cross-cultural interactions among Japanese, foreigners, and canines originating from throughout the world. Perry sent two of the spaniels, dubbed Miako and Shimoda, to Queen Victoria via Admiral Stirling of the British Navy. We can only guess what they may have actually looked like. The dogs are depicted in two paintings by W. T. Peters, a little-known New York artist who did not accompany Perry to Japan and never saw the dogs. Unrestrained by reality, Peters portrayed both dogs in a similar pose, perfectly positioned so as to offer a viewer a full view of their slight bodies and heads.[21] (See color plates 2 and 3.) Whether or not Victoria ever received the animals is unknown. There is no record of her doing so; they may have perished during the course of an ocean voyage. The sailors named the other two gift dogs Master Sam Spooner and Madame Yeddo (an alternate spelling for the shogunal capital of Edo). The inspiration for the former is unclear, but the pairing of a male Western name and a female Japanese one suggests that contemporary Orientalism may have been at play. Both of these dogs died at sea en route to the United States.[22] The commodore also sent two other pugs, named Yiddo (again, for Edo) and Jap, whom he had acquired by other means, to his daughter. Only one of these dogs survived the journey. A few years later, in 1860, an entourage of ambassadors from the shogunate visited the United States and called on Perry's widow at the home of her son-in-law, August Belmont, in New York City. It is said that when the group entered the house, the dog instantly and affectionately greeted its countrymen, a sight that moved Jane Perry to tears.[23] Interestingly, this reported greeting parallels the response of the "American dog" to its encounter with the teacher Griffis.

Despite such inauspicious beginnings, by the mid-1860s Japanese spaniels had become the rage in western Europe and the United States. The dogs were a resounding hit at dog shows. The first recorded prizewinner was "The Japanese Rose" at Islington in England in 1865. Official recognition of the breed soon followed, first by the Westminster Kennel Club in 1877, and then by the AKC in 1888. As in Tokugawa Japan, the *chin* was particularly appealing to women of high status or wealth in Victorian society. As Chamberlain put it, "one or two of them form charming ornaments to a lady's boudoir."[24] The devotion of Alexandra, the Princess of Wales (1844–1925), to the many Japanese dogs presented to her by the Rothschild family of financiers, was legendary.[25] Such celebrated artists as Édouard Manet (1832–83) and Pierre-Auguste Renoir (1841–1919) depicted the breed in their paintings.[26] The enthusiasm for the *chin* was part of a broader European and American craze for things seen as quintessentially Japanese, which became known as *japonisme*. Although Western artists and artisans admired the work and imitated the techniques of their Japanese counterparts, the island country was portrayed as an exotic, enchanted land. An Orientalist fascination with the Japanese spaniel, as well as its Chinese cousin, the Pekingese, were often emblematic of how their home countries were regarded by Westerners—as effeminate, decadent, and susceptible to Western imperial control.

As highlighted by a 1902 article in the *American Kennel Gazette,* the enthusiasm for and feminine connotations of the *chin* continued even after *japonisme* had waned somewhat in the West and Japan had become a geopolitical power of some measure. Its author, W. Ruloff Kip, recalled a recent trip to Japan and how one morning just before his return to the United States his courier Akiyama (a name he mistakenly translates as Summer Mountain rather than Fall Mountain) suggested that he and his friends take home a pair of Japanese spaniels. " 'They are very nice little dogs,' said Summer Mountain. 'All Japanese ladies have "Chin" dogs.' 'But we are not Japanese ladies, or any other kind of ladies,' I protested. 'We are three men.' 'You can give them to some ladies at home,' continued the crafty Oriental. 'Now that photograph you have always on your bureau, that is surely not your estimable mother—' 'Get them,' I said. 'Say no more.' After he was gone I regretted my decision, 'Three men and two ladies' dogs,' I sighed." After his *chin* captured several dog show prizes in the United States, however, Kip reevaluated the breed as "not as delicate as most people would have us think." Their bark, however, still conjured up feminized, Orientalist images for him. Their yap, he concluded, "is based on the best recognized type of Oriental vocal music, and if one has any imagination when they are singing he can hear the 'Semisen' [*shamisen*] accompaniment and see swaying, posturing, gaily-costumed Geishas, and smell that vague, peculiar odor which exhales from boxes which come direct from the Far East."[27] As illustrated by Kip's palpable Orientalism and the placement of the Japanese Spaniel on the 1933 "Dog Map of the World" as the country's representative canine, these highly feminized dogs stood as symbols of Japan well into the twentieth century. Conveniently for many Westerners, the Japanese spaniel and the Pekingese appeared to reflect the exotic and effeminate nature of the societies they were said to represent and to stand in stark contrast to the canines that accompanied them to the imperial realm.

A Dog-Eat-Dog World

If some Westerners brought back certain desirable canines from the imperial world, they often took along from the metropole English bulldogs, German shepherds, and an assortment of other colonial dogs such as the "American dog" adopted by Griffis. These dogs embodied canine imperialism and formed the vanguard of a movement that, like their human companions, swept across the planet, and, even more than their onetime human cohorts, continue to maintain global cultural supremacy today. Such canines were generally large, often pure-bred, and almost always powerful, dogs. In areas where they feared attack by natives or by wild animals, as in Africa, Westerners often took along at least two canines, one a large "attack" dog and the other a smaller "barking" dog.[28] In *Beasts and Man in India* (1891), John Lockwood Kipling (1837–1911), the famous author's father and longtime curator of the Lahore Museum, observed:

> [The] dog and the horse accompany [the British colonial] everywhere, for it is part of our insular vanity to declare that no other dogs or horses are half so good as ours. Packs of foxhounds are regularly imported; the subaltern, the private soldier, and the civilian bring bull-dogs, mastiffs, and terriers of every degree. Spaniels, retrievers, and greyhounds accompany sportsmen; the great Danes are occasionally seen, while ladies bring such pets as Maltese, Skyes, and Dandie Dinmonts, and dachshunds.[29]

In British India and throughout the imperial world, Westerners valued these dogs for hunting, as guards, or simply as companions. Toby, a Scottish terrier, likely fulfilled all three functions for his master, Sir Rutherford Alcock (1809–1897), the first British consul to Japan.[30] Alcock arrived in Edo in the summer of 1859. Following in the wake of Perry's "gunboat diplomacy," Alcock joined the U.S. diplomat Townsend Harris (1804–78) in pressuring the Tokugawa shogunate to make more concessions to Western demands. Japan was Alcock's second foreign assignment. He had served as consul in China since 1844, where he became known for his willingness to back up diplomacy with violence in order to enforce the extraterritorial privileges enjoyed by the British in the wake of the First Opium War (1839–42).[31] Alcock was apparently accompanied from the mainland by Toby. Unfortunately, the partnership came to a tragic end in September 1860, when on a return trip from becoming the first Westerner(s)—human and perhaps dog—to climb Mt. Fuji, Toby was accidentally scalded to death during a visit to the hot springs of nearby Atami. Alcock mourned the passing of his "constant and faithful companion," and lamented that "one must have led the isolated life of a Foreign Minister in Japan, to realise the blank which the loss even of an attached dog creates."[32]

Nearly two decades later, another terrier attached to the British foreign service in Japan also made a lasting impression. When the travel writer Bird visited the British legation in central Tokyo in 1878, she wrote of a thoroughly "English home" in the compound, complete with a Chinese butler, footman, cook, and servants, "two real English children of six and seven," and "a beautiful and attractive terrier named 'Rags.'" The "Skye dog," she continued, "unbends 'in the bosom of his family,' but ordinarily is as imposing in his demeanour as if he, and not his master, represented the dignity of the British Empire."[33] Although the size of a Skye terrier might lead one to believe that Bird was speaking tongue-in-cheek about Rags representing British imperial might, terriers were well known for their ability to track and destroy fox, badger, and other small game, and their temperament was (and still is) often far more imposing than their relatively small physique, which was probably larger and more physically powerful than today's Skye terriers.[34] As in the metropole, Europeans and Americans in imperial regions cherished such dogs for their loyalty and their usefulness, and esteemed them for their physical prowess, or at least their capacity for violence against other humans and creatures. It was canines like these whom Westerners came to be identified with, and which became the implicit benchmark against which Westerners and local peoples used to judge indigenous native dogs. Such comparisons, which depended on but amplified and exaggerated real ecological and behavioral differences, were central to the dynamic of canine imperialism. They were not without precedent.

Protocanine Imperialism

Although the flourishing of pet culture from the late eighteenth and nineteenth centuries onward certainly contributed to many Westerners taking dogs with them abroad during the age of New Imperialism, it was not the first time that canines had contributed to European expansion. Dogs traveled with Columbus and other European explorers on their journeys across the Atlantic, down the coast of Africa, and around the Cape of Hope to Asia in the fifteenth and sixteenth centuries. They also joined the conquistadors, merchants, missionaries, and slave traders who followed. In these different settings, Europeans physically and figuratively manipulated these early colonial dogs in ways that anticipated their uses hundreds of years later.

During the exploration, conquest, and rule of the Americas beginning in 1492, the Spanish, Portuguese, French, and English regularly trained large dogs, mainly mastiffs and greyhounds, to track, attack, and guard in their colonial endeavors. In the rough terrain of the New World, dogs became prized weapons, often considered more valuable than horses. Once victorious militarily, the Spanish were said to have pitted dogs against indigenous Americans accused of sedition and sexual crimes in public spectacles designed to intimidate the wider population.[35] European dogs, who were much larger than indigenous dogs in the Americas, appear to have surprised and inspired great fear among native peoples, who recalled in recorded oral accounts and visual depictions their awesome size, "burning eyes," constant panting and hanging tongues, and fearsome use.[36]

Although English commentators criticized the alleged excesses of Spanish rule, their countrymen resorted to similar techniques once they discovered the usefulness of dogs in their own colonies to track down Indians and runaway African slaves during the seventeenth, eighteenth, and nineteenth centuries.[37] Because the English, like the Spanish, considered Native Americans to be "brutish savages, which by reason of their godless ignorance, and blasphemous idolatry, are worse than…beasts," they had few qualms about treating them in the same category as nonhuman prey.[38] As historian Mark A. Mastromarino has written, Anglo-American colonists may have not used dogs merely for entertainment, but once they came to "believe that the only good Indian was a dead Indian, the adoption of such inhumane measures as hunting Indians with mastiffs and other dogs became inevitable."[39]

In sixteenth- and seventeenth-century Japan, the more circumscribed presence of Spanish and Portuguese explorers, missionaries, and traders gave rise to a more purely symbolic deployment of dogs. Here, too, big, powerful dogs accompanied Europeans, but militarily there was far greater parity on the Japanese archipelago than in the Americas. Although the inhabitants of the islands trailed Europeans in military technology, they quickly acquired and mastered the expertise they lacked, such as the manufacture of firearms. Within a century of contact, the country's leaders, conscious of the European appetite for conquest and wary of the subversive potential of Christianity, forced all but a small group of Dutch merchants out of the archipelago. In this context, Europeans, unlike the conquistadors in the Americas, had no opportunity to put their dogs to military use, and, even if they had the chance, Jesuit missionaries, who were at the forefront of interactions with people on the islands, would probably not have been inclined to do so. Perhaps because of these circumstances, dogs became a more malleable metaphor than in the New World. In general, the metaphorical use of dogs and other animals in colonial contexts seems to have been more pronounced, or at least qualitatively different, when there was less inequality in political and economic power between the disparate cultures.

In sixteenth- and seventeenth-century Japan, as in the Americas, certain types of dogs became strongly associated with Europeans. They appear frequently alongside Iberians in screens and other forms of Japanese artwork named for its subject matter, the figure of the Southern Barbarian (Nanbanjin). Japanese warlords, in turn, laid almost immediate claim to the physical strength, speed, and exotic nature of these newly arrived creatures in order to bolster their own status and political power.[40] They acquired the dogs as gifts or by purchase, and created compounds to breed and train dogs for fighting and hunting. Even after the banishing from Japan of all Europeans except for the Dutch, the Tokugawa shogunate and some regional rulers, or daimyō, continued to import dogs through the Dutch East Asia Company until at least the early eighteenth century.[41] The dog compounds and breeding facilities had disappeared long before Perry arrived in 1853, and the shogunate collapsed a decade and a half later; the wider canine population had largely absorbed the foreign animals, though their impact was still evident in the physical appearance of at least some dogs.

Visualizing the Colonial Dog

When Westerners and their dogs returned to Japan in the mid-nineteenth century, similar patterns reemerged. This time the United States and European countries possessed a clear military advantage and extracted unequal treaties that secured significant political and economic privileges in Japan. Still, Japan, unlike much of the world, was able to avoid outright colonization and, after the change of regimes from Tokugawa to Meiji in 1868, Japanese leaders embarked on a series of unprecedented political, economic, and social reforms that allowed the nation to become a world power in a generation. In this volatile geopolitical environment, dogs became entrapped in a discourse, which was spun in both words and images and grounded to some extent in actual human-canine interactions, about the nature of Japan and what it ought to become.

As they did elsewhere, Western diplomats, soldiers, missionaries, businessmen, and other visitors brought their dogs to Japan. And, like their sixteenth- and seventeenth-century ancestors, the local Japanese population imagined a strong connection between foreign dogs and their masters. Echoing earlier Southern Barbarian artwork, the mid-nineteenth-century prints known as "Yokohama pictures" (*Yokohama-e*) captured the strange manners and dress of the foreign community, many of whose members lived in the newly established treaty port of Yokohama. Artists of the day commonly portrayed Western soldiers, officials, merchants, and their families with canine companions. In an 1860 print, for example, Andō Hiroshige II (1826–69) depicted what appears to be a large borzoi-like greyhound alongside a fierce-looking and well-armed English soldier.[42] In the background, numerous dead ducks, presumably the kill of the soldier and his dog, hang from a broad rack.

Dogs appeared most frequently in the prints of Hashimoto Gyokuransai (also known as Utagawa Sadahide; 1807–ca. 1873). They are especially conspicuous in *Yokohama kaikō kenmonshi* (Report of things seen and heard in the open port of Yokohama; 1862), a widely read illustrated account of treaty port life. Here and elsewhere, Hashimoto, through his images as well as accompanying text, prominently portrayed foreigners with Western-bred dogs, sometimes as they interacted in the treaty ports but, in a few instances, as he imagined them in their home countries. The dogs depicted by Hashimoto are invariably large, physically imposing dogs. The immense and sometimes exaggerated size of the dogs, who from his illustrations appear usually to be pointers or greyhounds, lends their human masters an unmistakable air of authority. In the first print, a massive dog strides alongside its master's carriage as it moves down a street in Yokohama, as if shielding the occupants from Japanese onlookers. In the second print, a dog appears to be backing up the commands of its keeper, a Western merchant who appears to be giving an order to a local laborer. In the text, Hashimoto tells of the control that Westerners seem to exercise over their dogs, which put Japanese at the mercy of their commands. He describes how a large group of local residents, fascinated with the consumption of beef by Westerners, gathered around a shop located on the outskirts of Yokohama to watch a butcher at work, and began to excitedly discuss meat eating.

Because of all the chit-chat and commotion caused by the bothersome crowd, the foreigner, as only he could do, sicced about ten strange-looking dogs loose on the onlookers. Some of the dogs were smooth with bag-like hanging ears and panted heavily through large open mouths. Others were black and looked like lions, and still others looked like *chin*. When the people saw this dark swarm

1. Woodblock print of an English soldier and his dog by Andō Hiroshige II, from 1860.

車馬爭走る之図
是迄小圖出セ共
此車の形ハ又新
真馬を出も

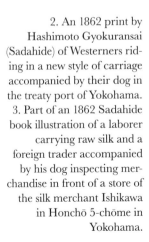

2. An 1862 print by Hashimoto Gyokuransai (Sadahide) of Westerners riding in a new style of carriage accompanied by their dog in the treaty port of Yokohama.
3. Part of an 1862 Sadahide book illustration of a laborer carrying raw silk and a foreign trader accompanied by his dog inspecting merchandise in front of a store of the silk merchant Ishikawa in Honchō 5-chōme in Yokohama.

with their open red mouths coming at them, they turned pale and started running, and the dogs chased after them.

This cleared the entrance to the butcher shop. Fortunately no one was bitten....When the people fled, many of them dropped their pocketbooks or lost their sandals, and these things lay in the middle of the street. They dared not return to retrieve them out of fear that the dogs milling around the shop would bite them. Just then three foreigners came down the street and, recognizing what was happening, they stopped between the dogs and the fallen items and motioned for the people to quickly grab their things. It was just as if Buddha had rescued them from hell. Everyone recovered their belongings and scurried away as fast as they could.[43]

In the prints of Hashimoto and other artists, dogs further contribute to their masters' aura of power by the fact that they diligently accompanied their owners wherever they went. Westerners and their dogs were presumed to be constant companions. As Hashimoto put it, "When foreigners are at home, a dog is laying about the house. And when foreigners have gone out, one can be sure if they are at home or not by determining whether a dog is present."[44] Numerous Hashimoto prints, as well as works by other artists, show well-built dogs following their masters through the streets, or domestic scenes of foreign children playing with dogs, or entire families with their pets.[45] One suggestive print shows a carriage ridden by an American. A massive dog trots faithfully at its side. In the background looms the silhouette of a large black ship, possibly an allusion to Perry's vessels of nearly a decade earlier.[46] Together the dog, the foreigner, and the ship subtly convey the military might and economic power of the West.

Hashimoto and other creators of "Yokohama pictures" were not the only ones who drew a visual association between Western imperialists and their dogs. In other representations of humans and dogs, national differences were overlaid with gender distinctions. The French illustrator and topical cartoonist, Georges Bigot (1860–1927), who lived in Japan from 1883 to 1899, frequently pictured Westerners accompanied by dogs in his prints for both foreign and domestic audiences. In contrast, he rarely depicted Japanese with dogs. Furthermore, Bigot's cartoons evince a distinct gendering of dogs, insofar as Western men appear with larger hunting dogs, while illustrations of Western women and families usually feature smaller pets.[47]

The frequent inclusion of dogs in Bigot's illustrations can in part be explained by the fact that he kept a beaglelike dog whom he called Aka (Red) or, even more affectionately, Aka-chan (Baby). Aka appears often in Bigot's artwork, especially his self-portraits. One such cartoon, which Bigot published in his magazine *Toba-e* (meaning "Toba pictures") on 31 August 1887, captures the privileged position of the colonial dog.[48] The print, captioned "Moyen de transporter son chien malade" (The way to transport a sick dog), depicts Bigot and his human and animal companions traveling down a rainy, dark mountainside on their way from Atami to Shūzenji Temple on the Izu Peninsula in Shizuoka Prefecture. Bigot, wearing classic nineteenth-century imperial khaki attire and a pith helmet, leads a

Japanese servant, who is carrying Aka piggy-back style, and a horse, laden with their belongings. In a letter to his mother in Paris dated several days earlier and on which Bigot had painted in watercolor himself and Aka on a beach, he explained how the dog had found his way onto the back of the Japanese underling.

> My dog was no longer able to keep up with us. He had been sick for two days, and had not eaten a thing. I thought it would be best if we let him ride on the horse's back, but my guides said that we could not do such a thing as putting him on the baggage. "Okay," I replied. "Well, then you guys can carry him. Here, secure him on your back quickly with your sash. Let's get going. We don't have any more candles, and if we don't hurry I am not sure how we are going to get out of here." So one of the men put the dog on his back with his forelegs around his neck. Aka's sulky expression was certainly an amusing sight. The man went pale fearing that he was going to be eaten by my dog and asked me stridently if he had anything to worry about. When Aka sniffed at his ears and the nape of his neck, he shook with fright. After we had traveled about one league, he liberated himself from the burden and with great pleasure took the dog off his back and handed him to his partner, whose turn it was to carry him. In this fashion, without a light and completely soaked, we finally arrived...near Ajiro about one in the morning.[49]

Bigot's illustrations, "Yokohama pictures," and other visual images revealed dog breeds and Western ways of dog keeping rarely before seen on the archipelago, nor, for that matter, throughout much of the colonized world. Other than the few house-dwelling lapdogs and hunting dogs who lived mainly in mountainous regions, by far most canines on the archipelago were native street dogs who freely roamed the streets and peripheries of human habitation. Unlike canines who accompanied Westerners to Japan, local street dogs were not kept by particular individuals. Some households probably adopted individual canines as watchdogs, if they had the means to feed the animal or property that they wanted to protect from other people or beasts. The historian Tsukamoto Manabu has suggested that street dogs maintained a symbiotic relationship with their human neighbors. Humans provided—either actively or passively—dogs with food scraps, and dogs foraged for sustenance through trash and waste. And because canines thought of the neighborhood or village as their territory, they functioned as guardians of the community, patrolling the area and warning their human neighbors of unfamiliar and suspicious intruders.[50]

The observations of mid-nineteenth-century Western visitors to Japan appear to confirm Tsukamoto's conclusions. Francis Hall (1822–1902), a reporter and businessman who lived in Kanagawa and Yokohama from 1859 to 1866, recorded in his diary that local dogs "appear to belong to the street rather than to individuals." A life on the street, though, did not necessarily mean a life of want. During a visit to Hakodate, a treaty port city on the northern island of Hokkaido, Hall found its canine inhabitants to be "the best fed and conditioned race of street monarchs I ever saw. They ranged the streets in bands seeming to have their

Moyen de transporter son chien malade
de Shisenji à Atami (onze heures du soir)

4. *A Clown on a Journey* by Georges Bigot, dated August 1887. The French caption reads, "The way to transport a sick dog, on the way to Atami from Shūzenji (about 11 p.m.)." Used with permission of the Yokohama Archives of History.

particular patrols and were fed from door to door."[51] Like such canines today, street dogs dwelling in economically vibrant areas probably thrived while those who did not may have had a more difficult time.

Several Western visitors to Japan in the nineteenth century noted the surprise of Japanese when they saw foreign dogs. Laurence Oliphant (1829–88), private secretary to Lord Elgin and chronicler of Elgin's mission to Japan in 1858, described how, during his first visit to Shimoda, Japanese seemed to take more interest in the canine foreigners than in the human ones.

> They manifested but little curiosity at us as we strolled about the streets, but I was amused to observe a crowd collected round about a dog belonging to one of our party, of the Shantung terrier breed, and which, though a purely Chinese dog, is scarcely to be distinguished from a Skye terrier. This long-haired specimen of the canine race created immense excitement and interest, both among Japanese dogs and men, as he trotted complacently along the streets of S[h]imoda.[52]

Approximately a decade later, a certain Mr. C. Barrow, clerk at J. C. Fraser and Company in Yokohama, set out to visit Miyanoshita, a village on the Izu

Peninsula. As his colleague J. P. Mollison recalled nearly forty years later in the *Japan Gazette,* at the time this trek on foot was a "very venturesome thing for one man alone." Indeed, Barrow likely made the trip in 1868 while civil war still gripped the country and when violence against foreigners remained commonplace. Barrow reached his destination without incident and gave much of the credit to his only companion, a large black retriever named Jack. According to Barrow, "Jack was a constant source of wonder and delight to the villagers of all ages, who had of course never seen a dog of the kind before. He proved to be a sort of passport to their goodwill, because of his good temper, obedience and docility, in spite of his huge size."[53]

Japanese were no doubt fascinated to see dogs who were physically different than those they had previously encountered. The artist Hashimoto, for example, marveled at the great number of dogs in the foreign quarter of Yokohama, but he was even more impressed by the "tremendous variety of dogs."[54] Other than the lapdog, most dogs in Japan resembled one another and were not far removed from the wolf in general physical appearance. Because of the limited influx of foreign dog blood into the canine gene pool during the years of strategic isolation of the Tokugawa period from the sixteenth to early eighteenth centuries, small variations probably existed in the appearance of dogs who lived in areas of contact with overseas dogs—in and near lowland urban environs—and dogs who lived beyond such zones—in more remote, mountainous regions. These differences are documented by a volume of *Fauna Japonica* that dealt with mammals, which was edited by Philipp Franz von Siebold (1796–1866) and written by Conrad Jacob Temminck (1778–1858). Siebold, a German physician who lived in the Dutch settlement of Deshima in Nagasaki from 1823 to 1829, was one of the first people to examine the Japanese archipelago's fauna and flora from a Western scientific perspective. He gathered his information either through direct observation in Nagasaki and during a visit to Edo or via Japanese whom Siebold became acquainted with at a school he established on the outskirts of Nagasaki. On his return to the Netherlands, Siebold cooperated with several zoologists, including Temminck, the first director of the National Science Museum of Natural History in Leiden, to publish his findings. Siebold and Temminck classified the archipelago's canine population into two broad groups, hunting dogs (*chien de chasse*) and street dogs (*chien de rue*), and described the latter as the product of uncontrolled interbreeding between the former and foreign dogs. Hunting and street dogs were similar phenotypically, but the *chien de rue* was stockier from the muzzle to the hindquarters and had longer hair, smaller eyes, and ears that were not completely erect like those of the hunting dog.[55] Interestingly, Siebold brought two live dogs back with him to Holland in 1829.[56] The fate of one of the canines is unclear, but it is said that Siebold regularly took walks with the other dog, a lean *chien de chasse* named Sakura, along the Rapenburg Canal that ran in front of his house in Leiden. Ever the natural scientist—and perhaps motivated by a dog keeper's sadness after a pet's passing—Siebold had taxidermists preserve Sakura after the dog's death in 1831. Sakura can still be seen to this day, along with Siebold's other scientific and ethnographic collections, in the SieboldHuis Museum occupying his former Leiden home.

Despite such urban/rural and other regional differences, dogs on the island chain did not exhibit the marked variety of form and hair length of European breeds, which prompted even Charles Darwin (1809–82) to wonder how all domesticated dogs could have sprung from the same species.[57] Apart from the *chin* and perhaps some hunting dogs (who if bred were produced for function rather than appearance), Tokugawa Japanese rarely bred for particular traits, and except for a few foreign dogs, additions to the gene pool had been relatively limited for several centuries. For all these reasons, it is not surprising that a glimpse of a foreign dog in nineteenth-century Japan carried considerable impact.

Next to their appearance, Japanese seemed most surprised by the demeanor of foreign dogs. Territorial packs of native street dogs greeted with hostility strangers who "invaded" their neighborhoods and could not be easily controlled even by resident humans. Foreign dogs, by contrast, seemed to move singly with their masters from one place to another without barking or growling at strangers and to answer readily to their owners' commands—including orders to chase away troublesome local inhabitants, such as in the case of the Yokohama butcher. Foreigners, as well as Japanese, regularly commented on these behavioral differences. Oliphant

5. *Canis Familiaris Japonicus* by Philipp Franz von Siebold, 1842. Siebold and his collaborator, Conrad Jacob Temminck, classified the canines on the Japanese archipelago into two broad groups, hunting dogs (*chien de chasse*), on the left-hand side, and street dogs (*chien de rue*), on the right.

distinguished between the "complacent" manner of the dog in his party and the "immense excitement and interest [of] Japanese dogs and men." The wonder of villagers at the "good temper, obedience and docility" of Barrow's dog Jack implied a similar if more implicit contrast. Drastically different dog deportment accentuated the obvious physical disparities between native and foreign dogs.

Local inhabitants were probably also startled by the customs of Western dog keepers. Although the raising of dogs by individuals was not unknown in Japan, it was not something that most people practiced or were even familiar with. The fascination registered in Hashimoto's observations about and numerous prints of dogs following foreigners around and moving freely around their homes was one of novelty born of unfamiliarity. The closest phenomenon in Japan was the keeping of lapdogs and hunting dogs, but it was limited in scale and was pursued deep within the interior of wealthy households, or else off in the mountains beyond the gaze of most. Owners of lapdogs or hunting dogs did not regard them as family pets or "man's best friend," as dog keepers of the Western middle classes had begun to do by the nineteenth century. A few Japanese may have "adopted" individual dogs (or been adopted by dogs) from the neighborhood pack, but their bonds were less formal, intimate, and enduring than was the case in contemporary Western pet keeping. Other than the *chin*, an "adopted" dog would have never been brought into one's home, and perhaps this was the reason why nineteenth-century Japanese regarded the *chin* as a separate species from other canines. Edward S. Morse (1838–1925), an American zoologist who taught at Tokyo University from 1877 to 1879, observed that Japanese did not pay "attention" to dogs and did not indulge in "petting."[58] Neither, apparently, was the practice of taking dogs for a walk common in Japan before Westerners arrived.

As elsewhere, when Westerners arrived in Japan beginning in the mid-nineteenth century, they and some local observers identified the dogs they brought with them and the manner with which Westerners interacted with the dogs as radically different than on the archipelago. As a result, Westerners and the colonial dogs came to be mutually associated in the minds of many. Such actual and imagined differences provided ripe ground for the rhetorical pairing of the colonial dogs with the native dog.

The Language of Civilization, or the "Currish Side of Canine Character"

In Japan and elsewhere, Westerners as well some indigenous elites regarded the colonial dog as an icon of enlightenment and domestication. By the same token, they disparaged native dogs as barbaric and savage. Nevertheless, explicit words of praise for the colonial dog were relatively rare. Just as discourses about whiteness or masculinity were submerged in most colonial contexts, the unstated, admirable qualities of the colonial dog provided an implicit foil for criticism of the native dog—and by extension, the native human. This pattern was manifest, in different inflections, throughout the imperial world. Westerners, and some members of the local upper classes, explicitly and implicitly compared the two groups of dogs using the languages of civilization and scientific racism. Even as they were speaking about dogs, they projected their preoccupations and prejudices about "Other" humans onto canines.

The concept of "civilization"—the notion that certain societies, primarily European ones, were more culturally advanced on a linear grid of development than other, "barbarian," societies—came to dominate European thinking during the eighteenth and nineteenth centuries. Discourses of civilization pervaded the second wave of imperialism and colonialism, and were imposed on the canine world. The colonial dog and its native foil became reference points for demonstrating the supposed civility of the Western colonizer and the savagery of the colonized. Observers contended that Western breeds were calm, peaceful, and brave animals, whereas native dogs were easily agitated, aggressive, but cowardly. They regarded the colonial dog as a loyal and trusted companion when compared to the native dog, which was said to be devious and to dislike "civilized" foreigners. In this way, colonial dogs were portrayed as culturally, if not intellectually, enlightened, and native dogs as backward and old-fashioned.

Wherever they ventured in the imperial realm, Westerners almost always described native dogs in this way. Percival Lowell (1855–1916), a senior American adviser to the Korean government in the 1880s, for example, characterized the canine of that country as a "hanger-on of civilization rather than a part of it," a statement that may have equally well described his sentiments about the nation as a whole.[59] John Lockwood Kipling, too, utilized the rhetoric of civilization to contrapose colonial and native dogs. He wrote that the "Indian pariah," or "pie-dog"

> reveals more of the currish side of canine character than English dogs and dog lovers are aware of. He uncovers more of his teeth when he snarls—and he often snarls—than the civilised dog; he slinks off with inverted tail at the mere hint of a blow or a caress, and his shrill bark echoes the long note of the great dog-father, the wolf, and the poor cousin the jackal. In a fight he does not abandon himself to the delight of battle with the stern joy of the English dog, but calculates odds and backs down with an ignoble care for his skin. In short, he is a *lendi* [shit], a cur, a coward.[60]

Many Westerners regarded everything in colonized and colonizable areas as substandard, including the intellect of dogs. A nineteenth-century foreign resident of one of the treaty ports in China complained: "Native dogs are useless for sport, as they seem to be devoid of that friendly intelligence so noticeable in our own breeds, while their powers of scent are much inferior."[61] The British writer Bird had similarly unkind words for the dogs she encountered in Korea. Writing in 1897, she claimed that the beasts were "neither the friend nor companion of man." She evidently found the dogs on the peninsula to be so savage and stupid that they were even "ignorant of Korean and every spoken language."[62]

Though they may have not used such strong language as Kipling or Bird, other Westerners and the Japanese who emulated them characterized Western breeds as the archetypes of resolute yet restrained domesticity and portrayed native dogs as an embodiment of belligerent and craven wildness. Recall Barrow's comments about the "huge size" yet "good temper, obedience and docility" of his dog Jack, and Oliphant's observations of the foreign dog strolling "complacently" through the milling streets of Shimoda in contrast to the "immense excitement [of] Japanese dogs and men." By conflating local humans and indigenous canines, Oliphant slyly suggested that the two groups shared a similar tendency toward excitability.

British Christian missionary Bernard Jean Bettelheim (1811–70), who resided in the Kingdom of Ryukyu from 1846 to 1854, portrayed dogs as models of how he wished the local "literati" would behave. Before his departure for the islands, missionary acquaintances in China had presented him, as he recorded in his journal, with "one very fine pointer" and a "2[n]d dog, somewhat of a Newfoundland & Chinese breed, a tried watchdog."[63] Bettelheim noted that he and his dogs were initially the object of great curiosity from both local people and canines, but by the next year what little goodwill had once existed had by then completely dissipated, perhaps in part because Bettelheim found almost no success in converting the islanders to his message. Tensions burst into the open after Ryukyuan authorities accused him of setting his dogs on assistants supplied by the kingdom, whom he believed, probably correctly, to be spies.[64] In a letter to the royal government, Bettelheim vehemently, and characteristically, denied using his dogs in that way and proceeded to claim that their manners were superior to those of the literati and that is why they were seeking to discredit his dogs. He declared:

> The matter is the literati envy the cleverness & politeness of these dogs, for the whole country seeing how well behaved these dogs are, plainly understand that it is not enough for man merely to honour his parents, love his offspring, and obey one's master, so much dogs are also able to learn. But man must pray, worship God and take care of his soul. This cleverness of my dogs it is why the mandarins brought forward an accusation against them. These dogs did not follow me on the day of the obsequies only, but always accompany me; they never run before, but always follow their master like a servant, and they (when with the master) never dare to bark or bite at any, not even on a fellow dog. The whole country knows this & therefore admires these dogs. How can the Vice Governor General say the dogs ran (or were driven) and bit people? I am the teacher of this country. The rules of propriety have to proceed from me; my alms are dispersed among the people (poor); I walk humbly among them like Confucy [Confucius], I teach the ignorant populace how they may obtain everlasting life with the only exception of the mandarins...; the people of Loochoo [Ryukyu] praise our conversation and religion. How say our dogs ran and bit people?[65]

While comparing himself to Jesus and Confucius, Bettelheim subtly contrasted the intelligence and behavior of his own dogs with that of the educated elite whom he saw as hindering his missionary efforts on the Ryukyu Islands.

The British diplomat Alcock's comparison between dogs and certain Japanese men was not nearly so subtle as Oliphant's or Bettelheim's. Alcock disparaged street dogs as the "only real nuisance of Japanese cities, in addition to the two-sworded Samourai [*sic*]."⁶⁶ Alcock may have not realized how apt his comparison was. Like street dogs, many members of the warrior class in the late Tokugawa period were *rōnin,* or roaming masterless samurai. Samurai *rōnin* existed for a variety of reasons—among others, the death or ouster of a lord and difficult economic conditions drove some warriors to seek their fortune elsewhere—but increasingly in the mid-nineteenth century, many were samurai who had forsaken their masters to support the imperial cause and drive out foreign "barbarians." Alcock was no stranger to the threat posed by *rōnin.* In 1861 he narrowly escaped death in a nighttime attack on the British legation, which at the time was based at the Tōzenji temple in Edo (renamed Tokyo in 1868), by samurai assassins who killed two of his countrymen and wounded his assistant, Oliphant. The actions of a stray dog who had earlier befriended Oliphant—its breed is unclear—had alerted him that night to the attack by barking furiously. Oliphant had "acquired the affections" of the dog during a break on a ride from Yokohama to Edo by feeding him scraps from his lunch. The dog "permanently attached himself" to the diplomat, and on the night of the attack was lying across the threshold of the door to his room.⁶⁷ The barking of another dog—its breed, too, unknown—who alerted other members of the legation to the assault, cost it its life at the hands of the samurai attackers. In contrast to the shogunate guards assigned to protect the British, Alcock wryly noted that the dog was "the only sentinel awake!"⁶⁸

Before the decade was over, "two-sworded ruffians" had attacked another of Alcock's colleagues stationed in the city, Sir Harry Parkes (1825–85), the British minister plenipotentiary to Japan from 1865 to 1883. The incident occurred as Parkes was returning home with his dog from a meeting with the Japanese foreign minister on 28 September 1869. "Providentially," Parkes recalled, the would-be assassin "missed both me and my dear old Shah."⁶⁹ Although Parkes seems to have felt a close bond with his canine companion, presumably a Western breed, its Oriental name, Shah, is suggestive. Perhaps many Westerners involved in imperial projects selected similar exotic appellations for their dogs, reflecting the worldwide scope and the day-to-day exoticism that it involved.⁷⁰ The use of Oriental names may highlight the liminal position and metaphorical pliability of dogs, who could be regarded as privileged enough to be a part of the colonial in-group, but simultaneously despised and degraded enough to be named as colonized Others. Such exotic names, though, may have just been terms of saccharine endearment, which may also be read as Orientalism, though of an entirely different kind. Either way, the hierarchal relationship between "master" and "pet" also symbolizes the unequal power arrangements that structured interactions between the colonizers and colonized.

Nearly every foreigner, it seems, had something negative to say about the native dogs she or he encountered in Japan. Lady Kate Lawson, a member of the Japan Society and of the Red Cross Society of Japan, may have considered herself a friend of the Japanese, but she was no fan of their dogs. With a typical British pride, she wrote in the early twentieth century that the "Japanese dog is not the friend and companion of his master as is his English brother. Those most often seen are either somewhat characterless poodles or wolfish outhouse creatures of the poorest breed."[71] In the eyes of many Westerners, native dogs manifested uncontrollable belligerence but in the end were craven, while their own dogs were docile and domesticated but powerful when called upon to fulfill the commands of their masters.

In the minds of many Westerners, native canines directed intense hostility particularly at foreigners and their dogs, rather than at their local human neighbors. "With the natives the animal lives on terms of mutual indifference," wrote the American advisor Lowell about local dogs in Korea, "but in the strange-looking foreigner he recognizes at once an enemy, of whom he is mortally afraid."[72] Three decades later, in another observation about Korea—by this time a Japanese colony—Mrs. Will Gordon in a report to the Japan Society of London claimed "jackal-like dogs...display a fierce eagerness and a terribly keen nose for foreigners." This conviction was reinforced in her mind one evening when a "wolfish dog dashed out with a savage rush, sending our *jinrikisha* [rickshaw] swerving madly, before the yells of the coolies made him shrink back into the gloom, but his savage bay of defiance followed us long after, and was taken up and echoed in different parts of the slumbering city."[73] The British businessman and travel writer Archibald John Little (1838–1908) recalled being bitten by a native dog in the western Chinese city of Ichang in 1883. Ironically referring to Westerners as barbarians, he asserted: "These dogs in China are the bane of one's existence; they have a mad antipathy to the barbarian, that the longest acquaintance fails to modify; the scent, appearance, or sound of his movements seems to infuriate them to madness; they rush out violently barking, and as a rule stop short of biting, but to any one with sensitive nerves there is no enjoyment in a walk outside the police-guarded roads of the larger [foreign] 'settlements.'"[74] The Yokohama businessman Hall had strikingly similar experiences with the canines he encountered in Japan. He observed, "Kanagawa abounds in a breed of wolfish curs that growl and bark furiously at the white stranger. They hang around the house, but we have given over shooting at them for they are legion." During his visit to the northern treaty port Hakodate, he described the well-fed street dogs as "formidable with their large size, wolfish head and eyes, and bristling necks and tails, but at the first sight of a *tojin* [foreigner] down drops the tail and away the animal goes to the nearest alleyway where he stands barking and howling as you pass and all his comrades take up the refrain and pass you on from dog to dog, band to band, street to street, and you find yourself heralded in advance wherever you go.... Their very yelp seems to say '*tojin, tojin.*'"[75]

Rudyard Kipling (1865–1936) echoed analogous sentiments in several of his many stories about India. In one piece, "Garm—A Hostage" (1925), he recalled taking care of Garm, an English bull terrier for a fellow British officer on the subcontinent. At first, the autobiographical narrator thinks the task to be troublesome, in addition to which his own dog, a smaller terrier, resents his presence. However, after the bull terrier single-handedly saves the terrier from a dozen native dogs, who "though utter cowards" routinely sought to ambush "English dogs," both master and pet come to respect the newcomer. The fight scene dramatizes Kipling's perception of "yellow pariah-dogs"—described as "half-wild, starving beasts"—and "English dogs" as mortal enemies. According to Kipling, it is only through cunning, by overwhelming numbers, or with a rabid bite that the "measley" [sic] pariah dog can prevail over the colonial dog, and on this occasion several of the former die trying in vain to kill the English terriers.[76] From India to Japan, many Western visitors seemed to believe that the native dog was a never-ending but hopelessly frustrated enemy of colonizer and the colonial dog.

Some Westerners asserted that such craftiness, belligerence, and cowardliness were an inborn or inbred characteristic of both dogs and humans in Asia. This was precisely the claim of Robert Fortune (1813–80), an English horticulturalist who visited Japan and China during the 1850s. In his travelogue *Yedo and Peking: A Narrative of a Journey to the Capitals of Japan and China*, 1863), Fortune made the following observation about canines in the former city:

> The dogs here [Edo] were the only animals which showed their enmity to us, and this they did in a manner not to be mistaken. They rushed out…and barked at us in the most furious manner; but they are cowardly withal, and generally keep at a prudent distance.
>
> These dogs appear to be of the same breed as the common Chinese dog, and both have probably sprung from the same stock. It is curious that they should have the same antipathy to foreigners as their masters. For however civil and even kind the natives of Japan and China appear to be, yet there is no doubt that nine-tenths of them hate and despise us. Apparently such feelings are born with them, and they really cannot help themselves. That we are allowed to live and travel and trade in these countries is only because one class makes money out of us, and another and larger one is afraid of our power. I fear we must come to the conclusion, however unwillingly, that these are the motives which keep Orientals on their good behavior, and force them to tolerate us amongst them. The poor dogs have the same feelings implanted in their nature, but they have not the same hypocrisy, and therefore their hate is visible.[77]

Fortune recognized perceptively how empires operate and acknowledged that most local people resented the presence of Western officials and merchants. He admitted to the inequalities of colonial practice, but he quickly dismissed, or rationalized, the disparities by comparing Japanese and Chinese people with less-than-human dogs. If Asian dogs and humans shared the same inborn "nature," Fortune intimated, then Western economic and political supremacy was justified.

In this manner, like the parade of Westerners who visited Japan before and after him, Fortune used civilizationist rhetoric when describing the indigenous canines he encountered. He and many other Westerners compared the street dogs of the country to those elsewhere in the imperial world, such as the "common Chinese dog." Less explicitly, but perhaps even more tellingly, Western commentators often contrasted these animals with the colonial dog, which they regarded as domesticated, physically powerful, loyal, and well-bred—in short, civilized. In doing so, these Westerners, though they probably did not realize it, were projecting their cavalier attitudes about people in colonized and colonizable areas onto the animals.

Scientific Racism: Of "Mongrels" and "Curs"

To justify their imperial and colonizing ventures around the world, Westerners drew not only on the ideas of civilization but also on Occidental science. The theories of Darwin that gained popularity during the second half of the nineteenth century greatly influenced Western colonial and imperial policies. Although in some instances Darwinian theory, as articulated in the pioneering *Origin of Species* (1859), challenged religious and other attitudes that aligned native peoples with nonhuman animals, Darwinian science was by no means free from cultural and human biases. Indeed, elements of what later became known as social Darwinism were imbedded in the mature work of Darwin himself. Darwin saw, for example, the emergence of morality in humans as little more than an evolution of animal social instincts. At one point in *The Descent of Man* (1871) the evolutionary philosopher compared human "savages" with dogs, in that both "imagine that natural objects and agencies are animated by spiritual or living essences." Furthermore, Darwin contended that dogs had intellectual and moral faculties rivaling those of "savage" inhabitants of Tierra del Fuego. Whereas Fuegians allegedly demonstrated no feelings of religious devotion to a higher being, a dog exhibited a "love for his master, associated with complete submission, some fear, and perhaps other feelings." Some believe, Darwin continued, "that a dog looks on his master as on a god."[78] Is this not the embodiment of the ideal colonial dog, whose devotion surpasses that of the "savage" native?

Assumptions of racial and cultural superiority in social Darwinism intensified the dichotomies of domestic and wild, civilized and savage, and equated them with colonizer and colonized. In turn, these notions were projected onto animals themselves. Westerners used the language of science and racism to claim the superiority of Western breeds over native ones, and of pure-blooded creatures over those of mixed blood. This was especially true for dogs, those prized pets who live in greater proximity and intimacy with people than any other nonhuman animal. Some Victorian bulldog enthusiasts, for example, maintained that the most serious threat to the breed was "infusion of foreign blood." Others argued that if the bulldog became detached from English soil it would inevitably degenerate. Concerns about degeneration echoed prevailing scientific theories about the deleterious affects of tropical, disease-ridden climates, as well as social Darwinist anxieties about miscegenation with inferior groups. One defender of the bulldog's

"British blood" even reasoned, in circular fashion, that foreign blood "must be inferior because it is foreign."[79]

The prospect of canine degeneration through miscegenation seemed inevitable for the elder Kipling. An unidentified "modern philosophical writer," he reported, "says the British Empire in India is but 'a romantic episode' destined to pass away and leave no recognisable trace." Not so, he countered; the British legacy was destined to remain in India forever. "Though we may pass away and be forgotten," Kipling predicted, "the dogs we loved will remain as permanent colonists." Staying on in India, though, was evidently not without its pitfalls for such colonialist canines. Mixing with lesser native breeds, and dwelling in the unfamiliar environment of India, Kipling *père* asserted, would inevitably lead to degeneration and deformity, both physical and moral.

> It appears to be a fact that the creole dog, born in India of imported parents, develops some of the characteristics of the indigenous animal. His head, especially his nose, grows longer and narrower, he loses substance in the neck, chest, and loins; he stands on higher legs and wags a longer tail than his British-born parents. The climate exerts a deteriorating influence on his moral qualities, and he loses some of the courage, temper, and fine spirits which are the birthright of a good dog in the West.[80]

If fear existed that the colonial dog might degenerate when exposed to the climes and wiles of the colonial tropics, it was a foregone conclusion in the minds of some Western canine experts and enthusiasts that degeneration was the explanation for the abhorrent state of indigenous canines. Such was the view of Robert Leighton (1859–1934), the author of a 1907 work titled *The New Book of the Dog*, who had a far more sympathetic view of native dogs. "Pariah dogs," which are "found in almost all Oriental towns prowling about their own particular encampment, and in measure protecting the greater encampments of their human friends," wrote Leighton, are "domestic dogs which have degenerated into semi-wildness, yet which remain, as by inherited habit, in association with mankind." Unlike Western dogs, he claimed, no native dogs composed a distinctive breed; instead they were "all mongrels." "By the process of indiscriminate interbreeding and influence of environment, they acquire local character," Leighton cautioned, but in his opinion they ought not to be regarded as a legitimate breed.[81]

Such racialized idioms as "mongrel," "bastard," and "kaffir" were pervasive in southern and central African nineteenth-century and early twentieth-century discourses, which reflected European anxieties about the mixing of the human races in Africa. European discussion about dogs in Africa tended to emphasize concerns about breed more than civilization, and the obsession with purity of blood seems to have grown as European colonial powers increasingly found their political grasp and moral authority on the continent threatened in the twentieth century. South African officials, for example, recommended in 1948—the same year that the apartheid government of the National Party came to power—that game laws license purebred dogs at one pound per head and that "mongrel" dogs be taxed at a higher rate, "particularly unsterilized bitches." The proposal thus echoed white African fears of being overwhelmed numerically and sexually by black Africans. As anthropologist Robert J. Gordon has noted, many whites believed that "mongrel bitches owned by Africans tended to breed indiscriminately like their owners."[82] As with the ideas of civilization, the language of scientific racism pervaded the canine world.

Japan's contact with Western imperialism in the nineteenth century coincided with an age of rampant Darwinism and social Darwinism throughout the imperial landscape. Morse, the American zoologist, commented on dogs frequently and is perhaps not coincidentally also the individual credited by some historians with having introduced Darwinian thought to Japan. In his writings on the country for Western audiences, Morse proved himself to be one of the most sympathetic observers of local society. Nevertheless, like nearly every other Westerner, he had few kind words for the dogs of the country.

In their rhetoric, Morse and other Westerners often used elements of scientific and racial discourse to characterize native dogs and to contrast them with the colonial dog. In Japan and elsewhere, Westerners portrayed native dogs as wolfish, jackal-like, or wild in behavior, appearance, and breed. Often they described street dogs as "mongrels, with a good deal of European admixture," which was indeed probably increasingly true as time passed.[83] More often, though, they commented that native dogs looked and acted more like wolves (or sometimes foxes) than the domesticated dog breeds with whom they were familiar. "Most of the dogs one sees in Japan," Morse recorded in his journal, later published as *Japan Day by Day* (1917), "are of a wolf variety; they do not bark but howl."[84] Similarly, George Hilaire Bousquet (1845–1937), a French legal adviser to the Meiji government, reported that, while traveling north of Tokyo in 1874, his group repeatedly had to protect its own canines from wolfish native dogs.

> These creatures with their heavy forms, enormous size, long wild hair, elongated snouts, small deep-set eyes and prominent fangs, are because of their hunter instincts far closer to wolves than the peaceful setter . . . who just came to hide between my legs. Our caravan was obliged several times since the beginning of our trip to defend our setters by throwing stones at these aggressors.[85]

Here we find one of the few admissions on the part of Westerners that native breeds might actually be stronger than the colonial dog.

Physically, and in some ways behaviorally, native dogs did indeed resemble wolves. Even today, some taxonomists point to the wolfish appearance and behavior of Japanese dog breeds and, conversely, the doglike appearances of the extinct wolves of Japan. Japanese dog-keeping practices, and the resulting blurry ecological boundary among street dogs, feral dogs, wild dogs, mountain dogs, and wolves actually made early canine crossbreeding a distinct possibility, as historian Brett Walker has noted.[86] Perhaps fuzzy biological realities gave rise to indistinct taxonomies. Classical and early modern naturalists, observers who applied Western science in the nineteenth century, and even biologists today offer no definitive answers for sorting out the confusion over how to classify the archipelago's canines.[87]

At the same time, Westerners and their aversion to "wolfish-looking" native dogs must be understood in the context of Western scientific and cultural prejudices. Many Westerners saw wolves and other wild canines as enemies of civilization who had to be forcefully eliminated. They often deployed dogs—either practically or metaphorically—as partners in extermination campaigns and so found the gray zone between *Canis familiaris* and *Canis lupus*, between tameness and wildness, between their trusted companions and wily adversaries, deeply unsettling.

Westerners regarded wolflike local dogs either as never having been completely domesticated or as having degenerated from a domesticated state. They alleged that the wild nature of native dogs was the result of interbreeding with lower species, such as the wolf or the fox. The observation of British naturalist Richard Lydekker in his *Royal Natural History* (1893) was typical of scientific and popular sentiments of the day:

> A brief allusion may be made here to those nondescript dogs found in troops in the towns and villages of Eastern Europe, Asia and Africa, and commonly designated pariah dogs. These animals vary greatly in different districts, but many present a very wolfish appearance, and it is probable that they often interbreed with the wolves and jackals of their respective countries, while in India they may perhaps also cross with wild dogs. Originally, however, these pariah dogs were undoubtedly domesticated breeds, which, from neglect, have reverted to a greater or lesser extent toward a wild state.[88]

In more figurative terms, too, Westerners in the imperial world distinguished between dogs and wolves when they deployed canines to explicitly describe "Other" humans they encountered. The South Pacific explorer Horatio Hale (1817–96), for example, concluded that the "Feejeans [Fijians] may be said to differ from the Polynesian as the wolf from the dog; both, when wild are equally fierce, but the ferocity of the one may be easily subdued, while that of the other is deep-seated and untameable [*sic*]." As historian Barry Alan Joyce points out, for "civilizing" Western imperialists such as Hale, some human groups such as Tahitians who had been broken or African Americans who had been domesticated by slavery were compared to dogs, while other groups such as Fijians and American Indians were said to be equivalent to wolves—savage, fearsome, and irredeemable.[89]

In Japan, the zoologist Morse characteristically drew on Darwinian science and Western anxieties about degeneration and aversions to wild canines when describing the canines of the northern island of Hokkaido:

> If it is possible to get a cross between a dog and a fox there is certainly fox blood in these creatures. Every village has a pack of dogs, and at night they are very

noisy, making sounds like cats, but more infernal; they howl and squeal, but never bark. Darwin had observed in his work on domesticated animals that when dogs relapse from their cultivated state to a semi-savage one, they lose the bark and take on the howl again. Wild creatures to which they are related never bark, but howl.[90]

In this way, Westerners contrasted the degenerate and devolved state of native dogs with the thoroughly evolved colonial dog, who, they boasted, was purebred. Such expressions reflected recurring colonialist obsessions about the mixing of races. As one English commentator remarked, "No one would plant weeds in a window box or a flower garden. Why have mongrels as pets?"[91]

Heaping pejoratives on the backs of native canines, Westerners invoked the late nineteenth-century language of hygienic science to describe them as diseased or particularly susceptible to disease. From Istanbul to Seoul, from Pretoria to Delhi, there was a strong association between the grime of the streets and the pariah dogs that were "forever prowling" them. A. V. Williams Jackson (1862–1937), a professor of Indo-Iranian languages at Columbia University, described the Ottoman capital's "thronged narrow streets" as a place "where hurrying feet can scarce find space to avoid the packs of mangy curs that do duty as town-scavengers."[92] The "miles of mud walls, deep eaves, green slimy ditches, and blackened smoke-holes," the British travel writer Bird wrote of Korea, were the "paradise of mangy dogs."[93] Some Westerners believed that the source of contagions, including rabies, was the detestable diet of native canines, who purportedly feasted on garbage, human waste (both feces and corpses), and other food unfit for a dog. Not only "civilized" people, but apparently their dogs, too, found native dogs despicable. According to Mrs. R. Lee (1791–1856), the English author of a popular 1852 collection of animal anecdotes from around the globe, "domesticated dogs will hunt and kill [dingos, the wild Australian dog], but show signs of great disgust afterwards, always, if they can, plunging themselves into water, as if to get rid of the contamination caused by such contact."[94]

In contrast with a country and a people that they generally praised for cleanliness, foreign observers viewed the street dogs of Japan as disorderly and downright filthy. A typical example is found in an 1888 editorial in the English-language *Japan Weekly Mail*, which commented on the mixed blood and sullied condition of native dogs. The newspaper, probably drawing on erroneous scientific theories circulating in Europe at the time, reported that the development of rabies was less severe in native breeds than in full-blooded Western dogs because of the former's "mongrel" nature.[95] Still, the paper warned, the wretched state of native dogs posed a grave threat to the health of the foreign community. It alleged that in Japan and China, hydrophobia occurred with greater frequency in foreign settlements than elsewhere in the country.

The development of the disease is not so formidable in the native as it is in foreign-bred animals, the reason being that the latter are more full-blooded. Yet there is room to believe that many of the wretched, mangey curs which

The Native Dog and the Colonial Dog   49

slink about the streets of Honmura [in Yokohama] and elsewhere in a half-comatose condition, are suffering from a mild form of hydrophobia, which they may transmit by biting or other infection to their stronger congeners of alien strain, which in turn may bite their masters. There are some pariahs daily on view whose case, in pity to themselves, demands the merciful employment of club or poison.[96]

In Meiji Japan, as elsewhere, the quality of this "mercy" would reveal itself in anti-rabies and other extermination campaigns, which were motivated in part by ideas of civilization and scientific racism and are the subject of the next chapter.

Postcolonial Dogs

In this chapter I have traced the path of the colonial dog as a means of shedding light on the dynamics of colonial humanity and global imperialism from the mid-nineteenth to the early twentieth century. The history of canine imperialism reveals a complicated configuration of relationships among humans, dogs, imperial structures, and the languages of nationalism, civilization, and scientific racism that humans have used to describe them. Although the bulk of the data marshaled here derives from the specific experience of Japan, it is clear that similar patterns emerged in other imperial contexts. Part of the reason for these historical commonalities is that Western imperialists had shared notions of the worth of particular dog breeds and modes of dog keeping wherever they ventured. Throughout far and near eastern Asia, Africa, Australia, the Americas, and other areas they deemed backward, Westerners repeatedly idealized dog breeds from the metropole while denigrating the native canines of the imperial periphery.

The common element that binds together these various colonial contexts—and the dynamic of canine imperialism—is the power apparatus of (human) imperialism itself. Over the course of the nineteenth century, as never before, Western colonizers spread their political authority, economic appetites, and ideologies of religion, civilization, race, and science across the globe. Wherever they went, they were accompanied by the colonial dog, whom they used to support their authority, both practically and, more significantly, on a symbolic level. In this manner, colonizers created an imaginary canine cartography that was structured by, and in turn helped to structure, the dynamics of colonial humanity and the harsh realities of imperialism.

In some areas of the postcolonial world the derogatory nuances of the colonial dog were not forgotten. In China, for instance, signs in Shanghai and other imperial concessions that read "Chinese and Dogs Not Admitted," thereby juxtaposing the two groups, became a potent symbol of Western imperialism in the nineteenth and early twentieth centuries, and continued to be a frequent topic of discussion after the Communist regime secured the country's sovereignty in 1949. The association between Chinese and canines was all the more humiliating because for centuries the country's rulers used the "dog" radical in characters to denigrate members of ethnic minorities living in imperial China's frontier regions.[97] Deploying dogs to disparage an "Other" was by no means the exclusive province of Western colonizers.

In some postcolonial societies, people reviled certain breeds of dogs identified with past colonial governments. Often it was the German shepherd dog, a breed despised as a symbol of imperial aggression and governance, because colonizers frequently deployed the dogs for guard and police work.[98] This was the case on the Korean Peninsula, which endured nearly four decades of oppressive control by Japan, and in the Congo, ruled ruthlessly by Belgium in the name of the Leopoldian civilizing mission from 1885 to 1960. The persistent link between certain dogs and colonial rule in the minds of the colonized was underscored by the experience of the American boxer George Foreman (1949–). When he arrived in Kinshasa, Zaire (now Congo), for his famous 1974 "rumble in the jungle" with his compatriot Muhammad Ali (1942–), Foreman emerged from the plane with Doggo, his massive shepherd dog. The imposing animal accompanied him almost everywhere, including into the ring for his weigh-in two days before the bout, in which he was knocked out and lost his world heavyweight title. Foreman figuratively heightened his own physical strength and manliness through his "mastery" of this menacing but loyal subordinate. Zairian dictator Mobutu Sese Seko (1930–97) added to Foreman's aura with his gift of another animal to Foreman: a lion cub. Mobutu's subjects, though, were appalled by Foreman's choice of dog breed, and their support turned even more to Ali, who had already captured widespread local support by emphasizing his African heritage. Foreman was bewildered by his cold reception.[99] Little did he know of the legacy of canine imperialism when he stepped onto the tarmac and out of his corner into the ring.

In most places, though, the colonial dog has largely been forgotten, especially in areas where imperialism did not leave long and festering memories. Amnesia may have set in for a couple of reasons. In a few countries, such as Japan, the native dog who had been denigrated and marginalized was rediscovered and valorized as an icon of purity, loyalty, and bravery. Concurrent with an upswing in nationalism and predominance of imperialism in early twentieth-century Japan, particularly during the 1930s, this movement transformed the native dog into a colonial dog itself, a breed that became recognized as legitimate within and beyond its borders. This transformation brings us back to the question posed in the introduction: Can the subaltern bark? Perhaps, but only when it is transformed into a colonial dog. In other words, as in the case of Japan, only when it became an imperial power, did its native dog become a colonial dog.

Forgetfulness may also have been facilitated when local elites continued to revere the same breeds esteemed by Westerners long after colonial rule and the imperial threat ended. This, too, was the case in Japan as well as in many other postcolonial societies. Although not through degeneration as John Lockwood Kipling predicted, the colonial dog remained as a permanent imperial legacy. Many postcolonial countries thoroughly adopted the dog-keeping ways and favorite breeds of their former colonial rulers. As a result, they have largely forgotten the imperial source of this naturalized and localized canine cartography. In addition, local elites sometimes embraced the Western imperialists' ideological aversion to native dogs, who were regarded as not completely domesticated and civilized. It is to the actual and metaphorical embrace of the Western colonial dog, and to persecution of the native dog, as seen in Japan and elsewhere in extensive campaigns against indigenous canines from the nineteenth to the early twentieth century, that we now turn.

2

CIVILIZING CANINES; OR, DOMESTICATING AND DESTROYING DOGS

In 1873 the artist Utagawa Yoshifuji (1828–87) created a print that invokes how the arrival of Western canine imperialism had radically reshaped human-canine relations in Japan in just over two decades. The print shows three dogs sitting down to a lunch of *hikkoshi soba*, a noodle dish eaten to celebrate the arrival of a new neighbor. Two of the dogs are native canines, as evidenced by their physical appearance and traditional Japanese clothing. The other dog is a Western canine wearing dark trousers and a navy-blue tunic. All three sport wooden tags hanging around their necks. In the accompanying text, the Western dog greets the native dogs, telling them that he has come from a faraway country to make his home in this land. To this, one of the local dogs replies, "You are welcome. Lately, there are bad dogs who trouble people, so dogs without tags are struck down and killed. For this, I am thankful."[1] The bad dogs, whom the local dog refers to are untagged native dogs, and as an indigenous canine, he is grateful for a tag that spares at least those dogs whose owners have registered them with the state. New regulations, such as the registration requirements, encouraged people to civilize dogs by turning them into pets through Western-style dog-keeping practices and threatened to eliminate them if they did not. The impact of "civilization" on dogs is shown by their tags, a practice that various local authorities began to require for the first time in the 1870s, and more metaphorically by their wearing of human clothing.

It would be easy to dismiss the railings against native dogs throughout the imperial world if such thinking and such talk had not led to actual changes that bore deadly consequences for canines, especially native dogs, and which served to discipline people as well. In a way that sharply diverged from other societies that were the object of Western imperialism, many elite and upwardly mobile Japanese quickly acquired an enthusiasm for Western breeds and dog-keeping practices, and used these animals to create and reinforce social-status structures. But as in other parts of the colonized and colonizable world, the Meiji government, influenced by imperial ideologies of civilization and scientific racism, began to implement policies to eliminate or regulate canines, whether street, feral, and wild dogs or wolves, often on the pretext of combating rabies and protecting domestic farm and game animals. Such steps were not without some precedent on the archipelago, but the new Meiji regime, as a modernizing nation-state equipped with unprecedented intrusive bureaucratic and policing powers, was able to increasingly extend a system of surveillance and control over its subjects, both human and nonhuman, within the country's newly defined borders. Until the government was able to successfully persuade the Western imperial powers to revise the unequal treaties and to escape its semicolonial status in the mid-1890s, it held less sway over foreign residents, and this served to privilege both them and their dogs and to disadvantage indigenous canines, who continued to be a target of imperial ire. As a result, seemingly mundane concerns about dogs were rarely unrelated to politics, either domestic or international.

As highlighted by the ecology of indigenous canines in Tokugawa Japan and elsewhere, humans often shared cities and towns with many other kinds of creatures—domesticated, feral, and wild. In much of the today's world, people have largely driven animals out of areas inhabited primarily by humans. This separation is, of course, the result of urbanization and economic change, but as historian Keith Thomas has argued, it is also the product of powerful sensibilities about what it means to be civilized.[2] Ideas that demanded a clear-cut distinction between culture and nature emerged during the Enlightenment and spread throughout much of the world during the age of New Imperialism, contributing to a disappearance of many animals from cityscapes. During much of the last two centuries, people in many parts of the world have often either eliminated beasts—killing them or restricting them to so-called natural areas such as highly regulated parks and reserves—or completely domesticated and commodified them, either as sources of food and other products or as pets. For many canines, these processes amounted to either completely becoming domestic companions of people or extermination at human hands.

The tendency of dogs to stray between domestication and wildness places them ambiguously between the dichotomies of culture and nature, within and beyond the reach of human domination. Nineteenth-century colonizers, as well as local elites who accepted Western dog-keeping practices in Japan and elsewhere, valued certain canines as "useful" when they acted as assistants, guards, and companions. They expected dogs to be fully domesticated and absolutely subservient to the commands of a human master. Perhaps this was one of the reasons that during the nineteenth century wolves evoked such dislike and denials that they were related in any way to Western dog breeds. Similarly, many nineteenth-century imperial and local authorities had almost no tolerance for the behavior of the street, feral, and wild dogs who wandered about cities and through the countryside exhibiting little fidelity or respect for the authority of humans. On the contrary, these animals seemed to express their greatest hostility toward unfamiliar-looking outsiders, who were often dressed differently. The utility and supposed loyalty of domesticated dogs was esteemed and taken as a sign of their civilized nature, while those canines who strayed beyond human control and ownership, who blurred the line between culture and nature, were put down. Imagining them as wolfish, mongrel, or rabid justified their elimination.

Within the ideological framework that valued Western breeds and denigrated dogs in the periphery, Western colonial regimes and the Meiji government, which avoided formal colonization but was strongly influenced by outside pressures, initiated campaigns to destroy canines—whether they were street, feral, and wild dogs, or wolves, dingoes, hyenas, jackals, and coyotes during the latter half of the nineteenth century. They did so to combat rabies and protect ranching, poultry operations, and hunting grounds. As a result, in some areas of the world, including the Japanese archipelago, humans drove wolves to extinction and drastically reduced the populations of other canines. Such efforts often targeted native dogs and have ensured the numerical and cultural supremacy of the colonial dogs in many countries to this day.

Nineteenth-century Western imperialism introduced new capitalist modes of exploiting the natural environment. Westerners and local elites who emulated them initiated more intensive ranching, farming, and hunting practices in colonized and colonizable areas. Canines played an important role in the support of and opposition to these projects. On the one hand, dogs—usually breeds from colonial metropoles—were deployed as herders or sentries, to fend off predators, both humans and animals, or as gundogs in the pursuit of prey. On the other hand, ranchers, farmers, and hunters despised canines—almost inevitably native animals—such as wolves, coyotes, and jackals, as well as wild, feral, and street dogs, as lethal marauders who ravaged livestock, domestic fowl, and wild game. In many areas of the imperial world, such as North America, Africa, India, Australia, and New Zealand, government officials made concerted efforts to exterminate canines, whom they often collectively referred to as wolves or mad wild canines, though many of the animals targeted were in fact domesticated dogs nominally kept by local people. These dogs' packlike behavior, habitation of roadways and the outskirts of populated areas, and limited attachment to humans, as well as their physical appearance, did not meet the expectations of what a "civilized" dog ought to be.

Authorities sometimes used the pretext of hydrophobia as an emotional and highly effective means to justify the eradication of canines. A number of historians in recent decades have explored the practical and rhetorical suppression of rabies in various countries during the late nineteenth century.[3] Perhaps because most of these studies focus on national societies in western Europe, the global nature of hydrophobia during the age of New Imperialism has gone largely unnoticed. Since the late twentieth century, the massive, but to a considerable extent regulated, flow of goods and people across political borders—a facet of globalization—has allowed for the almost instant spread of infectious diseases, which has so far been checked due to modern medical advances, international cooperation, and border controls. More than a century earlier, globalization in the form of Western imperialism and trade heightened a similar, though far less regulated, worldwide movement of people and other creatures that spread contagions such as rabies.

Although the rabies virus and other such contagions were often already present in much of the Japanese archipelago (except perhaps the northern island of Ezo [Hokkaido] until the early 1860s) and elsewhere, the increased movement of people and other creatures led to more frequent and severe outbreaks. In short, as Westerners embarked for empire accompanied by dogs, hydrophobia came along for the ride more than ever before.

Government efforts at canine control had consequences for humans as well as canines. Official policies aimed at dogs had the intent, and often the result, of regulating the human social order. The dogs whom authorities pronounced as threatening to people and farm and game animals often lived in the same areas as certain groups and classes of people who were similarly seen as unruly and un-controllable. Such canines were more likely to be indigenous or of mixed breed, whereas those owned by Westerners or well-to-do local people were more likely to be Western breeds. As a result, authorities were far more likely to round up dogs who dwelt in economically disadvantaged and ethnically different urban neigh-borhoods and rural areas than those owned by foreigners and local elites. For these and other reasons, in Japan and other parts of the imperial world foreign dogs became a symbol of the privilege and power of Western colonial and local elites, while street dogs came to represent urban and rural groups who challenged imperialism and the tremendous and often invasive authority of colonial govern-ments and modern nation-states.

Constructing Canine Class Cartographies

In mid-nineteenth-century Japan, as in the sixteenth century, it did not take long for local elites to acquire a taste for foreign dogs and the practices associated with them. The result was a mapping of the imperial canine geography onto local class hierarchies. Ownership of a colonial dog became a means for affluent and upwardly mobile Japanese to prove their "civilized" sophistication and to create and reinforce status structures. As early as the mid-1860s, a print appeared in the monthly magazine *Tōkyō kaika hanjō shi* (A record of Tokyo's enlightenment and prosperity) showing a kimono-clad female member of the local elite strolling along with a medium-sized Western dog on a leash.[4] Such a performance was one example of the widespread adoption of Western cultural forms during the early part of the Meiji era, one requiring not only an outlay of cash but a set of daily practices. Only elites had the financial means and social connections to acquire such animals, and the leisure time to engage in such activities.

Similar patterns occurred in other colonial contexts, such as the Indian Subcontinent, though they were not as widespread as in Japan. There, John Lockwood Kipling believed, "British influence" was stimulating "a slow but indubitable revolution…in favour of the dog." The "Hindu; and the Muhammadan,—the most conservative of races," he wrote, "may cherish his ancient grudge [against canines], but both are learning that the dog of good caste is a useful companion and friend." For Kipling, the dog of good caste was not the native but the colonial dog, a point he makes clear by asserting that the colonized were adopting the British "science, the care and lore of dogs" and that for them the "English dog has come to stand as a high-caste animal of respectable birth." Kipling assured his readers that "native ladies see that European animals are unlike the unclean creatures of the street, and are anxious to adopt them." The spaniel, bulldog, and other English breeds were "thought most highly of," he claimed, and English names were becoming "naturalised and Persianised after the liquid Oriental manner." Thus Spot, for example, had on the subcontinent reportedly degenerated into Eespot. One favorite "Indo-Anglian" dog name, though, ripe with irony, retained its original English form: "Bully."[5]

The civilized connotations embodied by Western dogs and their acquisition by local elites in Japan are particular evident in *Seiyō dōchū hizakurige* (A Western shank's mare; 1870–76), by the journalist and author Kanagaki Robun (1829–94) and two collaborators. This book humorously described the turmoil resulting from the introduction of Western culture in the early years of the Meiji period. Many of its illustrations depict dog bodies that bear a telling resemblance to the bodies of their owners. Hunched Japanese nonelites are positioned next to unkempt street dogs or small round puppies, while tall-standing Westernized elites are accompanied by lanky, well-groomed Western canines.[6] In one, for example, a Japanese figure is shown with a lean Western hound. He is a well-to-do, dignified, bearded "gentleman" clad in a Western coat and top hat, and he holds a walking stick in one hand and the dog's leash in the other. He stands tallest, literally and especially figuratively, among three male figures, positioned right to left on a two-page spread, who embody Japanese progression toward "civilization." The man on the right, labeled an "unenlightened person," represents a paragon of traditional Japan. He is a defiant-looking two-sworded samurai. His hair is bound in a topknot, and he is dressed in a *haori* jacket and in divided trousers (*hakama*), and wears *zōri*, thonged sandals, on his feet. In his hand, he clutches a folded fan, and two swords hang at his waist. Next to him, in the center of the picture, appears an eclectically dressed young man, designated as a "half-enlightened person." Some of his clothing is Japanese like that of the samurai, but his other apparel and implements are distinctly Western. He wears European footwear and a black short-brimmed cap that reveals a closely shorn hairstyle. In his left hand he dangles a Western-style umbrella, while he holds out a pocket watch in his right. The two less "enlightened" men face toward the "gentleman" on the left, as if to imply that he is the future of a "civilized" Japan.[7] The presence of the Western dog validates his supposedly sophisticated status, and he is apparently the only one of the three worthy of owning such a canine.

Although local Japanese did not express the same extreme aversion toward native dogs as did Western visitors, they recognized differences in behavior between colonial and native canines, and similarly employed the idiom of civilization to describe them. "The Story of Enlightened and Unenlightened Dogs" (Kaika to fukaika no inu no hanashi), probably published originally in a pamphlet titled *Bunmei kaika* (Civilization and enlightenment; 1874) and spread orally during

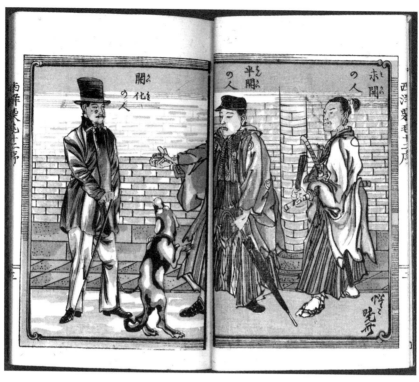

6. From left to right, "unenlightened person," "half enlightened person," and "enlightened person" with his hound, an illustration in Kanagaki Robun's *Seiyō dōchū hizakurige* (1870).

this period, provides a striking example.[8] As is obvious from the title, the story relied on the same civilizationist rhetoric that Westerners used to talk about canines. The story, of course, is not about dogs at all, but is instead a parable deployed by the powerful to persuade the populace to embrace the government's policy of Westernization through "civilization and enlightenment."

The story's canine cast of characters consists of two rival packs of native street dogs living in adjacent neighborhoods. One day, the leader of one pack meets with the boss of the other gang. He expresses his concern that, even though the world is changing around them through the influence of civilization and enlightenment, "we dogs are not adapting." "We dogs are still old-fashioned," remarks the canine critic, "still marking our territory by a single hedge or sewer ditch" and "feuding with the dogs on the next block." By contrast, Western dogs are supposedly enlightened because they eschew such "stingy things as fighting over a lousy block or half-block of territory," and instead "follow four and five feet behind their master's horse or buggy." "They rarely fight amongst themselves," continues the leader of the first pack, "and if one of our kind barks at them, they simply make a

face as if to say, 'I don't have time for your foolishness' and continue on their way."
He then proposes that street dogs stop doing "such unenlightened things as barking at people dressed in Western attire, and instead, like Western dogs, obtain the rights of freedom and independence that allow them to go anywhere without worrying about whose territory it is."

The leader of the second pack, unconvinced, rejects the suggestion. Apparently, as restaurants move their establishments from traditional neighborhoods to more up-and-coming quarters, the enlightened dogs who inhabit the latter have access to more leftovers than they can possibly eat, while their unenlightened counterparts, like those of the second pack, become increasingly miserable. The hungry canines' gloom, the tale moralizes, is a "result of their refusal to listen to the ideas of civilization and enlightenment." According to the literary scholar Ishii Kendō, the above story was one of the more effective parables produced by the cultural proponents of Westernization.[9] Perhaps it derived its persuasive power from its depictions of everyday life with which people could readily relate. Because of their daily contact with such dogs, audiences were able to recognize the behaviors described as relevant to, rather than distant and distinct from, their own experience.

Acquiring a Western breed was an option for only the up-and-coming members of society, the most well-to-do or well connected. Throughout the Meiji period, newspapers reported outrageous prices paid by the rich to import a particular breed, or the presenting of Western or other foreign dogs to the emperor and other government officials. Mary Crawford Fraser, wife of Hugh Fraser, British consul-general to Japan from 1889 to 1894, reported that the Meiji emperor was fond of dogs, especially a "tiny long-haired terrier, which was a present from Madame Sannomiya" and likely a Shantung terrier. "The little creature is quite a personage in the Palace," Fraser wrote, "and during this hot weather has a servant who sits beside it all day to fan the flies away and put bits of ice into its mouth. No one is allowed to wake it from sleep; and I believe there was terrible trouble one day when some unlucky person trod on its tail."[10] Emulating practices popular among Westerners in the treaty ports, many elite Japanese began to hunt birds and other small game assisted by purebred dogs, such as English setters and German pointers, which became some of the most expensive and the most sought after dog breeds in late-nineteenth- and early twentieth-century Japan. Two images illustrate this preoccupation, which was first adopted by the wealthy and then spread to the middle classes by the early twentieth century. The first, a mid-Meiji photograph showed the long-retired shogun, Tokugawa Yoshinobu (1837–1913), posing with his pointer, a supply of ammunition about his midsection and a shotgun slung over his shoulder.[11] Although Yoshinobu and his family lost political power to dissatisfied samurai who overthrew the Tokugawa regime in the name of the emperor in 1868, he was able to regain and maintain his social status in part by adopting new cultural practices, of which bird hunting with a Western dog was one. The second, the inaugural 1914 cover of the monthly boys' magazine *Shōnen kurabu* (Boys' club), displayed a print of a young adolescent male, dressed in a school uniform and armed with a gun, looking down at a pointer as birds fly in the background.[12] The cover of the magazine, one of the first marketed to the emerging middle class, aptly shows how middle-class emulation of upper-class practices (inspired by those of Westerners) furthered the spread of this adopted canine culture.

The supposedly sophisticated nature of Western canines was enhanced as early as the 1860s when a new word of English origin, *kame*, was coined for a dog of foreign breed. To the great amusement of anglophone Westerners, Japanese apparently created the expression when they heard foreigners calling to their dogs to "come here." The American zoologist Morse was one of many bemused observers who commented on the phenomenon: "You ask for the name of dog and the answer will be 'Kumhere.' Many think that is the Japanese name for dog, whereas the name has been adapted from the English and American who, in calling a dog, say, 'Come here!' 'Come here!'—and the Japanese in these parts have supposed that the word represents the English name for dog, which in Japanese is *inu*."[13]

If Japanese in the middle of the nineteenth century associated Western dogs with foreigners in the treaty ports, within a few decades the association had been extended to include the indigenous upper classes. By the 1880s, a foreign dog was practically an essential complement to a top hat or lacy dress, as exemplified by the center panel of an 1889 triptych by the print artist Inoue Tankei (or Inoue Yasuji; 1864–89) showing a well-to-do Japanese family enjoying a spring day in Tokyo's Asakusa Park with some sort of small hound.[14] Similar associations appear in a lithograph titled *Kiken bijin* (Elite beauty; 1888). The print shows a woman posing with what appears to be a spitz puppy arrayed in matching Western clothing.[15] (See color plate 5.) The woman's blue dress, with white, gold, and red trim, coordinated with a frilly collar of gold and red fabric around the dog's neck. The portrayal hearkens back to depictions of elite Tokugawa women with their lapdogs. At the same time, the artist is clearly familiar with contemporary dog-keeping practices in Europe, where elite society journals prescribed the proper clothing changes for a lapdog over the course of a day.[16] The lithograph quintessentially evokes the so-called Rokumeikan era of the 1880s, when the drive for Westernization reached its height and Tokyo's privileged gathered at the posh Deer-Cry Pavilion (Rokumeikan) to host foreign dignitaries and partake in ballroom dancing. Unlike the contemporaneous fascination with Western dogs, the enthusiasm for ballroom dancing did not last. It went out of fashion after conservative politicians shrilly criticized a Rokumeikan masquerade ball attended by high government officials including Prime Minister Itō Hirobumi and his "Dancing Cabinet," as a silly, demeaning attempt to win the approval of foreigners.

The more subtle practice of keeping a Western dog drew less criticism but did not escape it entirely. A few examples stand out. In a letter to the editor published in the daily *Yomiuri* newspaper in 1878, Nanba Shinshichirō, a resident of the Yaegaki neighborhood in Tokyo, expressed his dismay at the manners of his compatriots who imitated Western dog-keeping mores.

There seems to be no particular harm inflicted by the many people who arrogantly regard themselves as civilized and enlightened by dressing in Western clothing and walking a *kame* with a leash, but what is troublesome is when they bring their *kame* to beef-eating establishments and other restaurants, and on entering the premises, let the dog wander about twitching its nose in the dining areas of others. In Japan, we still partake of our food sitting on straw matting. Is it not improper for a dog to enter a Japanese-style room? I recently lost my appetite entirely and left a beef restaurant in the Asakusa area in disgust, because soon after I settled in and had my first drink, one of these *kame* suddenly dashed in and then ambled around my table. Why don't we prevent dogs from tracking their paws across Japanese-style rooms until we have decided to pull up the straw flooring [tatami] and start wearing our shoes inside?[17]

A couple of years later, another letter to the editor published in the *Yomiuri* from a reader signing himself Tokibō related an episode that he claimed reminiscent of the extravagant treatment of dogs during the rule of the fifth Tokugawa shogun Tsunayoshi (1646–1709). Influenced by Buddhist tenets about the importance of honoring all forms of life, Tsunayoshi had enacted a series of unpopular animal-protection measures that earned him the nickname Dog Shogun after his death, because he had been born in the year of the dog and because of his affinity for canines.[18] Just as ideas about civilization, zoonotic disease, and ranching and hunting concerns drove canine eradication in the final third decades of the nineteenth century, Buddhism and the Chinese zodiac calendar contributed to canine clemency in an earlier age. Different ideas in different periods of history produced drastically different consequences for dogs and people. Alluding to this earlier history, Tokibō wrote of a recent incident in which the *kame* of a wealthy household had allegedly barked fiercely at a man delivering goods. The visitor fended off the dog with a stick, only to be reprimanded by a household servant for treating the dog poorly. Referring to the dog in the most respectful language, the servant declared that the deliveryman ought even to be thankful that the dog had considered biting his dirty leg.[19] Elements of class criticism are clearly evident in Nanba's and Tokibō's letters, and the latter's mention of Tsunayoshi adds a political dimension to his censure.

In a similar manner, an 1888 open letter from writer Shiga Shigetaka (1863–1927) to Prime Minister Kuroda Kiyotaka (1840–1900) contained an implicit condemnation of the wealthy sport of bird hunting with dogs. Shiga wrote:

Although you are a man of affairs, we simply ask that when you go hunting with your dogs on official holidays or after work, you should get off at Hasuda or Koga stations and take a look at the wretched condition of the local inhabitants. . . . Only when the people of all the provinces of a nation are rich can the nation as a whole be rich; only when the nation is rich can its army be strong.[20]

For a nationalist and geographer like Shiga, Western hunting dogs represented a citified and extravagant foreign affectation, much as ballroom dancing might have done. Despite such criticisms as Nanba's, Tokibō's, and Shiga's, the rich and powerful did not give up their taste for Western breeds. A 1901 article in the *Yomiuri* noted that some fifty different non-Japanese breeds dwelt in Tokyo (constituting an estimated total of around six thousand dogs), and that native canines were disappearing.[21]

Japanese adoption of Western dog breeds and dog-keeping practices proceeded with remarkable speed. At first, local elites emulated Western canine culture mainly in the treaty ports, but these practices spread, through activities such as bird hunting, throughout the archipelago by the end of the century. This flexibility to accept outside practices corresponded with wider societal trends during the Meiji period. Such cultural assimilation was unmatched by other non-Western cultures faced with similar threats and opportunities posed by European and American imperialism. Not only did many Japanese adopt Western ways in their enthusiasm for the Western breeds, but they did so, through official government policies, by persecuting canines, especially indigenous ones, who did not adhere to the newly accepted standard of what it meant to be a civilized dog.

Campaigns against Native Canines
and Other Humans

From the 1870s onward, the Meiji regime used the threat of rabies and the menace posed to the livestock industry and sport hunting to translate crescendoing civilizationist and scientific racist expressions of distaste for native dogs and wolves into government policy. As articulated in the *Japan Weekly Mail,* it was ill-bred native "curs" who were seen as the biggest danger by the government and its foreign advisers, both official and self-appointed.[22] And so it was that native canines bore the brunt of half-century-long campaigns to cleanse Japan of hydrophobia, to eliminate so-called vermin from the countryside, and to civilize its streets. Foreign dogs largely escaped the campaigns because of their identification with Westerners and the native upper classes. By the late 1880s, Matsumori Taneyasu (1825–92), a natural historian in Yamagata Prefecture, noted that while the "seed" of foreign dogs was spreading rapidly, "Japanese dogs (*waken*) have been deliberately killed from time to time since the Meiji Restoration" in 1868.[23]

Extensive killing of canines was undertaken, in part, at the behest of the Meiji government's official advisers, and was motivated by ideas of civilization and racialized science as much as it was by economic and epidemiological concerns. Two figures who contributed importantly to the formulation of this policy were the Americans D. W. Ap Jones and Edwin Dun. One of many foreign employees hired by the government to assist Japan in its efforts to modernize, Jones (1851–unknown) resided in the country from 1873 to 1879. During his last four years there, he was entrusted with extensive authority by the Ministry of Home Affairs to oversee the creation of a sheep and dairy-cattle operation at the Shimōsa ranch in Chiba Prefecture, and to train a generation of animal-husbandry specialists from across the nation. Schooled in Western techniques and ideas, these fifty men went on to oversee and participate in livestock projects throughout the country.[24]

Like many other foreigners, Jones had little regard for native dogs, and when they began to attack sheep on the ranch, he was in a position to do something about it. Immediately after assuming his duties at the ranch, he requested that Chiba Prefecture begin to exterminate dogs within a broad area around Shimōsa. In a letter enlisting support from district and village officials, he reported many incidents of wild dogs killing sheep and ponies, and recalled the recent and widely reported death of an eight-year-old girl bitten by street dogs in nearby Tokyo.[25] Jones did not mention rabies specifically, but there was probably little need to do so. Just two years earlier, an outbreak in Tokyo had left nine people dead.

Jones employed the familiar rhetoric of civilization and scientific racism to condemn native dogs. While conceding that in Japan there were "some good dogs who have the ability to protect the property of their master and ward off burglars," he claimed that such dogs were "quite rare, and most dogs in Japan are offensive, despicable, and evil. These dogs were originally called the wolf-dogs of the eastern barbarians; they are of a savage nature, and are not the kind of dogs that a civilized people like the Japanese ought to keep."[26] Jones sought to vilify dogs in Chiba, and throughout Japan, by connecting them historically with the "eastern barbarians," the ethnically distinct, horse-riding Emishi people, who had lived in the northeastern reaches of the archipelago and long resisted the control of the premodern Yamato state. By doing so, Jones adopted, ironically, the same idiom of "barbarism" that xenophobic samurai had only recently employed to characterize Westerners like himself, and that Yamato elites a millennium earlier had employed against the nonagrarian peoples of the far northeast.

Apparently, Jones's request and rhetoric were effective. The prefecture immediately implemented a program that rewarded people for eliminating canines commensurate with the proximity of the animal to the ranch. Over the next decade, the government eradicated more than 1,200 canines annually in the area.[27] Probably few of these dogs were of Western origin. In 1876 Jones had Foreign Minister Terashima Munenori (1832–93) send letters to all foreign consulates in Tokyo informing them of the effort to crack down on "wild dogs" and cautioning them to keep their dogs on a leash when in Chiba.[28] In part, this was to ensure the safety of the Western sheep-herding dogs whom he had imported, but it was also to avoid accidentally killing any dogs of the Westerners and local elites who often hunted small game in the area. Just in case, he had signs posted at major crossroads near the ranch in Japanese, English, and French warning that "all dogs, either wild or domestic when let alone, shall immediately be caught and killed."[29] In a double irony, however, Jones's work for the government and time in Japan were cut short when he was seriously wounded in an attack by what the British diplomat Alcock had called the other "nuisance" of Japan—sword-wielding ruffians.

During his tenure as a foreign adviser on the northern island of Hokkaido, Edwin Dun (1848–1931), like Jones, exercised considerable influence over the development of the country's modern agricultural industry. Dun was employed by

7. Edwin Dun with a collielike sheepdog lying at his feet, another American adviser to the Kaitakushi, and fourteen of their Japanese students in an undated photograph. Used with permission of the Dun and Machimura Memorial Museum.

the Colonization Agency (Kaitakushi) from 1873 to 1883 and was charged with overseeing four expansive experimental farms in Hokkaido. An undated photograph shows Dun along with another American adviser and fourteen Japanese students, who came from throughout the archipelago to study Western ranching techniques. A collielike sheepdog lies between Dun's feet, probably one of at least six imported from the United States by the Kaitakushi to protect its burgeoning herds of sheep.[30]

In 1884 Dun left Hokkaido for Tokyo, where he became an official in the American legation for over a decade and lived until his death. Sometime during his stay in Tokyo, he acquired an English springer spaniel, a breed originally created for hunting and of significantly higher status than the sheepdogs he imported to Hokkaido. A photograph from around 1916 shows Dun with three of his younger boys, one of whom is holding the leash of the spaniel. The dog, whose name is unknown, has a tail that has not been docked, which indicates that the animal was probably not used for hunting but served primarily as a pet and for show. Ironically, one of the descendants of this dog probably became a Japanese colonial dog. Dun's oldest son, Hajime, became an oil executive for a government-controlled company in the Japanese colony of Taiwan, and a 1936 photograph shows him with his Japanese wife and children and a springer named Jon in a park in the southwestern city of Tainan.[31]

As did Jones in Chiba, Dun and his colleagues in Hokkaido sought to eradicate canines who were preying on livestock, particularly ponies and sheep. The Colonization Agency deployed two methods in this initiative: a bounty system and strychnine, "enough," as Dun later boasted, "to poison every living thing on the island." Their target was supposedly just wolves. Dun described lupines years later in his memoir in the most frightening and exaggerated of terms: "an enormous head and mouth armed with tremendous fangs and teeth...feet...three or four times larger than the feet of the largest dog which they resemble in shape, only the claws are much longer."[32] An examination of Kaitakushi correspondence, however, reveals that the vast majority of canines targeted and destroyed were not in fact wolves, but dogs kept by Ainu, the indigenous people of the island. Labeling them wolves, wild dogs (*yaken*), evil dogs (*akuken*), or mad dogs (*kyōken*) provided a convenient excuse for their slaughter.

The experience of Colonization Agency officials with dogs who dwelt in Ainu villages paralleled that of Westerners and local elites who attracted the hostility of street dogs on the southern Japanese islands. Iwane Seiichi, a Kaitakushi colleague of Dun's, described how each Ainu native (*dojin*) household kept a few dozen dogs, which roamed about villages. When Japanese (*wajin*) strangers approached, the dogs would rush at them in packs barking furiously, but because "Ainu loved these dogs as if they were their children" and feared that they would be harmed, they would quickly scold them and shoo them away. Iwane recalled how while passing once through the village of Monbetsu near the Shizunai experimental farm, he caught the attention of one or two dogs. These were immediately joined by many more and Iwane soon found himself surrounded. Desperate, he pulled out a knife and began slashing at the dogs, wounding one, and frightening the others, who finally scattered when a native woman emerged from a nearby home. The experience evidently strengthened Iwane's determination to eliminate Ainu dogs. On returning to the Shizunai ranch, he instructed that the dogs in the area of the village be slaughtered.[33]

This incident was not an isolated one but part of a systematic effort to extirpate canines whom the Colonization Agency regarded as "noxious" obstacles to its plan to breed horses and other livestock in Hokkaido. In January 1878, Kaitakushi officials ordered the eradication of "domesticated dogs kept by Ainu" (*dojin-ra chikuken*) and "wild dogs," whom they blamed for the deaths of horses and trampling of fields at the Niikappu ranch. The directive banned Ainu in the farm's vicinity from keeping dogs and established financial incentives for them to kill their own and other dogs as well as wolves by offering monetary rewards for pelts submitted to government offices.[34] A few months later, in April, officials at Kaitakushi's headquarters in the capital city of Sapporo raised the specter of rabies as a reason to eliminate dogs. Since 1861, when the virus probably entered Hokkaido for the first time, local authorities reported rabies outbreaks, first, in the treaty port of Hakodate and, later, in Sapporo. In 1878 Kaitakushi officials warned their employees that in addition to the threat posed by wild dogs to the livestock, poultry, and fishing industries, the "most" alarming danger was that these canines might go crazy with rabies during the approaching heat of summer and bite people.[35] Government offices around the island raised bounties on the pretext that destroying dogs would protect people and their livestock and fields. The Nemuro bureau in eastern Hokkaido, for example, offered fifteen *sen* (a *sen* is one-hundredth of a yen) for the hide of an unlicensed or wild dog.[36] When such warnings and monetary rewards failed to produce adequate results because of the unwillingness of many Ainu to part with their dogs, authorities resorted to toxins and bounty hunters, and sometimes organized dog-killing sweeps through the countryside. In fact, many bounty hunters were Ainu, who turned from hunting rapidly dwindling herds of deer to supply venison factories established by the Kaitakushi to eliminating predators such as dogs, wolves, bears, and crows, which the Kaitakushi thought threatened livestock and ranches and farms. In the end, the deer population, Ainu culture, and wolves and Ainu dogs were decimated. Ainu bounty hunters, though, were not alone in hunting down canines, especially as concern about hydrophobia grew. Though likely an exaggeration of the number of those involved, the *Yomiuri* newspaper reported that some 4,500 people anxious about rabies scoured the mountains of Esashi near Hakodate and succeeded in destroying two to three hundred "evil dogs" (*akuken*) in July 1882.[37]

The extermination of dogs was apparently routine enough that it became something of a spectator sport for some people. In his diary on Sunday, 10 February 1878, future Christian leader Uchimura Kanzō (1861–1868), at the time a student at Sapporo Agricultural College (now Hokkaido University), recorded in English that after discussing Christianity with a friend, he and five other friends went for a walk and observed the "extermination of houseless dogs [that] was going on then." "The boys," he continues, "liked to witness the cruel process, and we thought it was not a sin to do so even on Sundays."[38]

In these ways, in Chiba, Hokkaido, and elsewhere, government authorities throughout the archipelago translated the civilizationist and scientific racist condemnations of certain kinds of canines into a concerted effort to rid them from the streets and from throughout the countryside. To justify these efforts, officials, at times supported by Western advisers like Jones and Dun, employed practical concerns about the threat of such canines to livestock, sport hunting, and as vectors of rabies. But like many other Meiji developments, and like imperialism itself, these campaigns were neither new nor unique to Japan.

Domestic Precedents and Global Analogues

Although the campaigns against wolves and native dogs in Hokkaido and elsewhere on the archipelago were unprecedented in their scale and destruction and were inspired by a fear of rabies, a desire to protect a fledging livestock industry, and Western prejudices against wolves, the actual and rhetorical abuse of Ainu and "Other" peoples through violence against dogs, both physical and verbal, was not new nor was it isolated. The campaign in Hokkaido was part of a longer national and larger global movement, which had deadly consequences for wolves and indigenous canines and dire side-effects for peoples associated with them. The language of canine imperialism, especially civilization and scientific racism, may have been largely adopted from the West, but the use of dogs to denigrate other ethnic groups seems to have been universal and began long before the age of New Imperialism arrived in Japan.

In Ezo, as Hokkaido was known before its formal incorporation into the Meiji state in 1869, Japanese colonizers were said to have punished Ainu by binding the legs of their prized dogs and tossing them into rivers to drown from as early as the eighteenth century.[39] Similar to indigenous peoples in North America and Australia, Ainu aborigines valued canines for their hunting abilities and possibly because a creation legend connected their own people to dogs and wolves.[40] Such beliefs may have given some Ainu bounty hunters pause as they committed what some Ainu may have seen as tantamount to mythological patricide.[41] Many Japanese settlers and officials made the most of this myth to dehumanize the Ainu, claiming that they had a "common cur" for a father and a woman for a mother, thereby justifying their mistreatment and exploitation.[42] Such associations are visually apparent in a portrait of an Ainu chieftain and his dog by Kakizaki Hakyō (1764–1826), who was a member of the Matsumae warrior family that ruled the island during much of the Tokugawa period.[43] In this painting and in eleven others of Ainu leaders, Kakizaki exaggerated the physical characteristics of the Ainu to emphasize barbarity and bestial strength, which, according to historian Richard Siddle, implicitly glorified the Matsumae clan that had subjugated them.[44] To this day, many aborigines are reluctant to use "Ainu" to identify themselves because of the phonetic similarity between "Ainu" and "inu" (dog) as well as other negative stereotypes associated with the ethnic label.

The figurative and practical abuse of Ainu and their dogs resembled the interactions of Euro-American settlers with indigenous peoples and canines in North America, an environment that produced both Jones and Dun. Like Japanese intrusions in Hokkaido, American advances on the continent have not traditionally been acknowledged by historians to be about empire. Both contexts, though, can be aptly characterized as examples of imperialism, or as some scholars prefer to call it, "internal colonization." Not only did the Spanish and English of colonial times use dogs to hunt down Indians, but their post-Revolutionary progeny deployed them in both actual and metaphorical ways, as they pushed the borders of the new nation westward. Perhaps the best-known example is Seaman, a massive "Newfoundland dogg" who accompanied Meriwether Lewis (1774–1809) as he and William Clark (1770–1838), who brought along York, a black slave he had owned since childhood, explored the Louisiana Purchase from 1804 to 1806. Although Lewis considered Seaman a sagacious companion, the journal that he and Clark kept during their journey is rather matter-of-fact and has little commentary about Seaman and the dogs kept by Indians they encountered. Perhaps in this case, their actions speak louder than words: Lewis and Clark repeatedly purchased dogs from Indians to eat, but they probably would have never thought of devouring Seaman.[45] As was the case with Dun and his Japanese colleagues in Hokkaido,

8. A painting of the Ainu chieftain of Heshikai and his dog, by Kakizaki Hakyō (1790).

many other nineteenth-century American writers used the same civilizationist and social Darwinian rhetoric employed to describe native dogs by colonizers throughout the imperial world. Consider the 1874 observations of travel writer James F. Rusling (1834–1918) about the dogs in a southern Colorado Indian village:

> Dogs abounded everywhere. Each wigwam seemed to have a goodly supply, and the village at large a brigade besides. They were small wolfish-looking curs, as a rule, and the most vociferous and incessant yelpers I ever listened to. They had no regular bark—only a wild yelp, like their savage ancestors, the cayotes [sic] of the Plains. It is only the civilized dog that, "bays deep-mouthed welcome"—that has a full, open "bark"—and this he loses when he relapses to savagery again.[46]

Whether colonization was internal or external, in North America, Asia, or Africa, the vocabulary of canine imperialism was remarkably similar.

As did Japanese colonizers in Hokkaido, some Americans exploited the respect that many Indians exhibited for wolves and dogs by comparing "natives" to the continent's indigenous canines. They conventionally described the indigenous dogs of the frontier as creatures vastly inferior—like their human companions—to Old World pure breeds. Native dogs, they asserted, were "even a 'notch below' the mongrels of Europe."[47] The inferiority of American indigenous dogs, some commentators professed, was the result of their close affinity to wolves. Like colonizers elsewhere, English settlers in New England in the seventeenth century denigrated the indigenous dogs kept by Native Americans they encountered calling them "Currs," claiming they were "like their Wolves, and cannot barke but howle," and denying that Indians had the wherewithal to fully domesticate them.[48] By contrast, some Americans asserted, no such biological link connected wolves with European pedigreed dogs. In an 1803 essay, Benjamin Smith Barton (1766–1815), a renowned natural historian and early theorist of race, explained that the common lineage of Indian dogs and wolves was the reason that the former "will never attack or pursue the wolf, which common dogs readily do." Indian dogs, alleged Barton, "have less fidelity and will steal from their masters."[49] Thus, native dogs, like wolves, became imbued rhetorically with traits stereotypically ascribed during the period to Native American humans: namely, cunning and double-crossing treachery. As with the Ainu and many canines in Hokkaido, the ideological aversion to native canines and people in North America led to the decimation of both populations by the end of the nineteenth century.

The destruction of wild, feral, and street canines reached global proportions during the late nineteenth and twentieth centuries. As on the Hokkaido and American frontiers, government officials and settlers in other colonial contexts such as eastern and southern Africa, India, Australia, and New Zealand often classified domesticated dogs kept by indigenous populations alongside wild canine "vermin," and eliminated both kinds of dogs in their cynocide (dog-killing) campaigns.[50] Likewise, colonizers in many places regularly conflated wild canines with native and other oppressed ethnic or classes of people. In the Cape Colony, as historian Lance van Sittert has pointed out, in "settler parlance [black Africans]…became 'two-legged jackals' who went about accompanied by 'a host of dogs' preying on settler flocks."[51]

In Japan, the slaughter in Chiba and Hokkaido prefectures was part of a similar campaign to destroy undesirable canines throughout the archipelago. In the 1870s, the extermination of the archipelago's *Canidae* populations extended through the entire country, from Hokkaido to newly incorporated Okinawa in the south. By the turn of the century, the Meiji government, pushing forward modern meat-production operations, anxious about rabies, and influenced by the ideology of civilization and science, had driven Japanese wolves to extinction, decimated the wild dog population, and wiped out many of the street dogs who roamed populated areas and their outskirts. The cruelty and viciousness of human relations with wolves, wild and feral canines, and street dogs can in part be explained by people's actual and imagined warm and cordial interactions with fully domesticated dogs.

As was the case in Hokkaido, the denigration and elimination of native dogs and wolves in Japan did not necessarily begin with foreigners nor take place solely under the sway of adopted Western ideology. Rabies had afflicted the archipelago's canine populations much earlier, and some serious outbreaks had occurred during the eighteenth century. Hiraiwa Yonekichi (1898–1986), a zoologist in the early twentieth century who wrote extensively about wolves and dogs, speculated that already in the Tokugawa period such epidemics had set in motion a gradual erosion of respect for wolves and wild dogs who had traditionally existed in agricultural communities. Before the onslaught of rabies, he argued, farmers had esteemed these wild canines with a sort of spiritual reverence, viewing them as benevolent partners who contained crop-raiding herbivores such as wild boar and deer. Thereafter, early modern villagers began to fear wolves and wild canines as disease-crazed predators and organized hunts to exterminate them from surrounding mountains. Rabies had a similar if less severe effect on human relations with domesticated dogs during the Tokugawa period. Antirabies measures were usually limited to the killing of diseased dogs, but in certain hard-hit villages the keeping of dogs was banned entirely, and each household was expected to kill one healthy dog in hopes of slowing the spread of the disease.[52]

As was the case for wolves, inhabitants of the archipelago during the Tokugawa period held an ambiguous attitude toward domesticated dogs. City dwellers owned a few toy dogs as pets, and some mountain villagers kept hunting dogs, but the majority of canines roamed about urban neighborhoods and rural villages in packs. Because of the general obedience of dogs to human masters, and because street dogs specifically consumed human rubbish and actual humans such as the corpses of beggars and abandoned infants, people associated canines with abasement, death, and the profane. In contrast, canine characteristics such as their superb natural ability of scent, their apparent fidelity to a human master, their role as guards, and their capacity to abundantly reproduce led people to identify dogs with supernatural powers, such as the ability to find curses, ward off evil, and boost human fertility. Perhaps because of their immediate and very evident subjugation to people and extraordinary capabilities, dogs were believed to freely traverse from the human world into other worlds.[53] Residents of the archipelago were also influenced by Buddhist respect for all living things, as underscored by legal standing given to dogs by the fifth Tokugawa shogun Tsunayoshi. In short, mid-nineteenth-century Japanese probably regarded most dogs with considerable ambivalence and treated them with a measure of tolerance if not always kindness.

Some Tokugawa-era Japanese shared the worldview that regarded other ethnic groups as inferior and dehumanized them by belittling them as dogs or doglike. The metaphorical deployment of dogs was by no means isolated to the denigration of the Ainu. Popular Japanese beliefs during the mid-Tokugawa period portrayed Koreans as dogs and monsters.[54] Similarly, the National Learning and Shinto scholar Hirata Atsutane (1776–1843) described Westerners as having physical and behavioral attributes similar to canines.

> When they urinate they lift one leg, the way dogs do. Moreover, apparently because the backs of their feet do not reach to the ground, they fasten wooden heels to their shoes, which make them look all the more like dogs. This may explain also why a Dutchman's penis appears to be cut short at the end, just like a dog's. Though this may sound like a joke, it is quite true, not only of Dutchmen

but of Russians.... This may be the reason the Dutch are as lascivious as dogs and spend their entire nights at erotic practices.[55]

Common peasants, too, may have shared such sentiments, as illustrated by the belief of the teacher Griffis that farmers had poked out one of the eyes of his adopted "American" dog.

Long before and after the arrival of Griffis in the rural city of Fukui in 1871, colonizers and ideologues on the Japanese archipelago and around the world practically and metaphorically deployed dogs to support imperial expansion and claims of superiority vis-à-vis other ethnic groups. Canine imperialism was truly a global phenomenon with considerable precedent. And, in the late nineteenth century, it continued to extend its reach through the enlarged bureaucratic and policing powers of the modern nation-state at home as well as in colonial regimes abroad.

Public Health and Dogcatchers

Despite such practices, beliefs, and ideological precedents, the widespread slaughter of dogs by the Meiji government that began in the mid-1870s marked a significant departure from earlier Tokugawa practices. As highlighted by the two slogans that dominated the Meiji era, "civilization and enlightenment" and "rich country, strong army," Japanese leaders were determined to build a society and economy strong enough to overcome the unequal treaties that had been imposed on their country. Government officials regarded the creation of a public health system, like the establishment of a livestock industry, as essential to the nation-building process, and viewed street dogs and wild canines as expendable impediments to progress. Although rabies never posed as severe a threat to Japanese as other infectious diseases, such as tuberculosis, cholera, and measles, authorities often dealt with its possible bearers—canines—in a manner that far outweighed the danger.[56] The hygienic expectations of civilized subjecthood applied to all—both Japanese and other creatures—in modern Japan.

Concerned about the spread of disease and interested in promoting sanitation, national, regional, and municipal government bureaucrats made specific legal changes that broadened their ability to destroy dogs during the 1870s. They authorized anyone to kill a diseased dog, rather than delegating the task to police alone. Other local governments followed Chiba and Hokkaido prefectures' lead and began to round up dogs who were not sick by offering bounties for the pelt of any canine caught wandering the streets or countryside.[57] For the entrepreneur, this could be a lucrative business. Working together, two or three people could easily dispose of one to two hundred dogs daily and take home a handsome profit.[58] During these same years, Tokyo Prefecture issued the country's first edict regulating domesticated dogs. The measure defined the duties of dog owners, requiring them to put on their dogs a collar and tag (*chikukenhyō*) with the proprietor's name and address. The statute also mandated that owners must kill their dogs if they became hydrophobic, and specified that if any dog, diseased or not, bit or hurt a person, it was to be put down.[59] Measures like this one were often supported by rules that authorized the extermination of any unlicensed dog.

Government regulations and the effort to eliminate roaming dogs specifically, if not explicitly, targeted indigenous breeds. Native canines, or dogs of mixed breed, were precisely those who were likely to wander the streets or live on the edge of cities or villages. Contrary to the expectations of authorities, the new ordinances did not necessarily lead to drastic changes in human-dog interactions in urban neighborhoods and villages where the relationship between the two had traditionally been a communal and symbiotic one. Even if a particular individual had a liking for a dog and showed it special affinity, he or she was unlikely to take on responsibility for collaring and tagging the dog as mandated by the new regulations. And if a dog was not tagged, it could legally be destroyed.[60] Despite government efforts to eliminate dogs, loose ties between humans and dogs persisted at least until the early twentieth century, especially in rural areas. Folklorist Yanagita Kunio (1875–1962) recalled that in his native village in Hyōgo Prefecture in central Japan there were always four or five dogs wandering about, eating what little food was offered them, and sleeping where they could. Apparently not a single household in the community kept a dog.[61]

Little opposition greeted the new regulations and roundups of dogs. The specter of rabies, whether real or imagined, persuaded most people to abide by the rules without complaining. Because there was not a large constituency of dog owners, at least in the early Meiji period, the government did not need to worry about offending their sensibilities. Some people objected to the new canine policies, but their grievances were usually deflected in other directions. In some nineteenth- and twentieth-century societies, the dogcatcher came to represent the far-reaching and ominous nature of the modern state. In Meiji Japan, police officials often redirected any ire generated by dog regulations by delegating the task, as some domain authorities had done during the Tokugawa period, to *burakumin*, an outcaste group that had been the object of discrimination for hundreds of years.[62] As a result, *burakumin*, to whom the Meiji government had granted legal equality in 1871, became strongly associated with the figure of the *inukoroshiya* (dog killer), and the slaughter, butchering, and consumption of canines and other animals continued to be a persistent source of prejudice faced by this "invisible race."[63] Sometimes complaints about the elimination of dogs were aimed in other directions as well. For example, in a letter to the editor in 1877, an individual vented considerable spleen at foreign (canine) privilege and upper-class arrogance, while concern for native dogs appeared incidental:

> When a Japanese dog is spotted without a tag, people yell "Get it! Kill it!" and treat it as if it were the enemy, but why do they turn a blind eye when it is a Western dog? Is it that they treat them with reserve because the dogs, too, have come here from foreign lands? Recently one witnesses many [Western]

dogs biting and barking at passersby, but in the eyes of their owners even these evil dogs appear to be gentle creatures. Shouldn't people understand that no matter how expensive a dog may be, if it harms people, it ought to be speedily killed? Even dog fanatics ought to comprehend that humans are more important than dogs.[64]

The writer added further punch to his criticisms by using the penname "Furyō Ken" of Akasaka, which was a homonym of "Bad Dog" (*furyō-ken*). This pun, and his claim that he hailed from the upscale Tokyo neighborhood of Akasaka, added to the cutting humor of the letter.

As indicated by such complaints, the reach of the emerging nation-state, with its growing bureaucratic and policing powers, was extensive. Using the pretext that the health of imperial subjects was at stake and using the authority of legal regulations, national and local authorities increasingly extended their concerns to the roadsides and countryside where street dogs, unlicensed and therefore uncontrolled, dwelt. To eliminate this perceived threat, they turned to outcastes, whose low social status made them, rather than the state, the target of any criticism. And as "Bad Dog" recognized, it was native dogs rather than Western dogs who were the primary target of these campaigns.

Canine Extraterritoriality and the Crisis of Semi-Imperial Privilege

Foreign breeds, or *kame*, were often protected by virtue of being foreign. Such dogs were usually owned by Westerners or well-to-do Japanese who could afford these sorts of canines and who were more apt to collar, tag, and prevent them from wandering the streets. Even if an owner neglected to do these things, the physical appearance and social status of foreign dogs sometimes saved them, because authorities and dogcatchers did not want to risk being responsible for killing the pet of someone influential, whether a protected foreigner or a prominent Japanese. It was complaints from precisely such owners about dogs being immediately liquidated, along with objections to the killing of dogs in public, that prompted a revision of Tokyo's and Yokohama's domestic dog ordinances in the late 1870s and early 1880s. Like their human compatriots, many foreign dogs enjoyed a sort of canine extraterritorial immunity for much of the nineteenth century.

As highlighted by the central government's notification of foreign consulates about the elimination of dogs in Chiba by Jones, officials carefully avoided offending Westerners. Only after negotiations with each of the foreign diplomatic representatives in Yokohama did the governor of Kanagawa Prefecture implement a policy requiring dogs to be tagged in 1877.[65] Four years later, the central government ordered the creation of dog pounds where canines would be detained for a week rather than being killed at once. It also cautioned the police to be especially careful of how they handled the dogs of foreigners. The other notable

9. A page from Georges Bigot's "Heaving a Foreigner over a Cliff for Fun, Kobe, 24 August 1897." In the first frame, a native dog sniffs the rear end of a Western puppy, the pet of one of two Europeans walking to the lower waterfall with a Japanese friend. In the next frame, the men approach a wayside stall, where three coolies are drinking sake. The native dog sits next to the coolies, its head to the side as if to draw the attention of one of the laborers to the foreigners. The coolie exclaims, "Hey, look at that! It's some foreigners. Let's give them hell, because they're clueless" (*Ohé! Ohé! ijin ga kita; ijimeté yarō, wakarané kara*). Used with permission of the Yokohama Archives of History.

revision was a change from a per-head reward for canines to a daily salary for those who rounded up dogs. This modification, along with the initial impound-ment of dogs, made the work less lucrative. For a time, the changes mollified foreigners' complaints. At the turn of the century, however, after treaty revision allowed foreigners to live outside the treaty ports, problems arose once more, so that police began to round up dogs only late at night or early in the morning.[66]

The prospect of treaty revision, and especially the possibility of foreigners and Japanese living in the same neighborhoods, created anxieties within both groups. Again, these worries were projected onto dogs. During the 1870s, many Japanese were more immediately concerned with the possibility of foreigners traveling freely within the country (*naichi ryokō*) than they were with mixed resi-dence (*naichi zakkyo*), the latter of which required formal revision of the unequal treaties, and would be realized only in 1899. Interestingly, some early Meiji intel-lectuals, including the educator and government official Nishi Amane (1829–97), voiced almost as much unease about traveling canines as they did about their human companions. In a speech delivered in November 1874 to the Meirokusha, a society of leading Meiji advocates of "civilization and enlightenment," Nishi

10. The next page from "Heaving a Foreigner over a Cliff for Fun." After one of the coolies kicks the puppy, the foreigner cries, "Oh! My poor dog!!!!" To which they respond, "What, what the hell you talking about?" (*Nani, Nani, iounde??*). Used with permission of the Yokohama Archives of History.

proposed a gradual relaxation of laws restricting the travel of foreigners to prepare Japanese for this interaction. He acknowledged, however, that foreigners would likely inflict at least seven kinds of "injuries" (*gai*) if they were allowed to move unrestrained throughout the country. Fifth among these wrongs, Nishi declared, was that Japanese "will be troubled by the dogs that accompany them."[67] Fukuzawa Yukichi (1835–1901), generally considered the most important enlightenment thinker of the early Meiji period, disagreed with Nishi on the broader issue of travel by foreign persons, arguing that it was premature to permit it. However, he did not take the threat of their dogs too seriously. Fukuzawa's response to Nishi's canine concerns in the society's publication, *Meiroku zasshi*, seemed almost flippant: "We naturally need not be concerned with regulations to prevent foreigners from being accompanied by dogs. Whether they are accompanied by dogs or tigers is optional."[68]

As before, many foreigners continued to be concerned about what they might encounter on Japan's thoroughfares and byways. Through the last decades of the nineteenth century, Europeans and Americans repeatedly complained about the inability of the Japanese government to eradicate street dogs and the threat of rabies. However real or unreal the epidemiological concerns behind them, such anxious expressions functioned more often than not as coded language about treaty revision and the imminent loss of foreigners' privileged and protected status in Japan. Like Alcock's comparison of street dogs to masterless samurai, Western apprehensions about "wild and uncared for...brutes of all description [who]

Civilizing Canines; or, Domesticating and Destroying Dogs 75 wander about the streets with impunity," as the *Japan Weekly Mail* put it in 1897, were related to their worries about lower-class Japanese whom they might meet in the streets and byways after treaty revision was enacted.[69] Colonial and native dogs served as malleable metaphors to express such fears.

The satiric cartoons of the French expatriate Bigot are particularly evocative of foreign worries about the looming end to their exterritorial privileges. Bigot was highly critical of the Meiji government and opposed treaty revision because it would abolish the advantaged position of foreigners, including his own ability to publish his characteristically derisive cartoons. Though he sold his drawings to a variety of publications, Bigot was best known for the magazine *Toba-e*, launched in 1887, which was named for a twelfth-century Kyoto abbot who is said to have created ink hand scrolls (*chōjū giga*) depicting birds, frogs, rabbits, and other creatures engaging in humorous activities.[70] Bigot, in contrast, rarely portrayed nonhuman animals acting in anthropomorphic ways. Only rarely did beasts stand in for people, as in a few of Bigot's more biting cartoons of Japanese as monkeys aping Westerners by attempting to waltz and wear Western clothing at such venues as the Rokumeikan. Canines, especially his beagle Aka, appeared more than any other animal, but almost never did they stand in for individual human subjects. Instead, they mirrored more generally the behavior or culture of Japanese and Westerners as Bigot saw them.

One illustrated story titled "Heaving a Foreigner over a Cliff for Fun, Kobe, 24 August 1897" featured a Western and a native dog and underscored Bigot's worries about treaty revision. It advocated the "suppression," if not "elimination," of lower-class "rowdies," whom Bigot believed to be threatening to Westerners. The narrative, written in English, tells of a European embarking on a walk to a waterfall with a fellow foreigner and a Japanese friend, accompanied by a puppy of Western breed. As they walk, a native dog approaches the puppy and sniffs its rear end. The next frame depicts the three humans nearing a wayside stall where they notice three coolies drinking sake. Positioned alert next to the coolies, its head turned to the side as if to draw the attention of one of the laborers to the foreigners and their upper-class friend, sits the native dog. In the following frames, one of the coolies "wantonly" kicks the puppy who is "gambolling along in front of his master." When the foreigner protests, the three drunken coolies turn on him and proceed to toss him over the edge of a cliff. His two companions, mysteriously, have wandered off and are oblivious to his plight. Fortunately, a branch breaks the man's fall. After scaling back to the top of the ravine, he finds a policeman and files a complaint against the miscreants. The officer, however, only "reprimand[s] them in a fatherly way," telling them that it is "wrong to throw foreigners over cliffs." The story concludes with the following sardonic observation: "And this policemen was a member of that force which [some people] would have us understand is efficient and sufficient to protect foreign life and interests in Japan after Treaty Revision becomes an accomplished fact."[71] Bigot apparently was convinced that revision meant an end to his sixteen-year career in Japan. A month after the treaty went into effect in 1899, Bigot returned to his native France after divorcing his Japanese wife. It is not known whether or not he took along his beloved dog Aka.

Bigot's fears about treaty revision were probably largely without basis. For nearly a half-century, Westerners and their dogs had enjoyed a privileged existence thanks to the unequal treaties that the imperial powers had imposed on Japan. Such privilege gave them—both human and dog—little to fear, though this did not prevent the imaginations of at least some people from running wild. Who knows what their dogs thought.

Concerns about Animal Welfare

Increasingly in the late nineteenth century, the desire of many Westerners and some Japanese to rid the streets of unruly dogs collided with a growing interest in issues of animal welfare. From the late eighteenth century, a rising social concern for the proper treatment of nonhuman animals had emerged in Britain and, to a lesser degree, elsewhere in Europe and America. The manifestations of this phenomenon rippled outward toward Japan and other areas almost a century later.

Initially, concerns about the well-being of animals were expressed in a self-serving manner. Since at least the 1870s, Westerners had often protested against their own dogs being mistakenly picked up as strays and eliminated. By the 1880s, though, foreigners began to express less self-interested objections to the government's dog-control measures as they started to articulate them in terms of animal protection. A minority of foreigners, such as Morse, held Japanese treatment of nonhuman animals to be superior to that of the civilized West. In "pagan Japan," wrote Morse, "animals are always so kindly treated that you have to step out of the way or over hens, dogs, cats, and pigeons, and even the black crows." Japanese people, he specifically noted, never threw stones at dogs.[72] The comments of another, less sympathetic observer of Japanese society, support Morse's remarks. Major Henry Knollys, who visited the country during the 1880s, recorded:

> All ages and sexes appear immoderately fond of pets. Tame birds are habitually kept, not only in pairs in cages, but in dozens twittering and chirping and even singing to a deafening extent. Pariah-like dogs and tailless cats are so uncouth and hideous that it is difficult to muster up a semblance of affection for them, and yet they receive a considerable share of friendship....Indeed I consider the inhabitants not only humane—thoughtless or exceptional cruelty apart—but have a great regard for life *per se*, presumably the remains of the strict Buddhist doctrines on that point.[73]

Many Westerners, though, were less approving of Japanese animal ethics. Bigot expressed this view in several prints from the late 1880s in *Toba-e*, which regularly poked fun at the government. One cartoon, sarcastically titled "A Policeman with his Hands Full," shows a cop running toward a dog in the distance in a vain attempt to stop the animal from defecating on the ground.[74] Another one shows a police officer with his sword drawn chasing a scruffy-looking canine, who appears be of native or indistinct breed, in the Hibiya neighborhood in central Tokyo. In the caption of the latter cartoon, Bigot went so far as to compare the rounding up of stray dogs to the Massacre of the Innocents, King Herod's killing of the children of Bethlehem at the time of Jesus' birth.[75] Similar sentiments were voiced in a *Japan Weekly Mail* editorial of 1884, penned by an unnamed newspaper reporter. The editorial expressed indignation that, except for "those of the very highest culture, maltreatment of animals is quite as common in the better ranks of society as in the lowest." The writer called on Japan to make changes that would bring "credit upon her name," but conceded that it was not hopeful that anything could be done to alter the situation soon.[76]

Nevertheless, concerns about animal welfare rarely extended beyond the expatriate community. Because such sentiments were largely limited to a few foreigners, and even fewer Japanese (mostly those who had lived abroad), they did not gain broad cultural traction. It was not until 1902 that an animal-welfare organization was established in Japan, and that organization, the Society for the Prevention of Abuse to Animals (Dōbutsu gyakutai bōshi kai), was established largely at the behest of the government, which was concerned principally about protecting horses for military use. Six years later, the society expanded its attention

11. *Modern Japan (Massacre of the Innocents)* by Georges Bigot, dated 1888. The French caption reads "Hunting stray dogs in the Hibiya neighborhood." Used with the permission of Kōdansha.

to include the canine and feline populations. In 1914 volunteers formed the Japan Humane Society (Nihon jindō kai), the first private animal-welfare organization, albeit one with strong Western connections, in terms both of membership and philosophy. It would not be until the emergence of a professional middle class in the 1920s, and especially the maturing of that class in the 1960s and 1970s, that concerns about animal welfare gained wider social acceptance as well as a measure of political influence.

The Politics of Dogs

As evidenced by the authorities' campaigns to eradicate dogs, government efforts at canine control had the effect of regulating the human political and social order. While *kame* were identified with Westerners and local elites, street dogs were seen as unruly and disorderly, like certain classes of people, who often lived in the same poor neighborhoods as the canine constituency whom the government pronounced threatening. The state's attempts to regulate dogdom had the effect, as well as the objective, of controlling or attacking domestic political opponents, but thanks to the figurative pliability of canines, their enemies could easily use dogs to metaphorically bite back.

The identification of certain groups of people with these canines had the intent of discrediting the former by depicting them as animal-like, savage, and foolish. Such associations were probably the aim of government officials and their allies in their characterization of supporters of the people's rights movement (*jiyū minken undō*), which challenged the ruling Meiji oligarchy in the 1870s and 1880s. Tani Kanjō (1837–1911), a former general and high-ranking government official claimed of people's-rights activists: "They speak of civilization, but they act like Taiwanese savages. They always bark when they see a government official. Are people's-rightists human-dogs? (*Minkenka jinken ka*). That's why canine rights are all the rage now."[77] Tani attempted to maintain the government's grasp on moral authority instilled by civilizationist ideology by claiming that the actions, and even the voices, of the regime's opponents were as brutish as natives and as bestial as dogs.

Yet, an unflattering comparison to canines could be turned on its head because of the malleable metaphorical nature of dogs. The disregard for and fierce resistance to outside authority exhibited by street dogs made them apt symbols for government critics. Even in societies in which canines were regarded with particular distaste, such as in the late Ottoman Empire, opposition political cartoonists equated the street dogs of Istanbul with the urban masses: starving, oppressed, but defiantly protesting despotism and European imperial ambitions.[78] And, to cite a more recent example, biologist Alan Beck found that in 1970 many poor African American inner-city residents of Baltimore sided with stray dogs—even though they did not like the dogs' barking, defecating, and occasional biting—against white city authority in the form of the dogcatcher. Residents readily projected their dislike of the police onto the canines, whom they identified as fellow victims.[79] In nineteenth-century Japan, too, cartoonists critical of the Meiji government often portrayed supporters of the people's rights movement as native street dogs. One reason for their use of dogs was, as historian Peter Duus points out, for punning effect: the phonetic readings for the characters for dog (*ken*) and rights (*ken*) are identical.[80] Yet more substantially—beyond mere wordplay—dogs were an appropriate metaphor as evidenced by an 1880 cartoon by satirist Honda Kinkichirō (1850–1921) in the humor magazine *Marumaru chinbun*. The etching showed a group of catfish/officials hastily constructing a high wooden fence to keep out a large pack of barking dogs/people's rights supporters. Shortly before the publication of the cartoon, leaders of the movement had organized the Kokkai kisei dōmeikai (League to Establish a National Assembly) to conduct a national campaign for the creation of a constitution and parliament, and in response the government issued new regulations requiring prior police authorization for political associations and rallies. Honda's English caption reads: "Theg [*sic*] may use any efforts to keep those fierce brutes out: they will get through some day, though."[81] Street dogs' habitation of alleys and roadsides, their tendency to converge to confront a common enemy, and their hostility to unfamiliar outsiders made them a fitting symbol for political rabble-rousers. Another *Marumaru chinbun* article and illustration depicted the movement as a group of canines, dressed in

12. Cartoon by Honda Kinkichirō in *Marumaru chinbun*, 3 April 1880. The English caption reads: Theg [*sic*] may use any efforts to keep those fierce brutes out: they will get through some day, though."

suits and other attire, complaining about the extent of government controls that levied taxes on each animal, required every dog to wear a tag registered with state bureaucrats, and targeted native dogs in the suppression of rabies.[82] Clearly, the dogs were speaking for people and about human concerns.

Just as street dogs were equated with government opponents, popular associations between elites and foreign dogs, or *kame,* appeared in the rhetoric of those who agitated for political change. In his famous 1890 antigovernment, people's rights movement song "Oppekepē Song," actor and popular rights agitator Kawakami Otojirō (1864–1911) poked fun at a flaunting lady who "has no idea what her husband's job is, whose hair is arranged in the latest style, who uses highfalutin enlightened language, and has a trendy *kame.*"[83] Even more biting was "*sōku*" (running dog) or simply "*inu*" (dog), slurs favored by Communists and other leftists to describe the police and other allies of capitalism in the early twentieth century. The invectives were a derivative of the Chinese proverb "When cunning hares are all caught it is the turn of the faithful hound to be killed for meat" and had long been used to denigrate the blind obedience of people to authority in Japan. Communists, though, deployed the term with unprecedented frequency, probably because of the persistent fondness of the rich for purebred Western dogs. A 1919 article in *Aka* (Red), a Communist monthly that was banned by the government the following year, drew on such associations to criticize the lifestyles of the upper classes. Derisively titled "Twelve Hours of Labor by the Aristocratic Rich," the piece ridiculed a wealthy man who spent his night in the company of geisha, slept until one in the afternoon, and awoke to sumo wrestle with his "beloved" pointer.[84] More metaphorically but just as disparagingly, renowned proletarian writer Kobayashi Takiji (1903–1933) used the oft-used phrase the "running dogs of capitalism" to ridicule police officers in his 1929 short story, "*Fuzai jinushi*" (The absentee landlord): "These watchdogs wear caps, carry sabers, and do not play games. When Mutō, a union man, accompanied the tenants to negotiate an agreement...these dogs bit him and quickly took him into custody."[85] Four years later, those "watchdogs" lured Kobayashi out of hiding, and tortured him to death. As in the imperial realm, whether employed by economic and political elites or their opponents, the symbolic power and pliability of dogs made them a recurrent rhetorical weapon in domestic interclass frictions.

In a manner reminiscent of antirabies campaigns in nineteenth-century Britain and elsewhere, the Japanese government in the late nineteenth and early twentieth century targeted dogs belonging specifically to the lower socioeconomic strata of the human population. The relationship of social class to canine control was most evident in the widespread implementation of dog taxes in the mid-1890s, which were designed to encourage people who could not afford the tax to turn their dogs into the pound for extermination. After the rabies outbreak in Nagasaki in 1893, city officials implemented a dog tax and simultaneously authorized dogcatchers to "destroy" any unregistered canine.[86] A decade later, the daily *Yomiuri* reported many people had abandoned their dogs because of such taxes in Tokyo and that these were then rounded up as stray dogs by dog killers.[87]

Perhaps the policies were truly a success. Another article in the *Yomiuri* in 1903 implied as much. The piece, signed by a certain Matsuo, was one of a series of short commentaries composed by several different reporters that ran on the newspaper's front page. Each article was just one paragraph long and followed by an English translation—practically the only English that appeared in the paper. In this particular piece, Matsuo wrote: "The dogs which used to bark at people walking through back streets two or three years ago keep quite quiet nowadays. Nor do they bark at ladies in foreign costume or cyclists. That civilization is making steady progress in Japan may be noticed by the most cursory observer."[88] Why did Matsuo choose this dual-language column as an appropriate venue for his discourse on dogs? Maybe it was an attempt to give notice to the world that Japan had, like Western countries, at last attained the highest standards of civilization, even to the last dog. At the same time, one cannot help but wonder if canines had become civilized, or whether there were no barks merely because many of the dogs concerned had been eradicated. The revolutionary social and cultural changes that swept over its people since the Meiji Restoration may have rubbed off on dogs, but probably more consequential were the decades of elimination of certain types of canines for ideological and practical reasons. The "steady progress" of "civilization," it seems, had little room for street dogs.

The Strongest Dog on the Block

At the beginning of the twentieth century, Japan in substantial ways had in many respects drawn nearly even with the Great Powers in geopolitical terms. In 1894 the Meiji government fulfilled its forty-year-old goal of revising the unequal treaties, which five years later eliminated the extraterritorial privileges of foreigners but also forced the Japanese government to allow them to live outside of the treaty ports, a prospect once the source of considerable anxiety among Japanese and foreigners alike. In the following year, the country demonstrated its military might to the world at large by defeating the Qing Empire in the Sino-Japanese War, as a result of which it acquired its first overseas colony, Taiwan. Tellingly, Japanese authorities continued their campaign to extirpate street and wild dogs in the newly won island territory. Taking cues from policies at home and those of British and other Western officials in their far-flung empires, colonial police in Taiwan sought to "totally annihilate" (*zenmetsu*) such canines through a combination of taxes and rifles.[89]

Thus, by the end of the nineteenth century, Japan had completed its transformation from an independent but not completely sovereign object of imperialism into an emerging colonial empire. Nevertheless, for reasons of racial and cultural prejudice, Japan was denied equal membership in the imperialist club, and therefore it remained insecure about the fragility of its position. In addition to Taiwan, Japanese negotiators succeeded in compelling Chinese leaders to cede them the Liaodong Peninsula on the mainland, but in just over a week, Germany, Russia, and France demanded that the Japanese government renounce its claims to that territory, which, ironically, would enter Russian hands in less than three years' time. Still, the end of the century represented a defining moment in Japan's rise as a colonial power, even if it did not drastically alter the imperial map of the world.

Tectonic rumblings in imperial geopolitics triggered similar groans in the world of dogs. An event that occurred at the end of the century foreshadowed developments that would grow more conspicuous several decades later. The occasion was a dispute triggered by the creation of a statue of Saigō Takamori (1828–77) and his dog in late 1898 to commemorate the thirtieth anniversary of the Meiji Restoration. Saigō had been one of the principal leaders of the Restoration that brought the oligarchic regime to power, but nine years later he launched an unsuccessful rebellion against the government, in which he perished. Authorities' unveiling of the statue signaled graphically the regime's attempt to reorient and rehabilitate Saigō's political standing from that of a rebel against the Meiji state to a hero of the Restoration.[90] To this day, the statue remains a prominent landmark at an entrance to Ueno Park in Tokyo.

Ironically, the small, seemingly insignificant dog standing next to Saigō created almost as great a stir as the political repositioning of Saigō. Much public excitement and commentary greeted the unveiling of the statue. Committee members, including the art patron Kuki Ryūichi (1852–1931) and art critic Okakura Tenshin (1862–1913), selected the team of Takamura Kōun (1852–1934) and Gotō Sadayuki (1849–1902), sculptors who had been chosen to depict in bronze such political favorites as Kusunoki Masashige, a fourteenth-century warrior known for his devotion to the emperor, atop his horse in front of the imperial palace. Newspapers discussed the fact that Takamura represented Saigō in a casual robe-like *hitoe* hunting rabbits with his dog, rather than in a military outfit on the battlefield, a guise for which Saigō was much better known. Portraying Saigō in military garb might have left viewers wondering which uniform he was wearing: the one

13. The statue of Saigō Takamori and his dog by Takamura Kōun and Gotō Sadayuki, which was unveiled in Tokyo's Ueno Park in 1898. Photograph by author, 2003.

he had donned as a leader of the Meiji Restoration or the one that he later assumed as an enemy of the Meiji state. The dog drew a degree of attention dispro-
portionate to its size. As was the case with other members of the Meiji elite, Saigō
enjoyed hunting with dogs, many of whom were canines of Western origin. He
was said to have been particularly fond of a big fierce, floppy-eared dog who was
the grandson of a Western canine, originally kept by the Tokugawa shoguns.[91] In
order to depict Saigō's dog accurately, Gotō studied Western dogs in Yokohama,
but sometime during his preparations, he decided not to use Western dogs as a
model but to create the figure of a much smaller dog. Art historians think that
Satsuma partisans and Kuki may have persuaded Gotō to create Saigō's dog in the
image of the local Japanese Satsuma breed.[92] This proposal was surely motivated
by Satsuma pride and by the fear that portraying Saigō with a large Western dog
would make him look less formidable and defeat the purpose of dressing him in
casual Japanese attire, that is, it would make him seem like less of a man of the
common people. Four months before the statue was to be dedicated, Gotō unveiled a mock-up of a dog that appeared to be of indistinct or mixed origin. This
rendering seemed not to satisfy anyone. Some objected to the dog because it was
not big enough to be like Saigō's favorite Western dog. Other critics thought the
small dog did not look like a Satsuma dog and aimed their criticism at its droopy
ears. As an article in the daily *Hōchi* newspaper noted, its small floppy ears made it
look like a *chin* lapdog of Chinese origin rather than a Satsuma dog, which, like all
native dogs, was said to sport ears that "pricked up like a rabbit's."[93] In response,
Gotō recast a new canine bronze, with the same small body but almost rabbitlike
pointy ears, in time for the dedication ceremony in December 1898.

The timing is telling. It is striking that this controversy over the ears of a
seemingly innocuous dog sculpture followed closely in the wake of Japan's recent
geopolitical successes and setbacks: its victory in the Sino-Japanese War, its acquisition of Taiwan, and the retrocession of the Liaodong Peninsula. Undoubtedly,
concerns over the dog's appearance stemmed from a heightened sense of national
pride, coupled with anxiety, which was in turn projected in a canine direction.
The discomfort that some people felt with Gotō's portrayal of the dog as being of
mixed breed echoed worries about the most controversial provision of the treaty
revision due to be implemented in the following year, which allowed for the geographic intermingling of the races in neighborhoods outside of the treaty ports.
Furthermore, the perception of Chinese blood, even of a canine variety, as a
stain on the dignity of a newly canonized national hero bore ugly traces of a
popular chauvinism that the Sino-Japanese War had recently stirred into a frenzy,
and that would survive well into the following century. At any rate, the incident
marked one of the earliest articulations, however tentative and short-lived, of the
expression of pride in native dog breeds and a reaction against interbreeding, or
at least the artistic representation of crossbreeding between native dogs and those
of foreign origin.

Around this time, there were also other less subtle calls for favoring native
dogs over Western breeds. One such voice was the critic and novelist Uchida

Roan (1868–1929), who in 1901 published a short story, "*Inu monogatari*" (A dog's tale). The narrator, who calls himself "Tarō's dog," an "undefiled, pure Japanese dog (*Nihon inu*)," berates his human compatriots' enthusiasm for Western canines and disregard for indigenous dogs.[94] In the opening lines of the narrative, the dog describes how he was born as a street dog among rubbish in a vacant lot and was orphaned as a two-month-old puppy after his mother—who was lying by the side of the road at night—barked when a policeman accidentally stepped on her leg and then was killed on the false pretext that she was rabid. But this act, Tarō's dog asserts, was only the beginning of the injustices committed by Japanese against their nation's legitimate canines. Japan's domesticated dogs, he continues, had not descended from wolves or jackals, but from the dhole, a wild mountain canine found in India. Among all canines, the dog contends, the appearance of Japanese dogs with their pointed ears and curled tail is the truest to that of the dhole, perhaps because of "direct patrilineage." Tarō's dog bemoans the fact that Japan's dogs have not been properly recognized, even though canines such as Eskimo and Siberian dogs from "uncivilized" areas of the world had been. He claims, however, that unlike such canines, Japanese dogs have a magnificent 2,500-year history as hunters, fighters, and servants of a single emperor that shaped a "Yamato" race of dogs rivaling the best purebred Western canines. Why, he growls, don't Japanese realize this? Why have they desired Western dogs since the arrival of Perry's black ships until the inauguration of mixed residency? And most incomprehensible and unforgivable for him, why do Japanese look down on "half-breed" humans (*ainoko*) but adore "mongrel dogs" (*ainoko inu*) with their Western-looking faces? Tarō's dog concludes his tirade by demanding better treatment for native dogs, including himself: "Treat us Japanese dogs more kindly! Treat me more kindly! First of all, bring me at least a side of pork loin now and then." Though Uchida's tongue may have been firmly in his cheek, the story betrays genuine resentment over Japan's subordinate position within the imperial hierarchy, and it stimulated at least one future prominent aficionado of native dogs, who claimed years later that the tale sparked in his young mind an interest in indigenous canines.[95]

Perhaps no words better articulated how Japan's newly achieved imperial status influenced attitudes about the country's native dogs than those of Inokuma Ken'ichirō (1883–1911), an army colonel who served in Korea and Manchuria during the Russo-Japanese War in 1905. Recalling his wartime experiences in the latter region of northeastern China, which the Japanese government put partially under its influence as a result of the war, Inokuma wrote:

> Here I have had the chance to observe Manchurian dogs. They are drastically different than Japanese dogs (*Nihon no inu*). After Japanese dogs defecate, they undoubtedly kick sand over their feces with their back legs, but Manchurian dogs just defecate and go on their way. When Japanese dogs encounter each other, they probably start fighting, but Manchurian dogs just snarl at each other endlessly. They only snarl and rarely attack. As might be expected, the filth and complacency of Chinese dogs is just like their masters.[96]

Later in his account, Inokuma contrasted Chinese children with Japanese children in a similar fashion. As Japanese military and political power spread over the Asian Continent, using demeaning language about the area's subservient population—both human and canine—was an attempt to figuratively shore up Japan's heightened but uncertain position.

A full expression of and concrete actions based on these sentiments did not emerge until years later in the late 1920s and 1930s. Until then, the vast majority of people continued to favor foreign breeds over native canines as Japan sought to overcome and emulate Western imperialism by adopting the new regimes of ranching, hygiene, and civilization. In the process, many indigenous dogs continued to be eliminated or, at best, neglected. The controversy over Saigō's bronze canine companion, the literary outrage of Tarō's dog, and Inokuma's assumption of Japanese human and canine superiority were premonitions of a movement that would decades later transform native dogs into nationalized "Japanese" dogs, whose new-found status made them a symbol of imperial and wartime Japan, and protected them from the dogcatcher and from mass sacrificial slaughter near the end of the disastrous conflict with the Western colonial powers.

3

FASCISM'S FURRY FRIENDS

THE "LOYAL DOG" HACHIKŌ AND THE CREATION OF THE "JAPANESE" DOG

Thanks to his glorification, while he was alive and since, many people have heard of the tale of Hachikō (1923–35). Numerous photographs exist of the dog, including one that likely dates from around 1933 showing an aging, large, double-coated, cream-colored canine, hunched back on his hind legs, his right ear erect and his left ear drooping to the side, facing and gazing directly at the camera. At the time, Hachikō, still strongly built, stood at slightly over twenty-five inches at his shoulders and weighed about ninety to ninety-five pounds, fairly typical for an adult male Akita of the day. He had been born a decade earlier in late 1923 in the town of Ōdate in the northern Honshu prefecture of Akita. Two months later, in early 1924, Hachikō was shipped nearly twenty hours by rail to Ueno Eizaburō (1871–1925), a professor of agricultural engineering at Tokyo Imperial University who was fond of dogs.

For the next fifteen months, Hachikō walked with Ueno to the nearby Shibuya railway station in the morning and accompanied him home each evening until 21 May 1925, the day the professor collapsed and died while at work. Soon thereafter Hachikō was said to have begun his vigil outside the station. Apparently a common sight near Shibuya Station for years, Hachikō became the "Loyal Dog" (Chūken) Hachikō after media coverage, a textbook story about his wait, and a bronze likeness of him erected close to the station's main exit made him famous throughout and beyond Japan. The statue, which now stands in front of the station's northwest Hachikō Exit and next to an intersection where an estimated three hundred thousand people cross daily, is now best known by Tokyoites as a favorite landmark near which to rendezvous in the fashionable shopping and entertainment district of Shibuya. An even more authentic likeness of Hachikō, preserved by taxidermy, has for many years been on display at the National Science Museum in Ueno Park, where he stands next to one of the final wolves to be killed when lupines disappeared from the archipelago at the turn of the nineteenth century. Though long dead, Hachikō remains very much alive in popular memory. To name just a few examples, a 1971 children's picture book (an earlier version of which was published in 1934) about the dog remains in

14. An undated photograph of the "Loyal Dog" Hachikō that appeared on the opening pages of Kishi Kazutoshi's *Chūken Hachikō monogatari* (1934).

print today; in 1987 Shōchiku-Fuji released the movie *Hachikō monogatari* (The story of Hachikō), a maudlin retelling of his life, replete with an extended scene of Hachikō dreaming—in color—of playing with his deceased master under boughs of cherry blossoms; and a 1999 survey conducted by the national postal service for the selection of a series of commemorative stamps in which the public chose Hachikō as one of 170 images that best illustrate the Japanese experience in the twentieth century.[1] In the twenty-first century, Hachikō's fame appears to be reaching new levels. In the last few years, publishers have issued several children's books in English and French. And in 2009 *Hachi: A Dog's Tale*, a remake of the Japanese film, directed by Lasse Hollström, best known for *My Life as a Dog* (1985), and starring actor and Japanophile Richard Gere as a professor who adopts a stray Akita puppy, arrived in theaters throughout the world.[2] It is no surprise that visitors, both young and elderly, frequently exclaim, "Ah, it's Hachikō!" when they spot his stuffed figure at the museum.

What few people realize is that Hachikō played a prominent role in the culture of fascism as experienced in Japan. To characterize the Hachikō phenomenon as a warm and sentimental episode in a country slowly submerging into political turmoil and militarism, as the literary scholar Edwin Seidensticker did in his masterful history of Tokyo, may be true to some extent, but in the context of the 1930s the story of Hachikō has complex, even disturbing, implications.[3] Hachikō became famous precisely because dog enthusiasts and government bureaucrats cast the dog as an exemplar of what they defined as the country's and empire's canine ideal: Japanese in character, pure in blood, loyal to a single master, and a fearless fighter. Moreover, Hachikō captivated people, then as today, because of his living, breathing reality that amplified—and sometimes complicated—his incredible symbolic power.

In recent decades, scholars have written extensively about the deployment of the past and place in the imagination and invention of national communities and traditions.[4] Nonhuman animals, too, played a part in the formation of national, ethnic, and racial identities. Perhaps their most obvious use is as national symbols, like the American Bald Eagle, the Russian Bear, and the British Lion or Bulldog.[5] Beasts were also metaphorically manipulated in more subtle ways, as highlighted by the identification of certain dog breeds with particular nation-states beginning in the second half of the nineteenth century. Another more subtle example is the intimate connection that developed among fascism, nationalism, and canines in the course of the early twentieth century. The association goes beyond the cliché image of Hitler's personal fetishism in regard to his German shepherd dog Blondie. Rather, within the cultures of fascism, which were characterized by an idealization and glorification of nation, race, loyalty, and violence, dogs played an important role in defining the patriotic, pure, faithful, and ferocious qualities that were expected of the state's human, and nonhuman, subjects.

What it means to be human is understood in relation to the nonhuman—whether the divine or bestial—so animals serve as metaphors through which to assert the humanity and civilized nature of one's own group and the animality or barbaric character of "Others." While always based on supposed differences, such discourses usually place an emphasis either on defining the essential qualities of one's own group or the quintessential characteristics of other people. Westerners in colonized and colonizable areas in the nineteenth century explicitly commented on the character of the native dog and, by extension, native peoples, but spoke less often of the admirable qualities of the colonial dog or the colonizer, which were usually taken for granted. The reverse was the case in the imperial metropole, where discussions about canines usually centered on the admirable attributes of the newly nationalized dogs. This also occurred in the fascist rhetoric, especially in Japan, of the first half of the twentieth century. Japanese domestic discourses about canines overwhelmingly concerned themselves with describing the character of the national dog while using foreign or mixed breeds as foils.

Canines provided a powerful if subtle symbol in the language of fascism. Rapid industrialization, urbanization, and societal upheaval left many people uncomfortable with modernity. Suspicious of the universalism, individualism, and cosmopolitanism implicit in liberal thought, fascists offered their own exceptional and indigenous versions of civilization, based on the prowess of race, nation, and community. Influenced by Darwinian thought, they feared bourgeois degeneration and racial miscegenation, and celebrated violent struggle. As in the previous century, when people spoke about the character of dogs, they projected human attitudes about national and racial identity onto animals. The ubiquity, familiarity, and emotional connection of dogs, as well as their malleable symbolic power, made them an ideal vehicle by which to define identity. The nationalization of an everyday animal, purported to possess an ancient and intimate relationship with native place and people, served to augment and to emotionalize allegiance to the nation-state; distinct, indigenous breeds provided a graphic and comprehensible way for those concerned about human racial identity to express their views; dogs, celebrated in many cultures for their fidelity, offered a prosaic device to encourage individual submission to and sacrifice for the nation; and violence unleashed with a single command epitomized the control that many people wished to exercise over their world. Indeed, the relationship between a master or breeder and his dog may be seen as an archetype of the discipline and unity revered by fascist cultures.

The link between fascism and dogs was most readily apparent in two countries, Japan and Germany, during the first half of the twentieth century. In the fascist discourses of other places, different animal metaphors may have been more prominent, even if they were deployed in similar ways and for analogous ends. In Italy, for example, predators such as lions seem to have been the animals of choice. Although Mussolini reportedly was a fan of military dogs, he was frequently portrayed as a modern tamer of wild animals. He made a practice of being photographed "completely at ease visiting cages of lions"—who as it turns out had been defanged—and riding in the back of an automobile with a lion cub in his lap.[6]

Although some historians and political scientists have contested the characterization of 1930s Japan as authentically fascist, it is necessary both to recognize the particularities of time and place and to recognize the commonalities. Popular mass antiliberal and antisocialist nationalist movements and regimes that used a common language of unity, purity, and violence appeared in a number of modern nations that had previously seemed to be on a path toward expanding democracy in the early twentieth century.[7] Societies displaying these characteristics can be meaningfully grouped under the label "fascist" as long as we keep in mind that no two societies are the same. It is also important to remember that fascism's influence affected the entire globe, its thought and language infiltrating even such democratic countries as France, Britain, and the United States. Nevertheless, fascism's sway over Japan was far closer to the historical experience of Germany and Italy; yet each was fascist in its own way. Inserting a modifier before "fascism," as historian Andrew Gordon has with the phrase "imperial fascism," more accurately accounts for the historical and cultural particularities of 1930s Japan.[8] "Imperial" is especially appropriate because it alludes both to imperialism and the emperor system that mutually pervaded the country's fascist interlude. The fascisms of Japan, Germany, and Italy are perhaps most analogous in the realm of culture. While politics and ideology in Japan differed in some ways from the situation in Germany, Italy, and other countries that took a fascist turn in the interwar period, the cultural landscape showed a strong resemblance to its European counterparts.[9] As in Germany and Italy, many members of Japan's urban and educated middle class yearned for a pure, indigenous cultural aesthetic. They believed that it could be found in a "national political essence (*kokutai*)," a "range of ideological virtues that defined what it meant to be Japanese, as opposed to the 'other,'" and thought these communitarian values of the countryside or the distant past could restore a cultural and spiritual purity to a nation that had experienced foreign-influenced decadence of the city and a recent history of modernization and Westernization.[10]

There were not only striking parallels but also significant interactions between Japanese and German movements to protect and promote indigenous dogs. Germans influenced, and interacted with, Japanese government bureaucrats, military officials, zoologists, and dog enthusiasts on a number of levels. Many aficionados of "Japanese" dogs admired so-called German shepherd dogs—which were also a recent invention—and a few were members of groups that promoted the latter breed in Japan. The *Doitsu shepādo* (or sometimes *sepādo*), as the breed was formally referred to in Japanese, was frequently a benchmark of comparison for "Japanese" breeds, and some fanciers in Germany and Japan considered both types of dogs to be closely related, and therefore the purest and finest canines in the world. Finally, the two groups of enthusiasts spoke a shared language of fascism. As the historian Boria Sax has written: "The Nazis were constantly invoking dogs and wolves for the qualities they wanted to cultivate: loyalty, fierceness, courage, obedience, and sometimes even cruelty."[11]

Although it is hardly a cruel story, the legend of Hachikō provides a useful framework for probing the relationship between dogs and fascism. Hachikō was the key actor in the rediscovery and valorization of native dogs, long despised as disorderly, savage, and wolflike. Through the joint efforts of a group of private dog enthusiasts and the Ministry of Education, the native dog of Meiji times was in the course of the early twentieth century transformed into the "Japanese" dog, an icon of purity, loyalty, and bravery, superior to both Western dogs and the native dogs of Japan's colonies. Indeed, the creation of "Japanese" dogs, with Hachikō as its paragon, was one of the building blocks of a culture of imperial fascism that venerated the nation, celebrated purity, esteemed fidelity, and glorified violence.

Thanks to Japan's rise to imperial power status, "Japanese" dog breeds such as the Akita became colonial dogs, acknowledged as legitimate both domestically and abroad. Although Japan's disastrous defeat in the Second World War upset the official recognition of the Akita in Western countries, it did so only temporarily. Within a few decades, the Akita, a large, potentially fierce hunting dog and a symbol of Japanese loyalty, had completely eclipsed the lapdog *chin* as the representative canine of Japan and joined the pantheon of Western breeds that dominate today's canine cartography.

Nationalizing Native Dogs

The association of native dogs with the nation-state in Japan of the 1930s was part of a trend that had developed in Europe in the second half of the nineteenth-century and spread with imperialism and the global diffusion of Western modes of dog keeping and the ideology of animal pure-bloodism. Yet given indigenous canines' recent history, the extolling of native dogs in Japan was no small irony. Foreigners and local elites alike from the mid-nineteenth century had regarded native dogs as primitive, cowardly, and of mixed or wild breed. Within a remarkably short space of time, these same canines came to be cited as an example of what supposedly made Japan superior to the Western imperial powers. For decades rounded up for elimination by dogcatchers in the government's employ, "Japanese" dogs had by the early 1930s became immensely popular, serving as a status symbol for anyone with the means to acquire one. Once the target of derision, they were now a source of national and imperial pride.

The radical reappraisal of native dogs in Japan paralleled, even if it slightly trailed temporally, the nationalization of the shepherd dog in Germany. As with native dogs in Japan, the "Germanization" of the shepherd dog occurred comparatively late and produced a dramatic shift in popular attitudes. Until Max von Stephanitz (1863–1936), a retired Prussian cavalry captain, established the Verein für deutsche Schäferhunde (Society for the German Shepherd Dog) in 1899, the breed was largely undefined and little valued. Stephanitz tirelessly promoted the breed through his society's newsletter and the popular press. In 1901 he published a two-volume book, *Der deutsche Schäferhund in Wort und Bild* (The German shepherd dog in word and picture), which reached its fifteenth edition as early as 1914 and was subsequently translated into several languages, including English and Japanese.[12] Within a decade of its establishment, the group achieved phenomenal success in registering, breeding, and popularizing what Stephanitz called the "primeval Germanic dog."[13] Although four dogs were identified with Germany on the 1933 "Dog Map of the World" mentioned in chapter 1 of this book, the shepherd, even more than the Doberman pinscher, dachshund, and schnauzer, was seen as distinctively representative of Deutschland.

Although there were earlier expressions of pride in native dog breeds and dismay at their "mongrelization" in turn-of-the-century Japan, these sentiments did not crystallize until several decades later. There were probably several reasons for the delay. A clientele for canines—that is to say, a bourgeois middle class that was interested in and could afford to acquire and keep a dog—did not emerge in Japan until the 1920s. It was not until such a constituency appeared that the ownership of dogs, and in this case the keeping specifically of native dogs, became widespread enough for a reconsideration of the maligned canines to take place. Around this time, publishers began to issue dog-care and breed manuals aimed at well-to-do urbanites. Until the late 1920s, such publications rarely mentioned indigenous dogs. Nevertheless, a growing enthusiasm for canines in general and the maturation of a substantial group of people with the means to imitate the dog-keeping practices of the wealthy prepared the way for a movement to preserve native dogs.

Urbanization played an important role in the revaluation of indigenous canines, as well. The isolation from the countryside that is characteristic of citified modernity led in many countries to a desire to reconnect with the natural world, albeit in a domesticated form—or, as the historian Kathleen Kete has put it, to install a "beast in the boudoir."[14] As elsewhere, the roots and membership of the newly established dog clubs were overwhelmingly urban, and although some organizations were founded in rural areas during the late 1920s and 1930s, they almost always rose as a provincial response to attention from the city.

Shifts in the political and cultural climate during the late 1920s and 1930s made people more receptive to the promotion of native dogs. Nationalism and the veneration of native canine breeds were inseparable. The first expressions of concern for indigenous dogs coincided with rising nationalism at the end of the nineteenth century, and their full manifestation corresponded with what historians Tetsuo Najita and Harry Harootunian have called the "Japanese revolt against the West" in the 1930s. During this period, ideologues promoted national pride in the archipelago's natural environment, climate, and a pure, indigenous culture that was unsullied but supposedly threatened by foreign elements. The reclamation and praise of native dogs was a canine variant of this pervasive and powerful political, intellectual, and cultural groundswell of resistance to the purported corrosive influences of Western modernity.

In the realm of dogs, Saitō Hirokichi (who also used the pen name Saitō Hiroshi; 1900–64), the founder of the Nihon ken hozon kai (Society for the Preservation of the Japanese Dog), led the revolt. Born and raised in rural Yamagata Prefecture in northern Honshu, Saitō was one of many young people who poured into Tokyo and other cities from the countryside in the early twentieth century. A graduate of the prestigious Tokyo bijutsu gakkō (Tokyo Fine Arts Academy: now the Tokyo geijutsu daigaku), Saitō became a landscape architect. He later played a leading role in the design of a garden at the National Museum of Modern Art in Tokyo, which opened in 1952. An art lover, Saitō, as a guardian of the Yōmei archive that housed precious medieval cultural artifacts of the aristocratic Fujiwara and Konoe households, was instrumental in protecting the treasures from the bombing raids of the Second World War. Saitō's other love was dogs. In 1927 he joined the Eighth Artillery Division but was soon discharged because of health problems. Told by his doctor that he needed plenty of fresh air, and perhaps feeling in need of a mission, he decided to buy a dog and began to search, as he later recalled, for a pure indigenous canine like "those depicted in ancient scrolls."[15]

Saitō was unable to find a dog that met his standards in Tokyo, where, in his view, Western decadence and foreign blood had spread to the urban canine population. Even in the mountainous northern prefecture of Akita, soon to be known for a breed of the same name, he found it difficult to locate a dog that satisfied him.[16] Alarmed that, through interbreeding, native dogs were following wolves to what he believed was tantamount to extinction, Saitō established the Society in May 1928. He then spent much of the next several years traveling to remote highland regions throughout the archipelago to locate purebred dogs and to campaign for their protection. A photograph from 1931 shows Saitō dressed in

15. The founder of the Society for the Preservation of the Japanese Dog, Saitō Hirokichi, dressed in traditional hunting attire and searching for pure "Japanese" dogs in the Sanmen region of Niigata Prefecture in November 1931.

traditional hunting clothing while conducting research in the Sanmen region of Niigata Prefecture.[17]

While returning from one of those trips, Saitō encountered Hachikō somewhere in the vicinity of Shibuya Station. Like many ascents to stardom, Hachikō's was more staged than spontaneous. After this meeting, Saitō featured the dog on the pages of a Society newsletter in 1929. Several years later he realized that Hachikō had a potentially wider appeal and proposed a story about the dog to a reporter of the daily *Asahi* newspaper.[18] Although he was upset that the *Asahi* article stated that Hachikō was of "mixed breed" rather than a pureblooded Akita, Saitō was surely pleased with its placement and an accompanying large photograph of a forlorn-looking Hachikō in the paper's morning edition of 4 October 1932. "The Story of a Lovable Old Dog: A Seven-Year Expectant Wait for the Return of a Master Who Is No Longer of This World" told of the dog's unflagging fidelity and portrayed him as a righteous mediator of dogfights and a protective patron (*oyabun*) for smaller canines.[19] The article launched Hachikō's tremendous popularity, which probably escalated to a degree beyond what anyone, including Saitō, anticipated.

Saitō's timing could not have been better. There are good, historical reasons why this dog got his day in 1932 and why such an apotheosis occurring just a few years earlier is difficult to imagine. The Manchurian Incident (also known as the Mukden Incident), which began the previous year, marked the start of what was repeatedly proclaimed to be an extended "national emergency" (*hijōji*) and a time of tremendous anxiety. On 18 September, Japanese military officers used a staged explosion on a railway in northeastern China as a ploy to launch an attack on the troops of the local warlord. By January 1932, the entire region was effectively in the hands of the Japanese Kwantung Army, and the following month Tokyo established the Japanese puppet state of Manchukuo. The insubordination of military officers in Manchuria and the inability, or unwillingness, of civilian government authorities to constrain them, coupled with a series of assassinations of top government officials by military officers and right-wing radicals at home led to an end to party rule by mid-1932. After the 15 May killing of Prime Minister Inukai Tsuyoshi (1855–1932) by a group of navy officers and ultrarightists, top military leaders proceeded to dominate "national unity" cabinets. Thus began the country's descent into the long, dark valley of militarism and fascism. The unfolding sentimental tale of Hachikō surely brought release from the uncertainties of the early 1930s, but its very appeal stemmed from the fact that its underlying message subtly reinforced the upsurge in patriotism that sang praises to the virtues of Japan's unique "national polity" and demanded strict allegiance to the "imperial way."

As indicated by the name of his organization—the Society for the Preservation of the Japanese Dog—Saitō explicitly linked native canines to the nation. Just as Stephanitz had "Germanized" the shepherd dog several decades earlier, Saitō effectively nationalized native dogs on the archipelago by declaring them to be "Japanese," or *Nihon inu*. This simple linguistic move further transformed dogs that had previously been considered semiwild and uncivilized into worthy domesticated pets, desirable to the middle class. Before the influx of foreign dogs from the middle of the nineteenth century, local dogs were most commonly referred to simply as *inu* (dogs), a generic appellation that they and all canines retain to this day. From the mid-nineteenth century, the term *waken* (Japanese dog), in juxtaposition with *yōken* (Western dog), was sometimes used, typical of the *wa/yō* (Japanese/Western) binary constructed by many early Meiji elites who thought that many traditional cultural forms ought to be abandoned and replaced by more "civilized" Western ones. Although the term *waken* geographically identified indigenous dogs with the Japanese archipelago, it did not explicitly connect them to the modern nation. Some people even before the 1930s had used *Nihon inu* (Japanese dog), which more unequivocally tied native dogs to the nation-state, but thanks to Saitō's efforts, it quickly became an almost exclusively used label.

By the early 1930s, native canines had become a proud symbol of Japan, something unthinkable just a decade earlier. One visual example of this new status was the placement of five "Japanese" dogs on the Christmas and New Year's greeting cards sent to international guests by manager Inumaru Tetsuzō (1897–1981) of the Imperial Hotel in Tokyo, which had been designed by Frank Lloyd Wright, during the 1933–34 holiday season.[20] A degree of international appreciation seemed to confirm national recognition. During her widely covered visit to Japan in 1937, Helen Keller asked for an Akita dog after she heard the story of Hachikō. A police officer in Akita Prefecture gave her a puppy whose

With

The Season's Kind Remembrances and Every Good Wish for Christmastide and throughout the Coming Year.

From

T. Inumaru.

Manager.

Imperial Hotel, Tokyo.

16. Holiday greeting card from the Tokyo Imperial Hotel featuring native dogs, December 1933. Used with the permission of Christine Kim.

name, Kamikaze-gō ("divine wind"), referred to the tropical storms that had twice protected the archipelago from invading Mongol forces in the thirteenth century and that less than a decade later would become the label for the special attack forces (*tokkōtai*), composed primarily of young university students, that launched suicidal assaults against the United States during the final months of the Second World War. The dog's life was also unfortunately cut short. Just three months after arriving in the United States, he succumbed to distemper.[21] In response, the Ministry of Foreign Affairs arranged for one of his littermates to be sent to Keller in 1939.

Saitō did not link native dogs to the nation in name only. "Japanese" canines, he claimed, possessed a personality similar to the country's human population because of a long and close association between the archipelago's people and dogs. In a radio address in 1937 titled "What Kind of a Canine is a Japanese Dog?" aired by Nippon Hōsō Kyōkai (NHK), the government-controlled broadcasting company, Saitō made the following declaration:

> [The] dog's temperament is strongly influenced by the character of its master,
> but, because the Japanese dog has a long history, the character of the nation

has exerted influence on the entire breed. The various traits of the Japanese nation—difficulty in getting used to anyone outside its master's family, being intelligent but not adept in expressing emotions as compared to Western dogs, diffidence and stubbornness, and extreme courage—have been ingrained into the personality of Japanese dogs.[22]

Here and elsewhere, Saitō insisted that centuries of interaction between Japanese people and native dogs had caused a sort of Lamarckian inheritance of acquired characteristics whereby indigenous canines acquired a disposition like their human companions, which molded these canines into the dog of the Japanese family-state (*kazoku kokka*). Saitō even made the dog breed whom people kept the litmus test of their national identity with an oft-repeated phrase he was said to have coined, "*Nihonjin nara, Nihon-ken o kae*" (If you are Japanese, keep a Japanese dog!).[23] This statement implied that owning a non-"Japanese" dog was thoroughly un-Japanese.

Like Stephanitz, Saitō was able to spread his message and translate his ideas into action because he was an adept publicist, as evidenced by his frequent appearances in the press as well as on nationwide radio. Saitō communicated his ideas through the Society's journal and wrote or supplied information for numerous articles that were published in other magazines and national and local newspapers. Indeed, it was Saitō who submitted material for an article about Hachikō to the daily *Asahi* newspaper in 1932, thereby bringing the dog individual fame and "Japanese" dogs collective popularity. The length and prominent placement of a Saitō-authored piece that covered almost the entire third page of another national daily newspaper, the *Yomiuri*, in April 1929, and an article about "The Pure Japanese Breed of Dog" by a Society member in the *American Kennel Gazette* in May 1930, may have been the exception, but it indicates Saitō's ability to reach a wide, even international, audience even in the earliest days of the Society's existence.[24] Saitō was also able to boost the Society's membership and, probably more important, to enlist a number of influential figures to join the organization. In its inaugural April 1932 issue, the Society's magazine, *Nihon inu*, listed 140 people as members, including a number of top biologists, senior military officers, and powerful politicians, such as Nakano Seigō (1886–1943), a right-wing writer and populist.[25] By 1939 the Society's ranks expanded to 1,065 members.[26]

Equally important was Saitō's success in ensuring that government bureaucrats showed and maintained an interest in dogs. The Ministry of Education, at the recommendation of officials in its Bureau of Cultural Affairs, sanctioned the nationalization of native dogs by declaring seven different breeds as natural treasures worthy of government protection during the 1930s. The legal instrument through which this feat was accomplished was the Law for Preserving Scenery and Historic and Natural Monuments (Shiseki meisho tennen ki'nenbutsu hozon hō), a measure passed in 1919 as the result of lobbying by a coalition of historians, scientists, government officials, and other elites and modeled on similar regulations in the United States and Europe, and particularly Germany. Historian Julia Adeney Thomas has suggested that Japanese concerns with the physical environment were often expressed in abstract, rarified terms at the expense of real regulatory action, but this legislation, as well as the 1931 National Park Law, led to unprecedented if limited protections for cultural sites, natural landscapes, and animals before mobilization for war tempered such initiatives.[27] The preservation movement's principal proponent and theoretician was Miyoshi Manabu (1861–1939), a Tokyo Imperial University botanist who introduced German ideas of national monuments to Japan. As historian Shinoda Mariko has argued, Miyoshi's desire to preserve culture and nature was motivated by nationalism as well as by science. Miyoshi emphasized that preservation would enhance national dignity in three ways: by highlighting the length of Japan's history, by instilling geographical consciousness of Japanese territory in an age of imperial expansion, and by intensifying national unity and satisfying the nostalgia for the past that was threatened by industrialization and modernization.[28] Botanical objects, from shrine groves to rare plants, received most of the designations during the first two decades of the law's existence, but officials did not overlook zoological life that was unique to Japan, scarce elsewhere, or threatened with extinction.[29]

Native dogs fit the scientific requirements, as well as the ideological imperatives, of the law. The first advocate of designating canine natural treasures was Watase Shōzaburō (1862–1929), who argued that native dogs should be preserved for academic, cultural, and practical reasons. Watase, who graduated from Johns Hopkins University in 1899 and then studied in Germany before returning to Japan to assume a professorship at Tokyo Imperial University, joined Miyoshi and other scholars to advise the government about what sorts of natural and cultural objects deserved protection. In several articles in the early 1920s, Watase used a combination of scientific and nationalist language to make a case for native dogs. He claimed that because most dogs in the world were of "mixed breed," Japanese dogs, whose "pedigree stretched from the days of the gods," were of great interest to scientists. Although foreign researchers were importing the dogs for study, Watase lamented that Japanese zoologists showed little interest in local canines. He contended that research about "Japanese" dogs would assist in revealing the origins of the Japanese people, and that because native dogs were unrivaled in their ability to hunt beasts—though not birds—they ought to be preserved.[30] Watase's writings, however, neither gained much attention at the time nor led to any immediate action to preserve indigenous breeds. Watase was not involved in the creation of the Society for the Preservation of Japanese Dogs, and Saitō appears to have been unaware of Watase's writings or activities until after the latter's death. Nevertheless, once Saitō learned of them, he took full advantage of Watase's assertions and connections to lobby for official recognition. Sometime during the early years of the Society, he signed up one of Watase's junior professors at Tokyo Imperial University, zoologist Kaburagi Tokio (1890–1968), as a member of the Society. Kaburagi, who like Watase served as an official adviser to the Bureau of Cultural Affairs that made official recommendations about what animals should be designated as natural treasures, served as director (*rijichō*) of the Society from 1932 to 1933.

Although indigenous domesticated dogs were not the first animals to be given special status, they were probably the most celebrated. Even before Hachikō became the object of public adoration in late 1932, the Ministry of Education named the Akita breed an endangered national asset in July 1931. Over the next six years, the ministry granted similar status to the Kai, Kishū, Koshino (soon thereafter declared "extinct" because of interbreeding), Shiba, Shikoku, and Hokkaido breeds. Obtaining such recognition was no small task. It required the cooperation of central and regional bureaucrats, as well as the authorization of a prefectural governor. Society members worked closely with authorities on the national and local levels to complete the necessary paperwork, and frequently supplied information or articles from the Society's magazine as supporting documents.[31] A declaration of protection stringently regulated the sale, breeding, and movement—especially the export—of designated canines, prescriptions that continue to this day.

The Ministry of Education's rationale for preserving "Japanese" dogs echoed Saitō's argument that the character of the nation was ingrained in the personality of the country's canines. When the ministry announced its designation of the Shiba breed in 1936, its spokesperson proclaimed that the dogs were worthy of the honor because they "reflect the character of the Japanese people, and compared to foreign dogs demonstrate a particular vigor and have all the characteristics of a Japanese dog."[32]

As underscored by the ministry's insistence that the vigor of the Shiba breed surpassed that of foreign canines, fans of native dogs were anxious to show that their animals were as good as, if not better than, any pure-blooded Western breed. Claims about the superiority of native dogs vis-à-vis Western canines often appeared in articles in the specialized enthusiast and general press. The point was even made for young readers by Kishi Kazutoshi, author of *Chūken Hachikō monogatari* (The Story of the "Loyal dog" Hachikō):

> Mention the "Japanese dog," and the dogs of Japan who in the past have been treated like strays come to mind. Mention a dog show, and only Western dogs such as the shepherd, pointer, and terrier come to mind. What the Society for the Preservation of the Japanese Dog is making Japanese aware of is that the Japanese dog is by no means inferior, but, in fact, is far superior to Western dogs.[33]

Dog enthusiasts and education bureaucrats asserted that the timeless relationship between the archipelago's canine and human races, especially between the dogs and the country's emperors, made "Japanese" dogs better than others. Stephanitz used similar language to recall how in "time immemorial...the warlike proud German held in high esteem his courageous hunting comrade," the shepherd dog.[34] Reiterating the rhetoric of Saitō and other commentators, the children's author Kishi insisted that native dogs enjoyed a special bond with the people of Japan that had begun during the rule of the country's first (mythical) emperor, Jimmu, in 660 BCE.

> There are many dogs in present-day Japan, aren't there? For example, there are Western dogs such as the delightful German shepherd and bulldog; there are Japanese dogs that have been in Japan since ancient times; and then there seem to be quite a few of the type that are a mix between Japanese dogs and Western dogs.
>
> Japanese dogs have lived since very ancient times with the Japanese people and were raised in Japan. Therefore, one can say that from the days of Emperor Jimmu until today this dog has persisted as the pure Japanese dog.[35]

Kishi's words betrayed an anxiety about Western dogs and especially about dogs of mixed breed. The latter were numerous—probably far too numerous for the tastes of most native-dog enthusiasts. Kishi's principal message, however, depended on the (a)historical connection between native dogs and the Japanese

17. A postcard from the National Science Museum in Tokyo showing (from left to right) the stuffed Jirō and Hachikō. Jirō was one of two Sakhalin huskies who managed to survive for nearly a year after Japanese scientists were forced by inclement weather to abandon a pack of sled dogs when evacuating the Shōwa research station in Antarctica in the late 1950s. (See chapter 5 for more details.) Unseen in this photograph, standing on the other side of Hachikō, is one of the last wolves to be killed in Japan as the species was driven to extinction at the beginning of the twentieth century. Used with the permission of the National Science Museum.

throne, both of which were perceived as having preserved a constant, untainted bloodline since the dawn of time.

In addition to calling frequent attention to the alleged connections between the country's dog population and its imperial masters in the past, dog fanciers sought to create similar links in the present. As kennel clubs did in late nineteenth-century Britain and elsewhere, Society officials eagerly encouraged the participation of royalty and nobility in its dog shows. They also organized such events on holidays honoring the throne. The first dog show for Japanese dogs only was held on the roof of the Matsuya department store in Ginza in early November 1932 and coincided with a national holiday commemorating the birth of the late Meiji emperor.[36] The Society invited several members of the imperial household and presented them and, in absentia, the emperor with small statues of Hachikō.

Hachikō, the embodiment of the preeminence of Japan's newly nationalized dogs, attended this and subsequent shows as a special guest. At the first exhibition, he appeared together with Koma-go, another Akita dog, whom the Society had previously given to a relative of the emperor.[37] The Society awarded both dogs special collars to celebrate the event. The broad band of leather, stamped with the words "Commemorative Memento as Honorary Participant of the First Japanese-Dog Show—The Society for the Preservation of the Japanese Dog," still encircles the stuffed Hachikō in the National Science Museum. In death, as in life, Hachikō was collared by the nation and tagged as Japanese.

Blood and Breed

The Society's breeding standards and the government's moves to preserve native dogs reflected the complex nature of Japanese attitudes about racial identity during the 1930s. These attitudes represented two conflicting strains of thought, one that regarded Japanese as a racially homogenous people, and the other that considered Japanese to be of mixed racial origin. Reflecting the former view, the policies and rhetoric of dog enthusiasts and government preservationists betrayed a strident concern with the maintenance of pure blood. Society officials considered, and government bureaucrats recognized as "Japanese," only those groups of canines whose pedigree had been attested in the archipelago since the beginning of (Japanese) time. The primary threat driving "Japanese" dogs to extinction, they contended, were canines of Western and mixed breed. The officials' actions and statements mirrored wider societal anxieties about human purity of blood, the superiority of the Japanese race, and the specter of miscegenation.

Reflecting the latter view, enthusiasts and scientists speculated that the ancestors of "Japanese" dogs had likely come to the archipelago thousands of years earlier from the Asian Continent or the South Pacific. Such an explanation supported the government's efforts to assimilate and exploit the human population of Japan's formal and informal colonies. In this way, fanciers, scientists, and government preservationists enlarged the Japanese canine imperium even as Japan's empire expanded, making the country's political rule seem natural and organic.

The most pressing task for Saitō in the late 1920s and early 1930s was to determine precisely what a "Japanese" dog was. Saitō and others, from fanciers to zoologists, intensely debated how to define this standard in the Society's journal, *Nihon inu*, and in other dog fancier magazines, such as *Kokken* (National dog), a rival periodical issued by the short-lived Japanese Dog Association (Nihon inu kyōkai). In the end, Saitō exercised the greatest influence over the criteria that emerged and that were eventually embraced by the government.

The defining characteristic of the breeds that came to be considered Japanese was that their bloodlines were free of foreign adulteration. While recognizing that the archipelago's earliest canines may have arrived with humans from elsewhere thousands of years before, Saitō drew a clear distinction between those dogs and breeds that appeared on the peninsula more recently, even if their distinctive appearance had been shaped by breeders in Japan. Thus Saitō deemed such breeds as the lapdog *chin*, which he supposed had been imported from China during the relatively recent Tokugawa period and artificially shaped over many generations by breeders, to be "Japanized" but not "Japanese." Likewise, Saitō judged the Tosa, a fierce fighting breed that was created through interbreeding various Western dogs with native canines from the Tosa region beginning in the mid-nineteenth century, not to be Japanese.[38] In a 1935 letter in imperfect English addressed to foreign dog clubs, the Society's foreign secretary, Hata Ichirō (1901–69), a professor of French literature at Nihon University, took pains to point out that the Tosa should not be called a "pure Japanese dog," as had been claimed in foreign kennel gazettes. "This mistake is really excusable, although unfortunately it is far from the case, since a [T]osa is terribly a mixed breed." The only dogs that were truly Japanese, Hata declared, were "native dogs" of a "very ancient breed" that have "been living more or less in a similar form and shape from the days [of our] forefathers."[39]

For fanciers, this primordial connection to the archipelago was not the only reason that certain indigenous dogs outclassed purebred Western dogs. "Japanese" dogs, they claimed, had lived with humans but had not been interbred by them, so they remained in a natural and uncorrupted state. Among pure breeds, argued Hata in the Society's magazine, there were two types: primal breeds (*genshu*) and improved breeds (*kairyōshu*). Primal breeds were by far the rarer of the two. They had not been bred by humans, so that their "character and physiognomy had remained unchanged since the time of their appearance." Improved breeds, on the other hand, were dogs that had been bred over many generations to take on a fixed form, color, and character. Most Western dogs, he contended, though not "mixed breeds" (*zasshu*), were improved breeds, while "Japanese" dogs were primal breeds, having maintained an uninterrupted pure pedigree free from human interference.[40] Saitō suggested that the physical characteristics of improved breeds, such as the ears of a Doberman, were unnatural, whereas the appearance and personality of "Japanese" dogs were innate. Such language portended and reverberated with contemporary rhetoric in official texts, such as the 1937 *Kokutai no hongi* (Fundamentals of our national polity), about the unbroken and undefiled blood ties of the Japanese nation and the imperial line. It also ignored the irony that breeders and eugenicists were now intervening to improve and maintain those same Japanese canine and human races that they claimed were superior because they had been formed naturally.

Another commonality of many of the breeds designated as Japanese was that they inhabited mountainous upland areas rather than wetland, rice-farming regions. Saitō, like his Society colleague the folklorist Yanagita, regarded the country's mountainous regions as the literal repository of what was uniquely Japanese.[41] For Saitō, the mountains had provided a refuge for Japanese dogs far from the Western canines who had violated the blood of indigenous canines in the lowlands since as early as the sixteenth century, and especially since the mid-nineteenth century. Hoping to save these untainted dogs, Saitō spent much of the late 1920s and early 1930s exploring remote highland areas to find and protect dogs who "from before the Meiji period were deep in the mountains hunting bear, wild boar, and deer."[42] It was these dogs whom Saitō classified as Japanese. Only they were free from the legacy of Westernization that he believed had defiled Japan both physically and spiritually. Saitō and his fellow dog enthusiasts constantly recounted the ill effects of Meiji-era Westernization on the native canine population. Society member Takahisa Heishirō, for example, decried the period as one when "dog lovers, especially, hated native dogs" and people took pride in any dog that had floppy ears because they supposed that the trait meant that it was of Western breed.[43]

At the same time that Saitō and other Society members praised native upland dogs for being free of foreign canine blood, they celebrated their resemblance to wolves and possible blood links to their lupine cousins. Such admiration for the wolflike nature of native dogs was, of course, ironic. Westerners and local elites in Japan and other colonizable and colonized areas of the world had denigrated certain native dogs for their purported physical and behavioral similarities to wolves, and this disparagement led to efforts to eliminate indigenous canines— whether street, feral, or wild dogs or the wolves themselves.

During the interwar period, a new respect for wolves and other large predators emerged throughout the world, especially in areas where these animals were extinct and no longer an actual, or even imagined, threat. Attitudes toward canines once despised as wolflike changed, too. Possible biological links with wolves and a wolfish appearance and behavior became more appealing, particularly in those countries where fascism made the deepest inroads. Nowhere was this shift more apparent than in Germany. In his early writings, Stephanitz, whose rhetoric anticipated Nazi racial doctrines, claimed that only the "German" shepherd was entirely a descendant of an ancient medium-sized wolf, whereas many other dogs were recipients of varying amounts of jackal blood.[44] Hitler and other National Socialist leaders continually appropriated wolves for symbolic purposes, referring to themselves as wolves and their various headquarters as lairs.[45] The German government placed the wolf under protection in 1934, a first among modern nations and a gesture that was in fact symbolic, since wolves had been extinct within Germany's borders for almost a century.[46] Many prominent Nazis admired the shepherd dog because of its supposed wild, wolfish nature. The relationship between the three—Nazis, lupines, and shepherd dogs—is aptly captured by the name Hitler gave the first "German" shepherd he owned: Wolf.

Similar cultural trends were evident in 1930s Japan. Wolves were not deployed in the political sphere so frequently as they were in Germany, but the reasons for their extinction and their relationship with native dogs became a much discussed topic. The folklorist Yanagita in the pages of the Society for the Preservation of the Japanese Dog's magazine speculated that wolves may not have completely vanished from the archipelago at all, and even if they had, they probably interbred with dogs, so that wolf blood could still be found in native canines. If wolves had indeed disappeared, he conjectured that it was because "modern phenomena" had corroded their pack mentality and caused them to increase solo attacks on people, which prompted the successful human effort to exterminate them.[47] While Saitō and others rejected Yanagita's explanation of lupine extinction and his theory of a recent biological link between wolves and native breeds, they celebrated the idea of the wolflike nature of "Japanese" dogs, which made local varieties seem more natural, pure, and fearsome than their foreign cousins.[48]

Although there were striking parallels with Germany in discussions of canine blood and breed, there were also marked differences. Specifically, because of Japan's relatively shallow experience with animal husbandry, discussions about breeding neither preoccupied fanciers nor wielded the influence that they did elsewhere. In many Western countries, "breeding" animals *and* humans for superiority was important, as highlighted by the widespread popularity of eugenics, but nowhere else did such thinking become policy as it did under the Third Reich.[49] In early twentieth-century Germany, a number of advocates of eugenics and Aryan supremacy had backgrounds in zootechny or referenced animal breeding in their arguments for artificially improving human heredity. Stephanitz, for example, bombastically applied the principles of animal stirpiculture to human racial politics in his writings. Historians Wolfgang Wippermann and Detlef Berentzen, in fact, speculate that Hitler—a rabid fan of the shepherd dog—may have read Stephanitz's magnum opus, *The German Shepherd in Word and Picture*, as a young man. They argue that, at a minimum, Stephanitz and other enthusiasts influenced Nazi racial policies in their quest to create a pure, healthy, strong, and standardized race of dogs.[50] National Socialist educators, for example, used dog breeds to explain in readily understandable terms ethnogeny, the supremacy of the Aryan race, and the dangers of miscegenation.[51] In Japan, however, animal breeding had less impact on racial policies. Crossover between animal breeders and the relatively weak eugenics movement in Japan was much rarer, and any concern with human purity in the writings of canine enthusiasts was far more muted and implicit. That said, the rhetoric of Japanese dog enthusiasts clearly fed into wider societal concerns about racial identity, just as canine terminology helped to shape larger discussions of race.

In broader terms as well, the politics of race and empire in Japan differed significantly from that in Germany. Because Western notions of race were intertwined with a belief in the superiority of white races, many Japanese were uncomfortable with eugenic and racial thought.[52] Japanese nationalism, as historian Tessa Morris-Suzuki has pointed out, was generally centered on the idea of *Volk* or "national people" (*minzoku*) rather than "race" (*jinshu*).[53] One current of nationalism depicted Japanese as a racially homogenous people literally descended from a common bloodline whose uppermost branch was the Imperial Family. The competing mixed-blood view emerged only later, in the late nineteenth century, but grew rapidly along with imperial expansion. Japanese acquisition of an empire populated by ethnically similar peoples who lived in relatively close proximity to the metropole led some people to emphasize that Japanese were of diverse racial origins and to identify this hybridity as a source of national strength and imperial power.[54]

Such political realities were reflected in and supported by popular and scientific discourses about canines. Dog enthusiasts and academic researchers alike cited recent findings that ostensibly demonstrated ancient biological links between "Japanese" dogs and canines in Asia. The research of Society member Hasebe Kotondo (1882–1969), then a professor at Tōhoku Imperial University, is a case in point. Until the late 1930s, Hasebe accepted the fact that Japanese were a mixed-blood people with ancient biological links to the peoples of East and Southeast Asia. His 1935 summer research on prehistoric dogs confirmed this view and was mobilized to bolster the government's assimilationist policies in the Japanese puppet state of Manchukuo. Hasebe's work proved, as a daily *Yomiuri* newspaper headline proclaimed, "In the Dog World, Too, Japan and Manchuria Are Brothers." Through an examination of bones that he located in a Port Arthur (Lüshun) museum, Hasebe concluded that Manchurian canines were closely related to the first small-sized Japanese dogs. Hasebe's findings, the reporter concluded, "add another intimate strand in the web that links Japan and our ally Manchukuo."[55] The relationship later became even more intimate and assumed a distinctly gendered character. In June 1941, a *Yomiuri* correspondent reported from Kōfu in Yamanashi Prefecture that a male Japanese Kai dog named Torakō (Tiger) and a Manchurian she-wolf named Sekirōkō (Red Wolf) had produced a litter of three pups. The correspondent drew from the story much the same meaning that Hasebe's research had provoked six years earlier: "As might be expected from two allied countries, the three siblings get along well and are amply endowed. They have inherited intelligence (*eichi*) from their father and vitality (*kisei*) from their mother, and they will certainly become superb military dogs."[56]

During the 1930s, Saitō increasingly embraced theories that extended the Japanese canine realm even as the country's political empire grew. Late in 1935, he publicly signaled his approval for Hasebe's research in comments in the *Asahi* newspaper. Saitō did so in the context of advocating a new hypothesis, outlined by Stephanitz, that assumed historical links between "Japanese" dogs and canines on the Asian Continent. Stephanitz, in a letter to Saitō, suggested that "Japanese" dogs and "German" shepherds were intimate siblings, both breeds being the most closely related descendents of the ancient dogs of Central Asia. The dogs who moved eastward became "Japanese," while those who went west became "German" shepherds. In his letter, Stephanitz requested bones from a purebred Japanese dog. Not surprisingly, Saitō sent him a skull, other bones, and photographs of Hachikō, as well as a letter explaining Hasebe's research.[57] The two men promoted a lineage that traced their respective national dogs back to Central Asia, though probably for different reasons. From Stephanitz's viewpoint, the theory provided a canine analogue to Nazi doctrine, which identified Nordic, or Germanic, peoples as the purest members of an Aryan race that once dwelt in Central Asia. For Saitō, Stephanitz's proposition provided a historic link to the Asian Continent, increasing parts of which were becoming incorporated into the Japanese imperium.

With the assistance of colleagues, Saitō investigated canines in the Ryukyu Islands, Hokkaido, Taiwan, Korea, Manchuria, and the South Seas. The Society also established branches in several colonial cities and sought to promote "Japanese" dogs throughout and beyond the empire. In colonial Korea, Saitō gained the cooperation of Mori Tamezō (1884–unknown), a professor of zoology at Keijō Imperial University (present-day Seoul National University). In early 1937, an *Asahi* journalist reported that Saitō and Mori had discovered on Jindo, an island off the southwestern coast of Korea, what the article labeled "Japanese dogs raised in Korea," sporting pricked-up ears and curled tails. Saitō speculated that the dogs had originated either in the Japanese home islands (*naichi*) or in the northern part of the continent.[58] As a result of Saitō and Mori's research, alongside the seven breeds that the Ministry of Education designated "Japanese" national treasures during the 1930s, Japanese colonial authorities in Korea granted similar "Japanese" status to the Jindo in 1937 or 1938 and one other peninsular breed, the Poongsan, in 1942.[59] This bureaucratic canonization surely did not arise out of pure concern for the canines themselves, much less the Korean populace. Rather like other facets of colonial modernity, such as industrialization and the spread of primary education, it served the purposes of the imperial power. Such cultural policies, even when directed at canines, were part of a larger strategy on the part of Japanese leaders to naturalize their colonial rule on the peninsula by using everyday social customs and environmental objects to assimilate, and thereby to obliterate, Korea as an independent nation.

Whether with regard to dogs he deemed "Japanese" on the archipelago or on the Korean Peninsula, Saitō repeatedly emphasized two physical traits. All "Japanese" canines, as he declared in his radio speech in 1937, had to have "small, triangular ears that stand erect" and a "large and powerful curled tail."[60] Any animal that did not show these features was immediately regarded as suspect. Some people, including the respected zoologist Ishikawa Chiyomatsu (1861–1935), suggested that based on this standard Hachikō was not purebred because his tail slumped down when he walked and, even more noticeable, because his left ear drooped.[61] Questions about Hachikō's purity of blood initially arose, to Saitō's consternation, when the first article published about the dog in the *Asahi* newspaper stated that he was of "mixed breed." Then, and repeatedly over the years, Saitō emphatically defended the integrity of Hachikō's bloodline. He argued that the tail dropped and the ear flopped as a result of skin disease and not because of foreign contamination of the dog's pedigree.[62] He produced photographs of Hachikō, including one he claimed dated from 1925, as visual evidence that the dog's ear in his younger years did not droop.[63] Although supportive of Saitō's claims, these photographs do not provide definitive proof of Hachikō's pure breed or blood (which is an arbitrarily constructed human standard anyway), but they do reveal just how concerned Saitō and others were about this issue (then and, in the case, of Saitō, even years later). The photos do, however, allow Hachikō to contribute material evidence to the debate and to shape the discussion about his purported purity. In an even more corporeal fashion, Hachikō's body lent itself to the debate, though its form was drastically manipulated by human hands. Fortunately for Saitō, and indeed because of his influence, taxidermists working for the National Science Museum mounted Hachikō with his tail curled and both ears standing erect, so that he emerged looking like a young, healthy, pureblooded "Japanese" dog.[64]

If it had not been for Hachikō, or more accurately, photographs of Hachikō in his later years, Saitō and the taxidermists may have largely been successful in their attempt to get people to remember Hachikō as a young, healthy, pureblooded "Japanese" dog. A number of historians of natural history and science museums have observed that taxidermy seeks to conceal its work by creating the illusion that the mounts taxidermists create are purely natural specimens, neutral, and objective. As Samuel Alberti has put it, "after the labour of manufacture, still further efforts are expended to conceal this work" to make mounts appear "impartial," "authorless," and to hide "their constructedness."[65] Taxidermists might be able to pull this off for the innumerable mounts of anonymous biological specimens, but not so for an animal celebrity such as Hachikō, who had been photographed throughout his life and garnered so much attention. Older photographs of Hachikō's living, aging, and failing body—along with, as we shall see, the true-to-life statue of Hachikō—permitted the dog, even in death, to create doubt about the form in which he was resurrected. They also illustrate how the stuffed Hachikō was a cultural artifact more than a natural specimen and, as he was in life, a product of culture as much as of nature.

The formulation of a standard for what constituted a pure Japanese dog, praise for native upland dogs uncompromised by foreign strains, and discussions of links with other Asian canines reveal the projection of human concerns about racial purity into the realm of dogs. Victorian European obsessions with race and categorization and eugenic ideas in Germany and elsewhere influenced the development of Japanese discourses about dogs, but in many ways such discourses reflected the particular circumstances of Japan in the 1930s. Such connections, commonalities, and contrasts were also evident in discussions about canine fidelity.

Unfailing Fidelity

Preservationists were not the only bureaucrats in the Ministry of Education who were concerned about native dogs. Educators within the ministry, too, realized that native dogs like Hachikō—and other dogs in the service of the empire—could be elevated as icons of loyalty in imperial and wartime Japan. From the 1890s, the inculcation of the Confucian virtue of loyalty (*chū*) had been central to the mission of the national school system. Government officials and private spokespeople labored to instill in imperial subjects a strong sense of obligation and veneration for elders, teachers, superiors, the state, and, most of all, the emperor. Schoolteachers taught their pupils that they were part of a unique family-state, with the emperor at its head. Hachikō and other supposedly devoted dogs provided perfect pedagogical models for authorities to suffuse people, both young and old, with messages about duty to and sacrifice for the nation.

Many cultures have celebrated the faithfulness of dogs to humans. As Keith Thomas and Kathleen Kete, historians of Britain and France respectively, have described, canine fidelity was a frequently encountered trope in early modern England and nineteenth-century Paris.[66] One of the most famous of these dogs was Greyfriars Bobby, a Skye terrier who was said to have watched over his master's grave in Edinburgh for fourteen years until his own death in 1872.[67] Perhaps nowhere, though, were faithful dogs deployed so prominently as symbols as in the fascist rhetoric of the 1930s. In Germany, proto-Nazi and National Socialist commentators and educators often venerated canines as paragons of fidelity. Stephanitz praised the "German" shepherd as the "most loyal companion of humans."[68] It was precisely this supposed devout dedication that endeared the breed to Nazi officials, who enjoyed keeping dogs and other large predators as pets.[69]

Hachikō was of course not the first dog to be invoked to foster loyalty in Japan. In the early nineteenth century, the prolific writer Takizawa Bakin (1767–1848) published the 106 volume *Nansō Satomi hakken-den* (The eight dog chronicles of the Satomi clan of Nansō), a historical novel set in a time of medieval war that featured a band of sibling boy/dog warriors who embody both samurai virtues and bestial attributes of fidelity, self-sacrifice, and carnal desire.[70] The book was hugely popular in the late Tokugawa and early Meiji periods, and was still read widely in the early twentieth century and made into a motion picture in the 1930s. Earlier primary school textbooks also featured dogs. For example, an 1892 primer, which bore some similarities to an incident in *Hakken-den*, told the story of a faithful white dog who repaid his master's kindness by saving his life.[71] Children who learned about Hachikō at school were likely familiar with at least *Hakken-den*, which had strong didactic overtones, so the transition between Confucian ethics embodied by the eight dogs to the statist framework of fascist ethics may have been more of a sleight of hand than a departure. In this way, Hachikō may have worked especially well because loyal dogs were already a part of the pantheon of cultural symbols, familiar to imperial subjects, both young and old.[72]

If the deployment of dogs to spread ideas about race in Japan paled in comparison to Germany, the metaphorical mobilization of "Japanese" canines to foster loyalty was probably unrivaled. Such discourses extended to military dogs of Western breed in the employ of the army, especially "German" shepherd dogs. However, "Japanese" dogs were singled out even more often for their unconditional devotion. Commentators repeatedly asserted that the fidelity of indigenous dogs was unique among canines in that it was directed exclusively and unendingly to a single master. They were said to pine away at the passing of a master and to fight to the death in his or her defense. More than once, the faithfulness of Hachikō and other "Japanese" dogs was compared to the *bushidō* ethos that supposedly bound a samurai warrior to his lord and the allegiance that people felt for the emperor.

In addition to ideological motivations, a desire for economic profit buoyed the dog's rise to fame. In the months and years before and after his death, businesspeople were quick to cash in on the canine celebrity. Merchants introduced one product after another, capitalizing on and surely augmenting the popularity of the Loyal Dog. In 1934 they took advantage of the zodiac in the Year of the Dog. The Chinese astrological calendar could not have been kinder. Businesspeople manipulated Hachikō to sell everything from toys to kimonos, postcards to kitchenware, phonographs to books. The dog even appeared in *Arupusu taishō* (Alpine victory), a 1934 motion picture directed by Yamamoto Kajirō (1902–74).[73] The marketing of the dog continued into the next year after his death. The phenomenon became so conspicuous that at least one artist, Maekawa Senpan (1888–1960), could not resist parodying it. Just days after Hachikō's demise—his body was discovered near Shibuya Station on the morning of 8 March 1935 and his remains (except for his coat) were buried next to his long-deceased master's in nearby Aoyama Cemetery—a cartoon by Maekawa appeared in the *Yomiuri* newspaper. Depicting vendors hawking a variety of gastronomic delights, all with a Hachikō theme, it posed the question, "Is this what the anniversary of Hachikō's death will be like every year?"[74] In this instance, life appeared to imitate art. The commercial exploitation of Hachikō continued throughout the 1930s and persists to some degree to this day. Annual events, most prominently a memorial service in March and a festival in April, honor the dog, and until 2006 (when the space was taken over by the global chain store, the Body Shop), any number of Hachikō trinkets could be purchased throughout the year at a store called the Hachikō Shop located just outside the officially named Hachikō Square of Shibuya Station.

The Society for the Preservation of the Japanese Dog and its allies in the Ministry of Education reveled in the attention that Hachikō was generating, but by the same token they fiercely sought to maintain control of the manner in which the dog was portrayed. In late 1933, for example, anticipating even greater publicity during the upcoming Year of the Dog, a group of private entrepreneurs announced its intention to construct a wooden statue of Hachikō. Angered by

18. This cartoon by Maekawa Senpan asks, "Is this what the anniversary of Hachikō's death will be like every year?" Venders are hawking a variety of food items, all using Hachikō to advertise their wares. From left to right, *manjū* (bun stuffed with *azuki*-bean paste), *donburi* (big bowl of rice topped with meat), candy, rice crackers, *yaki* (cooked cake filled with bean jam), *zenzai* red bean soup, and *dango* (dumplings). *Yomiuri shinbun*, 18 March 1935. Used with permission of *Yomiuri shinbun*.

this attempt by outsiders literally to shape Hachikō's image and profit from it, Saitō and his influential backers formed a committee and sought to co-opt the proposal by suggesting that they work jointly to create a monument. When this overture failed, Saitō and his supporters outmaneuvered their rivals by swiftly launching a campaign in early 1934 to raise money to build their own statue.[75] The committee asked Andō Shō (1892–1945) to take on the task of sculpting, with but one condition. Andō had already created a plaster model of Hachikō the previous fall for an annual show at the Imperial Gallery of Art and in that work faithfully depicted Hachikō with a floppy left ear.[76] Such a design, the committee decided—at Saitō's insistence—would not do: Andō must depict the dog with both ears erect. Saitō's wish went unfulfilled, however, when the exigency of quickly completing the statue forced the sculptor to use his original model for the cast, and for perpetuity Hachikō was cast in bronze as a dog with a suspect ear.

The statue was dedicated in an elaborate hour-long ceremony on 21 April 1934. Several newspapers reported that crowds were so large that it was almost impossible to move. Photographic evidence seems to confirm the scale of the spectacle and the presence of many youngsters and Saitō at the center of the activities. Saitō's business allies are represented, too. One photo shows an employee of the Mikado Kennel, a dog shop that had just opened its doors across town, standing just to the right of the statue at the ceremony. Arrayed in white and red ribbons but beginning to show his age, Hachikō was the guest of honor. After speeches by dignitaries who included Saitō; the head of Shibuya Ward; the stationmaster; the Ministry of Education's Social Education Bureau chief; and the author of *The Story*

19. The original bronze Hachikō statue outside of Shibuya Station on the day of its dedication, 21 April 1934. The adult figure standing in front of the statue is Saitō, and the man just to the left of the statue, wearing the *happi* livery coat, is an employee of the Mikado Kennel. Notice the number of youngsters in the crowd. Used with permission of Mainichi Photo Bank.

of the "Loyal Dog" Hachikō, Kishi Kazutoshi; Ueno's niece Sakano Hisako unveiled the statue. A film crew, dispatched by the Ministry of Foreign Affairs, captured the scene for a talkie to be distributed overseas.[77] Politicians, too, got involved. A poem written by Yamamoto Teijirō (1870–1937)—who served as a Diet member, a minister of agriculture and forestry (1927–29; 1931–32), and, from 1935 on, as leader of the reactionary Kokutai meichō undō (Movement for the Clarification of the National Polity)—praised "The Conduct of the Loyal Dog (Chūken kō)" and was inscribed on the statue's base.[78] In a melancholy tone, Yamamoto's poem lauded the faithfulness of Hachikō and lamented the fickle nature of humans.[79]

Although Saitō gave birth to the Hachikō story and the business community cashed in on it, Ministry of Education bureaucrats largely dictated its interpretation and dissemination to a national, colonial, and even worldwide audience. Initially, ministry bureaucrats used Kishi's *Story of the "Loyal Dog" Hachikō* to spread their tailored message. Ministry officials promoted the book in classrooms by way of an army of teachers. One man half-joked years later that his teacher encouraged students so enthusiastically to buy the book that he wondered if the instructor was getting a percentage of the income.[80] Moral suasion, rather than financial profit, was a more likely motive. A newspaper advertisement proclaimed that the book was an "ethics primer that must reach every mountain and seaside village of the archipelago." Reading it, the ad declared, caused children to "feel the righteous heart of Hachikō, who embodies the Japanese spirit," and braced them in defying a "world gone decadent, where people wallow in luxury and idleness, and humanity has become thinner than paper."[81]

Official and popular media, artists, and performers joined forces with the ministry to celebrate the virtue of loyalty as embodied by Hachikō. Just weeks before the dedication ceremony, the Society for the Preservation of the Japanese Dog, the Ministry's Social Education Bureau, and the Kōkoku seishin kai (Imperial Spirit Society) sponsored a benefit concert of skits, songs, and comic acts that attracted more than three thousand people to the Japan Young People's Auditorium in the outer garden area of Meiji Shrine.[82] NHK repeatedly transmitted the story of Hachikō as part of its children's radio programming. Countless poems, books, and songs hailed the inexhaustible fidelity of Hachikō. A dance group performed a number called "The Marching Song of Hachikō," and verse by the poet Noguchi Ujō (1888–1945) likened the dog to the famous forty-seven samurai of Akō, who in the early eighteenth century demonstrated their devotion to their late lord by avenging his ritual suicide, and to samurai and soldiers from Nitta Yoshisada (1301–38) to General Nogi Maresuke (1849–1912) who showed their allegiance to emperors in life and death.[83]

The campaign was a rousing ideological and financial success. Although the committee secured large contributions from businesspeople, the fund-raising drive was primarily aimed at schoolchildren and enjoyed the full cooperation of the Education Ministry, school officials, and teachers. Even in the midst of a lingering economic depression, many children apparently responded. The small individual contributions made by youngsters on the Japanese islands, in colonial Taiwan and Korea, and in the puppet state of Manchukuo were collectively huge. Donations even arrived from outside the empire, including a large and well-publicized offering from schoolchildren in Los Angeles. The committee raised about 1,864 yen (the average yearly salary of a prefectural employee was 737 yen in 1934), more than enough to cover the cost of the statue. More important, for educators, adoration of Hachikō for his loyalty appeared to capture the minds of many people.

Ministry intervention ensured that the focus of the story would be loyalty rather than some other virtue or cause. For a brief time, Hachikō was acclaimed as a symbol of peace. When the tale attracted attention and monetary contributions from America, some pundits optimistically hailed Hachikō as an omen of improved relations with the United States. Other observers attempted to mobilize the dog to improve the plight of Tokyo's stray-dog population, among whose ranks Hachikō had surely sometimes wandered. After his master's untimely death, Ueno's widow Yaeko moved from the family home near Shibuya Station and worried that she could not care for a large dog and had entrusted Hachikō first to relatives in Asakusa on the other side of the city. After Hachikō repeatedly escaped and returned to the family home in Shibuya, where he at least once damaged some fields in the vicinity, Yaeko asked her former gardener, Kobayashi Kikuzaburō (1871–1954), who lived in the Shibuya neighborhood, to take care of the dog. It was from Kobayashi's home that Hachikō was said to have frequented Shibuya Station. Dogcatchers, in fact, nabbed Hachikō several times in the late 1920s and early 1930s, and on one occasion the dog may have come within hours of being eliminated by officers at the pound. Although Society and Ministry officials did not encourage the view of Hachikō as homeless, some people, initially at least, thought of him as a canine destitute. Early letters to the editor expressed pity for the dog, and children sent money so that Hachikō and other strays could be given milk, kept warm, and treated kindly.[84] Animal-welfare activists, such as those in the Japanese branch of the Humane Society, attempted to take advantage of these perceptions to promote more compassionate conditions in the city's notorious dog pounds.[85] The society made Hachikō an honorary member of its Pochi kurabu (Pooch Club), a group of select dogs from around the world, and its constituents called for better treatment of canines through newspaper articles and letters to the editor. The group also attached an ornament adorned with the club's name to Hachikō's collar, which dangles from the museum manikin to this day. The message stressed by animal-welfare activists, however, was largely overwhelmed by official and private voices praising the dog's devotion.

In the same month that Ministry officials helped raise the dog's bronze likeness outside Shibuya Station, they incorporated Hachikō further into the school curriculum by including his story in a new national ethics (*shūshin*) textbook for second-year students issued in April 1934. The painter Ishii Hakutei (1882–1958) provided an illustration for the story, depicting Hachikō with both ears erect—much to Saitō's relief, no doubt—waiting vainly but alertly outside of Shibuya Station. The tale, "On o wasureru na" (Don't forget your debts of gratitude), was rendered in the following manner.

> Hachikō was a cute dog. Soon after he was born, a person far away adopted Hachikō and cared tenderly for him just as if he were his own child. As a result, his weak body became very strong. Every day when Hachikō's master departed for work, the dog would see him off at the train station, and every evening when he would return, Hachikō was there waiting to greet him at the station. Then one day, Hachikō's master died. The dog, because he did not understand, searched for him daily. Hachikō would look for his master among all the people who got off at the station each time a train arrived. Many months passed in this manner.
>
> Even though one, two, three, ten years passed, Hachikō—grown old searching for his master—can be seen in front of the station every day.[86]

On the surface, the story appeared innocuous. But its title and the fact that it was linked both explicitly and implicitly to the more blatantly nationalist stories that filled contemporary textbooks underscored that Hachikō was a tool for indoctrination. The title did not capture the content of the story; rather, it didactically admonished children, "Don't forget your debts of gratitude." Other stories in the same reader exhorted youngsters to strengthen their bodies, to honor their ancestors and emperors past and present, and to be obedient.[87]

Hints of how the text—which was part of the ethics primer until 1940—may have been taught can be gleaned from instructors' manuals and educational magazines. The Ministry of Education's official teacher's manual, which provided a longer, more detailed version of the story and a historical overview of Hachikō's life and the dedication of the statue, simply stated that its objective was to teach children that they should "not ever forget the debts of gratitude they have received from people."[88] The author of another such column, Kobayashi Gen, asserted that although the episode was true, teachers should teach it as a fable and not explore the tale's veracity in the classroom. "Second-year students are meek," Kobayashi wrote, "and will meekly accept what you tell them." He challenged teachers to instill in youngsters a sense of their indebtedness because "for children not to forget their debts, they must first feel them." The debts that Kobayashi had in mind were made clear in the following paragraph. He suggested that the story be read in class on 6 March, the birthday of the Meiji empress. This day, he recommended, should be dedicated to the important task of encouraging children to "contemplate the magnanimity of the splendid virtues of the imperial throne and to nourish hearts that will repay this supreme debt."[89]

Some teachers testified to the power of the Hachikō story in the moral edification of young people. One primary school principal declared that Hachikō was a "good teacher to our schoolchildren, and a good friend to them." Another instructor vowed to convey the "love and loyalty of Hachikō for his dead master, to ponder deeply the eternal connection between the two, and to implement its lessons in my teaching."[90] Ono Susumi (1887–1953), a teacher from Hachikō's hometown of Ōdate, was so enthusiastic about the dog that he traveled to Tokyo to attend the dedication and then organized a campaign to build an identical statue, also fashioned by the sculptor Andō, in front of the Ōdate railway station. Unfortunately, Hachikō passed away just months before its completion. In July 1935, the statue was unveiled with considerable flourish. Participants included Ueno's widow and the former Shibuya stationmaster, Yoshikawa Chūichi, who had taken a liking to Hachikō during his tenure at the station, and a number of purebred Akita dogs from around Ōdate. One-hundred and twenty local second-year primary school students recited "Don't Forget Your Debts of Gratitude," and other children performed a song written by Ono and arranged by Odajima Jirō (also known as Odajima Jujin; 1885–1959), a composer of military and children's marches, that equated Hachikō with Mount Fuji, cherry blossoms, and the Rising Sun as a "national treasure" that "taught people never to forget their debts of gratitude."[91]

The use of Hachikō to foster devotion to authority in youngsters likely had its intended effect. Although measuring accurately how people respond to ideology is problematic, if not impossible, letters and essays by primary school students living in the Shibuya area and throughout Japan and preserved in the station's archive suggest that Hachikō did inspire in some children a desire to emulate his purported fidelity. One sixth-year student named Takayama Takao sent part of his allowance to help build the statue and explained, "I have been impressed that even a dog has such loyalty (*chūgi*), and have been taught by Hachikō that we humans must recognize our debts and show loyalty to the emperor and country."[92] Many youngsters in the Shibuya neighborhood reported making a special visit to the statue, seeing huge numbers of bouquets and wreaths, and feeling grief at his passing. A number of the compositions mouthed set phrases—describing Hachikō waiting vainly "on rainy evenings, on windy mornings, yesterday and today"—from a poem that appeared in Kishi's *Story of the "Loyal Dog" Hachikō*, which they had probably committed to memory at school or home. A few children linked Hachikō with other paragons of loyalty who appeared in their textbooks, such as Tōgō Heihachirō (1851–1934), naval hero of the Russo-Japanese War. A similarly embellished story of the admiral's unswerving loyalty and unsurpassed sense of duty to the state and emperor had become a staple of the school curriculum only recently, around 1930, the twenty-fifth anniversary of Japan's victory.[93]

Stories of dogs were ideal material for the government's efforts to inculcate the entire population with messages about duty to and sacrifice for the nation. More than anything, what made the Hachikō story so effective was that the protagonist was a dog, a seemingly benign, nonideological, commonplace companion that nearly everyone could relate to. Because the heroes of the Hachikō narrative and other stories were canines, they were appealing to children as well as adults. Perhaps the belief that they could control the story prompted Ministry of Education bureaucrats to make an exception to guidelines that discouraged the inclusion in textbooks of any topics related to characters still alive and to events still in the process of unfolding. There was, after all, no chance that Hachikō might actually speak up and contradict the dominant explanation of his motivations for loitering around the station. But his physical presence as preserved on film and what emerged from his body—as we shall see—left room for plenty of speculation that sometimes supported and at times undermined the official narrative.

The image of Hachikō as a model of dutiful devotion was not without its complications or its detractors, even within the Society for the Preservation of the Japanese Dog. Saitō's fellow Society member and canine researcher Hiraiwa Yonekichi harshly criticized the projection of human motivations onto Hachikō. In the April 1935 edition of *Kodomo no shi kenkyū* (Research on children's poetry), a magazine he founded and edited, Hiraiwa wrote that the "devotion of dogs does not stem from a sense of obligation for kindness received, but is based entirely on pure love." Despite the "dumbfounding" fuss over his alleged commitment to his master, he noted, Hachikō was still an unhappy dog who had lost his master. What Hiraiwa objected to most sharply was the use of Hachikō for the edification of children:

There have been many people who one after another appear to manipulate even Hachikō's name in a variety of ways. Now he is even being used as material to teach people's children. This is because from the standpoint of human morality, everyday occurrences in the world of dogs are seen as extraordinary acts of good that demonstrate immeasurable integrity. They clamor, "Don't forget your debts of gratitude." However, because there are no debts of gratitude in the world of dogs, there can be no forgetfulness. It is pathetic that only now, "man"—that ingrate animal—is kneeling down to worship and plead for guidance from the law of dogs.[94]

Saitō, for his part, did not see the deployment of the story as troubling. Although he conceded years later that Hachikō did not understand the concept of obligation, elsewhere, in reference to Hiraiwa's criticism, he countered that the "greatest result…was that children throughout the country became very fond of dogs."[95] Saitō's statement may have been true, but if so, it also bolsters the possibility that educators could make use of children's affinity for dogs to foster allegiance to the state and to the emperor.

Some observers outside the dog-fancying community found the fascination with Hachikō to be troubling as well. Perhaps the most prominent voice to speak out was the liberal critic Hasegawa Nyozekan (1875–1969). In the April 1935 issue of the literary magazine *Bungei shunjū*, Hasegawa criticized the uproar as sentimentalism gone awry. The public, he argued, influenced by a swirl of "rumor, sensational media reports, and theories," had entered a "self-hypnotic, collective psychotic" trance that allowed them to believe things that they had not experienced and that they could not rationally explain. This tendency, Hasegawa worried, might result in similar delusions about weightier social and political issues with more dangerous consequences than those created by the fervor over Hachikō. In his view, politicians, educators, and journalists had the responsibility to restrain this "national inclination" rather than take advantage of it. The nation's leaders, Hasegawa warned, were not doing so but instead were manipulating popular energies for their own benefit. During the recent years of politics by assassination, he noted, elites had fallen into the dangerous habit of either condoning forces from below with their inaction or obliquely encouraging them through pardons or drastically reduced sentences.[96]

Without using the word, Hasegawa was all but describing the culture of fascism. In the late 1920s and early 1930s, he openly argued that Japan was becoming fascist, the culmination of which process he saw in the Manchurian Incident. Hasegawa believed that the country's rapid modernization had created an identity crisis that left people longing for yesteryear and the country's democratic institutions and culture immature. He thought fascism in Japan was "built into the power structure itself" and was more "self-possessed and gradual" than the fanaticism of Mussolini.[97] Hasegawa, however, became less inclined to use the term after his book *Nihon fashizumu hihan* (Criticism of Japanese fascism; 1932) was banned and then reissued after being strongly censored, and following a brief arrest in 1933 for allegedly making a contribution to the Japanese Communist Party.[98] In his criticism of the Hachikō affair, Hasegawa appeared to affirm his earlier position that Japan had become fascist without his expressly employing the term.

While Saitō rationalized the objections of Hiraiwa, he dismissed offhand-edly the criticisms of intellectuals such as Hasegawa and the "misunderstand-ings" that they created.[99] Because loyalty, like purity, was so central to Hachikō's public persona, Saitō and his allies strongly contested any doubts raised about the dog's devotion and subtly expressed reservations about the "Japaneseness" of those who questioned the dog's motives. Shimizu Yoshitarō (1899–1941), the editor in chief of the *Kyūshū Nippon* newspaper, for example, fancied that people who criticized Hachikō were surely owners of Western dogs who had never expe-rienced the inherent loyalty of native dogs. Such suggestions were not unique to Japan. During both world wars, some British and American keepers of "German" dogs, such as the shepherd and dachshund, faced similar assertions that their choice of dog breed undermined their patriotic allegiance.[100] For his part, Shimizu reasoned that Western canines were quick to abandon their masters, even if they had been raised by them for a decade, and would immediately adapt to a new one. A "Japanese" dog would never do this, he contended, even if the animal had only been with an owner for just a number of months, as Hachikō had been with Professor Ueno before his premature death.[101]

Inflated claims of Hachikō's fidelity could not help but invite criticism, if not cynicism, in certain quarters. A number of observers, including the young writer Ōoka Shōhei (1909–88), ventured that the dog was not waiting for his master at all.[102] On the contrary, they deduced, the dog was merely hanging around the station and its surrounding shops waiting to be fed. Hachikō, it was rumored, was especially fond of chicken kebabs, or *yakitori*. Saitō and others, however, rejected any notion that Hachikō was a mere stray loitering in search of handouts. Even in death—or perhaps especially because of the circumstances of his death—the controversy about the actual motivations of Hachiko persisted. The official story is that Hachikō died due to the effects of filariasis and old age. However, accord-ing to a widely circulated rumor attributed to the attending taxidermist, several bamboo *yakitori* skewers were discovered in the dog's stomach during his autopsy, a factor that may quite easily have contributed to his demise.[103] In this manner, Hachikō spoke by disgorging from the depths of his body material artifacts that further complicated and constrained his metaphorical manipulation, which may have been Hachikō's attempt to have the last word.

Dogs Fit for Empire

In addition to purity and loyalty, "Japanese" dogs were often esteemed as being endowed with vigor and bravery. During the 1930s, they and some other breeds were militarized and, regardless of their biological sex, figuratively masculinized. It was probably no coincidence that the breeds Saitō defined and the Ministry of Education recognized as "Japanese" were all powerful hunting dogs. They seemed to embody loyalty, martial strength, and courage, qualities in great demand, espe-cially among males, as enthusiasm for imperialism and war pervaded the country. Is it any surprise that from the early 1930s ownership of "Japanese" dogs—as well as breeds frequently deployed by the military, such as the "German" shepherd—became wildly popular among Japanese both in the metropole and empire?

Stephanitz, too, promoted the shepherd dog as a martial canine. He touted the breed as unrivaled in its capacity to serve as a police and army dog. During the early twentieth century, national armies and colonial police forces throughout the world came to value the breed highly. The German army deployed the dogs in the country's possessions in Africa and during both world wars. Stephanitz was outraged when some reporters wrote unfavorably about the use of "German" shepherds to hunt native peoples in German Southwest Africa. He was also angered when the army opted to use English Airedale terriers rather than shepherd dogs in its rifle battalions.[104]

For his part, Saitō stipulated that physical power and ferocity were defining elements of the "Japanese" dog. The official breeding criteria of the Society specified that the "nature and expression" of "Japanese" dogs—whether of the large, medium, or small category—was "sharp and fierce."[105] Elsewhere, Saitō elaborated on what that standard meant. In the prominently positioned *Yomiuri* article published in 1929, he boasted that the incomparable courage and bravery of native dogs complemented their muscular build and was the source of a distinctive "masculine beauty."[106] As has been mentioned, Saitō and other commentators boasted that "Japanese" dogs were instilled with *bushidō*, the spirit of the samurai. Saitō claimed that like warriors of the past, but unlike Western canines, native breeds were poised and shrewd. He also supposed that in comparison to foreign dogs, indigenous breeds barked infrequently and that this stoicism demonstrated their courage. In Saitō's view, it was their toughness and the latent possibility of violence that qualified "Japanese" dogs for veneration. He even contended that not only behavior but also physical attributes, such as the size of the eyes, indicated a breed's bravery or lack thereof. Canines—again the point of reference was Western breeds—with big pupils were spineless cowards, whereas "Japanese" dogs with "small, slanted-eyes" were fearless.[107]

Society commentators boasted that ancient blood ties to wolves made "Japanese" dogs all the more fearless and fearsome. The wolflike appearance and behavior of native dogs, once seen as a sign of their cunningness yet at the same time cowardice, now became an indication of their intelligence *and* bravery. A lupine pedigree was also touted as producing more physically robust dogs. This contention was presented with impressive scientific backing. A *Yomiuri* newspaper journalist reported in 1936 on the research and preservation efforts of the Tokyo Imperial University biology professor and Society member Kaburagi Tokio. Among the breeds awarded with protected status, Kaburagi believed that particularly the Kishū and Kai were closely related to the wolf. The "blood of the fierce wolf," the reporter claimed, "makes them superior to Western breeds as military dogs." The Kai, he continued, drastically outperformed the "German" shepherd and other Western dogs in stamina tests.[108]

The indomitable spirit of "Japanese" dogs, which also apparently surpassed that of other canines, was another constant theme in the rhetoric of their fans.

References to the "vigor" (*kihaku*) of the canines appeared so often that the frequency of its use attracted attention. Yamada Shunryō, the author of a 1938 *Nihon inu* article, spent more than three pages recording every instance of the term and other related words in previous editions of the magazine and concluded, in a sort of circular logic, that "without vigor, the Japanese dog would not exist."[109] The existence of "Japanese" dogs did, in fact, partially depend on the enthusiasm that such rhetoric generated. Many urbanites were surely attracted by the opportunity of owning a primal beast of nature that was advertised in newspapers and highbrow journals such as *Chūō kōron* as being powerful and aggressive but thoroughly domesticated and obedient. The tremendous popularity of the dogs made their breeding and sale highly profitable ventures from the early 1930s onward, and by the second half of the decade, their possible extinction (through breeding with dogs of other or indistinct breeds) was less of a concern.

In the second half of the 1930s, fears about imminent disappearance were replaced by other anxieties once it was clear "Japanese" dogs had been successfully preserved. Some Society members expressed concern about the degeneration of native dogs that were increasingly being raised in cities rather than the countryside. One member wrote as follows: "Japanese are very pure, and this is precisely why people like canines such as the Japanese dog that are pure. The cities, of course, are full of people who have been influenced by Western thought and are no longer pure." What is to become of the Japanese dogs who dwell there, he worried.[110] In Germany, Stephanitz likewise fretted over the corruptive perversions of urban environments on shepherd dogs. He thought that dogs transplanted from their "hard but wholesome country school" to "large cities" would "surrender to the ways of the town, that Moloch who feeds on men."[111] In this sense, expressions of concern about canine purity revealed as much anxiety—and xenophobia—about foreign culture and ideas as they did unease about human racial purity.

"Japanese" dog lovers also were apprehensive about the proper role for the national dog. The question became all the more pressing as the conflict on the Asian Continent widened and military demand for canines increased from the mid-1930s. Imperial military authorities preferred three Western dog breeds—"German" shepherds, Doberman pinschers, and Airedale terriers, in that order—but probably 90 percent of all army dogs were shepherds.[112] Many government and private dog trainers considered native dogs unfit for military and police work because of their relatively small size (except for the Akita) and because of their difficulty in obeying the commands of anyone other than the person who had trained them. They also found that their hunting instinct was so strong that they often abandoned the task at hand to chase any game encountered. Not surprisingly, fans of the dogs, including the former army minister Araki Sadao (1877–1966), thought indigenous canines were up to the task. Araki, Saitō, and other fanciers were particularly proud of the dogs' physical endurance and ability to navigate obstacles, and repeatedly urged the military to conduct more research, training, and to mobilize Japanese dogs more widely.[113] From 1938 Society officials took the initiative and began to contribute some dogs to the army, including one Akita who was sent to the imperial frontier of Inner Mongolia to subdue wolves.[114]

Opinion on the matter, however, was not unified, even within the membership of the Society. One member, for example, argued against their deployment. It was not, in his opinion, because Japanese dogs were unsuitable for military use. On the contrary, they might well be, but if native canines were used in such a manner he worried that they might become just another working dog and lose their special "Japanese" characteristics: purity of blood, purity of devotion, and purity of resolve.[115]

These attributes supposedly embodied by the "Japanese" dog and its image as a masculine figure are palpable in a painting that probably dates from the early 1940s.[116] The polychrome painting, which was executed on a hanging silk scroll using traditional Japanese conventions (*nihonga*) and mounted on a golden background, shows a young girl standing behind a splendid but daunting-looking Shiba dog. The girl, her hair cropped short and clothed in a school uniform top with loose-fitting pantaloons (*monpe*)—which were required wear for war-related work—holds a rose at her left side. She and the dog, whose collar indicates that

20. A painting of a girl and her Japanese Shiba dog. The artist and title are unknown. It likely dates from the early 1940s. Used with the permission of Kogire-kai Auction House.

it is probably her pet, both gaze determinedly in the same direction, and his expression, stance, and position in front of her suggest that it can be relied on to shield the girl from any threat to the home islands.

The almost complete absence of Japanese dogs from the battlefield did not prevent them from appearing in imagined theaters of war. One such dog, aptly named Gunjingō (Soldier), was the hero of "The Bloodied Messenger" (Chimamire denrei), one of the purported true tales in *Shōhei o nakaseta gunba inu hato bukun monogatari* (Stories of gallant war horses, dogs, and pigeons that caused soldiers to weep).[117] The story relates how Gunjingō carried an urgent request for reinforcements after his small Imperial Army unit became surrounded by Chinese troops. To arrive at his destination, the book describes, the dog traverses a vast stretch of enemy territory. Again and again he fends off attacks from overwhelming numbers of wild Chinese dogs, canine ruffians said to be typical of the continent. Splattered with blood, Gunjingō successfully delivers the appeal for assistance, but by the time that backup forces arrive, the trapped group of infantrymen has already beaten back repeated onslaughts by the enemy. At the end of the passage, the comparison between humans and animals is made explicit as three Japanese soldiers reflect on the events of the day.

> A Japanese military dog surrounded by twenty-six Chinese wild dogs is just like a single Japanese soldier being attacked by twenty-six Chinese bandits.
>
> The Japanese dog killing eight wild dogs and breaking through to fulfill his important mission is exactly the same as what a Japanese soldier would do.
>
> Just as a Japanese soldier possesses the heart of Yamato, Japanese military animals, too, have that valiant spirit.[118]

This story was obviously allegorical. The message it bore was that Japanese—humans and dogs alike—were domesticated, strong, courageous, loyal, trustworthy, and civilized, while Chinese—at least those who opposed Japanese aggression—were wild, weak, cowardly, wily, and unenlightened. Canines served as highly malleable symbols to express attitudes of Japanese superiority and Chinese inferiority. Mere rhetoric, it may seem, but metaphors are often translated into policy. Some Imperial Army officers instructed their men to kill on sight any Chinese dogs that they encountered, describing them, surely disingenuously, as being more troublesome than the human enemy.[119] The animalized, imperialized human enemy, whether a threat or not, was sometimes treated little better.

Another "Japanese" dog who illustrated the rediscovery of native dogs and their mobilization for empire was a canine who, along with a pheasant and a monkey, accompanied the Peach Boy Momotarō to vanquish a horde of demons (*oni*) who periodically wreaked havoc on Japan, in one of the country's best-known folk tales. This story, John Dower has observed, became a perfect wartime symbolic expression of "Japan and its lesser Asian followers driving out the white imperialists and establishing their supremacy."[120] As one of Momotarō's animal subordinates, the dog was praised for his absolute loyalty and fierce bravery in

21. Momotarō, the Peach Boy, with one of his retainers, a thoroughly Japanized dog in the first-year language textbook version of the story that appeared in 1933.

crushing the foreign devils. Although not the primary hero of the story, it is the most prominent of the three vassals. Not surprisingly, Momotarō's dog also experienced a metamorphosis that mirrored the shift in popularity from Western dogs to "Japanese" breeds. It was transformed in textbooks and popular representations from usually being depicted as a Western breed during the nineteenth century to almost always being portrayed as a "Japanese" dog by the 1930s.[121]

In both their rhetoric and in practice, promoters of "Japanese" dogs regarded them, like their human compatriots, as superior. Despite talk of the common ancestry of canines throughout the empire, supposed kinship rested on the assumption that dogs on the home islands were a breed apart. Such language represented a canine parallel to pan-Asianism, which advocated "harmony" among the peoples of Japan's formal and informal empire, but positioned Japanese as the "older brother" among its younger, and therefore inferior, Asian siblings. The notion of the preeminence of "Japanese" dogs was implicit in the language of enthusiasts throughout the 1930s and was clearly articulated by Saitō in July 1940. The mission of the Society for the Preservation of the Japanese Dog, he stated, was to *"represent our country's domestic dog culture to those in Europe and the United States, and to lead the domestic dog cultures of the surrounding nations of Asia."* This representation and leadership hardly signified an equal relationship with canines either in the West or in Asia. After rhetorically asking what made Japanese breeds better than both the primitive pure breeds of Asia and the improved breeds of the West, Saitō declared:

> I reply without hesitation that it is a matter of character. No other dog has been the recipient of the superior attributes of the Japanese national spirit—*courage, composure, boldness, and loyalty*—that have been ingrained and preserved through interacting and dwelling with the Japanese nation for thousands of years. We may well discover that Japanese dogs, as one type among a primitive dog species, have a common ancestry with and a form similar to other domestic dogs on the continent or in the South Seas. However, the only canine to have received the spiritual influence of the Japanese people for thousands of years is the Japanese dog.[122]

In the 1930s Saitō had nationalized native dogs by claiming that their character reflected the personality of the Japanese people because of long and intimate interaction. By 1940 he unequivocally asserted that this relationship made them superior to canines anywhere. The transformation of canines on the archipelago was complete. As Japan became an imperial power, its native dog was transformed into a national dog and ultimately into a colonial dog. The bark, or perhaps the snarl, of the onetime subaltern reverberated at home, in Japan's expanding empire, and beyond.

In a largely unresolved irony, just as Hachikō's floppy left ear and his appetite for kebabs undermined pronouncements about his purported purity and the breed's unrivaled fidelity, his temperament weakened claims about "Japanese" dogs' incomparable martial spirit and bravery. As was related in *The Story of the "Loyal Dog" Hachikō*, but subsequently went unmentioned, the canine who was touted as the model "Japanese" dog and a guardian of smaller dogs seems in fact to have been quite fainthearted. While taking walks, Hachikō was apparently unnerved by gunfire resounding from military exercises at the nearby army base in Yoyogi and was even rattled by children shooting toy guns.[123]

Hachikō's Reincarnations

The creation of the "Japanese" dog sheds light on the relationship between animals and the formation of national, imperial, and racial identities in the early twentieth century. This history exposes the interconnections among humans, dogs, environmental protection, animal breeding, national education, and identity formation. It is clear that "fascism's furry friends" were not restricted to the Japanese archipelago. Parallels with the German experience, in particular, are conspicuous. One reason for such historical contiguities is that both countries emulated the late nineteenth-century nationalization of dog breeds elsewhere. Another reason for the commonalities is that Saitō and other enthusiasts sought inspiration in Stephanitz's efforts to promote the "German" shepherd. A final similarity is that both countries were pervaded by a culture of fascism, which radicalized and intensified nationalism and racism and that explicitly glorified the loyalty and violence that had been implicit in earlier civilizationist discourses. As this history has been framed by the story of Hachikō, it makes sense to follow the dog's paw prints into the final years of war, the postwar occupation, and the subsequent half-century of democracy and peace.

Like many youngsters who grew up hearing stories of the loyal dog who faithfully awaited his master's return, the bronze Hachikō at Shibuya Station did not survive the global conflagration. It, too, was sacrificed for the imperial cause. As the military retreated from the country's colonies and wartime spoils, Japan faced an extreme shortage of metal. In response, government authorities began to melt down public statues, and encouraged people to contribute household goods and other metallic items. Ignoring protests by Saitō that the Hachikō statue had irreplaceable artistic value, officials decided that even the Loyal Dog could not be spared. On 12 October 1944, Hachikō was toppled after a ceremony that mirrored, and perhaps surpassed, the fanfare of farewells held for soldiers departing for the front. Organizers draped the figure in a Rising Sun flag, and a large crowd gathered to participate in the spectacle. Speakers, including the station chief and a representative of the Society—which had otherwise suspended its activities—praised Hachikō for loyalty in life, for his fidelity to his master and the fellow "Japanese" canines whom he helped preserve, and, in death, for his transformation into bullets to "shoot down enemy planes."[124] Such a heroic transmutation, however, was not in fact Hachikō's fate. After the war, the *Asahi* newspaper informed its readers that, following the ceremony, the statue had been shipped south to a factory in the industrial city of Hamamatsu, where it was melted down to make spare train parts. The Loyal Dog, the paper speculated, was now probably running back and forth on the Tōkaidō railway line between Tokyo and Shizuoka.[125]

Within a few years of defeat, the statue was resurrected and would thereafter rest in peace. Like so much else before August 1945 that reappeared in the early postwar years, the new Hachikō simultaneously represented both the old and the new Japan. Attempts were made to cast the dog in the democratic and peaceful idioms of the immediate postwar era, but, like other images, the symbolism of Hachikō reverted, at least partially, to its pre-1945 connotations. During the summer of 1946, thirteen organizations led by the Tokyo Chamber of Commerce decided to bring Hachikō back to Shibuya Station. Once again, Saitō assumed a leadership role in the effort. The group claimed to be motivated, in part, by Westerners who—apparently familiar with the story thanks to the original publicity in the early 1930s and perhaps because of Helen Keller's interest in Hachikō and the Akita breed in the late 1930s—repeatedly descended on the area asking the whereabouts of the statue. All foreigners, though, were not so supportive or, at least, initially not so cooperative. Officials of the occupation military government, the Supreme Commander of the Allied Powers (SCAP), allowed for the plan to proceed but prohibited the statue from being called the Loyal Dog because of the

22. The farewell ceremony for the bronzed "Loyal Dog" Hachikō, 12 October 1944. The man is wrapping the statue in the Rising Sun flag. Used with permission of Mainichi Photo Bank.

nickname's association with the moral education of the pre-1945 era. As a result, restorationists proposed that the new statue be given a modified pet name, the "Beloved Dog" (*Aiken*).

The suggested change, however, stirred up opposition in other quarters. Some people protested that it would be inappropriate to refer to Hachikō as "beloved"; the dog was "loyal," they contended, and that was what he should be called. A seventeen-year-old Tokyo high school student, Sassa Atsuyuki, took precisely this position in a letter to the editor published in the *Asahi* newspaper in early 1948. Sassa (1930–), though, was no ordinary teenager. His father and late grandfather had both been well-known politicians.[126] On his graduation from Tokyo University, Sassa followed them into public service, climbing near the top of the civil service hierarchy of the National Police and Defense agencies, until he was appointed by Prime Minister Nakasone Yasuhiro (1918–) to head the Cabinet Security Affairs Office in the 1980s.[127] Demonstrating an eloquence that would serve him well years later as a prolific writer and television personality, the schoolboy Sassa disconnected the loyalty of Hachikō from the cultural and nationalist context of 1930s and imagined the story as a sentimental, universal tale of a dog and his master: "It shows an extreme lack of understanding to consider [Hachikō's] 'loyalty' feudal, as in the relationship between a lord and retainer.

Have not humans and dogs interacted as master and servant from olden days, and have not stories of the loyalty of dogs warmed hearts in both the West and the East?"[128]

In the face of such opposition, occupation officials soon relented and permitted the committee to use Hachikō's received pet name, "Loyal Dog." This about-face might be considered a cultural manifestation of what historians refer to as the occupation's "reverse course," a retreat from the democratization and demilitarization principles earlier espoused by the U.S. occupiers, who felt increasingly threatened by the unfolding cold war and the rise of militant labor unions and left-wing parties that sprang up as the result of early liberal reforms. At any rate, on 15 August 1948, the three-year anniversary of Japan's surrender, a statue of the Loyal Dog once again rose outside Shibuya Station. The ceremony was attended by a number of dignitaries from foreign embassies, and the dog that was once told to "shoot down enemy planes" was hailed, yet again, as a symbol of international peace and understanding.

Other continuities with the past could be observed. Andō Takeshi, (1923–), whose father sculpted the first Hachikō, was asked to recreate the statue. The younger Andō had returned from years of military service to find that his father, along with the original mold, had perished in an American air raid that destroyed their home during the final months of the war. The only bronze alloy that Takeshi could find to cast the statue was the remains of another statue created by his father, a bronze female figure titled "Ōzora ni" (In the firmament) that now lay baked and twisted among the rubble in the family's yard.[129] Using this material, he replicated his father's design to the last detail, including the controversial floppy left ear. Andō recalled that even in 1948 the shape of the ear remained a source of tension. He insisted, though, on staying true to the original statue and ignored requests, presumably from Saitō, to reconfigure the ear so that it stood upright like a purebred Akita.

Despite the evocations of the past, certain connotations of the new statue broke sharply with the prewar period. One semantic departure was necessitated by another occupation policy that had not yet been revoked. At the dedication ceremony, the three-cheer shout of *banzai* (literally, ten thousand years), which was strongly associated with militarism and emperor worship and banned by SCAP, was replaced by a dog who was induced to bark thrice as a final salute to Hachikō. Another dog, said to be Hachikō's grandchild Tetsu (Steel), was supposed to be in attendance at the ceremony, but mysteriously he went missing. Soon thereafter, police discovered that the dog had been stolen and ended up providing the protein for a sukiyaki dish, which usually consisted of thinly sliced beef, vegetables, tofu, and other ingredients cooked in a broth of soy sauce, *mirin* (sweet sake), and sugar. Tetsu's fate was probably the result of an ongoing food shortage that made *viande* of any kind a delicacy. Hachikō and his descendents, it seems, had bad luck with meat dishes.[130] Similar sensitivities to the new political environment help to explain why the committee decided not to include the sappy poem extolling Hachikō's devotion by the late right-wing politician Yamamoto Teijirō, which had been inscribed on the base of the previous statue. Instead, Saitō composed a more detached narrative of Hachikō's life and had it emblazoned, fittingly, in Japanese and English on large metal plates near the bronze canine.

A realignment of the committee's charter, too, was responsible for the changes in the physical memorial and dedication ceremony. In its mission statement, the group declared that the purpose of the new monument was to cultivate in children a "spirit of obligation, in addition to spreading a love for animals widely throughout society, and to foster hearts that appreciate uplifting children's culture." It was not clear what the committee wanted children to have a "spirit of obligation" toward or what they meant by "uplifting children's culture," but because the declaration encouraged youngsters to cultivate a concern for other living creatures, it appears that at last the animal-protection advocates had won a partial victory in the fight over Hachikō's meaning.

If "children's culture" referred to juvenile literature featuring Hachikō, then it, too, departed from the past in how it presented, or did not present, the story. As a result of occupation reforms that abolished ultranationalistic, Shintoistic, and militaristic teachings as well as the national ethics courses, Hachikō did not reappear on the pages of children's textbooks. He also vanished for a time from popular children's literature, which for a number of years featured stories almost exclusively about extraordinary dogs in the United States and Europe.[131] But just as the conservative Liberal Democratic Party government reintroduced a national ethics curriculum in the late 1950s as a part of educational reform measures, the use of Hachikō by school officials did not fade away completely. Ministry of Education officials still found the story morally edifying enough to certify the 1987 motion picture and a 1988 animated film about the Loyal Dog as "recommended movies" that parents ought to have their children see.[132] Interestingly, the appearance of the two films coincided with a rise in the popularity of "Japanese" dogs and nationalism during the 1980s. Although the Akita, Shiba, and other "Japanese" breeds are not as closely associated with the nation as they once were, the dogs are still marketed as somehow uniquely Japanese, and often pictured with other cultural emblems, such as cherry blossoms and Mount Fuji, to reinforce this image.[133]

One cannot help but wonder whether the physical and ideological transformations of Hachikō provided inspiration for novelist Abe Kōbō's short story "Te" (The hand). Abe (1924–93) specialized in Kafkaesque tales of metamorphosis. The story, first published in 1951, is told from the point of view of a military carrier pigeon whose keeper, "The Hand," uses the bird after the war as a sideshow attraction, but then sells him to serve as a model for a statue of a dove of peace to be built in the city square. The bird is transfigured into a stuffed model and then into a bronze statuette. Its final transmutation comes after government agents, who find the peace symbol and its advocates' offensive, persuade his onetime, now deranged, keeper to steal the figure. He is quickly arrested, and the story ends when the bronzed bird is melted down and made into pistol bullets, which are used to execute "The Hand" that once fed him.[134]

Appropriately enough, the return of the Loyal Dog to Shibuya Station occurred at about the same time as the revival of the Society for the Preservation of the Japanese Dog. The group had lapsed into inactivity during the final years of the war and ceased publication of its magazine in 1943 because of paper shortages. On the Society's reestablishment in 1948, its members faced challenges similar to those encountered nearly two decades earlier when Saitō launched the organization. During the war, hundreds of thousands of canines perished when they were conscripted for military use either as canine combatants or as material to clothe human soldiers. Some "Japanese" dogs, either because of their ineffectiveness as military dogs or because of their protected status, avoided such misfortune. Yet there was little that could protect many of the canines from indiscriminate U.S. bombing raids and the severe economic and nutritional deprivation of the final years of the war and the early occupation period. Saitō and his colleagues once again warned that "Japanese" dogs were facing extinction when they reestablished the Society. Some claimed that there were fewer than two dozen Akita left at the end of the war, but this was most certainly an exaggeration aimed to mobilize sympathy for the movement.[135]

Not surprisingly, the postwar task of increasing the numbers of purebred native dogs brought to mind the challenges that Saitō and his colleagues had faced nearly two decades before. Numerous authors in the Society's magazine praised the pioneering work of Saitō and rallied the Society's members to replicate his accomplishments as the savior of Japanese dogs. The postwar scientific community, too, honored Saitō as an accomplished canine biologist. Indeed, by the time of his death, he had published several books and dozens of articles on canines, as well as a book in German. Saitō also broadened his advocacy for animals as president of the Japan Society for the Prevention of Cruelty to Animals (Nihon dōbutsu aigo kyōkai), a post he occupied from 1948 until months before cancer felled him in 1964.

Some observers, though, believed that when it came to Hachikō, Saitō had gone too far. Several years before his death, Saitō admitted as much when he recalled that he had "nationalist or ultranationalist tendencies" in the 1930s.[136] As evidenced by Hiraiwa's criticism of Hachikō's textbook treatment, some of Saitō's colleagues disapproved of his politics and his lack of regard for science in promoting the dog before and after the war. One zoologist claimed that certain people regarded Saitō's training in the fine arts and his work designing gardens and teahouses as having engendered in him a strong nativist aesthetic and a corresponding anxiety about the Westernization of his country, which influenced how he viewed dogs. Some members of the scientific community regarded Saitō as an "ultranationalist," even in the postwar years. Saitō purportedly commented, for example, that he was proud of and even wanted to adopt the seventeen-year-old right-wing radical Yamaguchi Otaya (1943–60), who in October 1960 stabbed to death the Socialist Party chairman Asanuma Inejirō (1898–1960) on live nationwide television.[137] It is also rumored that Saitō's personality darkened drastically during the postwar period after a rabid dog bit him.

Setting such stories aside, one may be tempted to see Saitō and other fanciers of "Japanese" dogs as intellectuals schooled in European science who retreated to the apolitical pursuit of launching a kennel club and passively adapted to the political climate of the 1930s. This may have been the case. They may simply have liked dogs. However, Saitō's and his colleagues' search for and creation of a pure "Japanese" dog untainted by and superior to foreign canines, along with their emphasis on the purported loyalty and fierceness shown by Hachikō, suggests that their hobby was anything but a withdrawal from politics. The Western cultural ideas that they drew on—of purebred dogs as representatives of nations—harbored underlying assumptions of racism and nationalism that could not easily be erased; nor did Saitō and his colleagues attempt to do so. Instead, Saitō and his allies combined these ideas with a notion of Japanese uniqueness, obsessions with purity, and an admiration for loyalty and bravery to produce what on the surface were mere dog-breeding standards and a heart-warming story of a faithful dog. A closer look, though, indicates that the story of Hachikō and the movement to preserve "Japanese" dogs contributed, perhaps unintentionally but nevertheless powerfully, to the construction of the imperial fascist culture that would breed the destruction of human and animal life on an unprecedented scale, both within and beyond Japan's borders.

4

DOGS OF WAR

MOBILIZING ALL CREATURES
GREAT AND SMALL

While the "Loyal Dog" Hachikō and most other "Japanese" canines were militarized only in the realm of the imagination, many dogs actually went to war. During the First and Second World Wars, nearly every combatant nation employed dogs to perform military-related tasks. The widespread, systematic deployment of canines occurred even as the mechanization of warfare seemed to be rendering animals obsolete for military use. Scientific and technical advances in the ability to breed and train animals—on land and in the sea and air—and the practical value of beasts in battle, especially under certain conditions, such as in remote, adverse terrain, and for particular tasks, continued to make them a valuable strategic resource in the military conflicts of the twentieth century. Especially during the Second World War, dogs joined humans and other creatures—great and small—in larger numbers, with more precise organization and in more tactically important ways than ever before. An attention to military dogs highlights the uniquely twentieth-century phenomenon of total war—conflict that, as the historian Eric Hobsbawm has described, mobilizes entire societies and economies and "produces untold destruction and utterly dominates and transforms life" in all its varieties.[1] As the movie director Yamamoto Kajirō, who had just made a film about military horses, suggested in May 1941, "not only mechanized power, but all kinds of living things—horses, dogs, pigeons, and...various microscopic germs—are being mobilized for this war. Every organism that possibly can be is being deployed."[2] Indeed, the imperatives of total war prompted people throughout the world to marshal every breathing thing in the pursuit of victory.[3]

Along with this official exploitation of other animals for armed conflict, government and private voices figuratively manipulated dogs and other beasts to rally human populations in the pursuit of victory. The history of the activation of nonhuman animals for warfare has primarily been the territory of two groups of writers: a number of historians have extended their sights beyond the human domain to consider the use of beasts in war,[4] while large numbers of authors with a personal affection for or professional connection with animals have produced most of the historical or anecdotal narratives on the topic.[5] Although its scholarly value varies, the common denominator of the available literature is a focus on the actual performance of these creatures.[6] While paying attention to the practical use and actions of canines, I focus on the rhetorical wartime deployment of the "dogs of war." This common literary expression usually refers to the havoc that accompanies military hostilities. I use it to describe a set of relationships among state institutions, military organizations, canine-fancying groups, individual dog keepers, and canines, which actually and symbolically mobilized dogs—and people— for total war and empire.

By "dogs of war," I do not mean only "army dogs," but also police and guard dogs, who were widely deployed by military units, imperial agencies, and civilian colonizers. Although specialists and lay persons alike throughout the world divided working dogs into these three categories, they were by no means mutually exclusive; many canines performed multiple roles over the course of their lives. At the encouragement of governments, private owners of guard dogs often bred, raised, and then donated their animals to the military or police. Domestic and colonial police agencies sometimes transferred their canines to the army as demand for working dogs increased with the intensification of military conflict. Army and police dogs were at times "retired" to civilian life to become guard dogs. By the same token, the division of labor between jobs fulfilled by military, police, and even civilian guard dogs is blurry in many contexts. Japanese authorities, for example, stationed military police in most colonies until 1919 and posted several regular divisions, which often used dogs, in Korea and Manchuria until 1945. Whatever their duties, army, police, and guard dogs became colonial dogs, contributing in actual and symbolic ways to creating and maintaining imperial law and order.

The connotation of "havoc" in the literary meaning of "dogs of war" may also be appropriate. Despite being bred, trained, and handled to serve their military and colonial masters, dogs sometimes did less or went beyond what was expected. Like a variety of other "technologies," dogs became instruments of military and imperial control and violence by performing a number of specialized tasks. Yet, because dogs are autonomous, highly intelligent living beings whose actions cannot be entirely controlled by human masters, military, police, and guard "dogs of war" could produce uncontrolled and unexpected outcomes. Thus, dogs were not merely tools but agents of imperialism, not simply crime-solving devices but conscious deputies and active combatants rather than just military hardware. In turn, canines' practical yet unpredictable actions contributed to the symbolic uses to which they were put by people.

A by-product of the wars that racked the first half of the twentieth century was the popularization of dog breeds, such as the "German" shepherd, that were seen as useful on the battlefront, many of which were widely deployed in colonial contexts as well. In fact, the breeding, training, and trafficking of army, police, and guard dogs probably grew more energetically in colonial and client states, which were often beset by violence or its possibility, than in metropoles, though that growth was tied to the home country. Certainly this was the case for the Japanese empire and probably true in European and American empires as well. Furthermore, the use of dogs in these imperial zones often unfolded in tandem around the world, was mutually influenced by the deployment of canines elsewhere, and depended on interimperial and international trading networks. A consideration of canines, then, reveals the cultural and commercial threads that bound together and jointly bolstered empires internally and empires globally.

Army dogs were not numerically or tactically the most exploited animals during the First and Second World Wars, but they may have been the most important metaphorically.[7] Military, government, and private discourses about dogs were probably more prevalent and perhaps more penetrating than discussions about other creatures. This was because canines were much more widely owned by citizens and subjects of nation-states, because national armies relied heavily on private individuals to supply them with dogs, and because people lived in closer proximity and had stronger emotional connections with dogs than they did with other animals. Discussions about dogs were, at least, more personal. Canines that appeared in wartime media were more likely to be given names and anthropomorphized—sometimes even given the ability to speak—and attributed with personality traits, especially loyalty and bravery. The influence that propaganda had on people is nearly impossible to evaluate, but the intent and the primary target of such language are clear. Even as they sought to nurture intimate ties between people—especially youngsters—and canines, official and private voices took advantage of those bonds to dispatch both dogs and humans to war.

The figurative mobilization of canines emerged in every country that widely deployed dogs during the First and Second World Wars. Certainly, in some contexts other military animal metaphors, particularly warhorses, may have figured more prominently. In countries that did not actively employ army dogs and had an ideological distaste for canines, as was the case for Communist Chinese and, to a lesser extent, Chinese Nationalist forces, there was probably little discussion of army dogs.[8] Yet the rhetorical function of dogs described here sheds light on how other animal tropes were employed in wartime propaganda, and how the symbolic deployment of creatures is closely connected to their actual deployment, collective behavior, and individual actions.

Although actual and metaphorical militarization characterized many combatant nations during the First World War, Japan was not a major participant in that struggle, and the Imperial military did not begin an army-dog program until after the war ended in Europe. The practical and symbolic employment of canines was more universally extensive during the Second World War than in the previous one, just as every possible resource in each nation was marshaled. For Japan, the Second World War began with the Manchurian Incident in 1931 and widened drastically, first, after Japanese provocations near Beijing in July 1937, and further, with the attacks on Pearl Harbor and Southeast Asia in December 1941. For Japanese, the conflict was a long and exhausting Fifteen-Year-War and a wide and far-flung Asia-Pacific War, to use two common scholarly designations. Its length and its severity led to vast exploitation and sacrifice of humans and animals alike, both at home and across its vast empire.

Total War and "Silent Warriors"

In many countries, private dog-fancying organizations and militaries joined forces to mobilize canines for the two world wars, especially during the second global conflict. Often, breeders and trainers were the first to raise their voices to urge government, military, and colonial officials to deploy dogs. As canines proved their practical value in accomplishing certain tasks, armed forces tended to take greater control over the recruitment and training of dogs, and in the process came to exercise considerable authority over the private fancying groups as well.

Even though dogs had been employed in ancient conflicts and in earlier colonial conquests, the extensive and systematic use of canines for war first emerged in Europe in the latter half of the nineteenth century. Prussian forces successfully utilized dogs in the Franco-Prussia War of 1870, which prompted the French army to begin training dogs for battle. One principal advocate of this effort was Lieutenant J. Jupin, a veteran of that war. His *Les chiens militaires dans l'armée française* (Military dogs in the French army), published in 1887, attracted the attention of observers throughout the world.[9] In a review of the book, a reporter for the *New York Times* remarked:

> The nations of Europe, in their schemes of universal armament, are reaching the end of their human resources. From the Baltic to the Mediterranean all men must now bear arms. But the Governments, in their race for the means of conquest and of defense, require more combatants. Already various animals have been drafted into the service. The horse, as in all former times, hears the battle afar off. The dove, that symbol of peace, is now taught to be the messenger of war. And at last the dog, long an irregular and a partisan warrior, is being brought by the German spirit of organization within the lines of regular military service. The French are taking alarm at this, and a thick pamphlet, with illustrations, has been issued to show that they too should enlist dogs in their regiments.[10]

At the end of the review, the journalist urged the U.S. military to follow the French and German lead and begin to recruit and train canines for war.[11] Until the Second World War, though, U.S. officials largely ignored such calls.

Across the Pacific, Japanese military authorities followed with some interest the use of canines by European armed forces and police agencies at home and in their colonies in the late nineteenth and early twentieth centuries. They, too, initially took no concrete action toward organizing a military-dog program. Except as guard dogs, the deployment of canines for war had little precedent on the Japanese archipelago. Samurai warriors rarely used dogs in combat, although, as we have seen, some medieval warlords deployed large fierce dogs to symbolically project their status and political power from the sixteenth century. The newly constituted Meiji military contemplated employing dogs for strategic purposes. Officers evaluated the merits of military dogs in such publications as the leading army journal *Kaikōsha kiji*, but the army did not take any steps toward implementation until stimulated by the events of the First World War.

It was during this war that military officials recognized the possible tactical value of dogs. The manner in which the conflict was fought—widespread trench warfare with little movement of the battle lines—may have made dogs useful. Canines were employed in three principal ways: for ambulance assistance, messenger service, and sentry detail. Already the leader in the utilization of dogs before the war, Germany is said to have employed an estimated thirty thousand canines, as compared with reportedly twenty thousand between France and Britain. The animal studies scholar Jonathan Burt, however, has raised serious doubts about these numbers and especially the claims about the effectiveness of army dogs, but many people appear to have believed (and still believe) otherwise.[12] The U.S. military entered the conflict without any war dogs, except for a few sled dogs in Alaska, and relied entirely on the French and British for canine support. Despite such widespread wartime canine conscription, interwar disarmament led to cutbacks in some army-dog programs. The British army abandoned its program during the 1920s, and the U.S. military remained without a corps until 1942. The biggest impact that army dogs seem to have had on the United States in the wake of the First World War was as mascots. Stubby, a stray pit bull, became famous as an icon for the army's 26th "Yankee" Division, and Rin Tin Tin, a shepherd puppy found abandoned in a German trench by American doughboys, became famous as an interwar Hollywood movie-matinee star.[13] The movie studios cleverly shed the breed's Germanness by placing the dog (and his successors) in the American frontier during his decades-long appearances on the radio and on movie and television screens, and Rin Tin Tin often played the role of a brave, faithful ally of white settlers fighting off "savage" American Indians and low-class bandits. Thanks in large part to Rin Tin Tin's popularity, approximately one-third of the dogs registered with the AKC in 1927 were German shepherds, just a few years after the organization had formally recognized the breed.[14] Likewise, the Alsatian—as the (English) Kennel Club insisted on calling the breed due to war-provoked angst against anything affiliated with Germany—became one of the most popular dogs in Britain during the 1920s. While the principal Western military powers neglected their army-dog initiatives, Germany continued to develop its program throughout the 1920s and 1930s.

Even before the outbreak of war on the European Continent in 1914, dogs were proving themselves useful, especially for policing colonial areas. Among the European powers, Germany was probably the most innovative in deploying dogs for police work in its recently acquired possessions in Africa and its sphere of influence on the Shandong Peninsula in China in the late nineteenth and early twentieth centuries. Japanese colonial officials were not far behind and were ahead of police officials at home. Officers in colonial Taiwan and Korea began to use dogs in 1910, and two years later Tokyo police followed suit.

According to contemporary newspaper accounts, the dogs performed with great effectiveness in Japan's two colonies. In Taiwan dogs participated in a series of "great searches" (*daisōsa*) and "sweeping arrests" (*daikenkyo*) aimed at Taiwanese aborigines. These police actions were central to the colonial government's third and final offensive to suppress local resistance that lasted until 1915, when violent opposition against Japanese rule largely dissipated.[15] In the midst of a fierce but scattered guerilla movement in Korea after the Japanese occupation of the peninsula in 1905 and its annexation in 1910, top officials ordered that dogs be used for policing. Presumably these canines—including at least three dogs imported from Germany who were "taught Japanese" on their arrival—bolstered the efforts of army troops and civilian policemen to restore relative order in Korea by 1911.[16] Their purported successes in both colonies were apparently short-lived. By the 1920s, most of the dogs who had been imported from the European countries or their colonies had succumbed to disease, and reports of police dogs in the colonies or at home almost completely disappeared from Japanese newspapers throughout the empire until army dogs revived interest in using canines for police work because of their supposed heroics during the Manchurian Incident in 1931.

Spurred on by the reported accomplishments of army dogs in the First World War and police dogs in European colonies, as well as in Taiwan and Korea, Japanese military officials launched a small canine acquisition and training program in 1919. As a windfall of the conflict, the Imperial Army gained access to a limited but valuable population of shepherd dogs. In August 1914, Japanese leaders used the Anglo-Japanese alliance as a pretext to declare war on Germany and occupy the German-leased territories on the Shandong Peninsula, including the city of Qingdao. There, and in other Chinese cities such as Shanghai, the Japanese military found a number of shepherd dogs and other canines that were suitable as army dogs. These two cities became an important source of military dogs during the next few decades. One of the first soldiers sent to acquire dogs in the Chinese treaty ports after the First World War was a member of the Imperial Guard, Sawabe Kenjirō (1902–78), who found the canines to be so expensive that he could purchase only a few. After returning to civilian life a few years later, Sawabe drew on his experiences and opened the Mikado Kennel, one the country's first dog shops, in the downtown Tokyo neighborhood of Nihonbashi in 1934, and supported Saitō's campaign to build the statue of Hachikō and promote "Japanese" dogs. As noted in chapter 3, one of his employees, clad in a *happi* coat bearing the shop's name, can be seen standing next to the statue in a photo taken on the day of its dedication. The Kenpeitai military police evidently were not pleased that Sawabe selected the title of the emperor—the Mikado—for the name of his store. His having done so with all due respect for the emperor and his excellent connections with politically powerful people allowed him to weather the police's displeasure, and he soon became a principal supplier of dogs to the military.[17] In the early 1920s, though, Sawabe and other officers found dogs more difficult to come by. For a time, the military sometimes had to wait to be given dogs, usually by wealthy Japanese subjects. Canines, wherever they were acquired, were often sent to the Army Infantry School in Chiba, near Tokyo, the burgeoning program's training facility for dogs and their human handlers.

If Qingdao was the main site for acquisition and Chiba was the primary training area for military dogs, Manchuria became their proving ground. The Japanese government placed the northeastern Chinese region under its informal dominion after the end of the Russo-Japanese War in 1905, when it took over Russian leases, including a central railroad. During the next quarter century, Japan's colonial enterprise, the South Manchurian Railway (SMR), extended its vast business operations in the area, while Japan's Kwantung Army occupied territory around the train lines.

The development of army dogs prospered in Manchuria during the 1920s and 1930s, as did other emerging ventures in the region. In a canine sort of military-industrial complex, the Kwantung Army and SMR officials teamed with local Japanese settlers to import, breed, and raise dogs. They established the Manchurian Military-Dog Association (Manshū gun'yōken kyōkai) with the ambitious goal of "breeding in Manchuria all dogs working in the region."[18] Although it may have not been able to accomplish this task, the group was powerful, remaining independent even as other dog-fancying clubs were forced to merge during the next decade. The Kwantung Army created an independent canine-training school in early 1932. Instructors readied dogs, whether they were obtained locally, from Chiba, or abroad, and distributed them to the SMR, customs officials, and local police units. Next to the army, the SMR required the greatest number of dogs. From the late 1920s, the company stationed guard dogs and handlers to patrol mines, railway stations, and tracks from the interior to the port of Dalian (Dairen to the Japanese) in order to protect what at the time was perhaps the world's largest coal-production and transportation system. To outfit this security zone, SMR officials looked beyond the Japanese home islands and even the empire to purchase canines. They acquired some from the Society for the German Shepherd Dog, the group established by Max von Stephanitz. SMR officials also established an independent dog-training academy in Zhoushuizi near Dalian.[19] Within this complex network of breeding, distribution, and training, one typical route taken by military dogs was to be secured in Qingdao, trained in Chiba, and sent to Manchuria for further training and placement. This triangular imperial, commercial network highlights the tightly entangled relationship between dogs and the Japanese empire: only because Japan colonized Qingdao could it acquire the dogs it trained at home and sent to be agents of imperial war in Manchuria. This was precisely the route taken by Kongō and Nachi, two "German" shepherd dogs whose actions during the Manchurian Incident in 1931 made army messenger dogs famous throughout the empire. The dogs, it was said, joined in a skirmish and died after killing many enemy soldiers.

Private dog keepers in Manchuria, as in other contexts, fulfilled a vital role in propagating, raising, and supplying dogs to meet the demands of business, police, and military operations. In the dreamy language that was often used to describe the promise of Manchukuo, one former trainer described Manchuria as a "working dog's heaven."[20] Dogs, especially "German" shepherds, became iconic figures in Manchuria. They appear with surprising frequency in group portraits: one sits with Mr. Kozu, a Manchurian Colonization (Manshū Takushoku) Company employee, his wife, son, and company subordinates; another poses for a commemorative photo with three teachers and two students of a Japanese school on a snowy field in central Manchuria.[21] In photographic images and text in magazines that encouraged Japanese to migrate to Manchuria, working dogs, along with the fecund young mothers and wide-open vistas, came to represent an idealized northern imperial utopia. The author of an aptly titled article, "The Joy of Breeding," invoked the following scene: "Looking out onto a spectacular view, the young mother, the continental dog, and the plump and healthy second generation born in Manchuria play happily together on the second story of the shepherd's house."[22]

As in the Japanese empire, military officials and private breeders and trainers elsewhere made the development of army-dog programs a cooperative effort, and this collaboration inevitably led to greater state influence over kennel clubs. In Germany, Stephanitz and other training experts such as Konrad Most assisted the Wehrmacht in mustering dogs more widely and effectively. In Britain, retired colonel E. H. Richardson (1863–1948), who as a private citizen during the First World War persuaded the British army to establish a war-dog training school in 1916, failed in his attempts to resurrect an army-dog program after war broke out in Europe in 1939. He was told that it was a mechanical war and his services would not be needed.[23] After the British army was pushed off the Continent the following year, military officials changed their mind and the Royal Army Veterinary Corps solicited, ironically, the collaboration of the Royal Society for the Prevention of Cruelty to Animals to encourage the public to donate at least 2,500 dogs. In the United States, too, it was only through the repeated efforts of a

23. Three teachers, two students, and a shepherd dog, members of a settlement group from Nagano Prefecture, posing for a commemorative photograph in their village in central Manchuria sometime between 1939 and 1945. Used with permission of Kyōdo Shuppansha.

private network of volunteers, trainers, and breeders known as Dogs for Defense (DFD) that the military decided to employ army dogs in mid-1942. Initial wariness on the part of military brass soon gave way to efforts to gain more control over the programs, which through three hundred representatives across the continental United States, Alaska, and Hawaii successfully recruited approximately 17,000 dogs, of whom 10,000 underwent training.[24] The U.S. military at first delegated recruitment and training to the DFD, but it soon took over the latter task and became involved in the former one as well.

By comparison, the Japanese Imperial military's reach was wider and more heavy-handed. The Japan Shepherd Club (Nihon shepādo kurabu, or NSC), established in 1928, was in many ways a progressive social club composed of people such as corporate executives, journalists, and doctors. Military officials, unsatisfied with the group, attempted to steer it toward stronger support for the development of army dogs. Finding their efforts frustrated, they founded a new group, the Imperial Military Dog Association (Teikoku gun'yōken kyōkai, or KV) in 1931, and drew away some members of the NSC. Two years later, Army Minister Araki effectively ordered the NSC to disband. Still, some former NSC members refused to join the Imperial Military Dog Association and created a new group, the Japan Shepherd Association (Nihon shepādo kyōkai, or JSV). JSV mavericks continued to operate as a separate entity until the second National Mobilization Law in late 1941 forcibly consolidated all private organizations. The quasi-governmental Imperial Military Dog Association had long since eclipsed the power of any other group, growing from just over four hundred members in 1932 to around nine thousand organized into forty-seven branches by 1943.[25] The group's influence was, in fact, much larger than these figures indicate. In order for people to obtain a certificate of pedigree for their dogs, they did not have to become members of the association, but they were required to register their dogs. By 1942 the group listed some 41,000 purebred canines in its studbook.[26]

During the Second World War, both the Allied and Axis militaries employed canines in greater numbers and for a wider variety of tasks than in the previous conflict. One analyst estimates that around the world more than 250,000 canines served in some kind of military-related capacity.[27] In addition to Germany, Britain, and the United States, the Soviet Union created a massive army-dog program and was the only country known to have used "suicide" dogs to destroy tanks. Handlers trained the dogs to run to enemy tanks while carrying high-powered explosives on their backs, which were detonated remotely.[28] The Japanese military used canines as messengers, sentries, draft animals, trackers, and patrol auxiliaries. In January 1944, it maintained an estimated 815 dogs on the home islands, 3,260 in Manchuria, and 130 and 110, respectively, in the colonies of Korea and Taiwan. Based on these numbers, historians Hara Takeshi and Yasuoka Akio speculate that the army possessed a force of approximately ten thousand military dogs. These statistics, however, do not include canines in the employ of the navy, constabulary, and colonial police forces, or organizations such as the South Manchurian Railway.[29]

For Japan, these "silent warriors" (*mono o iwanu yūshitachi*), as they were often called, appear to have been far more valuable in the conflict on the continent than in fighting in the Pacific. Military dogs probably functioned most effectively when battle lines were stationary and relatively inactive, rather than in rapid and large-scale offensive or defensive maneuvers, so they were of little strategic use during the short-lived aerial and naval offensives and the protracted defensive struggle in the Pacific. For the American enemy, however, they purportedly performed superbly as scouts, helping U.S. marines prevent ambushes and locate hidden Japanese soldiers during the fierce island-hopping campaigns that began in 1943.[30]

Besides their tactical roles, canines provided companionship for soldiers. The psychological pleasure provided by a military dog was, of course, not among its officially prescribed duties in the Japanese and other armies. Some military officials and members of the media, though, seemed to informally recognize and tacitly encourage this function. One quasi-official Japanese army publication, in fact, named "comfort" and "inspiration" as two of three ways that army dogs aided soldiers.[31] At times, providing camaraderie may have been their only role. Author Imagawa Isao suggests that many dogs ultimately became mere pets or mascots, and sometimes they were abandoned, because soldiers at the front did not know how to handle them. Unlike the U.S. system, in which the military instructed handlers and dogs and sent them into action together as a team, the Imperial Army usually trained only dogs and then dispatched them to units that may have been unsure of how to deploy them properly.[32] They were often disappointed when the dogs did not perform "heroically" as stories had led them to expect.

By then it was too late. The dogs had already been mobilized for war. Yet this mobilization was not a top-down process. Private dog clubs, breeders, and trainers in Japan and elsewhere often proactively joined with government and military officials to create networks to prepare and dispatch dogs to empire and war. But, as we shall see, dogs in turn helped to ready and send people to war as well. At home, and in imperial areas, they were imagined, even if it was not always the case, to be reliable companions.

Imperial Japan's Colonial Dogs

Another role of "dogs of war," whether in battle or as a part of imperial occupation, was their ability to magnify the martial power and authority of their masters. There seems to be something particularly empowering in having a creature at one's command to torment other people, and something extremely humiliating about being on the receiving end of such an act. Throughout the world, military and law-enforcement agencies have activated dogs in this fashion to maintain colonial, wartime, and police controls.[33] Especially during the Second World War, dogs were employed systematically in such a manner. In Europe, the Gestapo and SS used dogs as an instrument and symbol of National Socialist terror in concentration camps and elsewhere. As a result, like the swastika and black jackboots, the

24. Military dogs on patrol with Japanese soldiers in China, 24 June 1938. Used with permission of Mainichi Photo Bank.

"German" shepherd dog has become an icon readily identified in popular culture with the Nazis.[34] Japanese colonial police and the Kenpeitai military police, too, utilized canines, usually shepherd dogs, to intimidate imperial subjects. In Hong Kong, for example, occupied residents of the city reported that the Kenpeitai set their dogs on persons who were found violating curfew or committing other minor offences, such as gathering dried grass for fuel.[35]

Like Western colonizers, many Japanese officials, businessmen, settlers, and other adventurers in Japan's formal and informal empire were in the company of dogs. As described in chapter 2, after the arrival of Westerners on the archipelago in the mid-nineteenth century, it did not take long for local elites to acquire a taste for foreign dogs and the practices associated with them. The ownership of a purebred Western dog quickly became a means for affluent and upwardly mobile Japanese to prove their sophistication and status. As their country attained an empire, Japanese often took along such canines and these recently adopted dog-keeping practices.

Japanese colonizers, like their Western counterparts, supposed their master-subject relationship with dogs as more civilized than local human-canine interactions, such as the gastronomic one often found in China and Korea. Of course, conspicuous consumption (of a nondietary nature), or what might be called in this instance colonial cultural capital, is alone not an adequate explanation. Influenced by the practices of foreigners living in Japan and popular images of the model colonizer—who was imagined as a British gentleman, adventuresome but thoroughly domesticated, dressed in khaki, and stalking wild game in some exotic land—hunting with dogs became a new preoccupation for many well-to-do Japanese expatriates. As in some Western colonial possessions, the imperialist's desire to eliminate competition for game may have contributed to early campaigns to eliminate indigenous canines in Taiwan and Korea. Finally, dogs provided companionship and camaraderie, as well as protection or some sense of security, which may have been in short supply in some imperial settings. As in Western colonies, canines—as sentries, hunting partners, or merely as companions—likely helped set apart their masters in the imperium.

As elsewhere, the extent and nature of dog keeping in the Japanese empire is difficult to measure and document. Certainly overseas dog keeping, as in the metropole, increased over time and was more prevalent among wealthier expatriates. A number of prominent colonial political, economic, and military leaders, such as Ugaki Kazushige (1868–1956), the governor-general of Korea from 1931 to 1937, were avid dog keepers. Visual evidence suggests that dogs were an important part of many colonizers' lives, at least significant enough to intentionally include them in family, group, and individual portraits. What appears to be a pointer, in a formal 1930s photograph with a Japanese textile executive, his wife, and two sons in Shanghai, is the focal point—held tightly in the arms of his master.[36] A snapshot of the family of a Japanese policeman in Taiwan taken at the Kirigaoka Shinto Shrine in Wu-she on the occasion of a father's and daughter's return from Japan in 1935 shows a retrieverlike dog lying at the feet of the group.[37] And a 1901 studio portrait portrays Soeda Juichi (1864–1929), the president of the Bank of Taiwan, as an Anglicized hunter. Soeda, who had studied at Cambridge University in the 1880s, is outfitted in his finest hunting attire—dressed in thoroughly British apparel, khaki britches, a single-breasted vest, jacket, and an ivy cap. At his feet sits an attentive and leashed English springer spaniel, a breed that bolsters his claim to elite Victorian rural gentility. In one arm, Soeda cradles a double-barreled twelve-gauge shotgun, and in the other he holds a half-dozen water hen and at least one duck, presumably killed by himself and his dog.[38] The visual and symbolic parallels between this staged photograph and Andō's 1860 woodblock print of the English soldier and his colonial dog (examined in chapter 1) are striking. Japan had truly gone from the subject to the object of imperialism in just a few decades.

Glimpses of individual dog-keeping practices are also evident in the activities of colonial dog clubs. In addition to the independent Manchurian Military-Dog Association, canine aficionados created branches of the Imperial Military Dog Association and the Society for the Preservation of the Japanese Dog in a number of cities throughout the empire. Canine-fancying groups, which were either organized by breed or function, promoted dog keeping and brought fans of dogs together to exhibit, train, and produce dogs, as well as hobnob.[39] The organizations also served as a means for police and military agencies to enlist canine recruits.

If army, police, and guard dogs provided security, comfort, and an excuse to congregate for colonizers, they often instilled fear in the colonized. Interaction

25. Soeda Juichi, president of the Bank of Taiwan, posing with an English springer spaniel in a photo studio in Taipei, 1901.

with some of these animals could be physically and psychologically painful, and perhaps even fatal. Training probably conditioned many dogs to be hostile to the colonized. One canine expert admitted as much during a 1935 round-table discussion of dog handlers who had recently returned from Manchuria. He reported that many working dogs "try to bite any tame or wild dog or any person who is not Japanese." "In particular," he bragged when speaking about one dog he had trained, "people and dogs both ran away when they saw Chōen."[40] Such comments, unfortunately, were not idle talk.

A series of incidents involving dogs in Korea during the early 1930s highlight the dangers for the colonized in their encounters with dogs such as Chōen. Between late 1933 to mid-1934, the *Donga ilbo*, a Korean-language daily newspaper generally sympathetic to Japanese rule, reported a number of attacks on Koreans by dogs kept by Japanese colonizers and an elite Korean.[41] The first incident occurred when army dogs attached to a cavalry supply division stationed in the northern city of Najin assaulted a large group of farmers. No fewer than forty-five people sustained injuries, including fourteen children. Perhaps recognizing the volatility of the situation, senior army officials quickly visited the victims and apologized. When some of the injured threatened to sue, officials

1. Hashimoto Gyokuransai (Sadahide) print of an American couple and their dog, 1860.
Used with permission of the Kanagawa Prefectural Museum of Cultural History.

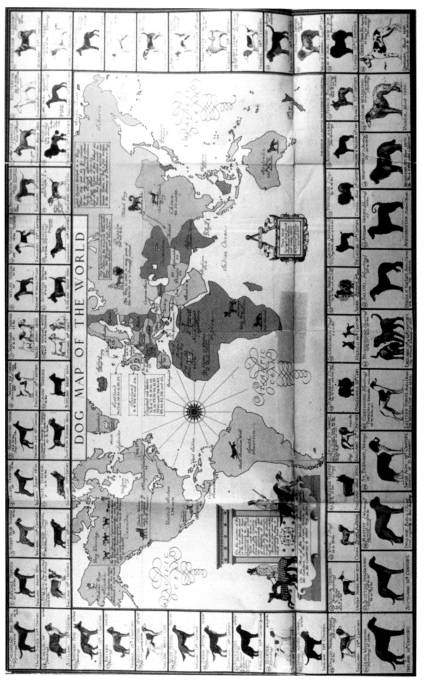

2. "Dog Map of the World: The Countries of Origin of Some Seventy Breeds of Domesticated Dogs, Half of Them Evolved in the British Isles!" *Illustrated London News*, 1933.

3. Painting by W. T. Peters of Miako (Miyako), a Japanese spaniel or *chin* presented to Commodore Matthew C. Perry by the Tokugawa shogunate.

4. Painting by W. T. Peters of Shimoda, another *chin* presented to Perry by the shogunate.

5. A lithograph, entitled *Kiken bijin* (Elite beauty), dated 1888. Artist unknown.
Used with permission of Chikuma shobō.

6. Norakuro launching an attack of the Regiment of Fierce Dogs on the January 1938 cover of a special New Year's supplement to the monthly boys' magazine *Shōnen kurabu* (Boys' club). Used with the permission of Kōdansha.

7. April 1944 cover of *Shōnen kurabu* (Boys' club). The caption between the magazine title and the dog reads, "We soon will be soldiers."

8. The Army Dog Memorial Statue erected on the grounds of Yasukuni Shrine in Tokyo in 1992. Used by permission of the photographer, Colin Tyner.

9. Painting of Hachikō waiting at Shibuya Station and poem, both of which appear in Kishi Kazutoshi's *Chūken Hachikō monogatari* (1934). The artist and author are unknown.

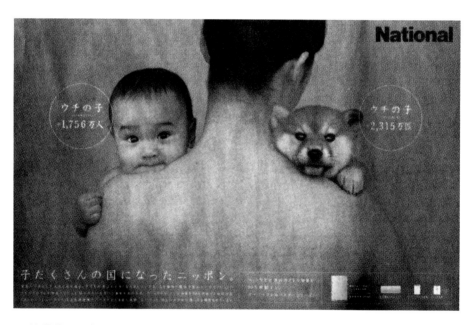

10. Full-spread newspaper advertisement for a Matsushita (Panasonic) electronic air-cleaning appliance. *Asahi shinbun*, 25 March 2005. Used with the permission of Matsushita.

countered by offering unlimited medical care and meted out punishments against division officers to persuade the aggrieved to drop their threatened suit.[42] Just days after the attack in Najin, two "German" shepherd dogs handled by a certain Mr. Okumura, the thirty-six-year-old caretaker at the Gowongyeon forest near the southeastern city of Pusan, severely bit a thirteen-year-old girl, Kim In Hwa. Okumura defended siccing the dogs on the girl, alleging that she had entered the property with the intent to steal. Kim's parents, who had immediately lodged a complaint with local government officials, denied Okumura's accusation and asserted their daughter had only entered the area to gather leaves to use for fuel.[43] These incidents roiled many Koreans, including representatives of the local assembly in Pusan who called the "use of guard dogs on the Kowongyeon grounds an insult to all Koreans." They submitted a resolution to ban the use of the dogs in the forest, and threatened to resign if it did not pass.[44] Some Japanese legislators were apparently willing to tacitly support the bill because the Koreans felt so strongly about the issue, but a majority of lawmakers opposed the proposal and it was defeated.[45] In protest, a few of the Korean representatives resigned and continued to push for the ban. A year later, in 1935, for reasons the newspaper did not explain, the Pusan government implemented a ban.[46] It is unclear why legislators shifted their position, but perhaps two other attacks by dogs contributed to the decision. In May and June 1934, canines owned by a certain Mr. Tanihata and a Korean counterpart, Mr. Wangsik, injured four people in another forest.[47]

Although these episodes, all of which took place within a six-month period, were the only dog attacks reported by *Donga ilbo* from 1920 to 1945, it is highly likely that there were many more confrontations between army, police, and guard dogs and the colonized. Japanese countermeasures evidently calmed Korean ire, but they did nothing to resolve the threat of violence posed by dogs. Removing such intimidation was surely not the intent of the colonizers. Rather the incidents and their so-called resolution only served to heighten fears, which would only disappear after colonial dogs and their masters did.[48]

Physically and figuratively, dogs lent their colonial masters an air of authority and expanded the breadth and depth of systems of surveillance and repression as a result of the canines' conditioned belligerence toward imperial subjects. As Fukushima Yoshie, a Japanese woman who settled in a town on the northeastern border of Manchuria in 1940, recalled:

> My husband bought a large dog from the army, a German Shepherd named Esu [Ace]. It was a good dog and watched over me while my husband was away. My husband told me that they trained dogs to bite only Manchurians. They'd dress someone in Manchu clothes and [the army] trained the dog to attack when he came into a room, taking a big bite of his calf. The man's life wouldn't be endangered, but he couldn't move. He could then be investigated to determine if he was a spy. Esu was brought up that way. We told [our servant] Chō-san never to wear Chinese clothes. My husband didn't tell me everything, but there must have been many other things he knew, because he had twice been a soldier.[49]

What were the other things Fukushima's husband knew, the things he never mentioned? Were these, too, related to dogs? Many of the colonized, like Chō-san, certainly knew something of them, too. The protection that a guard dog provided, the threat of such a dog, helped expand the suffocating nature of imperial rule beyond the levers of formal institutions and into the everyday lives of the colonized. For some, the threat posed by Japanese army dogs did not disappear with the end of war but continued to linger in the form of semiwild beasts. In their final days in power, Japanese army and police officials and colonizers unleashed working dogs in occupied areas, and for a time these feral animals continued to terrorize postcolonial peoples.[50]

The Teacher's Pet

Even as fighting and occupying armies deployed canines in novel ways and in unprecedented numbers during the Second World War, national education systems and private media mobilized dogs and other animals as never before. The greatest proportion of this cultural production was aimed at juveniles. In societies where stories of children, particularly boys, and their dogs had long existed as a subgenre within juvenile literature, and in places like Japan, where the genre was only as mature as the emerging enthusiasm for pet dogs, public and private rhetoric took advantage of such connections to mobilize youth for war and empire, even as they nurtured the relationships between dogs and male youngsters.

Two side-by-side images on the opening pages of the Ministry of Education's 1933 first-year language textbook captured how government- and privately produced rhetoric attempted to foster in children an interest in dogs while preparing youngsters for war. The primer was the first textbook ever to include colored illustrations, and the visual impact of these images on young readers, who probably encountered few such images in books and magazines, may have been considerable. The first illustration, on the fourth page, shows a young boy dressed in navy-blue kimono decorated with a pattern of white crests. He extends his right hand to an approaching white dog, which appears to be a pointer. The caption in simple *katakana* syllabary reads, "Come along, Shiro, come" (*Koi koi Shiro koi*). The child's hand and the dog's outstretched tail lead the reader's eye to the image on the next page: four advancing wooden toy soldiers dressed in khaki uniforms aligned in a straight row, who shoulder backpacks and rifles. The words on this page, too, are a command: "Forward, soldiers, march forward" (*Susume susume heitai susume*).[51] The placement of these images was not coincidental, but rather suggested a deliberately conceived relationship among boys, dogs, and "playing" war.

As Katherine C. Grier and Kathleen Kete have analyzed in the context of the nineteenth-century United States and western Europe, respectively, an affinity between children and animals—especially dogs—came to be thought of as natural and spontaneous in many societies with an emerging middle class.[52] This was precisely the opinion expressed by Chiba Haruo (1890–1943) and other education commentators in their analysis of the above images shortly after the

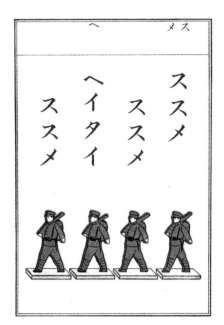

26. Pages four and five (which are inverted) of the 1933 national language textbook for first-year primary school students. On page four, the boy motions to the dog, and the caption reads, "Come along, Shiro, come!" (*Koi koi Shiro koi*). The script on the next page with the four toy soldiers is, "Forward, soldiers, march forward!" (*Susume susume heitai susume*).

publication of the textbook. Chiba wrote that dogs were an appropriate selection for the introductory textbook because they were a "member of the family," an "object of deep adoration and familiarity" for children, and a "natural part of children's play." The toy figures, Chiba noted, represented military service, which was a national duty for every male subject, and evoked the Japanese spirit (*Yamato damashii*) and a sense of nationalism. But playing war, too, he concluded, was a normal part of child's play.[53] Chiba appeared to recognize the political connotations and the constructed nature of the textbook's association between young males and soldiers, but he took for granted the affection of children for canines and the association between the two. The connection, however, is not a given, but in each society is a historically constructed cultural artifact. Another teacher's guide admitted as much in its explication of the purpose of the first image. Its goal, the guide stated, was to "foster in children feelings of affinity for dogs by creating an interest in playing with them and creating everyday interactions with them."[54]

To be sure, dogs did not make their debut in popular children's culture in Japan during the Asia-Pacific War. Textbook authors had included canines in primers for at least the past few decades. None of these, though, manipulated canine images for political purposes. In 1911, for example, the Ministry of Education included "Inu" (Dog) in the music curriculum. The song began with the words: "When I go outside, he comes bounding to me; no matter how far I go, he follows along; ah, Pochi is such a cute dog."[55] Likewise, stories about the relationship between boys and dogs, such as Futabatei Shimei's short novel *Heibon* (1907), had appeared in popular books and magazines for children for many years. By the 1930s, though, dogs had come to attract unprecedented attention, and government authorities charged with consolidating public support for war recognized the value of canines in grabbing the attention of youngsters. When NHK officials presented a petition to the Ministry of Communications to create a radio news show called *Children's News* in June 1932, they listed the "exploits of military dogs" at the top of a list of "news that holds special interest for children."[56]

The confluence of children, dogs, and war can be explained by larger trends. An enthusiasm for canines among the emerging middle class appeared around this time. From at least the 1920s, children's literature flourished as authors and publishers took advantage of the growing numbers of families who had financial leeway to buy books and magazines for their kids. The establishment of an army-dog program, along with the nationalism and war fever that began to pervade the country after the Manchurian Incident in 1931, added a military dimension. However one explains it, cultural discourses about dogs aimed primarily at young people flooded 1930s Japan as never before. The "Loyal Dog" Hachikō figured prominently, but other dogs, especially military dogs, elicited considerable attention as well. "Dogs of war" were a frequent motif in juvenile literature, cartoons, picture-story shows (*kamishibai*), board games (*sugoroku*), songs, motion pictures, paintings, and even children's kimono fabrics, which included such designs as helmeted puppies with boy soldiers strutting alongside tanks, battleships, and other weaponry.[57] Some of the images and stories portrayed fictional boys and their dogs contributing to the war effort, while others purported to recount factual incidents of real soldiers and military dogs in battle.[58]

The story of Kongō and Nachi and their exploits during the Manchurian Incident was primarily responsible for popularizing military dogs among people, both young and old. Although the tale is almost unknown in Japan today, at the time of its emergence it sparked an uproar that prefigured and rivaled the interest in Hachikō, which began a year later. The army dogs' message and path to popularity was similar to that of their civilian cousin. They were celebrated as models of loyalty, bravery, and as essentially Japanese. During the fighting that erupted after the railway explosion staged by the Kwantung Army on 18 September, Kongō and Nachi, as well as a third dog, Merī (Mary), disappeared while working as messengers. This much is known from a letter written in the following month by their handler, Captain Itakura Itaru, a trainer who first worked with dogs at the Chiba facility and then was transferred to Manchuria to oversee the deployment of military canines. He recounted that a search after the battle turned up two canine corpses, identified as Nachi and Merī, which he and his comrades buried after a small memorial service. Kongō's body was never found. Two months later on 27 November, Itakura became mortally wounded in an attack on his convoy and reportedly pleaded with his company commander to watch over the dogs' graves.[59]

This scene of a master following his dogs to the grave inspired the mass media, which, as historian Louise Young has recounted, became a "cheering gallery for the Kwantung Army" after the Manchurian Incident.[60] Like that of Hachikō, the story was first spread widely by newspapers and magazines, and then preserved in more enduring ways. On 7 July 1933, military and civil leaders gathered at Enmei Buddhist Temple in Itakura's hometown of Zushi in Kanagawa Prefecture to dedicate the Monument to the Loyal Dogs, a massive statue of a single dog sculpted by Aoyanagi Toshio honoring Kongō and Nachi, and another favorite dog of Itakura's named Jurī (Julie), who died in February 1932 after being sent to the captain's family from Manchuria. This ceremony took place nearly a year before Hachikō's bronze was unveiled in nearby Tokyo. There were other parallels as well. Organizers in Zushi targeted and raised much of the money to construct the statue through contributions from youngsters across Imperial Japan. Schoolchildren played an important role at the dedication ceremony, too. More than two thousand primary and secondary school students participated in the service, which was attended by political and military dignitaries such as Army Minister Araki, who was also president of the Imperial Military Dog Association, and General Minami Jirō (1874–1955), who was named commander of the Kwantung Army in Manchuria and ambassador to Manchukuo the following year. After Itakura's young son Yasuyuki—dressed in a navy uniform—unveiled the statue, other children draped medals over the neck of the dog statue, and the assembled crowd of students serenaded it with the following dedicatory song:

> The monument to the loyal dog is now complete,
> In memory of Kongō and Nachi's war feat
> And the deeds of Jurī,
> We all join in praise.[61]

Children throughout the archipelago soon learned of Kongō and Nachi's alleged courage and devotion when the Ministry of Education included "The Exploits of Dogs" (Inu no tegara) in the basic language textbook for fifth-year students in 1933, a year before Hachikō's tale appeared in the ethics primer. Textbook authors rendered the story in the following manner:

> It was the first night of the Manchurian Incident. Two military dogs, Kongō and Nachi, who accompanied our army and served as messengers, were caught in the midst of a severe attack and rushed ahead of our soldiers. They leapt into a swarm of enemy soldiers and with desperate courage bit the enemy one after another.
> At the end of the brutal battle, the enemy had fled from its positions. In the first light of dawn, the Rising Sun glittered high above. Thundering shouts of banzai rang through heaven and earth, but where were Kongō and Nachi? When called, they did not come.

The chief handler of the dogs searched vigilantly for them. Finally, their whereabouts were discovered. They lay in the midst of many dead soldiers strewn about. The dogs had received several bullets, and soaked with blood they were dead. A closer examination of their mouths revealed the shreds of the enemy's uniforms that they had fiercely bitten. The soldiers who saw this spontaneously began to cry.

Kongō and Nachi were the first to receive an honorific collar that can be considered the military dog's equivalent of the Order of the Golden Kite.[62]

While elements of the story were accurate—the dogs were indeed the inspiration for and first recipients of a new citation honoring military animals—the textbook tale took tremendous liberties with the account provided by Itakura. In his letter soon after the incident, which was published in the Japan Shepherd Club's December newsletter, Itakura did not mention that the dogs had attacked, and apparently killed, enemy soldiers.[63] These details, and perhaps others, were complete fabrications.

Another fiction that appeared in the story, and which did not match Itakura's version of events, was the names of the dogs that the soldiers had discovered. In the primer, it was no longer Nachi and Merī who were found dead, but Kongō and Nachi. Merī, in fact, had entirely disappeared from the story. The substitution of Kongō for Merī, a Japanese name instead of a Western one, effectively Japanized the dog. It is difficult to know for sure whether the switch was intentional or not, but certainly it made sense when one considers that the story's primary audience was children. A familiar Japanese name probably carried more emotional impact for youngsters than a foreign moniker. Children may also have known that Kongō and Nachi were the names of two Imperial Navy ships, which had probably been named after two sacred Shinto religious sites. The dog's original owner in Qingdao apparently named all the canines in the litter to which the two belonged after naval vessels—the males after battleships and the females after cruisers.[64] Kongō was the former and Nachi the latter, so the switch produced a Japanese pair of each gender, rather than a Japanese male and Western female.

If the rationale for the replacement of Merī by Kongō was uncertain, the intent of the Ministry of Education in including the story in the curriculum was not. In accompanying instruction manuals, education specialists asserted that a story that combined war and dogs would be of great interest to children. Its objective, one guide told teachers, was to cause "children to feel exhilaration at the acts of loyalty, bravery, and martial passion (*chūyū buretsu*) shown by Kongō and Nachi." Because children like tales of war and tales of martial passion and because they feel great affection for dogs, the manual explained, they would feel intense curiosity in a story in which dogs, who "were like friends to them, performed with martial passion to the end in a setting that was their favorite."[65] In another instruction manual, ministry bureaucrat Miyagawa Kikuyoshi (1891–1951) admonished teachers to "focus on the glorious exploits of the military dogs and to read with appreciation this inspirational deed performed to an incomparably heroic end." If teachers did so, he continued, they would "nourish in students' minds absolute martial spirit and a love for the nation."[66] In Miyagawa's commentary, the malleable symbolic nature of dogs is evident. On the one hand, Miyagawa elevated military dogs as exhibiting character traits that Japanese children ought to emulate, hailing them rather extravagantly as the "essential expression of the Yamato spirit, the exemplars of repaying accumulated debt, the incarnation of dauntless courage whose loyalty and bravery rank with the Imperial soldier, and which would even make a fierce god weep." On the other hand, he disparaged canines in general by declaring that if dogs were able to outperform children in their service to the nation, they—the youngsters—did not deserve to be called Japanese. Miyagawa thought that the fear of being outdone by a mere dog ought to provide motivation enough for children.[67]

While its effect on youngsters was unclear, the tale of Kongō and Nachi inspired publishers and movie studios to issue a steady stream of stories about dogs and other animals in the service of the military, nation, and empire during the 1930s and 1940s. The story of the two famous military dogs was reproduced in a number of different versions and formats. The publishers of the upscale children's monthly magazine *Kindābukku*, for example, included an illustrated adaptation in a special issue about canines in 1939. It showed the dogs leading a charge of Japanese soldiers into the fleeing ranks of cowardly looking Nationalist Chinese troops.[68] This rendering and other editions, as well as the original textbook story, all distorted Itakura's description of what happened. They were consistent, however, in glorifying the loyalty, bravery, and death of the dogs.

Although Kongō and Nachi became hugely famous, their silence was deafening. In part because the dogs achieved stardom because of their deaths rather than while they were alive, no still or moving images exist of them, and their remains went unpreserved. Unlike Hachikō, Kongō and Nachi left no bodily material evidence that could corroborate or undermine human representations of their actions.

As seen from the story of Kongō and Nachi, tales of army dogs often belittled the enemy and justified imperial ventures. This was done in several ways. Sometimes the country's foes were shown as unusually fearful of army dogs, as with the panicking Chinese troops running away from the two canine heroes. In other stories, adversaries were portrayed as being just as uncivilized and craven as wild dogs or wolves. In some instances, this comparison was explicit, as in the story described in chapter 3 of the "Japanese" army dog Gunjingō (Soldier), who routed the hordes of wild Chinese dogs.[69] Elsewhere, colonial peoples—especially Chinese—were compared with more docile canines—that is, puppies. In one such story, *Koinu to heitai-san* (The puppy and the soldier), author Yoshino Yumisuke tells of a Chinese dog who was adopted by a certain Captain Kuribayashi on the continent. When the dog, whom the captain gives a Japanese name, Tonsuke, repeatedly gets into trouble by doing things such as chewing up the shoelaces of soldiers' boots, Kuribayashi punishes the dog but continues to care for him tenderly. "Just as the captain punished that cute dog," another soldier tells Lin Baidao, a young Chinese boy who helps the Japanese soldiers, "Japan is punishing China

27. Kongō and Nachi leading an Imperial Army charge against fleeing Chinese Nationalist troops in the monthly children's magazine *Kindābukku,* November 1939. Used with the permission of Froebel-Kan Co., Ltd.

precisely because Japan cares for China." Tonsuke returns the captain's kindness by leading him to a cache of hidden weapons. Ultimately, Kuribayashi gives the puppy to Lin, but not before admonishing Tonsuke to "remember to follow my discipline. Become a dog that anyone would adore. Become a dog that people will know was raised by Japanese soldiers."[70] In this way, the ideal Chinese were depicted as being as pliable, obedient, and in need of being cared for like a puppy and child.

Authors and other image makers sometimes positioned dogs, both real and imagined, to portray wartime leaders in endearing terms. One such story from a German elementary school primer featuring Adolf Hitler attempted to show his humanity and kindness by highlighting his supposed concern for youngsters and animals. It told of two little girls using their own allowance money to buy a big sausage for his shepherd dog, Wolf, and flowers for the Führer on his birthday. After giving them a talk about the importance of the role of women and girls as mothers willing to sacrifice for the nation, Hitler cuts off a piece of the wiener, places it above Wolf's nose, and lets him jump for it. Such treatment elicited praise from the children, who were moved to exclaim, "My goodness, Herr Hitler, you really have an excellent way of training dogs!"[71] In addition to showing a more approachable side of Hitler, another message seemed to be that the ideal child would be just as teachable and compliant in executing Hitler's commands as his dogs. Similarly, many U.S. presidents, including most notably the wartime presidents Franklin D. Roosevelt and George W. Bush, have used "First Dogs" to humanize themselves and their families and to promote their political fortunes.[72] From November 1941, Fala, a Scottish terrier became Roosevelt's constant companion, frolicking with the press corps at the White House and elsewhere, traveling to Allied conferences and political events with him, and acting as an endearing ambassador for the president, particularly during his tight fourth presidential election campaign. His influence was so great that at the height of the campaign, Pulitzer Prize–winning journalist John H. Crider of the *New York Times* declared—with only slight exaggeration—that "Fala is no longer just a dog; he is a personage."[73] Although it may have not been intentional, Bush's dogs Barney, a Scottish terrier, and Spot, an English springer spaniel, created a similar effect on the day the president gave Saddam Hussein a forty-eight-hour deadline to leave Iraq in an evening speech shortly before launching an invasion of the country on 17 March 2003. As reported with a photograph on the front page by the *New York Times*, the president's only other public appearance on the day he prepared Americans for war was to emerge that morning on the South Lawn of the White House to play ball with Barney and Spot.[74]

Press coverage during the Second World War also used dogs to cast soldiers in a favorable light. In the United States, numerous photographs of soldiers and their dogs appeared in local newspapers. The U.S. connection between young males and their pet dogs was an established staple of popular children's literature, so such pictures likely heightened the feeling among people at home that the men who took care of these cherished childhood "buddies" were "our boys."[75] Meanwhile, Japanese media accounts and children's stories emphasized the kindnesses rendered by soldiers toward army or local animals. Newspaper reporters depicted military men going to great lengths to secure delicious food for army dogs and care for their health. They celebrated the intimate bond wrought between man and beast in the field, which often culminated in the death of both master and dog in battle. Writers sometimes portrayed the benevolence of soldiers as being so great that it turned animal foes, such as the dog and monkey—which according to tradition were irreconcilable adversaries—into friends. One such article told of the "compassion" of a Sergeant Okamoto who adopted a puppy and a baby primate in successive abandoned villages during his regiment's march through southern China.[76] Other correspondents alluded to the famous fairy tale of the peach boy Momotarō, who procured the support of a dog and a monkey, as well as a pheasant, to defeat ogres threatening Japan.

Another cartoon featuring a dog, Norakuro (Stray dog Kurokichi), contained similar messages, though its nature was more complicated. *Norakuro,* the name of the series and its main character, was the longest running and probably the most widely read cartoon of the 1930s.[77] The cartoon's popularity continues to this day. Like Hachikō, the public selected the image of Norakuro as one of the most representative to best illustrate the Japanese experience in the twentieth century.[78] It appeared in the monthly boys' magazine *Shōnen kurabu* (Boys' Club), issued by the publishing giant Kōdansha from January 1931 to October 1941, and was so well liked that it became the symbol of the magazine. Kōdansha also published the cartoon in fifteen volumes that sold well over a million copies during the 1930s. (See color plate 6.) The series was made into short animated films, and in an age before strict trademark legislation, it enriched entrepreneurs who capitalized on the dog's popularity by producing a wide variety of goods featuring Norakuro's image.

Unlike other "dogs of war," Norakuro did not explicitly promote bravery or loyalty. Postwar commentators have regarded his creator, Tagawa Suihō (given name, Takamizawa Nakatarō, 1889–1989), as a young avant-garde artist who was influenced by jazz music, foreign cartooning, including Pat Sullivan and Otto Messmer's Felix the Cat (1919) and Walt Disney's Mickey Mouse (1928), and progressive political thought, particularly anarchism. The series was indeed somewhat proletarian in its instincts. Norakuro, a stray orphaned mongrel, joins the army as a lowly second-class private and experiences numerous and humorous blunders as he progresses upward in rank until finally he retires as colonel. The cartoon was in many ways an irreverent look at the Imperial Army, and, as anthropologist Yamaguchi Masao (1931–) has argued, Norakuro and his fellow dogs' bloopers contested the myth of the Imperial military as immune to surrender, tears, or humor.[79] Some military officials apparently found the comparison of the emperor's army to a bunch of dogs so demeaning that for this and other reasons they ordered the publisher Kōdansha to stop printing the series in late 1941.

Even as Tagawa demythologized the mystique of the Imperial Army, he created an idealized picture of military life that was perhaps even further from reality. Norakuro and his fellow dogs, despite various gaffes, always triumph and, as in most cartoons, war is a harmless and entertaining affair, at least for the victorious animals. Although Tagawa challenged army ideals by, for example, having Norakuro and his bulldog commander surrender to enemy monkeys and crying while in captivity, the two inevitably escape and use information they obtained while imprisoned to rout the simians. This imagined world was a favorite of a cohort of youngsters who grew up reading the cartoon, so much so that they refer to themselves as the "Norakuro generation." Indeed, the circulation of *Shōnen kurabu* reached 750,000 in 1936, but its actual readership was believed to be several times that number, since each copy was passed around among friends.[80] A survey conducted by the Ministry of Education in the same year found that almost 80 percent of sixth-year students who answered read the magazine frequently. The popularity of Norakuro introduced soldiering to millions of youngsters, many of whom entered the armed forces and went to war with such images in their heads. Unfortunately, many of them never returned. The male age cohort that sustained the most Japanese war dead during the Asian-Pacific War was born in 1922, which coincidently was the Year of the Dog according to the Chinese zodiac. These men were nine years old when Kōdansha began publishing *Norakuro* and nineteen when the company suspended the series in 1941.

Perhaps what made *Norakuro* so engaging was that in some ways fiction closely matched reality. For material, Tagawa drew on his two-year stint in the army after the First World War. He spent part of that time taking care of military messenger pigeons in colonial Korea, and participated in punitive raids against horse thieves. Tagawa's firsthand experience as an enlisted soldier enabled him to create a cartoon that was in many ways true to military life, especially in the series' early years, which chronicled Norakuro's adventures as a part of the Regiment of Fierce Dogs (*mōken rentai*). The regimental rules, for example, strongly resembled the "Imperial Rescript to Soldiers and Sailors," an official code of ethics issued in 1882 that defined military service in terms of absolute loyalty to the state and emperor.[81] Moreover, Norakuro's adventures closely mirrored those of actual geopolitical events in a way that made the cartoon interesting and timely. When full-scale fighting erupted in China between the Imperial Army and Chinese Nationalist troops in 1937, Norakuro and his fellow dogs went to war against pigs who were threatened by bears, a scenario that was instantly recognizable as the three-way rivalry among Japan, China, and Russia. In this way, Norakuro interested and educated youngsters about military and foreign affairs and prepared them to participate in these ventures. *Norakuro* functioned much like its comic strip series contemporary, *The Adventures of Tintin*, created by francophone Belgian artist Hergé, the pen name of Georges Remi (1907–83). Like Norakuro, the protagonist, Tintin, who was accompanied by his faithful and "talking" fox terrier, Snowy, provided its youthful readers with virtual tours of imperial lands and rival regimes, including the Belgian Congo and the Soviet Union, and familiarized them with the intrigues of geopolitics and empire.[82]

Although in some ways iconoclastic, *Norakuro* bolstered the themes of success and loyalty, which were central motifs of government textbooks as well as popular children's publications as seen in *Shōnen kurabu*. A well-known slogan of the day, in fact, pointed to the ideal schoolboy as holding "textbook in the right hand, *Shōnen kurabu* in the left hand."[83] Norakuro became a symbol of advancement (*risshin shusse*), as evidenced by a popular tune about him that was even sung in the schools. The ditty included the lines: "A stray dog, an orphan without a home, now part of a regiment of fierce dogs, his popularity resounds everywhere."[84] Norakuro's image as an "underdog" who overcame staggering odds to rise from enlisted to officer status may have provided inspiration for economically disadvantaged and undereducated young men, for whom military service provided the preeminent path of mobility and masculinity. The fidelity exhibited by Norakuro was not nearly as obvious as it was in other popular and official literature, but the dog, despite his various blunders, always remained true to his fellow canines, adhering to the regiment's and Imperial military's precept to "never forget loyalty for a single moment."[85] The only time he did not follow this ideal, which evidently angered some military officials and likely contributed to the government's decision to order Kōdansha to stop publishing the series, was when Norakuro returned victorious from the war in China only to retire from the army and depart for Manchuria to reap a profit in the empire.

Though some military men may have regarded Norakuro's resignation from the emperor's army as a serious betrayal of a higher cause, in this instance as well as during his entire army career, Norakuro fully supported imperialist war. Throughout the 1930s, Norakuro went to war battling gorillas, mountain monkeys, pigs, and other creatures that were thinly disguised and unflattering representations of Japan's enemies. Chinese were invariably portrayed as pigs because of their culinary fondness for pork, and because their traditional queue hairstyle was said to resemble a pigtail. The canines, though depicted as blundering and of various breeds, still exemplified Japan's martial strength, courage, and superiority, while other beasts were portrayed as backward, weak, and dim-witted. Norakuro also familiarized children with the rhetoric of empire and pan-Asianism. When Norakuro went into business in Manchukuo, he collaborated with four other creatures who represented the constituent ethnic groups of Manchuria—a Korean dog named Kongō (Diamond), Ho-kun from the country of Chinese pigs, Ran-kun of the Mongolian sheep nation, and Kan-kun of the Manchurian goats—to develop the region's resources and attain a "realm of peace and prosperity" (ōdo rakudo) and the "harmony of five peoples" (gozoku kyōwa). Both of these slogans were identical to those used in the puppet state of Manchukuo, and the selection of a dog to represent Koreans alongside Norakuro and his Japanese canine compatriots may reflect late 1930s colonial policies that sought to forcibly assimilate Koreans to become Japanese both in name and in reality and, as signified by the slogan "Japan and Korea as one body" (Naisen ittai), to strip them of their Korean cultural and racial identity.

Asked years later why he chose to use canines in the cartoon, Tagawa's reply seemed to echo the words of the education commentator Chiba's analysis of the relationship between children and dogs featured in the 1933 first-year textbook: "Children like dogs, so I thought I'd make a dog the protagonist. I had the dog do things children enjoy. Children like to play soldiers, so I had the dog play soldiers."[86] Tagawa's logic was that because children like to pretend to be soldiers, he had the fictional dogs play soldiers. But the reverse logic was equally true and was surely of greater historical consequence. Popular culture, just like official literature, actively fostered affinity for dogs—both real and fictional—in children and at the same time took advantage of that familiarity to encourage an interest in becoming a soldier and to cultivate values that supported militarism and imperialism.

The relationship among children, dogs, and war in popular juvenile culture and official literature is illustrated by a Shōnen kurabu cover from April 1944. (See color plate 7.) It shows a smiling boy hugging a large "German" shepherd dog. In one hand the boy holds a folded piece of paper, which is evidently a conscription notice. He is dressed in a school uniform and appears to be too young to be eligible for military service, even by the standards of mid-1944, when Japan's war situation was growing increasingly desperate and government officials were sending teenagers to defend the rapidly collapsing empire. The caption reads: "We will soon be soldiers." From this phrase it is unclear who has been called up—the boy, the dog, or both. The ambiguity, intentional or not, was appropriate. Both dog and boy had been mobilized for war and empire.

"Army Dogs Come from the Home"

The rhetoric of the "dogs of war" encouraged people to offer their pets to the military to become army dogs. Military authorities solicited other animals as well, but armies throughout the world during the Second World War relied heavily on the public for canines. In all combatant nations, such collection efforts were vital in providing a supply of military dogs. The traffic in dogs linked, in both actual and symbolic ways, the home front to the battlefront, families with military organizations, and children with soldiers. Indeed, "Army dogs come from the home" (*gun'yōken wa katei kara*) became an oft-repeated slogan in Japan, and a similar awareness was created in other countries, such as Britain, Germany, and the United States. Dogs were by far the most widespread household pet, and the one with the most intimate connection to children and their families. Increasingly, they were regarded as a "member of the family." Thus, the donation of the "family dog" to the military produced a sense of personally participating in the war effort. As one promoter of the Dogs for Defense recruitment program put it, "If you have an idea that somebody who gives a dog for war isn't sacrificing anything, you have never had a dog who was a member of your family. You have never had a little girl or a little boy whose affection was given to a dog."[87]

In Japan and elsewhere, donating a dog to the military became a way for people to prove their patriotism. Campaign coordinators, usually dog-fancying club officials, focused their enlistment efforts on dog-club members, but they soon widened their reach to the general public to satisfy the military's insatiable demand for canines. Organizers commended people for their contributions in newspaper articles and with awards and certificates. Parades, sponsored by dog clubs and the military, were another way for people to publicly demonstrate their loyalty, with keepers marching alongside dogs who would soon be shipped to the front. During the 1930s and 1940s, people with dogs draped in swastikas walked through German towns, and military personnel accompanied by canines strode down main streets in American cities.[88] The Imperial Military Dog Association and other groups made such displays a regular occurrence in Japan after the Manchurian Incident. Some two hundred canines and their owners composed one such procession that marched from the statue of Saigō Takamori and his dog in Ueno Park, down the main Shōwa thoroughfare, and to a close in front of the Imperial Palace in the summer of 1933.[89]

Dogs departed for the front with similar fanfare. Sometimes dog keepers announced a dog's departure to friends and associates via postcards, and they usually sent off dogs clad in a Rising Sun flag or other garment on which words of congratulations were written. Some canines bound for military duty were first consecrated at shrines and temples, such as the Sensōji (Asakusa Kannon) Temple in Tokyo.[90] A dog's departure became a celebratory event, at least for some people. Sawabe Shōzō (1936–), son of the owner of the Mikado Kennel, recalls as a youngster marching from the family home and business in Nihonbashi to nearby Tokyo station to send off his favorite shepherd dog during the final years of the war. As he walked, Sawabe remembers crying while he, his family, and neighbors sang the 1937 hit song, *Roei no uta* (Bivouac ballad). The song, among the winners of a public contest for army battle anthems sponsored by the Osaka *Mainichi* and Tokyo *Nichinichi* newspapers after the outbreak of the China War (Second Sino-Japanese War) in July 1937, was regularly sung on the occasion to human soldiers

28. Dogs marching in an air-defense preparedness parade in June 1941. Used with permission of Mainichi Photo Bank.

departing for the front, and its inclusion on a phonograph of these ballads helped sell more than six hundred thousand records in the first six months of the album's release. Sawabe could still recite the lyrics verbatim nearly seventy years later:

> Valiantly promising, "We shall triumph,"
> We departed from our country,
> We can't die unless we do so heroically,
> Each time the bugle sounds to charge,
> In my mind's eye the flag is waving. [91]

For many people, contributing a dog became an opportunity to affirm their support for the war and express their willingness to sacrifice themselves heroically for the emperor and empire in mortal conflict.

Often participation did not end with farewell. Many military organizations, both Allied and Axis, made efforts to notify contributors about the status of their dogs without revealing any strategic secrets such as the location of units. The British army and Royal Air Force sent former dog owners letters and certificates awarded to dogs, such as Don, a shepherd dog, "For Loyal and Faithful Service...to Britain and all the free peoples of the World in time of War."[92] In Japan, government and private groups encouraged people to maintain a connection with their dogs. The Imperial Military Dog Association admonished former dog keepers to correspond with the soldier in charge of their former dog in the field, and to send items such as food and clothing to their dog and its handler. In turn, soldiers sometimes responded, keeping onetime owners posted about a dog's performance and health. Private and government organizations also organized ceremonies at public venues like the Ueno Zoological Gardens in order to honor canines and other animals who had departed, whether for the front or from this world.[93] And, at times, the army would send former owners mementos, such as the collar, after a military dog's "glorious" demise on the battlefield.

As with other military-dog rhetoric, children were often the focus of these campaigns. As the historian William M. Tuttle Jr. has described in the context of wartime America, this was just one of many ways that adults rallied youngsters to participate in the war effort.[94] Newspaper photographs and publicity shoots in Japan and other combatant countries frequently depicted youngsters watching military-dog demonstrations, raising money to support canine corps, or sending dogs off to the front.[95] Schools and dog-recruitment agencies joined together to appeal to children for more dogs. One such event was held at P.S. 66 in New York City, where at a school assembly a ten-year-old girl presented "Skippy," a shepherd-collie mix, to the president of Dogs for Defense while the rest of the student body sang "The K-9 Corps" march.[96] In many countries, juvenile literature—such as Helen Orr Watson's *Trooper, U.S. Army Dog*—played on the theme of the emotional struggle faced by youngsters in deciding to donate their prized companion.[97] Often these were melancholy tales; some were upbeat to the point of absurdity. One Japanese story of the latter variety appeared in April 1932, soon after the Manchurian Incident. It told of Masao's dog, Jonī (Johnny), who became despondent after Teru, a dog kept by Masao's friend Ichirō, was conscripted. Concerned about the dog's depression and urged on by his son, Masao's father wrote a letter to the authorities requesting that Jonī be called up as soon as possible. Soon a draft notice arrived and the family and Jonī were overjoyed.[98] In this way, dogs—both real and imagined—led many young men into the military.

During the early years of Japan's war effort, much of this rhetoric was aimed primarily at boys, but as time passed it appeared to be increasingly directed at girls. Females, the discourse seemed to teach, should tenderly raise and send army dogs off to war, who, regardless of their actual biological sex, were almost inevitably imagined as masculine. This action was analogous to, and preparatory for, sending males off to war. One motion picture, *Sensen ni hoeyu* (Barks at the battlefront), highlighted this message. Independently produced by the Tōyō movie studio in 1936, the film was one of many works inspired by the story of Kongō and Nachi.[99] Although no copies of the film appear to have survived the war, its basic plot can be surmised from contemporary reviews. One critic praised its producers for the movie's realistic use of dogs, which included "moving, tear-jerking scenes" of dogs being hit by gunfire.[100] The film told of a teenage girl of a well-to-do family and her dog Esu (Ace). At the beginning of the picture, the family's shepherd dog delivers a new litter and the girl declares that she will present "our emperor's army" with the best dogs as soon as they have been weaned. "Ah," her friend exclaims, "a dog soldier? Oh, how handsome! Our baby brother is going to be a

29. A young military German shepherd jumping over a soldier's arm as children and others look on, 1934. Used with permission of Mainichi Photo Bank.

hero on the battlefield." Esu is sent to Manchuria where he teams with a female shepherd dog, Doru (Doll), to form a two-gender pair. Together, they apprehend an enemy spy, with no human intervention until after the capture. At the end of the most detailed review, Esu and Doru depart for the front, presumably to become heroic martyrs—like Kongō and Nachi—in a blaze of gunfire.[101]

Who knows how the film was received, but as life appeared to imitate art a few years later, it seems clear that it had an audience and some influence. In 1939, three years after the motion picture's release, the *Tōkyō shinbun* daily newspaper featured the "beautiful story of a silent partisan and a young lady."[102] The latter was Teshima Tamie, a student at a higher girls' school and a member of a wealthy family residing in the upscale Meguro neighborhood of the city. The former was Aren Homare, her shepherd dog. In August 1938, Aren, as Teshima wrote in an enthusiast newsletter, "left my small loving hand for the large loving hand of the military," specifically the 14th Division based in Manchuria.[103] A photograph, one of a number preserved by Teshima, taken in front of her elegant home on the morning of Aren's departure shows Tamie with her mother and two younger brothers, dressed in formal attire and holding two celebratory banners, on each side of the dog. Aren, who has a Rising Sun flag hanging from her neck, is sitting on her

30. A photograph from the Imperial Military Dog Association's monthly magazine, *Gun'yōken* (Military dogs), of a girl in the Asakusa neighborhood soliciting contributions on behalf of the Tokyo Military Dog Training Research Group for dogs departing for the front, July 1938.

hind legs and looking directly at the photographer, presumably Tamie's father, who trained her. Aren's posture and the fact that she appears to be not wearing a leash indicate that she is conforming to the training she received and comfortable with the situation, though she likely does not understand what it is leading to and what the implications may be. These are conjectures, but they are not any more tenuous than assumptions one might make about humans based on textual evidence. The photographic evidence allows Aren a way to "speak," though still somewhat obliquely and nevertheless fleetingly. The lack of any photos of Aren in

31. Teshima Tamie, second from right, with Aren Homare and her two brothers and mother standing in front of the family's home on the day that they sent off Aren to the 14th Division based in Manchuria, August 1938. Used with permission of Yasukuni Shrine.

Manchuria completely silence her and leave her history to be entirely crafted and told by people, however they please.

Unlike the fictional Esu, Aren's demise at the front was due to the disease filariasis, but, according to the *Tōkyō shinbun*, her death was still heroic. The article quoted Teshima as stating, "As a woman, I cannot stand on the frontline, so I asked Aren to go fight for me."[104] In this manner, Teshima echoed the rhetoric of her prescribed gender role: it was her duty to send family members, whether a dog or male relative, to war in her place. Teshima pasted newspaper advertisements for the movie *Sensen ni hoeyu* in an album, so the movie likely contributed in some way to her determination to give the dog to the military. Her father's active membership in the Tokyo Branch of the Imperial Military Dog Association was also certainly a factor in her fulfilling this expectation.

The prescribed duty of dispatching dogs to war, though, reached a far wider audience than daughters of wealthy dog fanciers. Authors of children's books and classroom teachers exhorted youngsters to send their dogs off to become the next Kongō and Nachi and urged them to become pen pals with the soldiers who worked with their dogs. Furthermore, probably millions of primary school children intoned a story and song describing these actions from 1942 onward.

"Gunken Tone" (Tone, the army dog), a story in the national language textbook for fifth-year primary school students, told of Fumiko, a young girl who received a shepherd puppy from her neighbors. The Ministry of Education's official teacher's guide declared that the purpose of the story was "especially to connect these silent warriors to the lives of children."[105] The little puppy's parents were both military dogs, and Fumiko hoped that the little canine would become one, too. Accordingly, she took great care to ensure that his body would be strong and healthy and taught him to be obedient. She named the pup Tone, after a powerful river near her grandfather's house in central Honshu. Soon Tone had become the largest canine in the neighborhood, so imposing that passersby crossed over to the other side of the road when he approached. The night before contributing Tone, Fumiko made him a large meal, and the next day she sent him off with a small Rising Sun flag hanging from his neck. Soon Tone was in northern China. A soldier kept Fumiko informed of his superb performance as a tracker, sentry, and messenger. One day, he reported, the troops faced an overwhelming enemy and Tone had to deliver a message to ensure the success of a counterattack. He accomplished the mission through a torrent of bullets, but he was wounded. The soldier went to his rescue despite a relentless barrage of gunfire. The attack was successful and Tone, who had survived, the soldier wrote, was sure to receive the army's commendation for valiant animals, the honor inspired by Kongō and Nachi. As she read the note, Fumiko burst into tears of joy at Tone's bravery.[106]

After reading this story, children sang the accompanying song:

> At the order to move, you dash forward.
> Beloved army dog, you dash forward.
> Rat-a-tat-tat, rat-a-tat-tat,
> Bang, bang, in a hail of bullets.
> Shoot that dog! Fire away!
> Don't miss! Don't miss! Fire away!
> Rat-a-tat-tat, rat-a-tat-tat,
> Bang, bang, the enemy's bullets.
> Attaboy, attaboy, Tone, come, come.
> Come to me, Come to me. Tone, come, come.
> Rat-a-tat-tat, rat-a-tat-tat.
> Bang, bang, in a hail of bullets.[107]

What did children imagine as they read this tale and chanted these lyrics? Other than the appearance of Tone on children's kimono patterns and later statements that the ditty was popular among youngsters at the time, it is difficult to know.[108] By 1942 most families no longer had a canine worthy to become an army dog—if they ever did. Fortunately, the war ended within a few years, though it did so only after often indiscriminate U.S. bombing of civilian areas and disease brought on by malnutrition took many lives—young and old. Primary school students, however, had no idea when and how the war would end, and they were still being told that victory was attainable. "Tone, the Army Dog," both in prose and in verse, continued to conjure up visions of human and canine battlefield heroism for boys and domestic sacrifice for girls.

In such ways, real dogs like Aren and imagined ones like Tone served to both physically and metaphorical connect the home front to the battlefront. In this context, too, the actual and figurative deployment of canines was mutually reinforcing. Though such actions and rhetoric may seem fairly benign, the results for people and dogs, as they mobilized each other for war, were devastating.

"Dying Like a Dog"

In Japan and elsewhere, spokespersons for the military and for dog-enthusiast groups couched their appeals for dogs in the language of sacrifice. They told people that canines would fulfill essential roles in the defense of the nation and empire. Dogs were hailed as exemplary warriors who (usually) silently and obediently carried out orders and loyally and bravely protected their masters. Dog keepers understood their canines might perish while in the army's employ and, even if they did not, that their dogs would probably not return home.[109] Perhaps giving up the family pet prepared people to endure greater losses.

The majority of dog keepers in combatant countries, however, did not own dogs suitable for army service. In the United States in the early 1940s, for example, it was said that only 10 percent of the country's approximately twenty million dogs were big enough—at least twenty inches tall or more at the shoulder—for war duty. Militaries and dog-fancying organizations found ways, nevertheless, for these animals and their owners to contribute to the war effort—to "do their bit." In the United States, for example, the owner of a prize-winning show dog came up with a clever scheme to enlist all canines barred from service because of size to do their part by raising funds to defray the administrative costs of Dogs for Defense. A *Newsweek* reporter concisely summed up the program, which was said to be inspired by President Roosevelt's undersized dog Fala: "It works via the master's pocketbook." Organizers encouraged dog keepers to enroll their animals in a "civilian canine corps," with the size of the owner's financial contribution determining the dog's rank. At the low end, a dollar could make Rover a private or seaman. For a more generous donation of one hundred dollars, Fido would be designated a general or admiral. In return, the keeper received a certificate and the dog a signature paw print on a celluloid collar tag.[110] Organizers enlisted youth groups, including Girl Scout troops, to enroll dogs in the fund. The activities of one such thirteen-year-old Manhattan girl and the language used to describe her and her dog closely resembled that used to characterize Teshima Tamie and her shepherd Aren. In July 1943, the *New York Times* reported that Gwen Elder had enrolled her fox terrier, Sandy, in the navy because her father was connected with the merchant marine. "Actually Sandy is too small to go on active duty," the piece continued, "but the money he pays to enroll will be used to train larger dogs as regular Army and Navy sentries.... Gwen ... is engaging in one of the many Girl Scout activities, which include nurse's aid and salvage work, making dolls for nurseries and helping out on floating hospitals for underprivileged children."[111] As did Teshima and Aren, Gwen and Sandy performed roles deemed appropriate for their gender and size.

In Japan, as the country's strategic fortunes and resources deteriorated, government leaders asked keepers of small dogs to make a greater sacrifice. Beginning as early as 1940, and reaching a nation and empirewide scope by mid-1944, officials of the Ministry of Welfare and (from 1943) the Ministry of Munitions urged imperial subjects to offer up all dogs for the war effort. The campaign, which employed much the same language as the earlier (and ongoing) effort to gather canines suitable to become army dogs, used local government and neighborhood associations (tonarigumi) to spread the message and exert pressure on every household to comply. A tonarigumi notice in the Tokyo suburb of Hachiōji in late 1944, for example, urged people in its opening sentence to "form special canine-attack corps—great loyal dogs that will charge into the bodies of the enemy—so that we can triumph. Dogs will fulfill a wonderful role as valuable weapons in the decisive battle."[112] Such rhetoric was, of course, probably largely figurative. Lapdogs and other small canines were not likely going to become vicious army attack dogs. Instead, small dogs were to be put to death and their body parts would be exploited in various ways by the military. In essence, the authorities deployed the sacrifice of dogs as a model for people to emulate. In the months that followed, government, military, and local leaders began to organize people, such as females, young children, and the elderly who had been considered physically unfit for regular military service, into special human-attack corps to bravely repel the American foe in the war's ultimate showdown.

Government leaders did present, or at least raise, some practical reasons for the drive to enlist all canines—whatever their size—for the defense of the nation. First, proponents of the idea regarded dogs as needlessly devouring food that was better consumed by more useful beasts such as farm animals, and saw canines themselves as an object of human consumption. Similar concerns arose in Britain. In 1940 Parliament passed the Waste of Food Order, requiring pet owners to feed their animals only food that was abundant, grown in the United Kingdom, or not edible for humans.[113] During a February 1940 Japanese Diet session, lower-house member Kita Reikichi suggested to Army Minister Hata Shunroku (1879–1962) that the government should round up and slaughter all canines—except those suitable as military dogs—as well as felines, in order to increase the amount of fodder for livestock and poultry. Hata replied that he recognized that the supply of feed was a serious problem, but he expressed concerns about alienating canine lovers on whom the military relied for army dogs.[114] Such anxieties, in part, may have discouraged government bureaucrats from launching an extensive campaign to eliminate household pets until 1944. It did not prevent them, however, from attempting to persuade people to dispose of their dogs or, at least, prevent their increase. One such call came in the form of a letter from a Ministry of Welfare technician named Ikeda to the *Yomiuri* newspaper, published on 27 March 1941. Ikeda applied his ministry's campaign to encourage people to have more children to canine reproduction, but in negative terms: "Households who do not desire to be fruitful and multiply (*umeyo fuyaseyo*) should spay the female dog as estrus is approaching." In addition, citing Germany as a positive example, Ikeda suggested that people should consider eating canine venison and overcome "traditions that until now have made us think we could not possibly eat dogs."[115] Although Ikeda was probably not aware of it, the so-called traditions he spoke of were relatively recent and invented. As historians and archeologists have shown, many people on the Japanese archipelago, including and perhaps especially social elites such as samurai, regularly consumed dog meat well into the Tokugawa period.[116] Since then, smaller segments of the population, particularly those who could not afford an alternative source of protein or who possessed a culinary canine culture, such as *burakumin* outcastes and migrant Koreans, continued to eat dogs. Police officials further encouraged the dietary intake of canine flesh by authorizing the sale of dog, as well as frog, meat the following month in April 1941.[117] Although pointing out the nutritional value of canine *viande* probably never became a persuasive tool to justify the elimination of pet dogs, during the final years of the war an increasing number of people may have, consciously and unknowingly, been partaking of dog, be they donated household pets or stray, feral, and wild canines.

Officials more forcefully asserted a second rationale for people to dispense with their pet dogs. The 1944 Hachiōji circular—after calling on people to contribute dogs for the defense of the nation—immediately added, "and [donations] will aid in preventing hydrophobia." The flyer and other official voices portrayed the threat posed by the disease in the most alarming terms. The reverse side of the notice included two lengthy paragraphs describing the horrors of the disease, which it erroneously claimed killed 100 percent of those bitten.[118] According to government figures, rabies spiked during the early 1940s, and more than seven hundred rabid dogs were eliminated nationwide in 1944.[119] These numbers, though, are suspect. A related rationale given for donating dogs—a shortage of veterinarians (because of conscription)—provides one reason to doubt the statistics. While a scarcity of animal doctors may have led to an increase in rabies due to decreased preventative care, having fewer vets probably led local officials to simply eliminate stray dogs and claim the dead animals were hydrophobic without performing a proper evaluation. More canines probably did roam the streets and outskirts of cities as it became difficult for people to find leftovers for their pets and as bombing destroyed residential neighborhoods. People were led to believe that aerial attacks drove canines into a crazed frenzy, as was reported after a bombing raid on the southwestern industrial city of Kitakyūshū in mid-1944.[120] In any case, government authorities seemed to heighten and capitalize on anxieties about rabid canines to impress on people that if they did not turn in their dogs, their trusted companions might turn on them.

A third rationale was the idea that pets were an unnecessary luxury for a population at war. This sentiment was common in all combatant countries and may explain, in part, the dog-show origins of Dogs for Defense in the United States. Breeders and fanciers of show dogs surely did not want their hobby and animals to be regarded as frivolous and irrelevant. In Japan, disapproval of any extravagance was voiced both officially through government policy and socially in the form of neighborhood gossip. Because most of the population had only secured the financial means to acquire and maintain a pet dog in the last few decades, if at all, a strong association between dog keeping and wealth lingered. As in the late nineteenth century and as recently as during rabies outbreaks a decade earlier, government officials used positive and negative financial incentives to encourage dog keepers to discard their pets. In April 1941, Tokyo prefectural bureaucrats substantially raised the annual tax levied on dogs to 4.84 yen. As well, from 1933 until 1944 they increased the amount paid for a dog donated for disposal from 40 *sen* (one-hundredth of a yen) to 3 yen. Tokyo administrators also instituted a ban on the walking of dogs and the movement of canines in and out of the city in May 1944.[121] Officials justified the regulation as necessary to prevent the spread of hydrophobia, but a corollary message was that this was no time for people to be out strolling with a dog. Many people recall experiencing societal pressure from nearby residents to dispose of their dogs, before and after the commencement of the dog-donation drives directed by neighborhood associations.[122]

A final rationale for the disposal of household pets was that their bodies would be used to physically bolster the military effort. In his 1940 statement, Diet member Kita suggested that dogs and cats might fulfill the armed forces demand for leather. Other campaign advocates claimed that the fur of animals could be used to make warm clothing for soldiers fighting in northern China and headgear for pilots and sailors. During both world wars, the British Dogs' Wool Association appealed to the public to send them canine fur in order to make military clothes and fill pillows "for the supply of Hospital wool for comforts for the Sick and Wounded."[123] Unlike in Japan, however, the association only asked people to sacrifice their dog's hair not their pet's lives. Japanese organizers even claimed canine bodily fluids would be used as machine oil.

In the face of such talk, canine clubs and individual dog keepers offered little opposition. In the early 1940s, some veterinary groups and the Humane Society voiced concerns about the regulations, but the possibility of a broad, unified resistance quickly dissipated after government authorities assured the leaders of the major dog-fancying groups, such as the Society for the Preservation of the Japanese Dog and the Imperial Military Dog Association, that the dogs they represented were not threatened. Officials exempted purebred "Japanese" dogs, canines fit for military or police use, and those used for hunting for sustenance.[124] No organization represented the vast majority of small, so-called worthless household pets. A few small breeds, such as the *chin*, once regarded overseas as representative of Japan but rejected by the Society for the Preservation of the Japanese Dog as not genuinely "Japanese," almost entirely disappeared during the war and were only revived on the archipelago by importing dogs from the United States in the early postwar years.

Tens and perhaps hundreds of thousands of people on the home islands and throughout the Japanese empire answered the official and private appeals to hand over their canines "for the sake of the nation." As early as 1943, the liberal journalist-critic Kiyosawa Kiyoshi (1890–1945) noted in his secret diary that "this spring in Minami-Azumi [in Nagano Prefecture], they killed all the dogs and presented the hides to the army."[125] Nakashima Satoru, who participated in the drive as a young veterinarian, estimated that during the height of the campaign in Kanagawa from 20 July to 10 August 1944 as many as seventeen thousand dogs were donated in that prefecture alone. He recalls seeing one man who, after accepting the token compensation for his donated dog, ran to a nearby butcher with the money and returned with a final meal for the doomed animal.[126] As with canines bound for military service, some people sent off their dogs with celebratory gestures, clothing them in a Rising Sun flag or some other item. Parents and sometimes children escorted their dogs to the appointed location. While the campaign did not seem to specifically target youngsters, children frequently were the primary caretakers or had the closest relationship with household pets. They were enlisted in other ways as well. During the early 1940s, teachers helped students convert small animal enclosures housing rabbits and fowl established at many primary schools into mini meat, fur, and down production facilities.[127]

Some dog keepers refused to part with their animals. Those with the means or connections to do so moved them inside or sent them to live with landowners to avoid attracting the notice of neighbors and local officials. Was this a political move, a sign of disloyalty? Or were such people simply wealthy, well-connected, or so attached to their dog(s) that they were willing to defy the authorities and neighborhood pressure? Turning over a dog cannot necessarily be read as a sign of loyalty. Rather in the face of official and societal coercion and without the means to feed them many people probably had little choice but to submit.

A frequent expression common to both campaigns to solicit canines to become military dogs or to be sacrificed for their fur, meat, body fluids, or simply to get rid of them was *inujini*, literally a "dog's death." In a different context, soldiers and civilians used the word far more often. The connotation was not positive. To die like a dog meant to throw away one's life for no purpose. It was a fate that soldiers, and other people, wanted to avoid, for themselves and for their dogs. The young Teshima Tamie, for example, wrote after her dog's death due to illness in Manchuria that if he had not joined the army but had died at home of natural causes that his passing would have been ignoble *inujini*.[128] Likewise, authorities promised that dogs donated for disposal—whether strays or pets—would not face a dog's death because they would be dying gloriously for the nation. As the Hachiōji notice put it, dogs would become "valuable weapons in the decisive battle" with the enemy. In another Tokyo neighborhood, sloganeers urged people to sacrifice their dogs "for the sake of humanity."[129] But humanity—the Japanese as a nation—was soon asked to ready itself to die in mass. In preparation for the decisive battle, government and military leaders urged people to loyally defend their homeland as the way to avoid a "dog's death," though not death itself. In this manner, dogs were mobilized both practically and rhetorically as models for people of how to offer up their lives in the culmination of an indoctrination process that sociologist Kazuko Tsurumi has aptly called "socialization for death."[130]

Although the remains of some canines were fashioned into warm clothing for soldiers or consumed as meat, it is likely that authorities allowed the corpses of many donated dogs and other animals to go to waste. Officials probably found it to be a logistical impossibility to convert the innumerable animal bodies into clothing and food, if they ever intended to faithfully fulfill that promise. Many corpses likely just rotted in warehouses or were quietly dumped in remote locations. In a semiautobiographical novel based on his childhood experiences growing up in rural Shikoku during the war, Ōe Kenzaburō (1935–), who was awarded the Nobel Prize for Literature in 1994, described how his fellow villagers willingly gave up all of their dogs to a dog killer who came to requisition their pelts for military use, only to later find the skins abandoned on the outskirts of the village.[131] Another man recalled as a boy coming upon a huge heap of reeking carcasses in the mountains outside of Tokyo during the final year of the war. Only on hearing about the donation drive years later did he realize what they were.[132] Whether at home or at the battlefront, many canines, not to mention humans, died a dog's death. Their rapidly decomposing carcasses were dogs' only—though ephemeral—way for them to testify of their fate.

Dogged Memories

The history of dogs and warfare illustrates several strands of interactions among humans, dogs, military institutions, and the wartime rhetoric of mobilization and sacrifice for the nation-state. In Japan, the United States, Germany, and elsewhere, government, military, and private officials deployed dogs with the intent and the result of rallying people for total war. Indeed, though it is difficult to measure, much less compare, such phenomena, the metaphorical mobilization of dogs and other animals probably surpassed their military value.

Since the Second World War, military dogs have lost much of their metaphorical resonance, if not their tactical value. This decline in symbolic power has been directly linked to changes in actual practices. While militaries continued their employment of dogs, they generally established direct contracts with large kennels to ensure a steady and reliable supply of canines. This shift effectively eliminated the need to rely on average citizens for dogs. An increasing number of people during the latter half of the twentieth century, moreover, have become generally more suspicious of the nation-state and jingoism, and less forgiving of some forms of anthropomorphism. More recent discussions of military dogs, at least in the United States—one of the few countries to have repeatedly gone to war since 1945—have been framed either by concerns of dog lovers and animal rights activists about the military's alleged inhumane treatment and disposal of canines after their practical usefulness had been exhausted, or by efforts of some veterans groups to create memorials honoring army dogs.

In Japan, it is almost exclusively in the realm of war memory that canines continue to be deployed. Because Japan's postwar military, commonly known as the Self-Defense Force, has only been deployed overseas in an extremely limited fashion because of strict constitutional constraints, its use of dogs has never been an issue.[133] As might be expected, both the Left and the Right invoked canine examples from the Asia-Pacific War to suit their objectives. Some pacifists focused on the government effort to encourage people to contribute their small "useless" dogs during the final years of the conflict. Most prominently, during the 1980s, activists published two children's books—a nonfiction account and a piece of historical fiction—as well as an essay in the leftist monthly *Sekai* about the "useless-dog" collection campaign.[134] Each of these accounts presented these canines as the ultimate martyrs in a nation of victims abused by a military regime. In short, dogs were in part standing in for people.

Those on the conservative side of the political spectrum prefer to remember other canines who died in the conflict—those who served as military dogs. The most conspicuous example of this memory production is the Army Dog Memorial Statue (Gunken irei zō) erected on the grounds of Yasukuni Shrine in 1993. (See color plate 8.) Located in central Tokyo, the Shinto shrine is dedicated to Japanese war dead, including soldiers convicted of wartime crimes, and visits to the site by top politicians have sparked considerable domestic and international debate about how Japanese view the past. On 20 March, Animal Welfare Day, the shrine association and a major army veterans group, Kaikōsha, dedicated the statue, which, according to its plaque, honors

> military dogs—which were most often shepherds—who served with our officers and soldiers as loyal comrades in arms fighting on the front lines from the outbreak of the Manchurian Incident in September of the sixth year of Shōwa (1931) until the close of the Greater East Asia War [Pacific War] in August of the twentieth year of the said imperial era. Many of them succumbed to enemy bullets or died of illness, and not a single one returned to its homeland even if it was alive at the termination of hostilities.[135]

Although the statue, which was sculpted by war veteran Ichihashi Toshio (1919–2005), is not a duplicate of the one that honored Kongō and Nachi in Zushi, there are several links between it and the bronze that memorialized the canine heroes of the Manchurian Incident. The shrine's Yūshūkan Military and War Memorial Museum, which stands in front of the statue, proudly houses one of the honorific collars presented to Kongō and Nachi and a miniature replica of the Zushi bronze, which like the original Hachikō statue was melted down during the final years of the war.

If the great movie director Akira Kurosawa (1910–98) is any measure of national memory, the war, in the guise of a military dog, still haunts the dreams of many Japanese. In his film, *Yume (Dreams)*, released forty-five years after the war's end in 1990 and near the end of his life, Kurosawa, who had assisted Yamamoto Kajirō with his 1941 film about military horses (mentioned at the beginning of the chapter), depicted eight dreams based on his own. In the fourth segment, an eighteen-minute nightmare, an army officer, who looks to be around forty, is returning home after being held as a prisoner of war. He is shown walking along a deserted road at dusk and coming upon a dark concrete tunnel. Suddenly a vicious, snarling military German shepherd dog, carrying mortars on its back, rushes out of the tunnel, threatening the officer. Clearly frightened, the officer manages to edge away from the dog and completes what seems like an endless walk through the nearly pitch-black passageway into the dim light at the other end. He finds, however, that he has not escaped the past, as he is followed out of the tunnel by something even more ominous: the embodied ghost of one of his men, Private Noguchi, his face and hands a pale blue, indicating he is dead. The soldier appears not to realize, or to not want to admit, that he is dead, but the officer convinces him, telling him how he died in his arms, and reluctantly Noguchi stumbles back into the tunnel. Almost immediately, though, the commander's entire 3rd Platoon marches out to report that they are "returning to base" with "no casualties." They too are dead, their skin pale blue. The commander tells them the platoon was "annihilated" and expresses his guilt for sending them to die and that he alone has survived. He wishes that he "could place all responsibility on the stupidity of war" but admits his own "thoughtlessness" and "misconduct." "They may call you 'heroes,'" he continues, "but you died like dogs" (*Senshi towa ie, demo inujini da*). He pleads for them to "Go back and rest in peace" and orders them to "About face!" and "Forward march!" back into the tunnel. As they do, he salutes them but then collapses to his knees, perhaps both from grief as well as from relief. But the latter is short-lived as once again the military dog emerges from the tunnel, barking even more fiercely and snapping at him as the scene comes to an end. For Kurosawa's generation, at least, there seems to be no end to the dogged memories of war.

In Japan's former colonial and wartime possessions, the role of dogs has not been forgotten either. As in other postcolonial regions in Asia and Africa, some people in Taiwan, China, and Korea associate shepherd dogs with Japan's oppressive imperial rule and wartime aggression. Many older Koreans despise "German" shepherds as a symbol of Japan's four-decade colonization of the peninsula. In Taiwan, Japanese have at times been collectively referred to as "dogs." Islanders described the departure of their longtime colonial rulers and the arrival of Chinese Nationalists from the mainland in 1945 as "the dogs go and the pigs come" (*Gou tui zhu lai*).[136] The saying captured the ambiguous perception that Japanese imperialists were noisy and nosy but provided order and stability like guard dogs, and reflected the image of Japanese authorities and settlers accompanied by such canines.

The view from mainland China is not so ambiguous. Several Chinese films produced during the 1960s identify Japanese soldiers with shepherd dogs and imply that Japanese officers tried to compensate for their small stature with the massive animals.[137] More recent films, such as director Ang Lee's *Lust, Caution* (2007), also consciously associate military and guard dogs with the Japanese as well as Chinese collaborators. Elsewhere, these associations are on display. The Museum of Japanese Occupation of Manchuria (Dongbei lunxian shi chenlieguan) in Changchun and the September 18 Incident Historical Museum ("Jiu yiba" lishi bowuguan) in Mukden, which commemorate the Manchurian Incident, prominently exhibit a number of large statues of fierce-looking Japanese army dogs, who were said to eat the intestines of their Chinese victims. Although one might question the intent of such museums, which appeared across China during the 1990s in what seemed to be a staged government effort to stir up anti-Japanese sentiment and Chinese nationalism—and distract the population from discontent with growing economic disparities and the Communist Party's monopoly on power—the action depicted has a historical basis. Furthermore, because of traditional Han Chinese and more recent Communist scorn for dogs and dog keeping, the portrayal of Japanese Imperial Army soldiers using army dogs has added rhetorical weight and emphasizes the supposed barbaric, doggish character of Japanese. An even deeper religious and cultural dislike for canines exists among Arab Muslims, so that the use of military dogs in searches of homes and in the torture of prisoners by U.S. troops at the Abu Ghraib prison during the occupation of Iraq, which began in 2003, has become and will likely long be a symbol of U.S. imperial excesses in the early twenty-first century.

While dogs may be denigrated for cultural reasons in some areas and associated with imperial wrongs, they often evoke a more positive image of economic prosperity throughout much of the world. This is true in places like China and sometimes even the Middle East. Purebred dogs and the modes of dog keeping that spread across the globe with Western expansion in the mid-nineteenth century continued to envelope the world in the latter half of the twentieth century, and they often symbolize a level of financial well-being that many people dream of emulating. It is to the dog's status as a metaphor of consumption and cultural capital, as highlighted by more recent history—both in and beyond Japan—that we turn to next.

32. A bronze diorama showing Japanese soldiers and army dogs invading Chinese territory during the Manchurian Incident in September 1931. Museum of Japanese Occupation of Manchuria (Dongbei lunxian shi chenlie guan) in Changchun, 2007. Photograph by Thomas David DuBois and used with his permission.

5

A DOG'S WORLD

THE COMMODIFICATION OF CONTEMPORARY DOG KEEPING

In the spring of 1946, just over a half a year after the Japanese government's surrender brought an end to the Second World War, the former army-dog specialist and owner of the Mikado Kennel, Sawabe Kenjirō, reopened his shop across the street from the Takashimaya department store in the downtown Tokyo neighborhood of Nihonbashi. The U.S. firebombing of 9 March 1945, which claimed approximately 120,000 lives and 23,000 homes, destroyed Sawabe's shop and two wings of the Takashimaya store. Six months later, when the American occupiers arrived, they requisitioned what remained of the main Takashimaya building for office space. On resurrecting his shop, Sawabe changed its name from the Mikado, which had honored the emperor, to the Washington Dog Shop (Washinton inuten), an appellation that deferred to Japan's new imperial rulers. The switch not only seemed like the neighborly thing to do, it proved to be a wise business decision, too, as many of Sawabe's early customers were American soldiers and their families.

The Sawabe family store conducted business at this location for the next six decades, although it was soon dwarfed by Takashimaya, which was returned by occupation authorities to its owners in the late 1940s and rebuilt in 1952. During the Mikado's first decade in business, Sawabe catered to Tokyo's wealthy citizens until wartime opportunities prompted him to focus on supplying the military with dogs. For the first few decades after the war, the Washington Dog Shop primarily served wealthy Japanese, who usually purchased Western dogs, and Americans and other foreigners, who often bought Japanese breeds. More recently, the extended Sawabe family expanded their business ventures beyond the well-placed shop, opening branches inside department stores, a veterinary office, and a pet hotel to sell puppies and an array of canine-related goods and services to a far greater number of dog keepers.

The experience of the Sawabe family business highlights several of the principal trends of dog keeping in Japan since the end of the Second World War, trends it has shared with many countries, including the United States and western European nations, but also with many non-Western industrialized societies. These developments are at least threefold. First, thanks in large part to the powerful influence of postwar American culture, the breeds and dog-keeping practices spread by nineteenth-century canine imperialism proliferated with increasing acceleration during the second half of the twentieth century. As a result, dogs and dog keeping exhibit a progressively more homogenous appearance throughout the world. Even when native dogs, such as the Japanese Akita, were able to achieve a degree of global recognition and acceptance, they were merely incorporated within a familiar configuration firmly established by earlier canine imperialism. Second, the middle class, rather than just the upper class, became the dominant hegemonic force in spreading cultural mores, including dog-keeping practices in the latter half of the twentieth century. In Japan, as elsewhere, possession of a purebred dog and treating the dog as a pet became a way for a growing number of people to affirm that they had achieved a middle-class level of economic prosperity and were living a modern, "cultured" lifestyle. In part because of this symbolic value, dog keeping spread rapidly as many more people became, in effect, not just keepers but consumers of canines. Third, dogs not only became pets, they were more than ever transformed into products, according to the often cruel logic of consumer capitalism. Ownership of a particular breed of dog at a certain time conferred social capital on owners and signified fashion and sophistication. In the last several decades in Japan, a country where many people think of themselves and just about everyone else as members of the middle class, there is less need to demonstrate that one belongs. Instead, people deploy dogs, as well as other products, to construct self or group identities, and to create new stratifications and distinctions that include and exclude other people within the imagined middle class.

The dog is, of course, not the only animal endowed with symbolic meaning. Humans use numerous other animals to express identity. Dogs, though, are the most widely kept and the most visible. Indeed, in 2006 approximately 13 million dogs resided in nearly 20 percent of all households in Japan, and the numbers were even greater in the United States (around 39%) and the European Union (over 20%).[1] Furthermore, the variation and malleability of dogs' shapes, colors, sizes, and temperaments make them ideal for the exhibition of individual and collective identity. Usually active and social creatures, many dogs demand physical activity, which presents opportunities for keepers to parade their wares, often in the form of walks. As sociologist and critic Thorstein Veblen (1857–1929) pointed out over a century ago, the value of "prevailing styles of pet dogs" is an example of "conspicuous consumption," the term he coined to describe the ways people acquire items to establish their social position.[2] An examination of the practical and figurative value of pet dogs in the late twentieth century shows their significance in the social and cultural landscapes of the contemporary world.

Canine Cultural Imperialism and the Middle-Class Family Dog

Japan emerged from the Second World War a devastated and poverty-stricken country. In addition to the millions of people who died, tens, perhaps hundreds, of thousands of dogs perished either as army dogs or as offerings to the military. During the early months and years of the occupation, many people could barely find sufficient food for themselves, much less for dogs. As during the final years of the war, canines sometimes provided protein for a hungry population. In the subsequent decades, however, many people came to regard a pet dog as an essential part of their lives, a companion for whom they would expend considerable money and emotional investment. What accounted for this change? What motivated people to keep a dog? A liking for dogs, though certainly a factor, does not entirely explain the desire to acquire and maintain a pet dog. No less significantly, dog ownership was associated with economic affluence and an idealized view of the modern middle-class family as portrayed in American popular culture that flooded Japan during this era. These associations undoubtedly contributed to the dramatic rise in dog ownership.

The postwar spread of dog keeping was, of course, grounded in the past. As in the second half of the nineteenth century, many people identified certain dog breeds and modes of dog keeping with financial prosperity in the early twentieth century. Since at least the 1920s and 1930s in Japan, as in the United States and western Europe, dogs were depicted as members of the family (*kazoku no ichiin*), especially nuclear households, and as a supplement to the cultured, modern life. In *Umarete wa mita keredo* (*I Was Born, But...*; 1932), one of the "common man" films of director Ozu Yasujirō (1903–63), a salaried worker and his family are portrayed as having achieved the good life when they move to a new single-family home in the suburbs. Their house is complete with a lawn, a white picket fence, and a bull terrier named Esu (Ace), who has its own wooden doghouse. The family treats Esu, who was likely purchased at a dog shop like the Mikado, as an important part of the household. When the dog falls sick, for example, the father immediately summons a veterinarian to the house to treat its ailment. The film presents an idealized view of a middle-class family that has the economic means to obtain and maintain luxuries such as a pedigreed dog. Associations between economic wealth, the exotic foreign, and purebred Western dogs are also evident in interwar art and literature. An example from the latter is Tanizaki Jun'ichirō's 1928 novel, *Tade kuu mushi* (translated as *Some Prefer Nettles*). The author's status-conscious protagonists own two dogs, a collie named Peony, as well as a greyhound named Lindy (short for Lindbergh), who was purchased in Shanghai. In addition, another character observes that foreign women use dogs as a sort of ornament to enhance their beauty as they stroll in public.[3] Only the most well-to-do people could afford to buy purebred dogs in Shanghai or those offered by the Mikado in prewar days, but the shop's location across the street from Takashimaya was surely designed to whet the appetite of the masses who yearned to secure the kind of economic success pictured in Ozu's film and Tanizaki's novel. Department stores had an even more direct hand in fostering enthusiasm for dogs, as highlighted by the use of their roofs for dog shows from the 1920s.[4] Both department stores and pet shops created a desire for the novel and exotic, if not necessarily for lasting fulfillment.

For at least the first decade after the war, ownership of a dog continued to be strongly associated with the economically wealthy and politically powerful. As was the case with many of its pre-1945 counterparts, the largest dog-fancying group in the postwar period, the Japan Kennel Club (Japan keneru kurabu, JKC), was essentially a rich men's club from the time of its establishment in 1950. Its forerunner, the All Japan Guard Dog Association (Zen Nihon keibi ken kyōkai), was founded the previous year, financed by Sawabe and other businessmen, and counted many of the most influential political and corporate figures of the day among its leaders and members. In fact, the group's first honorary chairmen were Shidehara Kijūrō (1872–1951), who served briefly as prime minister from late 1945 to mid-1946, and Ishibashi Tanzan (1884–1973), finance minister in the next cabinet. Such elite individuals, who could afford to buy and keep a dog in the aftermath of the war, were the kind of people who became the Washington Dog Shop's top Japanese customers.

In addition to owning a dog being a way to exhibit status, the giving of dogs as presents sometimes facilitated the building and maintenance of personal relationships among the political and economic elect. One prominent example was Yoshida Shigeru (1878–1967), who served as prime minister twice, from 1946 to 1947 and again from 1948 to 1954, before assuming the role of elder statesman. Perhaps in part because of his prewar diplomatic experiences overseas in such locations as London, Yoshida was an avid dog lover. When he traveled to San Francisco to sign the treaty that brought an end to the occupation in 1952, Yoshida returned with two cairn terriers, whom he named San Fran and Cisco. The dogs were likely presents from U.S. officials and may have symbolized for Yoshida the concessions he secured under the treaty and the alliance with United States. Japanese journalists, in fact, sometimes referred to the presence of the U.S. military in Japan as the country's "watchdog" (banken), a source of postoccupation protection that allowed Japan to concentrate on economic recovery and development, just as Yoshida desired.[5] Six years later, the former prime minister professed to owning more than twenty dogs at his Ōiso estate, including "German" shepherds and two more cairn terriers, the latter a gift from the Tokyo editor of Reader's Digest.[6] A loyal customer of the Washington Dog Shop, Yoshida sometimes bestowed dogs on other politicians and officials, a practice reminiscent of the exchanges of canines among sixteenth-century warlords, who presented large powerful dogs to fellow warlords to curry favor and solidify alliances. Yoshida reportedly had a habit of beginning telephone conversations with colleagues to whom he had given a dog by inquiring about the animal's health before addressing more serious matters.[7] Dogs, then, operated as a living reminder of patronage.

Other members of the early postwar elite, as well as some members of the middle class, deployed dogs for a more practical use: security. As signified by the name of the All Japan Guard Dog Association, many people valued dogs during the late 1940s and early 1950s for the protection they might provide. Such guard dogs, often chained to a post, were still a fairly common sight outside some rural and suburban homes decades later. As he had during the war, Sawabe trafficked in shepherd dogs and other breeds that could act as sentries, though now their opponent was domestic intruders rather than colonial subjects or enemy soldiers. These dogs were expensive and domestically limited in their supply, however, and during the early postwar years it was still difficult to obtain dogs from overseas. Some people selected "Japanese" breeds or, more often, the spitz, a breed developed in Japan from dogs imported from Canada, the United States, and Manchuria in the 1920s. The spitz exhibited an active nature and shrill bark that enhanced its value as a guard dog, yet it was small enough to dwell indoors.[8] In the following decades, as more people moved into apartment complexes, the spitz's yap became its Achilles paw, and its popularity plummeted until breeders developed dogs with a softer bark or none at all. In the late 1940s and 1950s, however, the spitz dogs' soft, thick, snow-white double coat, and their resemblance to Western breeds, made them appealing to many Japanese. Their relative affordability and availability, compared to "Japanese" and foreign breeds, contributed to their popularity. Indeed, almost three times as many spitzes were registered with the JKC than any other breed in 1955, the first year for which statistics are available.[9]

Most people, however, did not have the means to purchase purebred dogs during the first decades after the war. For many, the only way to acquire a dog was to be given an extra puppy or to adopt a stray wandering the streets. As many elderly Japanese recall today, dogs at that time were an item to receive rather than to purchase. Indeed, children adopting a stray dog against opposition from their mother became a theme in a number of movies in the 1950s and 1960s.[10] Some films, such as *Non-chan kumo ni noru* (Non-chan riding on the clouds), presented a more idyllic picture. Released in 1955, a decade after defeat and the year government officials proclaimed that the Japanese economy had recovered to prewar levels, the film offered an idealized view of a postwar middle-class family living in the suburbs of Tokyo. Its depiction was much like that of *I Was Born, But…* In fact, the name of the family dog was the same, Esu, as was proudly painted on its doghouse.[11] The movie was based on a children's book, first published in 1947, in which the dog is claimed from the streets.[12] The film, however, did not specify how the family acquired the animal. Regardless of the dog's origin, the film seemed to suggest that a home was complete when it included a dog.

Perhaps as important as its prewar roots, dog keeping in the second half of the twentieth century was a reflection of Western and American cultural forces that penetrated Japan and much of the globe. The occupation of Japan by the United States military from September 1945 to April 1952 and the powerful American cultural influences that have pervaded the country ever since reinforced the image of dog keeping as a symbol of a financially secure and cultured life. The domestic habits of U.S. soldiers and their families stationed overseas strengthened the impression that dogs were an important element of American home life. Even stronger and more saturating, the offerings of American popular culture transmitted through a variety of media repeatedly confirmed this vision in Japan and throughout the world. The global sway of U.S. political, military, and economic power contributed to the spread of a sort of canine cultural imperialism that promoted particular dog breeds, dog-keeping practices, and canine-related products and services. Even the name of the premier postwar dog-fancying organization, the Japan Kennel Club (JKC), emulated the American Kennel Club, as well as the (English) Kennel Club. Indeed, throughout the world, the domination of Western breeds in the official twenty-first-century canine cartography is almost absolute.

The appearance of what might be called the "neocolonial" dog did not arrive in Japan immediately, at least not with common occupation personnel. General MacArthur, who oversaw the occupation from September 1945 until April 1951, did not allow U.S. soldiers to bring dogs to Japan until Christmas 1948, when—as a holiday gesture—he reversed the policy. Blackie, a cocker spaniel, however, had slipped into Japan with MacArthur's family in 1946. Japanese were aware of the fondness of MacArthur and many Americans for dogs, and they soon presented him with two "Japanese" breeds—an Akita and a Shiba, who joined Blackie at the family's home in the U.S. embassy compound.[13]

Whether they brought dogs from abroad, received them as presents, or, even more likely, acquired them from local suppliers such as Sawabe, U.S. military families other than MacArthur's, were often imagined as dog keepers by Japanese. One example stands out. In his 1973 novel, *Aoba shigereru* (Thick green leaves), which appears to draw on the author's experiences as a teenager during the occupation, the novelist Inoue Hisashi (1934–2010) describes a high-ranking U.S. officer and his wife who take along an extremely expensive, purebred spitz on a train trip to the countryside. In a scene ripe with irony, a Shiba dog being taken to breed with another Shiba by the story's protagonist Minoru, a young Japanese boy, gets away from him and proceeds to mount the spitz. After the dogs stop mating, the Shiba runs off and Minoru, too, makes a rapid retreat. To his surprise, the local newspaper features the story the next day and reports that the officer's wife reacted cheerfully to her dog's heated encounter with the Shiba, declaring, "If even the dogs of Japan and America are engaging in fraternization, why can't we humans get along, too? Let's nourish mutual goodwill and not lose to the dogs."[14]

Though probably rarely in this manner, U.S. military families in Japan contributed to the vision of the dog as complementing a modern, affluent lifestyle during and for many years after the occupation. U.S. military bases, which were imagined by many people as a model of the "bright life" (*akarui seikatsu*) with their PXes stocked with bountiful material amenities, served not only to communicate the supposed importance of a dog in American life but also as an aqueduct for the transfer of dogs to the local population.[15] The long ocean journey and customs restrictions made it difficult for Americans returning to the United States to take back dogs until commercial air travel become a viable option in the 1960s. Some Americans apparently preferred granting their dogs a "peaceful death" rather than taking the supposed risk of entrusting them with Japanese, but others either gave their animals to Japanese friends or sold them to intermediaries such as Sawabe.

There was one breed, though, some Americans went to great lengths to bring back to the United States: the Akita. Already somewhat famous overseas thanks to Hachikō and Helen Keller, the Akita obtained a broader following in the United States as returning GIs, often flouting Japanese restrictions against the export of a "national treasure," brought the dogs back with them when their tours of Japan ended. The dogs' association as a former enemy did not seem to dampen their appeal. Rather, their purported loyal devotion and reserved dignity, stereotypical qualities Americans strongly identified with Japan, appear to have given them special cachet. By the mid-1950s, American enthusiasts formed several competing kennel clubs dedicated to the breed. In 1956 the AKC admitted the Akita into its "miscellaneous" class and, after the divisions within the enthusiast community were finally resolved, bestowed regular breed status on it in 1973.[16] Ironically, defeat and occupation helped complete the transformation, begun by Japan's early twentieth-century geopolitical rise, of a once maligned native dog into a globally recognized breed. The culmination of the Akita's metamorphosis occurred during the first few decades of the cold war, and the official acceptance of and popular enthusiasm for the dogs mirrored American middlebrow fascination with things Japanese. Akita fanciers in Japan, though, were not thrilled with this development. Reflecting in part entrenched notions of racial and cultural purity, and bolstered by some physical disparities between the two groups of dogs, they have refused to acknowledge that the American Akita is equivalent to the breed recognized in Japan.

Interestingly, the postwar occupation of Germany had similar effects for another canine, the German shepherd. Far more than the Akita, the shepherd was already hugely popular in the United States thanks to the First World War and the popularity of Rin Tin Tin during the interwar years. However, as with the Akita, defeat and occupation provided another boost to the German shepherd in the United States. Many GIs returned with dogs acquired from occupied Germans desperate to feed themselves and their families, and unable to care for their dogs. The breed's close association with Nazi Germany may have helped rather than harmed its popularity. One example is illustrative. In 1951 the *Los Angeles Times* featured a story about an enormous German shepherd who had been obtained from a returning soldier. Its owner, a Mrs. William Kenward—who claimed relation to a sixth-century English king—asserted that the dog, named Baron von Zeiglerhoff, once belonged to Hermann Goering and was later used by the SS as a guard dog at the Bergen-Belsen prisoner-of-war and concentration camp, but that in both instances it had purportedly performed contrary to expectations, even "seeing off" prisoners as they escaped from the camp.[17] Ownership of such a dog, the article implied, conferred on its keepers special status, just as Mrs. Kenward's supposed royal ancestry did. Perhaps inspired by this newspaper story, the popular American TV series *Hogan's Heroes*, which appeared weekly on the CBS network from 1965 to 1971, featured a shepherd guard dog who treated prisoners fiercely when his Luftwaffe master, Colonel Klink, was present, but affectionately licked the face of the French corporal LeBeau and other prisoners when he was not. This behavior was the result of the training the dogs received at the kennel that supplied the dogs for Stalag 13, which was operated by an Allied sympathizer. In this way, the sitcom, like the *L.A. Times* article, reminded viewers of the shepherd breed's relationship to German National Socialism while the relationship is presented in a sanitized manner—as are the Nazis generally—that avoids a serious consideration of the dogs' use and abuse.

The middle-class American way of life as depicted in cartoons, movies, and television imported from the United States to Japan and other cold war allies often portrayed dogs as an essential part of the good life and contributed to the popularity of dog keeping and enthusiasm for particular breeds, especially Western ones. The Bumsteads—Dagwood and Blondie, along with their dog Daisy—provided a glimpse of American family life when the comic strip ran on the pages of the daily *Asahi* newspaper from January 1949 to April 1951. The impact of American-produced movies and television was even greater. After Disney's *Lady and the Tramp* arrived in Japanese theaters in 1955, the cocker spaniel soon surpassed the spitz as the most popular breed in Japan.[18] In the film, distributed locally as *Wanwan monogatari* (A story about dogs), Mutt, the rakish street-smart canine tramp declares, "When a baby moves in, a dog moves out," but the film probably had the opposite effect in real life. The enthusiasm of young children for dogs appearing on movie and television screens likely led many parents to acquire a dog.

The long-running television series *Lassie* produced similar results. KR Television, which became Tokyo Broadcasting Station in 1960, aired the show as *Meiken Rasshī* (The famous dog Lassie) for almost a decade, from 1957 to 1966. It played during prime time, at 6:15 on Sunday evenings. In addition to introducing cold war middle-class American values of honesty, hard work, and family togetherness to Japanese audiences, *Lassie* was responsible for making collies one of the most sought-after breeds in Japan. Although the dog's size did not make the breed particularly suitable for the cramped living conditions of the islands, for five years during the early 1960s the number of collies registered by the JKC trailed only cocker spaniels.[19] *Lassie*'s influence continued long after 1966 through television reruns, broadcasts of movie versions, and a Japanese animated adaptation. The enthusiasm for collies that it generated among youngsters is evident from a 1975 letter to the *Asahi* in which an eight-year-old girl living in Yokohama named Imai Takako exclaimed, "Probably not many dogs are as smart as Lassie, but I want a dog just like Lassie all the same."

Purveyors of canines were quick to take advantage of television and American-permeated popular culture to market their dogs. In the late 1950s, Sawabe and his sons made appearances in numerous television programs, including *Inu no kaikata* (How to raise a dog), a special produced by Nihon Television.[20] In 1959 the Washington Dog Shop teamed with Meiji Seika confectionary company to promote the Milk Chocolate Deluxe candy bar. Meiji executives, anxious to attract the taste buds of youngsters to the Deluxe—made from a recipe licensed from the American chocolate maker Hershey—promised to give away five hundred puppies to people whose names were selected in a lottery among those fortunate enough to find a sticker of a dog on the inside of a Deluxe wrapper. Sawabe's youngest son, Shōzō, who had just completed his veterinary studies at Nihon University, recalls that the promotion made him one of the nation's busiest veterinarians as he rushed about the country administering vaccinations and ensuring the health of the puppies to be given away. Shōzō's support of the Washington Dog Shop did not end there, as the demand for Western dogs continued to climb. While he furthered his education in veterinary medicine at the University of Pennsylvania graduate school and worked at a local clinic from 1960 to 1964, his father instructed him to attend dog shows across the United States to purchase top dogs to send to Japan. Shōzō recalls buying a collie for seven thousand dollars cash at the Westminster Dog Show in New York. The amount, the form of payment, and probably the fact that the buyer was Japanese were enough to land him on the local television news.[21]

The heightened interest in and greater concern for dogs generally in the late 1950s was evidenced by the intense sentiments ignited by the plight of a team of sled dogs abandoned by Japanese scientists in Antarctica in 1958. The expedition to the South Pole, which began in November 1956 and was the first by the country since before the war, generated tremendous television coverage and public curiosity as an important step in restoring Japan's international prestige. But when unanticipated bad weather forced researchers to make an emergency evacuation of their Shōwa base and leave fifteen Sakhalin huskies (*Karafuto-ken*) behind in February 1958, the attention of the media and people shifted completely to the fate of the canines. This shift can in part be explained by images, both print and television, of the dogs before 1958 that heightened public sympathy for the animals. As Jonathan Burt has asserted, greater concern for animals is another by-product of the increasing ubiquity of still and moving photographic images of actual animals in the twentieth century.[22] Attempts in the next weeks to rescue the dogs failed before the change of seasons and formation of impassable ice shelves made the camp inaccessible until summer again arrived in the Southern Hemisphere. Appeals made by concerned citizens to U.S. president Dwight Eisenhower to send in the navy were to no avail. A year later, in January 1959, when researchers returned to the camp, they found to their astonishment that two of the dogs, brothers Jirō (1956–60) and Tarō (1956–70), had somehow survived eleven months on the frigid continent on their own.

Interestingly, the person responsible for popularizing the "Loyal Dog" Hachikō, Saitō Hirokichi, became involved in this canine controversy, too. As president of the Japan Society for the Prevention of Cruelty to Animals, the most powerful animal welfare group in the early postwar years, Saitō once again decided a statue would be an appropriate memorial. He began a fund-raising drive to erect life-size figures of Jirō, Tarō, and their departed canine companions on a thirty-nine by fifteen foot pedestal, which was dedicated as "Nankyoku de hataraita Karafuto-ken no kinenzō" (Memorial statue to the Sakhalin huskies who worked in Antarctica) on 20 September 1959, the first day of Animal Welfare Week. No doubt Saitō drew on his previous experiences with Hachikō: he aimed the campaign for contributions at primary and junior high school children; so-licited Andō Takeshi, the sculptor who had recreated the second statue of the "faithful" dog ten years earlier, to cast the bronzes of the huskies; and secured a prime location for the statues at the base of Tokyo Tower, the world's tallest self-supporting steel structure, a rather tacky—but taller—knockoff of the Eiffel Tower that had been completed the year before.[23] There were other similarities between Hachikō and Jirō and Tarō, who are probably the three most famous dogs in Japan today. In a poll conducted by the national postal service, Jirō and Tarō, along with Hachikō and Norakuro, were chosen by the public as images that best exemplified the twentieth century as it came to a close in 1999.[24] Also, like Hachikō, Jirō and Tarō achieved immortality, thanks to a taxidermic resur-rection. After Jirō died in 1960, undertakers cremated his innards and deposited the ashes in a pet cemetery at the Jindaiji Temple in suburban Tokyo, while spe-cialists preserved his figure and displayed him next to Hachikō at the National Science Museum. His brother, too, is on public display. After living a decade in the botanical gardens of Hokkaido University, Tarō passed away in 1970, and his stuffed body is exhibited in a museum building on the grounds of the arboretum. Like Laika (ca. 1953–57), a mixed-breed dog who became the first mammal to orbit Earth on a Soviet spaceship in 1957, Tarō and Jirō fulfilled an emerging he-roic role for dogs in the realm of science.[25] Although the publicity sparked by the remarkable ordeal of Tarō, Jirō, and their fellow sled dogs did not lead to popular-ity for the Sakhalin husky among dog keepers, contemporary television exposure and subsequent retellings of the story in children's literature and two major mo-tion pictures—a highly regarded 1983 Japanese production, *Nankyoku monogatari* (*Antarctica*) by director Koreyoshi Kurahara, and a 2005 Disney adaptation, *Eight Below*—continue to influence generations of youngsters to take an interest in and perhaps have compassion for canines.

At the same time, media depictions of typical American family life helped form an image of what possessions and values constituted a middle-class lifestyle. As a result, many Japanese came to equate the middle class with consumer items, like electric appliances, automobiles, and home ownership, as well as ideas of fam-ily, diligence, and loyalty.[26] As anthropologist Marilyn Ivy has noted, "Those peo-ple who had acquired those things were, purely and simply, the middle class."[27] The possession of a dog may not have been regarded as quite so essential to this equation as other items; "my dog" (*mai doggu*) never achieved the popularity of "my home" (*mai hōmu*) or "my car" (*mai kā*) as an Anglicized expression or as a rhetorical symbol of the most coveted material objects. Nevertheless, in Japan as elsewhere, a dog was regarded as a perfect addition to the ideal middle-class home and family.

The "family dog" (*kateiken*) was generally imagined as a small dog. Postwar Japanese families seem to have preferred small dogs for two reasons. First, a lack of living space, especially in urban areas where a majority of people lived by the late 1950s, discouraged even people who owned single-family dwellings from keeping a large dog. Except for homeowners in movies, space outside for a

33. "Memorial Statue to the Sakhalin Huskies Who Worked in Antarctica" at the base of Tokyo Tower. The monument was dedicated by the Japan Society for the Prevention of Cruelty to Animals in 1959. Photograph by author, 2003.

doghouse, much less a lawn, was minimal. Second, because many fathers working long hours were largely absent from the home, families tended to acquire a dog that could be easily handled regardless of the age and gender of its keepers. In particular, the family dog became closely associated with mothers and children. A father's connection with the family pet was more tenuous. From the late 1960s and early 1970s, a time when the social costs of rapid economic growth began to gain attention, the family dog came to be regarded, paradoxically, as the only ally of the male salaried worker (*sararīman*). One memorable joke by entertainer Sada Masashi (1952–) told of fathers returning home after a long day in the office to find their wives sulking and children who would no longer talk to them. Only the family dog would faithfully give them their full attention.

Before the decade of rapid economic growth and its social downsides could be contemplated, the family dog was thought to be a complementary member of the modern household. This vision of the family dog was aptly illustrated by a 1958 newspaper advertisement for Jintan health products. Jintan products, the ad claimed, did no less than "establish the guidelines for happiness" by "maintaining a healthy balance" and "conveying a pleasant atmosphere." A large photograph included in the advertisement supposedly portrayed that happiness. It depicted a scene of a nuclear family gathered in the living room of a single-family home. The father, apparently a salaried white-collar worker, judging from his tie and cardigan, sits on a chair to the rear, newspaper in hand. He appears to be contently gazing on his family or drifting off to sleep. His wife, dressed in a kimono and *haori* coat, sits on a chair to his left, attentively observing two young boys playing with an electric train set. Other electronic consumer items, a box stereo and a television, as well as shelves full of books, surround the family, demonstrating the fact that this household has acquired two highly desired manufactured products and also places an importance on education. Clothing, home furnishings, and the habit of sitting in chairs all signal that the family is financially stable and culturally sophisticated. Finally, as if to round out the scene, what appears to be a Norfolk terrier lies at the woman's feet.[28] The photo, of course, does not necessarily reflect reality. Men likely did not lounge around in a tie, and few women wore an expensive kimono and *haori* at home. There are other features that are inconsistent with the times, but the advertisement portrays the ideal Americanized and cultured middle-class home, complete with the family dog.

These developments in the world of dogs highlight how prewar trends contributed to the postwar landscape and how developments during the first fifteen postwar years laid the foundation for the rest of the century. The tremendous sway of American culture spread by the seven-year-long occupation, the ongoing presence of bases, and commercial and entertainment influences created a vision of middle-class, family-centered consumerism in which the dog was a desirable member. Paradoxically, this valuation of dogs as essential companions led to their increased commodification as products that could be bought, sold, and thrown out.

Companion/Products

Social commentators and business analysts claim that Japan is today in the midst of a "canine frenzy."[29] As this book has revealed, though, the current enthusiasm for pet dogs is simply the latest in a long and growing passion for dog keeping, and part of a much broader global phenomenon. The widespread affection for dogs and the financial means to keep, and in many cases pamper them as household pets, is also the by-product of economic prosperity in many countries since the second half of the twentieth century.

Although contemporary ways of dog keeping in Japan can be traced to the arrival of Westerners in the mid-nineteenth century and the adoption of their "civilized" modes by local elites in that century and then by an emerging middle class in the next, a widespread interest in dogs developed most dramatically with postwar economic growth and has been shaped by society becoming more and more middle class. Whereas earlier discussions of dogs and dog keeping in Japan were often concerned about civilization and loyalty and shaped by severe national, racial, and class anxieties, more recent discourses, which have taken place within a more stable geopolitical climate and a less confrontational, more equitable domestic economy, have been much less political and more focused on individual consumption. If language about the "cultured" life provided an excuse to consume and largely disguised the cultural imperialist underpinnings of that consumption during the early postwar years, by the late twentieth century the acquisition of things became an end in itself, was less American and more global in its cross-cultural influences, and demanded little justification and almost no self-reflection.

Today, the keeping of—and talk about—dogs in Japan, although not without certain particularities, is much the same as everywhere else in the industrialized world. The breeds kept and the goods and services offered to dog owners are essentially the same.[30] Dog keepers can purchase almost any of countless numbers of breeds and take advantage of a huge (approximately one trillion yen) and

34. Newspaper advertisement for Jintan health products, which, according to the caption, "establish the guidelines for happiness" by "maintaining a healthy balance" and "conveying a pleasant atmosphere." *Mainichi shinbun*, 3 January 1958. Used with permission of Morishita Jintan Co., Ltd.

flourishing industry of pet-sitting services, fee-charging dog parks, pet-training schools, pet hotels, pet cafes, beauty salons for pets, and pet cemeteries. As in many countries, people are spending a greater percentage of their income on household animals and treating them increasingly like human family members. New global trends in dog keeping, especially in the realm of accessories sold in upscale boutiques, are as likely to start in Tokyo or Osaka as they are in New York or Paris.

In Japan, the vast majority of dogs have been completely transformed into pets in the last half-century, and during recent decades these practices have spread to a broad segment of the population. A pet is typically defined as a domesticated animal that is kept for companionship or for the beauty of its appearance rather than for economic or utilitarian reasons. Although the ability of dogs to act as guards contributed to their diffusion in the prewar and early postwar years, since then this function has been far less of a factor in prompting their acquisition, as a result of decreased concern about crime, the spread of electronic surveillance devices, and changing notions of dog keeping. The new emphasis on dogs as domestic pets or as aesthetic objects is suggested by the title of the monthly magazine inaugurated by the Japan Kennel Club in 1952, *Kateiken* (Family dog). Even the concept of "pet" is becoming outmoded. As in the United States and elsewhere, people in Japan have come to think of dogs not as pets, but as companions or even as family members, as evidenced by recent preferences for phrases such as "'let's live' pleasantly with a dog" *(inu to tanoshiku 'kurasō')* rather than earlier expressions like "'raising' a pet" *(petto no 'kaikata')*.[31]

Even as dogs have become valued members of households as pets and companions, they have been transformed into consumer products. A consumer product may be provisionally defined as a thing produced by labor that is acquired through the exchange of capital. Products are made, sold and purchased, used, and routinely thrown away when they are no longer useful or have gone out of style. As the psychiatrist Ōhira Ken wrote in his longtime best-selling account of obsessive materialism in contemporary Japanese society, dogs have a dual meaning as a "family member" and an "animate stuffed toy," as an "object of deep friendship" and a "thing to be bought and sold."[32] The tension between the complimentary and contradictory position of dogs as living pets or companions and property has intensified as their popularity has grown. Businesses and individuals that aggressively produce dogs through intensive breeding and marketing and selling dogs as if they were manufactured goods have proliferated together with growing opportunities for profit. Indeed, the line between the technological and genetic manipulation of living animal pets and the creation of cyberpets is increasingly ambiguous. These cyberpets include Bandai's Tamagotchi virtual creature released in 1996, Sony's robotic dog Aibo, whose relatively short (product) life spanned from 1999 to 2006, and most recently Sega Toy's Yume Inu DX (Dream Inu DX), which responds by walking, cuddling, wagging its tail, making guttural sounds, and barking to a variety of tactile and verbal commands—six English words or phrases including, interestingly, not "bark" but "speak!" That Sega's dog responds exclusively to English-language commands, not to mention the preponderance of English names for military dogs even in the midst of the war, may signal some of the strangely infolded dimensions of empire. For the Sega robot dog, whether those legacies date from the Western imperialism of the nineteenth century or are of a more recent variety of cultural imperialism or are some combination of the two and other factors is unclear.

In Japan, the contradiction of dogs as both a pet and a product became readily apparent by the late 1960s. In 1963, near the beginning of a decade of rapid economic growth, several entrepreneurs established a new company, Tokyo Chikuken, to exploit the rising popularity of dogs. Within five years, they built the firm into one of the most financially successful in an industry that as a whole was booming. The company opened many dog shops and launched many of the country's first canine beauty salons, dog hotels, and medical clinics specializing in dogs. It advertised on television and in print publications, sent salespersons peddling dogs door to door, and stationed representatives in cities overseas such as London, Chicago, and New York to purchase dogs for export to Japan. By the late 1960s, Tokyo Chikuken was importing almost a thousand dogs per month from Britain alone. Offering people a chance to combine "pleasure with profit" (*kyōmi to jitsueki*), company executives pioneered a new business model. In exchange for a sizeable payment and a promise to purchase all dog food and veterinary services from Tokyo Chikuken, sales representatives provided people with a female dog, who was paired with male dogs to produce puppies. The company promised to purchase each of the puppies for a determined price and to transfer ownership of the bitch and to return the deposit once she had given birth to twenty puppies. The economic motivation to produce puppies in mass turned many dogs into breeding and birthing machines, creating innumerable puppy mills. Tokyo Chikuken executive also founded a subsidiary that began to certify dogs as purebred, allowing it and its customers to bypass older organizations such as the JKC and the Society for the Preservation of the Japanese Dog. For a time, Tokyo Chikuken's business plan worked well, but in early 1970 it collapsed along with the company when media scrutiny and a subsequent police investigation revealed deception of customers and tax evasion, as well as animal cruelty.[33]

The last charge was extended to Japan as a whole by London tabloids, which vociferously accused the country of being a "hell for dogs." The accusation was first leveled in 1968 but quickly resolved. The next year, however, a journalist at *The People*, a daily scandal sheet, published no fewer than three articles detailing exploitation and abuse of "British-bred-and-born" dogs in "Japanese canine concentration camps." The first article, titled "This Is How They Die," appeared as the top story and included a shocking photograph of an Asian-looking man dressed in robes and about to club a whimpering dog to death. The photo was widely dismissed in Japan as spurious, as was the claim that Japan was a "less civilized country without a single law against the abuse of animals."[34] Still, despite the obvious journalistic flaws in the reportage, the contentions of exploitation and abuse were based, at least partially, in reality.

The series created an uproar and a minor diplomatic crisis in both countries. Many British animal-rights activists and some breeders called for a ban on the export of dogs to Japan and for a boycott of Japanese goods. One woman visited the Japanese embassy in London, declared that she would never buy another item "made in Japan," and left her stainless steel Japanese-made silverware wrapped in the newspaper in which the first article had appeared.[35] Fury over the mistreatment of dogs probably was not the only issue at play. Lingering grudges over the Second World War and resentment about the spectacular economic rise of Japan and the competition it posed for Britain, now bereft of its own expansive empire, probably contributed to outrage over the maltreatment of "British" dogs. In Japan, too, the allegations caused considerable distress. Some Japanese found assertions that they, like their Korean neighbors, ate or once ate dogs—although many of their ancestors probably did—to be particularly disturbing.[36] Other commentators in Japan questioned whether their compatriots were dog lovers or not, a coded rhetoric that questioned, in effect, whether Japan was a modern, civilized nation. One guest columnist, Kase Toshikazu (1903–2004), Japan's first ambassador to the United Nations, writing in the *Asahi* newspaper, turned the controversy into an issue of class. Conceding that among "civilized countries" only Japan abandoned so many dogs, Kase contended that once incomes increased and the middle class expanded, the problem would be resolved and the entire nation's people (*zenkokumin*) would become dog lovers.[37] Although Tokyo Chikuken's commodification of dogs in a sort of pyramid scheme may have been an anomaly, it underscored the contradictions inherent in the commercialization of pets. Many of the same ethical excesses, while not always illegal, continue to this day.

Such contradictions are present in every modern society and are manifested in the way that dogs are bred, sold, and disposed of. Ironically, in Britain, whose residents are said to be unrivaled in their devotion to dogs, animal shelters are obliged to destroy hundreds of thousands of dogs each year. In the United States, also widely regarded as a country of dog lovers, it is estimated that perhaps a third of dogs are abandoned or given up for adoption before they reach their second birthday, and half of those are euthanized. Indeed, on average, American households keep their pet dogs for only two years, and probably a third of its canine population dies in animal shelters.[38] As historian Sabata Toyoyuki (1926–2001) observed during the flare-up over the treatment of "British" dogs, the difference between Japan and Western countries may have amounted to simply the preferred method of disposal. In Britain and other Western societies, he suggested, people had few qualms about taking dogs to the pound to be put to sleep, but most Japanese did not have the heart to do this, so they simply abandoned their pets instead, which usually in the end resulted in the same dreary fate—death in a pound.[39] Indeed, as dog ownership grew dramatically in Japan during the 1960s, abandoned dogs became a dilemma, not unlike other environmental and social costs that were a consequence of high growth. Newspapers regularly featured stories of stray dogs wandering alone or in packs about cities and rural areas and attacking people, sometimes with fatal results.[40] Only after a tightening of dog-keeping regulations, a campaign to educate the public about their responsibilities as pet owners, and the expansion of local government facilities to dispose of dogs—all of which were a reaction to the Tokyo Chikuken scandal and foreign criticism—did the problem of stray dogs begin to be contained in the early 1970s. While stray dogs are far less of a problem now than before, the disposal of dogs continues to this day, perhaps more tidily managed but nevertheless on a mass scale. Japanese Ministry of Environment officials estimate that more than one hundred thousand dogs who have been either turned in by their owners or captured by dogcatchers are annually eliminated nationwide at so-called health centers.[41]

As elsewhere, the ongoing disposal and death of unwanted dogs in Japan rarely attracts public attention or opposition, except when the process, like that of the life-producing puppy mills, becomes readily visible and therefore offensive to human sensibilities. Such was the case in Kitami, a city on the northern island of Hokkaido, in 1986. Municipal officials placed a doggie box (wanwan bokkusu) next to the government offices, providing dog-owners with the convenience of simply pulling off to the side of the road and dumping an unwanted dog down a chute into a metal container, just as if discarding an obsolete product. Protests from dog lovers and negative publicity led to the removal of the dumpsters.[42] As long as the disposal and elimination of dogs remains out of sight, it gains little public attention, except from the most fervent activists. Hoping to deter abandonment and increase the recovery of lost dogs, animal lovers successfully persuaded politicians in 2005 to pass legislation requiring all dogs sold to be implanted with a microchip that can be used to identify their owner. The gap between pet animals and cyberpets grows narrower still.

As in the late 1950s and 1960s and as in other countries, the mass media continues to strongly influence which dog breeds become popular. Like the cocker spaniel and the collie and the American films and television shows that bred their popularity, there is a clear connection between dogs featured by the media and those that become fashionable. Movies, television programs, comic books, and appearances by celebrities with their pet dogs are among the most prominent influences that shape the public's rapidly changing appetite and consumption of dogs.[43] Television commercials, too, have a tremendous impact, as demonstrated by the recent enthusiasm for the Chihuahua. In 2002, Aiful, one of many consumer-credit companies that specialize in making high-interest consumer loans, began a series of humorously absurd but hugely popular commercials featuring Kū-chan, a pale tan Chihuahua with big droopy eyes.[44] An appearance by a Japanese actress on television with her pet Chihuahua, as well as the arrival of the Hollywood motion picture *Legally Blonde* (2001) and its sequel, *Legally Blonde 2: Red, White and Blond* (2003), in which a Chihuahua played a prominent supporting (and sometimes starring) role, also contributed to the craze for the breed.[45] The same phenomenon was evident in a series of Taco Bell commercials in the United States that featured two Chihuahua dogs, first Dinky and soon thereafter Gidget. In the first Aiful commercial that was aired, a young woman who looks about twenty years old pleads with her middle-aged father to purchase Kū-chan, who gazes at them through a pet shop window, leading to the rhyming question, "Dō suru, Aifuru?" (What to do, Aiful?). In subsequent commercials, the dog has been shown engaging in activities such as snowboarding, getting married, and disappearing for days only to show up on the doorstep with a mate and dozens of offspring in tow, all of which require an expenditure of cash and lead the man to wonder repeatedly, "What to do, Aiful?" Not only did Kū-chan temporarily improve the seedy image of Aiful—for a while few people could not utter the long-familiar query "dō suru" without having the alliterative "Aifuru" pop into their minds—but the TV dog made the Chihuahua one of the most sought-after breeds. For a couple of years, individual Chihuahuas sold by the thousands, and sometimes for as much as 800,000 yen (around $7,400) apiece.[46]

Who is buying these dogs and why? As highlighted by the Aiful spot, young women are perceived to be the primary patrons of Chihuahuas and other dogs. If dogs became militarized and masculinized during the 1930s, dog keeping and dogs have been gradually feminized since the Second World War. Small dogs, like felines in Japan and other societies, have long been associated with femininity.[47] In the last half-century, while the preference for particular breeds of dogs has waxed and waned, there has been an overall miniaturization of the overall dog population in Japan, the United States, and elsewhere. In 2002 over half of the dogs in Japan were varieties weighing less than ten kilograms (twenty-two pounds). More recently, the aging of owners of the large Akita dog has led to a drastic drop in the number of registered dogs, while the smaller Shiba breed has become hugely popular, which is partially related to its size.[48] As we have seen, the family dog of the 1950s and 1960s, as symbolized by Lady and Lassie, was identified with mothers and children. Likewise, during the following decades, three of the most popular breeds, all lapdogs and known collectively as "Maru-Pome-Yōkī" (Maltese-Pomeranian-Yorkshire terrier), became strongly associated with female bar hostesses and other leisured women, who were said to desire a pet for companionship.[49] Such a correlation is not surprising given that similar connections were made between wealthy women during the Tokugawa and Meiji periods and are, as literary and animal studies specialist Susan McHugh has described, common in many societies throughout time across the world.[50] In terms of contemporary Japan, sociologists generally agree that while women have a distinctive dearth of power due to lower earnings and lack of access to high-level posts in the business and political worlds, they have much greater control over everyday life and consumption.[51] In the last several decades, marketers have recognized that single working women and high school girls possess tremendous say in determining what trends become chic and command significant spending power. For many of these women, especially young, single working females, small dogs have become an essential fashion accessory. The enthusiasm for tiny dogs, which are inevitably described as adorable, cuddly, and infantile, seems to be a canine variant of the "cute [kawaii] culture," which has been a dominant force in Japanese popular culture since the 1980s.[52] American society exhibits similar developments. A 2006 *New York Times* article titled "Woman's Best Friend, or Accessory?" identified a "nationwide trend toward smaller dogs" and quoted a female executive who remarked that pint-sized canines were a "handbag with a heartbeat."[53]

The demand for small, cute, "loveable" dogs leads to another widespread excess within the global pet industry. Dealers have found that puppies sell at the highest prices during the time they are fifty to sixty days old, and that their value drops off rapidly once this period passes, so almost all dogs are separated from their mothers and become the objects of a business transaction when they are but five weeks old. This short span of time arrives just days after the pups have been weaned and before they have sufficiently developed physically and socially. With little success, many veterinarians and animal-welfare advocates urge buyers and sellers to wait at least three months before removing them from their mothers and siblings.[54]

Why people are spending an increased amount of their incomes on purebred puppies is a complex issue, but it is clear that Veblen's concept of conspicuous consumption is part of the answer. As sociologist Pierre Bourdieu has argued, acts of consumption have become the primary means for people to position and distinguish themselves in societies where the "middle class" is a taken-for-granted social stratum in which just about everyone is lumped together. The acquisition and possession of consumer goods enables people to establish self-identity by creating connections among and distinctions from people who do and do not own the items in question.[55] Dog breeds act as brands by which people define who they are, both individually and as part of a group. Identification with a particular breed or brand can bring people together. In the past, dog-fancying organizations and dog shows produced this effect. More recently, a less formal manifestation of such canine-influenced group formation is the phenomenon whereby owners of the same breed make contact with one another through specialty magazines or the Internet and gather at a designated park to chat, eat, and play jointly with their canine companions.

Among pets and other domesticated animals, dogs are particularly suited to enabling consumption and the creation of relationships with other people. Like other consumer items, dogs come in a multiplicity of forms, hues, sizes, and personalities to suit consumers. Because dogs are tame and socially interactive (although, unlike some humans, they do not seem to discriminate—socially or sexually—on the basis of breed), they can easily accompany people outside their keeper's domestic space to be put on display through such activities as walks, drives, visits to the park, and shopping. Dog keepers, especially young women, can often be seen with tiny dogs while in public, and an increasing number of stores, restaurants, hotels, and apartment complexes are accommodating such dog keepers. Particularly when it comes to miniature breeds, dogs seem to be the ones taking people for a walk, rather than the other way around, as they often go along for a ride, are carried in an expensive designer bag, are cuddled in the arms of their owner, or are even wheeled around inside a "baby" stroller.

Although dogs may assist their keepers in forming relationships with other people, they may also hamper, or at least be taking the place of, interactions with other humans. Some academic and popular observers view the current "canine frenzy" as symptomatic of larger trends in Japanese society. They speculate that the increased enthusiasm for pet animals relates to changes in community and family relations that have led to social ills and isolation.[56] Some onlookers think that falling fertility rates, longer life expectancy, higher divorce rates, and especially the postponement or rejection of marriage are leading people to substitute relationships with nonhuman pets for ties with other humans.[57] Small-dog ownership is most strongly associated with so-called parasite singles, who are almost always imagined as women in their twenties and thirties who delay or reject marriage and continue to rely on their parents for financial support. A number of observers, including some conservative politicians, have blamed them for contributing to the country's economic and population crisis: the birthrate has sunk to 1.34 per woman, well below replacement levels.[58] In short, faithful dogs—both real and robotic—may be taking the place not only of faithless people, but of people altogether. Commentators have repeatedly expressed similar concerns about pet keeping in Western societies, but because of severe restrictions on immigration, Japan is aging far more rapidly than Europe and the United States and is already facing a variety of related socioeconomic problems. At the beginning of the twenty-first century, domestic and international observers alike have belittled the current passion for small indoor dogs as symbolic of a society beset with deep uncertainties.

One fitting visual example of the escalating numbers and high profile of dogs in the contemporary world was the appearance of an award-winning newspaper advertisement for a Matsushita electronic air-cleaning appliance in March 2006.[59] (See color plate 10.) The copy of the two-page full-spread ad reads "Nippon, a country blessed with many children" (*Kodakusan no kuni ni natta Nippon*) and shows the top backside of an unclothed female figure who holds two young creatures who peer directly into the camera over her bare shoulders. On her left, she holds a "Japanese" infant. The baby, according to the caption is a "child of the family" (*uchi no ko*)—one of "approximately 17.56 million children under the age of fifteen years old" in Japan. On the right, cuddled against the woman's neck, is another "child of the family," a tan and white "Japanese" Shiba dog, who is one of "approximately 23.15 million pet dogs and cats" dwelling on the islands.[60] Because pets, the text states, outnumber children as "members of families," Matsushita has engineered an electrical device that suppresses 99 percent of animal scurf that can be a cause of human allergies. The ad plays on public anxieties about depressed human birthrates and on the popularity of pets, especially small dogs such as the Shiba, which is now among the most popular dogs in Japan.[61] Indeed, there almost appears to be an inverse relationship between pet dogs and children. As the number of childless women and couples has increased, so has the number of dogs.[62]

Because of changes in human-animal relations in Japan and throughout the modern world, dogs have probably never before been so intensively bred, precisely groomed, better fed, or longer lived. The bond between people and canines seems to have never been stronger. People treat pet dogs not merely as the "family dog" but as well as and sometimes even better than other family members, or as the only other member of a "family." These relationships are changing how sociologists define the family unit.[63] Never have animal-rights movements been so active or enjoying so much political clout. Increased sympathy for animal rights, as illustrated by the uproar over the abandonment of the huskies on Antarctica, may to some extent stem from the increased visibility of actual animals thanks to still and moving photographic images. As Harriet Ritvo has suggested, we currently live on an "Animal Planet," or at least in an animal moment, with TV programming and even cable networks entirely devoted to animal-related content.[64] If this is an animal moment, it is one with an extremely pervasive canine hue, which spans the globe from New York to Beijing, Rio de Janeiro to New Delhi.[65] Many people no longer dismiss pet or companion dogs as frivolous luxuries. Rather, their companionship is valued by a variety of experts as therapeutic for all humans—not just for the elderly and the ill. Some keepers and dogs are probably engaging more than ever in physical activities, such as playing Frisbee, which seems designed as much for dogs as they are for people. These activities, unlike dog shows, seem to challenge the abilities of dogs rather than just the human manipulation of canines. Dogs have won the admiration of the public and therefore the interest of business, and gained increasing attention in the academy; they have even acquired their own "manifesto."[66] Canines have also returned to the classroom, not as disembodied models of loyalty and bravery to mobilize youngsters for war and death, but as real live animals for students to physically interact with and whom educators hope will teach students the value of compassion and life.[67] Dogs may be bought and sold, used to sell things, thoroughly commodified and commercialized, but they are certainly no longer subaltern. Their bark has never resounded so loud and clear.

Yet, one wonders about the quality of some dogs' lives. In Japan and elsewhere, many dogs, especially small dogs but even those of a larger variety, spend much of their time inside, and not only in urban areas. Indeed, quite a few dogs could not survive outside of a human-controlled environment. Because of intensive breeding to conform to arbitrary standards, many purebred dogs are physically weak and fragile, debilitated by congenital abnormalities and ailments. Human-induced genetic problems, though, appear to be particularly severe in Japan's canine population: "Rampant inbreeding has given [dogs in Japan] some of the highest rates of genetic defects in the world, sometimes four times higher than in the United States and Europe."[68] As a result, many dogs seem to have lost their once-prized instincts and capabilities. Indeed, many dogs in Japan and elsewhere spend their days in a manner that stands in sharp contrast to how most canines lived a century and a half ago, before Western imperialism introduced new dogs and novel modes of dog keeping. Like an increasing number of their human companions, many are overweight and overstressed, owing to excessive food consumption and being cooped up inside all day with little exercise.[69] Indeed, the small dogs that have come to be regarded as emblematic of postmodern, postindustrial Japan at the beginning of the twenty-first century are thoroughly unlike the wily native dogs that roamed the streets and fields in the nineteenth century. Nor do most of them resemble physically or figuratively "Japanese" or military dogs, which represented the country and its people in the 1930s and 1940s. Instead, ironically, today's tiny indoor dogs stand shoulder to shoulder with the *chin*, the pampered but fragile toy dog that was seen as the symbol of Japan a century and a half ago, where this book began.

Coda: The Triumph and the Troubles of the Colonial Dog

As highlighted by the continuing obsession with breeds and the commodification of canines in Japan and other societies, the vestiges of canine imperialism are still readily apparent today. If we were to graphically represent these developments, in a manner like the 1933 "Dog Map of the World" discussed in chapter 1, what would they look like? As it has been since the nineteenth century, Western kennel clubs and breeds of British, American, and western European origin would still dominate today's "Dog Map of the World." Three kennel clubs exercise tremendous power worldwide over breed standards and registries: the (English) Kennel Club, the AKC, and the Federation Cynologique Internationale (FCI), an organization established in 1911 by continental European political elites from Belgium, Germany, France, Austria, and the Netherlands to blunt the influence of British breeding and commercial interests. Firmly entrenched at the apex of dogdom power, each organization recognizes only one kennel club from other countries (and domestically for the English and American kennel clubs, a single club per breed) as affiliates, with whom they coordinate the rules that govern the breeding, registration, and exchange of purebred dogs. Not surprisingly, these three organizations represent almost all of the major Western imperial powers of the nineteenth and twentieth centuries.

If one were to combine the breeds recognized by these organizations with those acknowledged by their junior partners in other parts of the world, the aggregate would look a lot like the original "Dog Map of the World," which aptly captured the canine cartography of New Imperialism. The vast majority of some four hundred codified and recognized breeds depicted on such a map would still be of Western origin, heirs of the colonial dogs who accompanied Westerners into the imperial world from the nineteenth century onward. Today's map would feature a few more native dogs from once colonized or semicolonized areas than appeared on the 1933 map—dogs like the *chin* which were often valued for their exotic allure. In fact, a number of canines from postcolonial areas, which were once denigrated as pariahs, wolflike, and the object of official persecution, are now regarded as legitimate and purebred strains. The Akita and several other "Japanese" native dogs—beneficiaries of Japan's transformation from an object to a subject of imperialism—were among the first of such postimperial additions to our updated map.

Unlike "Japanese" dogs, many postcolonial native dogs did not acquire legitimacy by becoming colonial dogs. The transformation of Japan and its chosen canines is relatively unique in that respect. But other elements of their remarkable metamorphosis have been replicated. Local fanciers have bound their dogs to the modern nation-state by stressing their supposed connection to the nation in a distant past, glorified them for their purity of blood and attributes such as loyalty and bravery, and endeared them to members of the middle class. Economic power, international trade, and a widely diffused national diaspora have replaced geopolitical imperial might as elements instrumental in boosting a newly nationalized dog to global prominence. The national dogs of (South) Korea and Israel provide examples of one-time native pariah dogs who have achieved this ascent.

After Korea regained its independence from Japan and the peninsula was divided politically in 1945, each of the two states that claimed to be the true representative of the Korean people chose a dog breed as its own. In the south, the government of President Park Chung Hee (1917–79) declared the Jindo, one of the breeds the Japanese colonial government had declared to be a "Japanese" national treasure in the late 1930s and early 1940s, to be Korea's representative canine during the intense nationalism of the early 1960s. The Park government of course made no mention of any colonial precedent during the period of Japanese rule. As was (and still is) the case in Japan, the declaration strictly regulated the breeding, sale, and movement of the designated dogs, all in the name of protecting the breed's purity of blood and preventing its "extinction."[70] The breed's fans suggested that the Jindo was especially worthy of selection because the dogs had ostensibly long been fierce defenders of the Korean nation. Proponents claimed that on the day before the armada of Japanese warlord Hideyoshi (1537–98) invaded Korea in the late sixteenth century, thousands of Jindo had faced the sea and barked viciously in the direction of the Japanese islands. In response to the South's declaration, the North Korean regime chose the Poongsan, the other breed designated by the Japanese colonial government, as Korea's true national dog.[71] Given North Korea's international isolation, the Poongsan is virtually unknown beyond the peninsula. The Jindo, however, thanks in part to South Korea's tremendous economic rise in the last several decades and the large Korean diaspora in the United States and elsewhere, has captured widespread global recognition.[72]

Perhaps in an attempt to avoid the inevitable politics associated with the Jindo's codification and promotion by Japanese colonial authorities, the South Korean government recently seems to be downplaying the Jindo in favor of the Sapsaree (also known as the Sapsal) a shaggy canine that looks like an Old English sheepdog. Unlike the Jindo, the Sapsaree did not benefit from Japanese rule but were its victims. Similar to other dogs who could not be used as working dogs, a purported 1.5 million Sapsaree were systematically killed so that their fur could be used for Imperial Army clothing. Recent accounts of this slaughter, like that of Japanese rhetoric about indigenous dogs in the 1930s, make explicit comparisons between the character of the human nation and the Sapsaree. As the *Koreana*, a quarterly magazine supported by the South Korean government and dedicated to introducing international readers to Korea's culture and arts, put it: "Not only were dogs that did not conform to Japanese standards exterminated, but those breeds that were considered pugnacious and natural fighters were butchered as well. The Sapsaree—so similar in temperament to the Korean people—was a natural target."[73] And in another striking similarity to descriptions of Japanese dogs in the early twentieth century, fans of the Sapsaree hail the dogs for surviving the postindependence "inflow of western culture and popularity of foreign breeds as pets [that] pushed the Sapsaree even closer toward the edge of extinction."[74] In 1992 the Republic of Korea designated the Sapsaree as National Treasure No. 368, and the Korean Embassy in Washington sponsored a lecture to introduce the breed to Americans in 2006.[75] The timing of these moves clearly reflects and contributes to a dominant national narrative that portrays the colonial (and postcolonial) period in terms of victimization. In addition, Korean diplomats and the breed's fans seem to be using the breed to counter negative Western views of Koreans' appetite for other dogs as meat.

Israel's national canine, the Canaan Dog, followed a similar trajectory as that of the Korean(ized) dogs, but one which has even more in common with "Japanese" dogs. Like most canines in the Middle East, the animals that came to be called the Canaan Dog had previously received little respect or care, living on the peripheries of villages. As in Japan, South Korea, and elsewhere, the codification of the dogs into an officially recognized and protected breed coincided with the rise of nationalism in the early twentieth century. When European Jews, including many who had adopted the dog-keeping mores of the continent, migrated to Palestine in the early twentieth century to establish a Zionist state, they looked around for a dog that they could call their own. According to the canine's admirers, the Canaan dog's history paralleled that of the Jews themselves: they possessed ancient roots in the "promised land" as guards for the camps and herds of ancient Israelites; they were of "noble" and "aristocratic" stock; and when the Israelites were scattered, the dogs dispersed and lived on the margins of Bedouin society, but were reunited with God's "chosen people" on their return. From the late 1930s, they were bred and trained to fight alongside Jewish paramilitary forces during the War of Independence (1948 Arab-Israeli War). Not only have they been nationalized, they have now become a sort of colonial dog, acting as guards for Israeli settlements scattered throughout the Palestinian West Bank. The nationalization of the Canaan dog was not without its challenges, though. For many years, fanciers faced an uphill battle to convince the general Jewish Israeli public, many of whom preferred Western breeds, to not lump Canaan dogs together with other street "mongrels," whom most people had long pejoratively referred to as "Arab dogs"—who were, ironically, at least part Canaan.[76] The Canaan dog is now recognized at home and abroad, including by all three of the major international kennel clubs. As in Japan and elsewhere, the obsession with the purity of canine blood in national dogs in Korea and Israel reflects anxieties about perceived threats to national human racial and cultural purity. Similar patterns of the reevaluation, nationalization, and popularization of native dogs are evident in other contexts as well.[77]

If the triumph of the colonial dog is clear in contemporary canine cartography, so are its troubles. Kennel and breeding clubs, which created, popularized, and whose survival depends on purebred dogs, wield less influence than they once did and are increasingly the targets of critics who charge that they put profits and arbitrary and antiquated standards of purity over the welfare of dogs. Such bad publicity and changing consumer trends have led to a steady decline in the number of dogs being registered with the clubs, but purebred dogs still exercise considerable cultural hegemony throughout the world.

But what of these dogs? As we have seen, people have certainly treated purebred dogs with greater kindness in the past, but all this human attention and especially intervention in their reproductive processes seems to have become a curse rather than a blessing. Intensive breeding practices that value appearance over health, temperament, and utility have led to dogs inflicted with a host of physiological and psychological disorders. Purebred bulldogs, one of the first breeds to be codified and long the symbol of British imperial might, suffer from a variety of ills and can only reproduce through artificial insemination. The German shepherd breed, arguably the epitome of the colonial dog thanks to the efforts of Stephanitz, the adoration of Hitler and other Nazis, and the dogs' widespread adoption in the imperial world, faces severe behavioral and congenital cytoskeletal troubles. Even native dogs who have more recently been standardized as legitimate breeds, such as the Akita, must cope with similar debilitating genetic disorders, from hip dysplasia to severe eye problems. Some biologists predict that breeds like these "caught in...eugenic breeding practices are headed for extinction."[78] Yes, the subaltern could bark once it became a colonial dog, but after so much inbreeding, perhaps it cannot do so very vigorously. Ironically, the street dogs that still wander on the edge of human inhabitation in many areas of the world may be far better off than many dogs that are caught in the stifling embrace of national and commercial adoration.

Despite such setbacks, the ideological underpinnings of canine imperialism remain remarkably vibrant. The primary vocabulary of breed, civilization, and loyalty maintains currency in the dog world even as the nineteenth-century political and social forces such as imperialism and racism, which once provided underlying conceptual support, have been renounced. The notion of breed, in particular, continues to carry tremendous influence. Despite the tight connections between breed and race, the idea of breed goes largely unquestioned even though the concept of race has lost its scientific validity if not its social relevance. Most people take breed for granted as if it were entirely natural and not a human construct. Dogs are still referred to primarily according to their breed name, or if they don't appear to adhere to a particular breed's prescribed physical appearance, then they are referred to as being of mixed-breed, a mutt, or to use a word that is still used with little hesitation when talking about dogs, a mongrel. It is almost impossible to talk about dogs without using this vocabulary. If this were merely an intellectual exercise that would be fine, but the continuing influence of this sort of thinking has dire consequences for dogs who do not physically conform to breeding standards and as a result are eliminated because of a supposed impurity or defect, and for humans because it serves to subtly bolster lingering and resurgent notions of racial and class hierarchy.

In contrast to breed, civilizationist discourses have almost entirely disappeared from discussions about dogs and, for that matter, about humans. Yet the underlying expectation that dogs ought to adhere to a set of standards defined as civilized in the nineteenth century persists. People expect that canines ought to be and act completely domesticated, to conform to human control by not straying but staying close by (and even next to or under the same roof as) their human companion(s), and if they hunt at all, it should be for humans rather than for themselves. If dogs do not adhere to these expectations, they can expect to end up in the pound or worse. In short, most people still expect dogs to not transgress the boundaries between culture and nature, domesticity and wildness.

Loyalty, too, continues to be an attribute expected of dogs. People celebrate devoted and brave dogs, past and present. In the last few decades, many people have been less inclined to create—or at least characterize—relationships with their dogs as hierarchical. Instead of pets, dogs are "companions." Yet actually attempting to create an egalitarian relationship with dogs, who appear to thrive within a stable social order, may be psychologically unhealthy for canines. Life, as with history, ought to be a collaborative (ad)venture that considers the needs of all creatures—both human and nonhuman—involved.

This history, perhaps unavoidably, has focused more on humans than on dogs. Like most discussions of nonhuman creatures, as the historian Donna Haraway has observed, this book has "polish[ed] an animal mirror to look for ourselves."[79] Still, throughout I have attempted to catch a glimpse, however fleeting and tenuous, of actual dogs, especially through sources such as photographic images and stuffed bodies coproduced by canines, while recognizing that these materials, too, are unavoidably mediated and shaped by people. One of my underlying arguments is that—though dogs are almost always and completely spoken for—the symbolic deployment of nonhuman animals is closely connected to their actual interactions with humans. The figurative deployment of dogs has been dependent on certain dogs, as individuals and as breeds, behaving in specific ways. Because canine behavior is the product of biological breeding, sustained contact with particular human cultures, and interaction between individual canines and humans, dogs have some degree of culture that intertwines with and, to some extent, reflects human societies with whom they associate. Examining human-canine relations across time and place contributes to the recognition that dogs, as well as other animals, share cultures *and* histories with particular groups of people.

Such an acknowledgement may amount to a partial concession to those voices in this book that clearly projected national, racial, economic, gendered, and other culturally constructed categories onto canines. Although the idioms of civilization, race, and loyalty were fundamentally flawed and often projected wrongly, or at least to an excess, onto dogs, many human observations about dogs were probably based to an extent on actual behavioral differences that were a product not only of the biological realities created and amplified by artificial selection but also of patterns of conduct acquired through contact with specific human cultures. Unlike the depiction of human "racial groups" being endowed with a similar set of fixed traits and particular intellectual and personality characteristics, dogs of the same breed do to a degree exhibit similar characteristics. Unlike for human races, there is an identifiable link between biological character and behavior, though this by no means precludes individual canine agency. The pronouncements of the Society for the Preservation of the Japanese Dog and the Ministry of Education that indigenous breeds such as Hachikō "reflect the character of the Japanese people" or, for that matter, Korean statements that the Sapsaree are "pugnacious" and have a "temperament" like that of the Korean people, were certainly colored by the times, but they may have not been completely off the mark. Indeed, more objective studies by zoologists undertaken since the turn of the millennium suggest that "Japanese" breeds are more wary of strangers while dogs of European extraction tend to more quickly let down their guard with people other than their keeper.[80] Such findings neither validate nor justify the claims and actions of those discussed in this book who metaphorically manipulated dogs for a variety of purposes; but they do confirm there is a close but uneasy relationship between the actual behavior of dogs, which to an extent may be the result of selective breeding and intensive training, and their figurative deployment by humans. That reality is what makes the enforcement, both material and metaphorical, of human hierarchies by nonhuman actors, so subtle and so powerful.

Dogs do not merely reflect what is projected onto them. Their behavior, actions, and culture shape their relationships with people and affect human discussions about them. Because dogs and other animals, including people, share and shape the past and the present, our histories, cultures, and natures are inseparably intertwined. It is time we humans more fully acknowledge and more wisely value the assorted barks, bellows, bleats, brays, and cries of our fellow creatures that inhabit our cultures, our histories, and our world. More than simply being our mirrors, dogs and other creatures are our partners in a shared environment, culture, and history, the nature of which is a joint creation, and which encompasses the fate of all species.

NOTES

Introduction

1. See, for example, Virginia De John Anderson, *Creatures of Empire: How Domestic Animals Transformed Early America* (Oxford: Oxford University Press, 2004); Alfred W. Crosby, *Ecological Imperialism: The Biological Expansion of Europe, 900–1900* (Cambridge: Cambridge University Press, 1986); Mark A. Mastromarino, "Teaching Old Dogs New Tricks: The English Mastiff and the Anglo-American Experience," *The Historian; A Journal of History* 49 (1986): 10–25; Elinor G. K. Melville, *A Plague of Sheep: Environmental Consequences of the Conquest of Mexico* (Cambridge: Cambridge University Press, 1994); and John Grier Varner and Jeannette Johnson Varner, *Dogs of the Conquest* (Norman: University of Oklahoma Press, 1983).

2. Although substantial historical research has been published on the symbolic use of animals brought from colonial areas to the metropole, work concerning the figurative deployment of beasts in regions that were the object of imperialism has only begun to emerge. See, for example, James Boyd, "Horse Power: The Japanese Army, Mongolia, and the Horse," *Japan Forum* 22, no. 1–2 (2010): 23–42; Lance van Sittert and Sandra Swart, *Canis Africanis: A Dog History of Southern Africa* (Leiden: Brill, 2008); Greg Bankoff and Sandra Swart, *Breeds of Empire: The "Invention" of the Horse in Southeast Asia and Southern Africa 1500–1950* (Copenhagen: NIAS Press, 2007); Robert J. Gordon, "Fido: Dog Tales of Colonialism in Namibia," in *Social History and African Environments*, ed. William Beinart and JoAnn McGregor (Athens: Ohio University Press, 2003), 240–54; and Nancy J. Jacobs, "The Great Bophuthatswana Donkey Massacre: Discourse on the Ass and the Politics of Class and Grass," *American Historical Review* 106 (2001): 485–507.

3. Keith Thomas, *Man and the Natural World: Changing Attitudes in England, 1500–1800* (Oxford: Oxford University Press, 1983), 106.

4. Tsukamoto Manabu, *Shōrui o meguru seiji: Genroku no fōkuroa* (Tokyo: Heibonsha, 1993), 184.

5. Ibid., 184–204.

6. Japan was not the only non-Western imperial power in the twentieth century. The Qing Empire and the Ottoman Empire, until their respective collapses in 1912 and 1923, each acted in some ways like a modern imperial power.

7. James Serpell, "From Paragon to Pariah: Some Reflections on Human Attitudes towards Dogs," in *The Domestic Dog: Its Evolution, Behaviour, and Interactions with People*, ed. James Serpell (Cambridge: Cambridge University Press, 1995), 245–56.

8. Ibid. For examples in other geographic and temporal contexts, see Susan McHugh, *Dog* (London: Reaktion Books, 2004); Yamada Takako, *Ainu no sekaikan* (Tokyo: Kōdansha, 1994),

246–52; Edward Muir, *Mad Blood Stirring: Vendetta and Factions in Friuli during the Renaissance* (Baltimore: John Hopkins University Press, 1993), 222–38; and David Gordon White, *Myths of the Dog-Man* (Chicago: University of Chicago Press, 1991), 11–21.

9. John Borneman, "Race, Ethnicity, Species, Breed: Totemism and Horse-Breed Classification in America," *Comparative Studies in Society and History* 30, no. 1 (January 1988): 48.

10. Ibid.

11. Eiko Ikegami, *The Taming of the Samurai: Honorific Individualism and the Making of Modern Japan* (Cambridge: Harvard University Press, 1995).

12. Michael Pollan, *The Botany of Desire: A Plant's-Eye View of the World* (New York: Random House, 2001), xvi.

13. Raymond Coppinger and Lorna Coppinger, *Dogs: A New Understanding of Canine Origin, Behavior, and Evolution* (Chicago: University of Chicago Press, 2001), 28; Stephen Budiansky, *The Truth about Dogs: An Inquiry into the Ancestry, Social Conventions, Mental Habits, and Moral Fiber of Canis Familiaris* (New York: Penguin, 2000), 5–7.

14. Edmund Russell, "Evolutionary History: Prospectus for a New Field," *Environmental History* 8, no. 2 (April 2003): 204–28.

15. Anderson, *Creatures of Empire*, 211.

16. Ibid., 5.

17. Gayatri Chakravorty Spivak, "Can the Subaltern Speak?" in *Marxism and the Interpretation of Culture*, ed. Cary Nelson and Lawrence Grossberg (Urbana: University of Illinois Press, 1998), 271–313.

18. Erica Fudge, "A Left-Handed Blow: Writing the History of Animals," in *Representing Animals*, ed. Nigel Rothfels (Bloomington: Indiana University Press, 2002), 3–18.

19. Stanley Coren, *How to Speak Dog* (New York: Fireside, 2001).

20. Erica Fudge, *Pets* (Stocksfield, UK: Acumen, 2008), 63.

21. James C. Scott's theories about domination and resistance, which like Spivak's ideas have typically only been applied to subaltern peoples, are also useful in contemplating human-animal interactions. Do canines, like peasants and other subaltern groups, wield "weapons of the weak" and submit to subordination vis-à-vis humans while maintaining a degree of autonomy and a "voice under domination"? Scott, *Weapons of the Weak: Everyday Forms of Peasant Resistance* (New Haven: Yale University Press, 1985); Scott, *Domination and the Arts of Resistance: Hidden Transcripts* (New Haven: Yale University Press, 1990).

22. Harriet Ritvo, *The Animal Estate: The English and Other Creatures in the Victorian Age* (Cambridge: Harvard University Press, 1987), 5. Emphasis added.

23. Hilda Kean, *Animal Rights: Political and Social Change in Britain since 1800* (London: Reaktion, 1998); Jonathan Burt, *Animals in Film* (London: Reaktion, 2002). In contrast, John Berger and Steve Baker have argued that the increasing visibility of animals as symbols, signs, and images in the twentieth century has resulted despite, or perhaps because of, alienation from and the disappearance of actual animals, other than pets, from the human world. John Berger, "Why Look at Animals?" in John Berger, *About Looking* (New York: Pantheon, 1980), 1–28; Steve Baker, *The Postmodern Animal* (London: Reaktion, 2000), 7–25.

24. Donna Haraway, "Teddy Bear Patriarchy: Taxidermy in the Garden of Eden, New York City, 1908–1936," *Social Text* 11 (Winter 1984–85): 34.

25. Claude Lévi-Strauss, *Totemism*, trans. Rodney Needham (Boston: Beacon Press, 1964), 89.

1. The Native Dog and the Colonial Dog

1. Isabella Bird, *Unbeaten Tracks in Japan* (1880; London: John Murray, 1885), 86. Fujihara is near Nikkō in Tochigi Prefecture. Bird also recorded: "As animals are not used for milk,

draught, or food, and there are no pasture lands, both the country and the farm-yards have a singular silence and an inanimate look; a mean-looking dog and few fowls being the only representatives of domestic animal life. I long for the lowing of cattle and the bleating of sheep." Ibid., 45. For an analysis of Bird's travel writings about Japan, see Lorraine Sterry, *Victorian Women Travelers in Meiji Japan: Discovering a "New" Land* (London: Global Oriental, 2009), 238–79.

2. George Fleming, *Travels on Horseback in Mantchu Tartary: Being a Summer's Ride beyond the Great Wall of China* (London: Hurst and Blackett, 1863), 233–34.

3. Coppinger and Coppinger, *Dogs*, 69–83.

4. William Elliot Griffis, *The Mikado's Empire*, 6th ed. (New York: Harper and Brothers, 1890), 451.

5. How Griffis knew the dog's eye was injured in this way is unclear. From his passage about the dog in *The Mikado's Empire* it appears that he encountered the dog for the first time some time after the alleged attack. Neither do his journals and correspondence mention the dog, nor does the animal appear in any of the dozen or so photographs in his Fukui scrapbooks. However, the fact that Griffis believed that farmers made a strong association between foreign dogs and Westerners, and would violently act on that view, is revealing.

6. Kathleen Kete, *The Beast in the Boudoir: Petkeeping in Nineteenth-Century Paris* (Berkeley: University of California Press, 1994), 2.

7. See the following path-breaking works by Ritvo: *The Animal Estate: The English and Other Creatures in the Victorian Age* (Cambridge: Harvard University Press, 1987); *The Platypus and the Mermaid and Other Figments of the Classifying Imagination* (Cambridge: Harvard University Press, 1997); "Pride and Pedigree: The Evolution of the Victorian Dog Fancy," *Victorian Studies* 29, no. 2 (Winter 1986): 227–53.

8. Thomas, *Man and the Natural World*, 102.

9. Ritvo, *Animal Estate*, 84.

10. Ibid., 101.

11. Ibid.

12. Parker Gillmore, *The Hunter's Arcadia* (London: Chapman and Hall, 1886), 70. See also 28, 133. For other examples from the literature of British big game hunters, who almost always hunted with prized Western hunting dogs and less often with local canines, see R. Gordon Cumming, *Five Years of a Hunter's Life in the Far Interior of South Africa*, 2 vols. (New York: Harper and Brothers, 1850), 1:290, 2:84; Frederick Courtney Selous, *A Hunter's Wanderings in Africa* (London: MacMillan, 1907), 389; Colonel R. Meinertzhagen, *Kenya Diary, 1902–1906* (Edinburgh: Oliver and Boyd, 1957), 133, 170–73. For secondary scholarship on imperial hunting, see J. A. Mangan and Callum McKenzie, "'Pig-Sticking is the Greatest Fun': Martial Conditioning on the Hunting Fields of Empire," in *Militarism, Sport, Europe: War without Weapons*, ed. J. A. Mangan (London: Routledge, 2003), 97–119; Edward I. Steinhart, "The Imperial Hunt in Colonial Kenya, c. 1880–1909," in *Animals in Human Histories*, ed. Mary Henninger-Voss (Rochester, NY: University of Rochester Press, 2002), 144–81; Joseph Sramek, "Face Him Like a Briton": Tiger Hunting, Imperialism, and British Masculinity in Colonial India, 1800–1875," *Victorian Studies* 47, no. 4 (2006): 659–80; William K. Storey, "Big Cats and Imperialism: Lion and Tiger Hunting in Kenya and Northern India, 1898–1930," *Journal of World History* 2, no. 2 (1991): 135–73. Historian John M. MacKenzie has noted that for the celebrated big game hunters of the nineteenth century, the "dog represented devotion and obedience but also a cruel hunting auxiliary." John M. MacKenzie, *Empire of Hunting: Hunting, Conservation and British Imperialism* (Manchester, UK: Manchester University Press, 1988), 32.

13. Ritvo, *Animal Estate*, 101.

14. Joseph Patterson Sims, "Dog Map of the World: The Countries of Origin of Some Seventy Breeds of Domesticated Dogs, Half of Them Evolved in the British Isles!" (London: Illustrated

London News, 1933). Sims (1890–1953), a prominent architect who was chairman of the Philadelphia trial board of the American Kennel Club, first published the map as "Where Your Dog Comes From: Unusual Map Shows the Native Dogs of the Various Countries of the World," *American Kennel Gazette* 50, no. 8 (1 August 1933), 25–26, 124–25. Although I refer to it as the English Kennel Club, the official name of this pioneering organization is simply and tellingly The Kennel Club.

15. Thomas, *Man and the Natural World*, 108.

16. Ritvo, *Animal Estate*, 93; Borneman, "Race, Ethnicity, Species, Breed," 26.

17. Thomas, *Man and the Natural World*, 108; Ritvo, "Pride and Pedigree," 50–51.

18. Mary E. Thurston, *The Lost History of the Canine Race: Our 15,000-Year Love Affair with Dogs* (Kansas City, MO: Andrews and McMeel, 1996), 109.

19. John M. MacKenzie, "The Imperial Pioneer and Hunter and the British Masculine Stereotype in Late Victorian and Edwardian Times," in *Manliness and Morality: Middle-Class Masculinity in Britain and America, 1800–1940*, ed. J. A. Mangan and James Walvin (New York: St. Martin's Press, 1987), 179.

20. Basil Hall Chamberlain, *Japanese Things; Being Notes on Various Subjects Connected with Japan, For the Use of Travelers and Others* (1890; Tokyo: Tuttle, 1971), 401. The first *chin* is said to have come to the archipelago in 732.

21. V. W. F. Collier, *Dogs of China and Japan, in Nature and Art* (London: Heinemann, 1921), 177–78. Miyako is in the present-day orthography. Mi[y]ako and Shimoda are both place names, the former referring to the imperial capital, today's Kyoto, and the latter to a small port that was designated as the first harbor to be open to foreign ships in 1854 and the location of the initial U.S. consulate in Japan in 1856 as a result of Perry's diplomatic negotiations with shogunal representatives.

22. Francis L. Hawks, *Narrative of the Expedition of an American Squadron to the China Seas and Japan* (1856; Mineola, NY: Dover, 2000), 369, 392; Henry P. Davis, ed., *The New Dog Encyclopedia*, (Harrisburg, PA.: Stackpole, 1970), 670–77. The origins of Master Sam Spooner's name may have to do with a certain D. C. Spooner, a partner of Russell and Company and vice consul in Macao, who put his "magnificent Chinese estate . . . at the squadron's disposal for headquarters" while Perry was waiting to sail for the Ryukyu Islands and then Japan. See Matthew C. Perry, *The Japan Expedition: 1852–1854: The Personal Journal of Commodore Matthew C. Perry*, ed. Roger Pineau (Washington: Smithsonian Press, 1968), 56. Several years later, shogunate officials presented two *chin* to the first U.S. consul-general Townsend Harris (1804–78), who arrived on the archipelago in 1856 to exert more pressure on the regime to concede to U.S. demands. Harris gave the dogs identical names to those that Perry had given two of the dogs he received. Harris called them Jedo (an alternative rendering of the shogunal capital of Edo) and Miako (once again, Miyako, referring to the former imperial capital). Townsend Harris, *The Complete Journal of Townsend Harris, First American Consul and Minister to Japan*, 2nd ed. (Rutland, VT.: Charles E. Tuttle, 1959, 270; Shio Sakanishi, ed., *Some Unpublished Letters of Townsend Harris* (New York: Japan Reference Library, 1941), unpaginated.

23. Masao Miyoshi, *As We Saw Them: The First Japanese Embassy to the United States* (New York: Kodansha, 1994), 52. It is interesting to note that Perry's grandson, August Belmont Jr., served as president of the American Kennel Club from 1888 to 1916.

24. Chamberlain, *Japanese Things*, 401.

25. Pamela Cross Stern and Tom Mather, *The Complete Japanese Chin* (New York: Howell Book House, 1997), 16–19.

26. Robert Rosenblum, *The Dog in Art from Rococo to Post-Modernism* (New York: H. N. Abrams, 1988), 52–56.

27. W. Ruloff Kip, "How Rhinebeck Fuji and Rhinebeck Chindi Came from Japan," *American Kennel Gazette* 14 (31 October 1902): 285. For an analysis of the imperial British

fascination with the Pekingese, see Sarah Cheang, "Women, Pets, and Imperialism: The British Pekingese Dog and Nostalgia for Old China," *Journal of British Studies* 45 (April 2006): 359–87.

28. Gordon, "Fido," 241.

29. Note the division of canines between large and small ones according to the gender of their colonial owner. John Lockwood Kipling, *Beast and Man in India: A Popular Sketch of Indian Animals in Their Relations with the People* (London: MacMillan, 1891), 307. Kipling uses "subaltern" in its original sense (and thus quite differently from Spivak) to refer to a commissioned British military officer below the rank of captain. For a later view, including some telling photographs, of British dog keeping in colonial India, see Charles Allen, ed., *Plain Tales from the Raj: Images of British India in the Twentieth Century* (London: André Deutsch, 1975).

30. One must be careful not to equate present-day breeds with dogs who were called by the same name, or a different name (Scottish terriers were once frequently referred to as Aberdeen terriers) before most breeds became standardized in the mid- to late nineteenth century. Alcock's Scottish terrier may have been much larger (perhaps by as much as eight inches) and more muscular than modern-day Scottish terriers. Nineteenth-century terriers reportedly had an excellent scenting ability and powerful legs well suited for digging in pursuit of animals burrowed underground. Breeding has led to a smaller pet dog less well known for (though certainly not bereft of) its tracking abilities, but terriers have evidently neither lost their feisty nature nor their high-pitched bark. See John T. Marvin, *The Book of All Terriers* (New York: Howell Book House, 1976), 27–31.

31. Hugh Cortazzi, "Sir Rutherford Alcock: Minister at Edo, 1859–62," *British Envoys in Japan, 1859–1972*, ed. Hugh Cortazzi (Folkestone, UK: Global Orient, 2004), 9.

32. Rutherford Alcock, *The Capital of the Tycoon: A Narrative of a Three Years' Residence in Japan*, 2 vols. (London: Longman, 1863), 1:434–35; Meiji bunka kenkyū kai, ed., *Meiji bunka zenshū: Bekkan, Meiji jibutsu kigen* (Tokyo: Nihon hyōronsha, 1984), 1451.

33. Bird, *Unbeaten Tracks in Japan*, 14.

34. As with the Scottish terrier, a nineteenth-century Skye terrier was probably not only larger but also more physically powerful than today's animals of the same name, who have been bred for appearance over function. See note 30. For an insightful discussion of the relationship between hunting (with dogs) and masculinity in the American South, see Ted Ownby, *Subduing Satan: Religion, Recreation, and Manhood in the Rural South, 1865–1920* (Chapel Hill: University of North Carolina Press, 1990), 21–37.

35. Varner and Varner, *Dogs of the Conquest*, 193; Marion Schwarz, *A History of Dogs in the Early Americas* (New Haven: Yale University Press, 1977), 161–64.

36. See, for example, James Lockhart, ed., *We People Here: Nahuatl Accounts of the Conquest of Mexico* (Berkeley: University of California Press, 1993), 80, 97, 111, 273.

37. For more on English criticism of the Spanish and later abolitionist condemnation of the use of Indian-hunting and slave-catching "bloodhounds," see John Campbell, "The Seminoles, Bloodhounds, and Abolitionism," *Journal of Southern History* 72, no. 2 (May 2006): 259–302.

38. Thomas, *Man and the Natural World*, 42. French soldiers attempting to crush the Haitian Revolution deployed dogs purchased in Cuba for torture and on the battlefield, sometimes with disastrous consequences, such as during the skirmish near Port-au-Prince in 1803, when the dogs who were "ignorant of color prejudice" attacked fleeing French soldiers rather than black insurgents. Laurent Dubois, *Avengers of the New World: The Story of the Haitian Revolution* (Cambridge: Belknap Press, 2004), 292–93. For a more in-depth look at such deployments, see Sara E. Johnson, "'You Should Give Them Blacks to Eat': Waging Inter-American Wars of Torture and Terror," *American Quarterly* 61, no. 1 (March 2009): 65–92.

39. Mastromarino, "Teaching Old Dogs New Tricks," 25.

40. Tsukamoto, *Shōrui o meguru seiji*, 184–204.

41. Paul van der Velde and Rudolf Bachofner, eds., *The Deshima Diaries: Marginalia, 1700–1740* (Tokyo: Japan-Netherlands Institute, 1992), 280. Chinese merchants, too, may have participated in the canine trade.

42. Hugh Cortazzi, *Victorians in Japan: In and around the Treaty Ports* (London: Athlone, 1987), 174, fig. 1. This dog appears to be a greyhound, but it almost looks like a goat. The shape of its feet indicate that the latter is not the case, but the difficulty in distinguishing whether it is a dog or a goat aptly illustrates how nonphotographic images can easily, whether consciously or unintentionally, be depicted and interpreted in a way that is entirely beyond the control of the purported subjects, especially when they are nonhuman creatures.

43. Hashimoto Gyokuransai [Utagawa Sadahide], *Yokohama kaikō kenmonshi* (1862; Tokyo: Meicho kankōkai, 1967), 21–22.

44. Ibid., 15.

45. For other examples, see Hashimoto, *Yokohama kaikō kenmonshi*, 88–89, 96–97, 128–31, 168–71, 185–86, 193, 220–21; Kanagawa kenritsu rekishi hakubutsukan, ed., *Yokohama uki-yoe to sora tobu eshi Gountei Sadahide* (Yokohama: Kanagawa Kenritsu Rekishi Hakubutsukan, 1997), 44, 49, 52, 55, 59, 75, 97, 114; Ann Yonemura, *Yokohama: Prints from Nineteenth-Century Japan* (Washington, DC: Smithsonian Press, 1990), 79, 86–87,113, 117, 132, 134, 182–83; J. E. Hoare, *Japan's Treaty Ports and Foreign Settlements: The Uninvited Guests, 1859–1899* (Folkestone, UK: Japan Library, 1994), title page.

46. Okada Akio, *Inu to neko* (Tokyo: Mainichi shinbunsha, 1980), 119. Yet another Hashimoto print depicts a Westerner attempting to take a photograph of American ships in the harbor as three large Western dogs stare into the lens, wriggle between his legs, and chew on the camera stand. See Hashimoto, *Yokohama kaikō kenmonshi*, 112.

47. Shimizu Isao, *Meiji mangakan* (Tokyo: Kōdansha, 1979), 89, 94, 105.

48. Haga Tōru et al., *Bigō sobyō korekushon*, vol. 2, *Meiji no seisō* (Tokyo: Iwanami shoten, 1989), 35. The print is entitled, *Pierrot en Voyage* (*A Clown on a Journey*). Bigot often referred to or portrayed himself as a clown in his artwork.

49. Utsunomiya bijutsukan, *Bigot: Retrospective* (Utsunomiya: Utsunomiya Bijutsukan, 1998), 86–88.

50. Tsukamoto Manabu, *Edo jidaijin to dōbutsu* (Tokyo: Nihon editā sukūru shuppan, 1995), 235.

51. F. G. Notehelfer, ed., *Japan through American Eyes: The Journal of Francis Hall, Kangawa and Yokohama, 1859–1866* (Princeton: Princeton University Press, 1992), 360, 252.

52. Laurence Oliphant, *Elgin's Mission to China and Japan* (1859; Hong Kong: Oxford University Press, 1970), 89–90. Though Westerners no longer refer to any breed of dogs as Shantung terriers, these canines are probably related to dogs that became standardized as the Tibetan terrier breed. Collier, *Dogs of China and Japan*, 183; Author's correspondence with Pat Nelson of the Tibetan Terrier Club of America and Barbara Kolk of the AKC, 7 March 2007.

53. Cortazzi, *Victorians in Japan*, 215; Daily Press, *The Chronicle and Directory for China, Japan, and the Philippines, for the Year 1869* (Hong Kong: Daily Press, 1869), 58.

54. Hashimoto, *Yokohama kaikō kenmonshi*, 8.

55. Philipp Franz von Siebold with Conrad Jacob Temminck, *Fauna Japonica* (1842–44; Tokyo: Shokubutsu Bunken Hankō kai, 1934), 36–38, Mammalia table 10. For a more detailed analysis, see Kuga Kōun, "Shīboruto to Nihon no inu," *Shīboruto kenkyū* (November 1985): 93–112.

56. Arlette Kouwenhoven and Matthi Forrer, *Siebold and Japan: His Life and Work* (Leiden: Hotei, 2000), 85.

57. Charles Darwin, *On the Origin of Species by Means of Natural Selection; The Descent of Man and Selection in Relation to Sex*, Great Books of the Western World, vol. 49 (Chicago: Encyclopedia Britannica, 1955), 347.

58. Edward S. Morse, *Japan Day by Day, 1877, 1878–79, 1882–83*, 2 vols. (Boston: Houghton Mifflin, 1917), 1:388.

59. Percival Lowell, *Chosön: The Land of the Morning Calm; A Sketch of Korea* (Boston: Ticknor, 1886), 234.

60. Kipling, *Beast and Man in India*, 297.

61. Frances Wood, *No Dogs and Not Many Chinese: Treaty Port Life in China, 1843–1943* (London: John Murray, 1998), 122.

62. Isabella L. Bird, *Korea and Her Neighbors: A Narrative of Travel, with an Account of the Recent Vicissitudes and Present Position of the Country* (1897; Rutland, VT.: Charles E. Tuttle, 1986), 45.

63. A. P. Jenkins, ed., *The Journal and Official Correspondence of Bernard Jean Bettelheim 1845–54, Part 1 (1845–51)*, (Haebaru, Okinawa: Okinawa-ken kyōiku iinkai, 2005), 81.

64. For the accusation, see *Ryūkyū Ōkoku Hyōjoshomonjo*, ed. Ryūkyū Ōkoku Hyōjoshomonjo henshū iinkai, 20 vols. (Urasoe, Okinawa: Urasoe-shi kyōiku iinkai, 1989), 3:246.

65. Jenkins, *Journal*, 282–83.

66. Alcock, *Capital of the Tycoon*, 1:200. Of masterless samurai, that other threat of the streets, Alcock recorded: "I met in the 'tokaido' [highway] many officers, some in groups and others alone, armed with their two swords (about as dangerous and deadly weapons as men can well possess), and evidently intoxicated. They were drunk in various degrees, but all—the best of them—were in a state utterly unfit to be at large in a great thoroughfare, or trusted with weapons by which they might in an instant inflict fatal wounds or grievous injury.... They are not only insolent, and as a general rule offensive in their gestures and speech when they meet foreigners, but are very prone to put themselves directly in the path, and either dispute the passage with an air of menace, or sometimes even attempt to strike either horse or rider." Ibid., 127.

67. Laurence Oliphant, *Episodes in a Life of Adventure, or Moss from a Rolling Stone* (1887; Richmond: Curzon Press, 2000), 189–200.

68. Alcock, *The Capital of the Tycoon*, 2:165. The dogs might not appreciate a sign at Tōzenji today indicating that dogs are not welcome on the temple grounds.

69. Frederick Victor Dickens, *The Life of Sir Harry Parkes II* (1894; Wilmington, DE: Scholarly Resources, 1973), 149. This attack should not be confused with a more famous ambush that had occurred the previous year on March 23 as Parkes proceeded to his first interview with the Meiji emperor. In that assault, Parkes came even closer to death. The incident led to an imperial edict prohibiting attacks on foreigners. The whereabouts of Shah during the earlier attack is unclear.

70. In a similar vein, E. N. Lambert, a young assistant at the Yokohama branch of the Hongkong and Shanghai Banking Corporation and resident of the city's foreign enclave of Yamate in the early twentieth century, named one of his dogs Togo, either in honor or in disdain of Admiral Tōgō Heihachirō (1848–1934), who by defeating Russia's Baltic fleet in the Sea of Japan became the hero of the Russo-Japanese War of 1904–5. "E. N. Lambert Photo Album, No. 11" (Ac1–211c), photo no. 38, Yokohama Archives of History.

71. Lady Kate Lawson, *Highways and Homes of Japan* (London: Adelphi Terrace, 1920), 212.

72. Lowell, *Chosön*, 235.

73. Mrs. Will Gordon, "Glimpses of Old Korea," *Transactions and Proceedings of Japan Society, London* 16 (1918): 103, 111.

74. Archibald John Little, *Through the Yang-tse Gorges, or Trade and Travel in Western China* (London: Samson Low, Marston, and Company, 1898), 37–38. Little and his wife Alicia were not uniformly hostile to Chinese dogs, in particular small lapdogs. Together they adopted three local dogs—a Shantung terrier, a Peking pug, and a black Chow, that he tellingly named "Nigger," and she devoted a chapter, entitled "A Little Peking Pug," to mourn the death of Shing-erh (Little Apricot) in her book *Intimate China*. Mrs. Archibald Little, *Intimate China* (London: Hutchinson and Co., 1899), 38–39, 68, 446–56.

75. Notehelfer, *Japan through American Eyes*, 103, 252.

76. Rudyard Kipling, "Garm—A Hostage," in his *Collected Dog Stories* (Garden City, NY: Doubleday, 1934), 19–44.

77. Robert Fortune, *Yedo and Peking: A Narrative of a Journey to the Capitals of Japan and China* (London: Murray, 1863), 96–97.

78. Charles Darwin, *Descent of Man*, 303.

79. Ritvo, "Pride and Pedigree," 251. The italics are in the original.

80. Kipling, *Beast and Man in India*, 306, 309.

81. Robert Leighton, *The New Book of the Dog: A Comprehensive Natural History of British Dogs and Their Foreign Relatives, with Chapters on Law, Breeding, Kennel Management, and Veterinary Treatment* (London: Cassell, 1907), 524.

82. Gordon, "Fido," 247–49. See also Jacob Tropp, "Dogs, Poison, and the Meaning of Colonial Intervention in the Transkei, South Africa," *Journal of African History* 43 (2002): 455–56.

83. Ernest Mason Satow and A. G. S. Hawes, *A Handbook for Travellers in Central and Northern Japan* (Yokohama: Kelly, 1881), 40. See also, Mrs. Hugh Fraser, *Letters from Japan: A Record of Modern Life in the Island Empire* (London: MacMillan, 1905), 129.

84. Morse, *Japan Day by Day*, 1:388. An encounter with a "savage, wolfish-looking dog" appears elsewhere in Morse's journal (1:103). Morse's description of that dog as "bark[ing] viciously," and then "retreating and howling" partially contradicts his claim above that most native dogs "do not bark but howl."

85. George Hilaire Bousquet, *Le Japon de nos jours* (Paris: Hachette, 1877), 209. Any praise for native dogs by Westerners was often immediately tempered by qualifications or dismissals. The British horticulturalist Fortune, for example, praised the deer-hunting abilities of Chinese dogs remarking that "they are clever" but added, "they are not, however, to be compared for a moment with our English dogs." Robert Fortune, *A Journey to the Tea Countries of China* (London: John Murray, 1852), 152–53.

86. Brett L. Walker, *The Lost Wolves of Japan* (Seattle: University of Washington Press, 2005), 52.

87. Recent scientific research, using microsatellite typing, phylogenetic analysis, and genetic clustering methods to differentiate different dog breeds, suggests that the modern breeds with the closest genetic relationship to wolves and early pariah dogs include breeds from Africa, the Middle East, the Arctic, and Asia, such as native "Japanese" breeds. Heidi G. Parker et al., "Genetic Structure of the Purebred Domestic Dog," *Science* 304 (21 May 2004): 1163.

88. Richard Lydekker, ed., *The Royal Natural History*, 6 vols. (London: F. Warne, 1893), 1:520. See also, Alfred Edmund Brehm, *Brehm's Life of Animals: A Complete Natural History for Popular Home Instruction and for the Use of Schools*, 7 vols. (Chicago: Marquis, 1896), 1:206–8.

89. Hale, as quoted in Barry Alan Joyce, *The Shaping of American Ethnography: The Wilkes Exploring Expedition, 1838–1842* (Lincoln: University of Nebraska Press, 2001), 119. See also Joyce, "'As the Wolf from the Dog': American Overseas Exploration and the Compartmentalization of Humankind: 1838–1859" (PhD diss., University of California–Riverside, 1995), 5.

90. Morse, *Japan Day by Day*, 2:18.

91. George Taylor, *Man's Friend, the Dog* (New York: Stokes, 1891), 7.

92. A. V. Williams Jackson, *From Constantinople to the Home of Omar Khayyam* (1911; Piscataway, NJ: Gorgias Press, 2002), 2. See also, Fleming, *Travels on Horseback in Mantchu Tartary*, 234–35.

93. Bird, *Korea and her Neighbors*, 45. Likewise, the British travel writer Fleming wrote of dogs in western China: "Uncared for by the Chinese, hunted by Europeans, to whom it proves an endless source of annoyance by its nocturnal howlings, barkings, and noisy fights, and covered with mange and sores, the service it renders is yet great; for without it and the pig, as sanitary agents, heaven only knows what the Central Flowery Land would become in a short time. Its mission is a most disgusting one, and we would rather see this faithful and devoted friend of man cared for by the family, than find it the devourer of their filth, and the object of their disregard."

"The work is gone through in a systematic manner; every dog having its allotment in a certain district of a town from which it must not intrude upon that of others, without the penalty of being half worried. Their tastes, as may be inferred, are not over nice, for they hesitate at no kind of diet. Can anyone who has seen these canine vultures in the deserted villages in the neighborhood of Peking a few days after an engagement, forget the sensation of horror he experienced, when inadvertently he startled a swarm of them from feasting on the body of a dead Chinaman in some lonely spot?" Fleming, *Travels on Horseback*, 234–35.

94. R. Lee, *Anecdotes of the Habits and Instincts of Animals* (Philadelphia: Lindsay, 1852), 85.

95. In England during the 1880s, several highly regarded scientists blamed an increase in rabies on inbreeding and the resultant excitability of pedigreed dogs. See John K. Walton, "Mad Dogs and Englishmen: The Conflict over Rabies in Late Victorian England" *Journal of Social History* 13 (1979): 227.

96. *Japan Weekly Mail*, 8 March 1883, 132.

97. Robert A. Bickers and Jeffrey N. Wasserstrom, "Shanghai's 'Dogs and Chinese Not Admitted' Sign: Legend, History, and Memory," *China Quarterly* 142 (June 1995): 444–66; Wood, *No Dogs and Not Many Chinese*, 2. The former authors cast doubt on the actual existence of such signs but recognize that it is the perception of a dehumanizing epithet that matters. In a manner similar to violence allegedly committed by Japanese soldiers using army dogs in China during the 1930s and 1940s, Communist government officials, historians, and journalists have actively manipulated stories of the "Chinese and No Dogs Admitted" signs to stir up antiforeign sentiment and nationalism.

98. Even though such dogs were certainly not all German shepherds, they almost always were perceived as such. I will return to the German shepherd as the quintessential colonial dog in chapter 4. For a more focused examination of how the breed came to be identified with Imperial and Nazi Germany and then other masters throughout the colonial world, see Aaron Skabelund, "Breeding Racism: The Imperial Battlefields of the 'German' Shepherd," *Society and Animals* 16, no. 4 (Winter 2008): 354–71.

99. For more on this incident, see *When We Were Kings*, a documentary directed by Leon Gast, 92 min., released by Gramercy Pictures, 1996. I am grateful to Gregory Mann for first drawing my attention to this film. Foreman's poor selection of canine breed and the reaction of Zairians caught the attention of contemporary American sportswriters, too. Shirley Povish, "Ali Declares War, Then Takes Wing, Foreman Dogs It," *Washington Post*, 28 October 1974, D1. Another writer recorded a different spelling for Foreman's dog: "Daggo." David Anderson, "George Foreman and Pol Parrot," *New York Times*, 25 October 1974, 45. Two other African examples of the postcolonial grudge held against certain dog breeds associated with European imperialism are highlighted in the fictional stories of Ngũgĩ wa Thiong'o, *A Grain of Wheat* (Oxford: Heinemann, 1967) and J. M. Coetzee, *Disgrace* (New York: Viking, 1999).

2. Civilizing Canines; or, Domesticating and Destroying Dogs

1. Okada, *Inu to neko*, 125–26.

2. Thomas, *Man and the Natural World*. For a broader argument, with application to human-animal relations, about the spread of ideas of what it meant to be civilized, see Norbert Elias, *The Civilizing Process* (Oxford: Blackwell, 1994). For an example of the civilizing process and its impact on attitudes about nature and animals in early twentieth-century Sweden, see Jonas Frykman and Orvar Löfgren, *Culture Builders: A Historical Anthropology of the Middle-Class Life* (New Brunswick, NJ: Rutgers University Press, 1987), 42–87.

3. Kete, *Beast in the Boudoir*, 97–114; Ritvo, *Animal Estate*, 167–202; Walton, "Mad Dogs and Englishman;" Neil Pemberton and Michael Worboys, *Mad Dogs and Englishmen: Rabies in Britain, 1830–2000* (London: Palgrave Macmillan, 2007).

4. Hagiwara Otohiko, *Tōkyō kaika hanjō shi* (March 1865), in *Meiji bunka zenshū*, 28 vols., ed. Meiji bunka kenkyūkai (Tokyo: Nihon hyōronsha, 1968), 8:231.

5. Kipling, *Beast and Man in India*, 306–8.

6. Kanagaki Robun, Ochiai Yoshiiku, and Kan Fusao, *Seiyō dōchū hizakurige* (Tokyo: Bankyūkaku, 1870), vol. 1, 5v–6r; 19r; vol. 7, 16v–17r; vol. 15, 25v–26r. For a more in-depth analysis of *Seiyō dōchū hizakurige*, see John Pierre Mertz, "Internalizing Social Difference: Kanagaki Robun's *Shanks' Mare to Western Seas*," in *New Directions in the Study of Meiji Japan*, ed. Helen Hardacre and Adam L. Kern (Leiden,: Brill, 1997), 219–28.

7. Ibid., vol. 12, 2v–3r.

8. "Kaika no inu to fukaika no inu no hanashi," in *Meiji bunka zenshū*, 24:33–34.

9. Ibid., 24:2.

10. Fraser, *Letters from Japan*, 132–33.

11. "Tokushū: Tokugawa Yoshinobu," *Taiyō*, no. 449 (April 1998): cover.

12. *Shōnen kurabu* 1, no. 1 (November 1914): cover.

13. Morse, *Japan Day by Day*, 1:246. See also Griffis, *Mikado's Empire*, 451.

14. Mary Crawford Fraser, *A Diplomat's Wife in Japan: Sketches at the Turn of the Century*, ed. Hugh Cortazzi (New York: Weatherhill, 1982), 112, fig. 1.

15. Haga Tōru, Ogi Shinzō, and Maeda Ai, eds., *Meiji Taishō zu shi*, 17 vols. (Tokyo: Chikuma shobō, 1978), 1:250. The artist is unknown.

16. Kete, *Beast in the Boudoir*, 84–87; Walton, "Mad Dogs and Englishman," 222.

17. Nanba Shinshichirō, "Yosebumi," *Yomiuri shinbun*, 7 March 1878, 4.

18. Harold Bolitho, "The Dog Shogun," in *Self and Biography: Essays on the Individual and Society in Asia*, ed. Gungwu Wang (Sydney: Sydney University Press for the Australian Academy of the Humanities, 1975), 123–39. For more on Tsunayoshi and the politics of canine protection, see Tsukamoto, *Shōrui o meguru seiji*; Beatrice M. Bodart-Bailey, *The Dog Shogun: The Personality and Policies of Tokugawa Tsunayoshi* (Honolulu: University of Hawaii Press, 2006).

19. Tokibō, "Yosebumi," *Yomiuri Shinbun*, 18 May 1880, 4.

20. Shiga Shigetaka, "Shin naikaku sōridaijin ni shomō su," *Shiga Jūkō zenshū*, 8 vols. (Tokyo: Shiga Jūkō zenshū hankō kai, 1927–29), 1:9–10. For more on hunting in late nineteenth-century Japan, see Okada, *Inu to neko*, 128–43.

21. "Tōkyō shinai kasanaru kaiinu to kaineko," *Yomiuri shinbun*, 27 October 1901, 4.

22. *Japan Weekly Mail*, 8 March 1883, 132.

23. Taniguchi Kengo, *Inu no Nihon shi: Ningen to tomo ni ayunda ichiman nen no monogatari* (Tokyo: PHP Kenkyūjo, 2000), 191–92.

24. Jones was probably particularly interested in ensuring the commercial success of Shimōsa, because, unlike most foreigners, he exempted himself from extraterritorial privileges in order to circumvent an injunction against foreign advisers having a personal stake in the profits of quasi-government projects. Hazel J. Jones, *Lives Machines: Hired Foreigners and Meiji Japan* (Vancouver: University of British Columbia Press, 1980), 176.

25. Kunaichō, ed., *Shimōsa goryō bokuyōshi* (Tokyo: Kunaichō, 1974), 90. I was unable to find this statement by Jones in English. This is my translation from a Japanese secondary source of what he presumably said.

26. Ibid., 90–91.

27. Tsukamoto, *Edo jidaijin to dōbutsu*, 164.

28. "Chiba kenka bokuyōjō kinbō yaken bokusatu kisoku hakkō ni tsuki kaku kōshi ne tsūchi no ken" is quoted in full in Tsunoyama Yukihiro, "O-yatoi gaikokujin Appu Jonzu (hoi)," *Kansai daigaku keizai ronshū* 38 (1987): 38–39. For more on Jones, see Tsunoyama, "O-yatoi gaikokujin Appu Jonzu: Shimousa bokuyōjō ni okeru men'yō kaiiku," *Kansai daigaku keizai ronshū* 37, no. 6 (1986): 585–618.

29. "Yaken bokusatsu ni tsuite no teiji bun," Yokota Masao Papers, Sanrizuka Museum of the Imperial Household Ranch, Narita, Japan.

30. Edwin Dun photo album, unpaginated, Dun and Machimura Memorial Museum, Sapporo, Japan.

31. Ibid.

32. Edwin Dun, *Reminiscences of Nearly a Half Century in Japan* [MS., n.d.]., 37, Resource Collection for Northern Studies, Hokkaido University Library, Sapporo. For more on Edwin Dun and the elimination of canines in Hokkaido, with an emphasis on the killing of lupines, see Walker, *Lost Wolves of Japan*, 129–83. For an additional biographical overview, see Fumiko Fujita, *American Pioneers and the Japanese Frontier: American Experts in Nineteenth-Century Japan* (Westport, CT: Greenwood Press, 1994): 77–87.

33. Yamada Kazuyuki, "'Hokkaidō ijū kaiko roku' to Iwane Seichi," *Shizunai bungei* 11 (1991): 54–55.

34. "Niikappu bokujō bokuba oyobi hatachi o sonshō suru yaken sakkaku hō no ken," (25 January 1878), in *Honchō-bu katatsu shorui* (02422, no. 6), Hokkaido Prefectural Archives, Sapporo.

35. "Mushu no yaken bokusatsusha he teate kin shikyū no ken," (8 April 1878), in *Shusai roku* (A4–54, no. 51), Hokkaido Prefectural Archives, Sapporo.

36. Hokkaidō Keisatsu Henshū Iinkai, ed., *Hokkaidō keisatsu shi* (Sapporo: Hokkaidō Keisatsu Honbu, 1968), 188–89.

37. "Hokkaidō Esashi ni sakukon akuken," *Yomiuri shinbun*, 16 July 1882, 2.

38. Kanzō Uchimura, *The Diary of a Japanese Convert* (New York: Fleming H. Revell, 1895), 25.

39. Brett L. Walker, *The Conquest of Ainu Lands: Ecology and Culture in Japanese Expansion, 1590–1800* (Berkeley: University of California, 2001), 160.

40. For more on the legend linking Ainu ancestrally with dogs and its abuses, see Sasaki Toshikazu, "Inu wa senzo nari ya—Ainu no sōsei setsuwa to Wazo dōso ron," in *Kita kara no Nihon shi*, ed. Hokkaidō-Tōhoku Kenkyūkai, 2 vols. (Tokyo: Sanseidō, 1990), 2:189–225.

41. Walker, *Conquest of Ainu Lands*, 169.

42. John Batchelor, "Findings after 62 Years in Japan," *Hokkaidō shakai jigyō* 18 (1939): 32. For other examples, see Bird, *Unbeaten Tracks in Japan*, 233, 315; Walker, *Conquest of Ainu Lands*, 230. For more on Ainu-Japanese relations, see David Howell, *Capitalism from Within: Economy, Society, and the State in a Japanese Fishery* (Berkeley: University of California Press, 1995).

43. Kakizaki Hakyō, *Ishū Retsuzō* (1790; Hakodate: Tosho rikai, 1988), 11.

44. Richard Siddle, *Race, Resistance and the Ainu of Japan* (London: Routledge, 1996), 49.

45. Mark Derr, *A Dog's History of America: How Our Best Friend Explored, Conquered, and Settled a Continent* (New York: North Point Press, 2004), 107–21.

46. James F. Rusling, *Across America; or, The Great West and the Pacific Coast* (New York: Sheldon and Company, 1874), 117–18. For other examples from the nineteenth-century western United States, see John E. Baur, *Dogs on the Frontier* (1964; Fairfax, VA: Delinger's, 1982), 6, 17, 20–21, 26–27.

47. Thurston, *Lost History of the Canine Race*, 160.

48. Anderson, *Creatures of Empire*, 34.

49. Thurston, *Lost History of the Canine Race*, 160.

50. For an example from British India, see Jesse S. Palsetia, "Mad Dogs and Parsis: The Bombay Dog Riots of 1832," *Journal of the Royal Asiatic Society* 11, no. 1 (2001): 13–30. For examples from southern Africa, see Gordon, "Fido," 240–54; Tropp, "Dogs, Poison and the Meaning of Colonial Intervention in the Transkei, South Africa," 451–72. For Australia, see James Boyce, "Canine Revolution: The Social and Environmental Impact of the Introduction of the Dog to Tasmania," *Environmental History* 11, no. 1 (2006): 102–29; Merryl Parker, "The Cunning Dingo," *Society and Animals* 15, no. 1 (2007): 69–78. For New Zealand, see Ian Wedde, "Walking the Dog," in *Knowing Animals*, ed. Laurence Simmons and Philip Armstrong (Leiden: Brill, 2007), 279. For an examination of campaigns to eliminate wolves in the United

States, see Jon T. Coleman, *Vicious: Wolves and Men in America* (New Haven: Yale University Press, 2004).

51. Lance van Sittert, "'Keeping the Enemy at Bay': The Extermination of Wild Carnivora in the Cape Colony, 1889–1910," *Environmental History* 3, no. 3 (July 1998): 352.

52. Tsukamoto, *Edo jidaijin to dōbutsu*, 162–163. See also Walker, *Lost Wolves of Japan*, 96–128.

53. *Nihon minzoku daijiten*, s.v. "Inu," 2 vols., 1:119.

54. Tsukamoto Akira, "Jingū kōgō densetsu to kinsei Nihon to Chōsen-kan," *Shinrin* 76, no. 6 (1996): 1–33.

55. Hirata Atsutane, "Ibuki oroshi," *Hirata Atsutane zenshū*, 15 vols. (Tokyo: Meicho shuppan, 1976–1981), 15:137–38; English translation in Donald Keene, *The Japanese Discovery of Europe, 1720–1830* (Stanford: Stanford University Press, 1969), 170. In similar, if more subtle terms, the Buddhist priest-poet Gesshō (1817–58) wrote the following verse on hearing that the port of Shimoda had been opened to foreigners: "For seven miles by the river the dogs and sheep forage. / The hues of spring visit the wastes of quake-ridden earth. / Only the cherry blossoms take not on the rank barbarian stench, / But breathe to the morning sun the fragrance of a nation's soul." Donald Keene, ed., *Anthology of Japanese Literature: Earliest Era to Mid-Nineteenth Century* (Rutland, VT.: Tuttle, 1975), 439.

56. For an overview of the development of hygienic and public health regimes in Japan, see Ono Yoshirō, *"Seiketsu" no kindai* (Tokyo: Kōdansha, 1997).

57. See, for example, Kawano Mitsunaga, ed., *Ōita-ken keisatsu shi* (Ōita: Ōita-ken Keisatsu-bu, 1943), 1485–88.

58. Imagawa Isao, *Inu no gendai shi* (Tokyo: Gendai shokan, 1996), 86.

59. Ibid., 85.

60. "Chikukenhyō no nai inu ya kyōken wa bokusatsu," *Tōkyō koshinbun*, 1 July 1880, in *Meiji nyūsu jiten*, ed. Edamatsu Shigeyuki, Sugiura Tadashi, and Yagi Kyōsuke, 9 vols. (Tokyo: Mainichi komyunikēshonzu, 1983–86), 2:42.

61. Yanagita Kunio, "Mame no ha to taiyō," in *Yanagita Kunio zenshū*, 32 vols. (Tokyo: Chikuma shobō, 1989), 2:298.

62. For more on *burakumin* and dogs during the Tokugawa period and earlier, see Nunobiki Toshio, "Hashika inu," *Nihon rekishi* 331 (December 1975): 75–81; Amino Yoshihiko, *Nihon no rekishi o yominaosu* (Tokyo: Chikuma gakugei bunkō, 2005), 81–142.

63. The phrase is from George De Vos and Hiroshi Wagatsuma, *Japan's Invisible Race* (Berkeley: University of California Press, 1967). For examples of discrimination stemming from the identification of *burakumin* with the elimination of dogs, see Mikiso Hane, *Peasants, Rebels, and Outcastes: The Underside of Modern Japan* (New York: Pantheon, 1982), 146, 152, 164; "Yosebumi," *Yomiuri shinbun*, 30 May 1877, 3; "Genshakai nishiki no ura (Inu koroshi no uchimaku)," *Yomiuri shinbun*, 1–8 April 1902, 4.

64. "Yosebumi," *Yomiuri shinbun*, 10 August 1877, 4.

65. "Yosebumi," *Yomiuri shinbun*, 10 February 1877, 2.

66. Imagawa, *Inu no gendai shi*, 87–90.

67. Nishi Amane, "Travel by Foreigners within the Country (Naichi Ryokō)," in *Meiroku Zasshi: Journal of the Japanese Enlightenment*, trans. William Reynolds Braisted (Cambridge: Harvard University Press, 1976), 287–93.

68. Fukuzawa Yukichi, "Refuting Nishi's Discussion on Travel by Foreigners in the Country," in *Meiroku Zasshi*, 319–24.

69. *Japan Weekly Mail*, 7 August 1897, 141.

70. Julia Meech-Pekarik, *The World of the Meiji Print: Impressions of a New Civilization* (New York: Weatherhill, 1987), 187.

71. S. Bigot, *Le Japon en 1897* (Tokyo: publisher unknown, 1897), unpaginated, Paul C. Blum Collection, Yokohama Archives of History. The waterfalls mentioned in the story are probably

the Nunobiki cascades in Kobe, which along with Yokohama was a major treaty-port city. Another cartoon in the same volume imagines the "charming country of Japan" after the amended treaties have been implemented. It depicts foreigners and their dogs strolling down an avenue in head-to-toe (or -tail) armor. The new apparel, reads the French caption, is "now being used by foreign residents and tourists in Japan" to protect themselves, presumably from Japanese people and street dogs.

72. Morse, *Japan Day by Day*, 1:264. See also 1:193–94; Griffis, *Mikado's Empire*, 390; Fraser, *Letters from Japan*, 129. For more on foreign views of the treatment of animals in nineteenth-century Japan, see Watanabe Kyōji, *Yukishi yo no omokage* (Fukuoka: Ashi shobō, 1998), 403–36.

73. Henry Knollys, *Sketches of Life in Japan* (London: Chapman and Hall, 1887), 139–40.

74. Shimizu Isao, *Bigō ga mita Nihonjin* (Tokyo: Kōdansha, 2001), 45.

75. Haga, *Bigō sobyō korekushyon*, 2:84.

76. "The Treatment of Animals," *Japan Weekly Mail*, 13 September 1884, 258–60.

77. Yasumaru Yoshio, "Minshū undo ni okeru 'kindai,'" in *Nihon kindai shisō taikei*, ed. Yasumaru Yoshio and Fukaya Katsumi, 23 vols. (Tokyo: Iwanami shoten, 1989), 21:455.

78. Palmira Brummett, *Image and Imperialism in the Ottoman Revolutionary Press, 1908–1911* (Albany: State University of New York Press, 2000), 262–66.

79. Alan M. Beck, *The Ecology of Stray Dogs: A Study of Free-Ranging Urban Animals* (Baltimore: York Press, 1973), 40.

80. Peter Duus, "Presidential Address: Weapons of the Weak, Weapons of the Strong—The Development of the Japanese Political Cartoon," *Journal of Asian Studies* 60, no. 4 (2001): 993.

81. Honda Kinkichirō, "Kenhei o kizuite minken o fusegu," *Marumaru chinbun* (3 April 1880): 2456–57. For more on the dichotomy between officials (*kan*) and the people (*min*), see Carol Gluck, *Japan's Modern Myths: Ideology in the Late Meiji Period* (Princeton: Princeton University Press, 1985), 60–67.

82. *Marumaru chinbun* (9 March 1878): 806–8.

83. Soeda Tomomichi, *Enka no Meiji Taishō shi* (Tokyo: Tōsui shobo, 1982), 26.

84. "Kizoku fugō no jūni jikan rōdō," *Aka* (1 October 1919): 6.

85. Kobayashi Takiji, "The Factory Ship" and "The Absentee Landlord," trans. Frank Motofuji (Tokyo: University of Tokyo Press, 1973), 175.

86. "Chikuken zei fuka no gi," *Yomiuri shinbun*, 3 June 1893, 2.

87. "Shiba kōen no yaken," *Yomiuri shinbun*, 21 November 1903, 3.

88. Matsuo, "Sono hi sono hi," *Yomiuri shinbun*, 30 May 1903, 1.

89. "Yaken bokusatsu no kōseiseki," (28 January 1903), and "Kaiinu kazei no setsu," (7 February 1903), *Taiwan nichinichi shinpō*. After taking control of Korea in 1905, Japanese colonial authorities initiated similar campaigns in that territorial possession as well. See Abe Yoshio, "On the Corean and Japanese Wolves," *Journal of Science of the Hiroshima University* 1 (1930): ser. B, div. 1, (Zoology), 33–38.

90. Takashi Fujitani, *Splendid Monarchy: Power and Pageantry in Modern Japan* (Berkeley: University of California Press, 1998), 91–92.

91. In illustrations in newspapers and elsewhere during and in the years after his death, Saigō was portrayed with several different dogs, including a canine that was probably the grandson of the Western dog. Saigō and this dog can be seen on the cover of the former's English-language biography: Mark Ravina, *The Last Samurai: The Life and Battles of Saigō Takamori* (Hoboken, NJ: John Wiley and Sons, 2004). For other illustrations, see Emi Chizuko, "Saigō Takamori dōzō kō: Sono kensetsu katei o chūshin ni," *Bunka shigengaku* 3 (31 March 2005): 73–75.

92. Yoshida Chizuko, "Saigō-san no aiken," *Ueno* 417 (January 1994): 16–17; Emi, "Saigō Takamori dōzō kō," 75. Art historians Yoshida and Emi both concede that there is a lot of uncertainly about Gotō's design decisions and their sequence. Yoshida indicates that Gotō may have created a mock-up and then scrapped it, but she is unsure of the timing. The Satsuma

dog may have also been known as the Sakarajima dog. There are no dogs called by this name now. See Kōhō-shitsu, "Ueno no mori no Saigō no inu," *Katei-ken* (January 1985): 12–14.

93. "Nanshū Dōzō no aiken ga mondai," *Hōchi shinbun*, 18 August 1898, in *Meiji nyūsu jiten*, 6:274.

94. Uchida Roan, "Inu monogatari," in *Uchida Roan zenshū*, ed. Nomura Takashi, 13 vols. (Tokyo: Yumani shobō, 1986), 11:381–405. Uchida's use of an animal as a storyteller anticipated Natsume Soseki's feline narrator in his famous novel *Wagahai wa neko de aru (I am a Cat)* in 1905.

95. Takahisa Heishirō, *Nihon inu no kaikata* (Tokyo: Shun'yōdō, 1933), 222.

96. Inokuma Ken'ichirō, *Tekketsu* (Tokyo: Meiji shuppansha, 1911), 196.

3. Fascism's Furry Friends

1. Kume Gen'ichi, *Hachikō*, illustrated by Ishida Takeo (Tokyo: Kinnohoshisha, 1971); Ministry of Finance, Printing Bureau, *20-seiki dezain kitte*, 23 February 2000, no. 7.

2. Pamela S. Turner, *Hachiko: The True Story of a Loyal Dog*, illustrated by Yana Nascimbene (Boston: Houghton Mifflin, 2004); Lesléa Newman, *Hachiko Waits*, illustrated by Machiyo Kodaira (New York: Henry Holt, 2004); Claude Helft, *Hatchiko, chien de Tokyo*, illustrated by Jiang Hong Chen (Paris: Picquier Jeunesse, 2005); Shizuko O. Koster, *Hachi-ko: The Samurai Dog* (Baltimore: PublishAmerica, 2007); and Julie Chrystan, *Hachiko: The True Story of the Royal Dogs of Japan and One Faithful Akita* (Beverly Hills, CA: Dove Books, 2009).

3. Edwin Seidensticker, *Tokyo Rising: The City since the Great Earthquake* (New York: Knopf, 1990), 123.

4. Benedict Anderson, *Imagined Communities* (London: Verso, 1983); Eric J. Hobsbawm and Terence Ranger, eds., *The Invention of Tradition* (Cambridge: Cambridge University Press, 1983); Anthony D. Smith, *The Ethnic Origins of Nations* (New York: Basil Blackwell, 1986), 175–208.

5. Steve Baker, *Picturing the Beast: Animals, Identity, and Representation* (1993; Champaign: University of Illinois Press, 2001), 33–73.

6. See Simonetta Falasca-Zamponi, *Fascist Spectacle: The Aesthetics of Power in Mussolini's Italy* (Berkeley: University of California Press, 1997), 68–70, 149–62; *Mussolini: Italy's Nightmare*, 50 min., A&E Home Video, 1995.

7. Robert O. Paxton, "The Five Stages of Fascism," *Journal of Modern History* 70 (March 1998): 1–23.

8. Andrew Gordon, *Labor and Imperial Democracy in Prewar Japan* (Berkeley: University of California Press, 1991), 333–39.

9. E. Bruce Reynolds, ed., *Japan in the Fascist Era* (New York: Palgrave Macmillan, 2004); Harry Harootunian, *Overcome by Modernity: History, Culture, and Community in Interwar Japan* (Princeton: Princeton University Press, 2000), 62–63; Leslie Pincus, *Authenticating Culture in Imperial Japan: Kuki Shūzō and the Rise of National Aesthetics* (Berkeley: University of California Press, 1995), 216.

10. Tetsuo Najita and H. D. Harootunian, "Japanese Revolt against the West: Political and Cultural Criticism in the Twentieth Century," in *Cambridge History of Japan*, vol. 6, *The Twentieth Century*, ed. Peter Duus (Cambridge: Cambridge University Press, 1988), 714.

11. Boria Sax, *Animals in the Third Reich: Pets, Scapegoats, and the Holocaust* (New York: Continuum, 2000), 75. The National Socialists in Germany, who made a practice of "imagining the nation in nature," to invoke Thomas M. Lekan's book title, mobilized other large predators and ungulates, as well as the physical land, for symbolic purposes. Thomas M. Lekan, *Imagining the Nation in Nature: Landscape Preservation and German Identity, 1885–1945* (Cambridge: Harvard University Press, 2004). The Nazis morally elevated certain nonhuman creatures, associated certain beasts with themselves, and animalized groups of human "Others." Arnold Arluke

and Clinton R. Sanders, "Boundary Work in Nazi Germany," in *Regarding Animals,* ed. Arluke and Sanders (Philadelphia: Temple University Press, 1996), 132–66.

12. The book was published in English as *The German Shepherd in Word and Picture,* trans. Carrington Charke and rev. Joseph Schwabacher (Jena, DEU: Anton Kämfe, 1923), and in Japanese as *Doitsu shepādo inu: Kaisetsu to shashin,* 5 vols., trans. Arisaka Mitsutaka and Karita Hideo (Tokyo: Teikoku gun'yōken kyōkai, 1934–36).

13. Sax, *Animals in the Third Reich,* 83; Wolfgang Wippermann and Detlef Berentzen, *Die Deutschen und ihre Hunde: Ein Sonderweg der Mentalitätsgeschichte?* (Berlin: Siedler, 1999), 67.

14. Kete, *Beast in the Boudoir.* For examples of similar trends in industrializing and urbanizing early modern Britain, see Thomas, *Man and the Natural World.*

15. Saitō Hirokichi, *Nihon no inu to ōkami* (Tokyo: Sekkaisha, 1964), 332.

16. The canines of this region were probably more commonly known at this time as Ōdate dogs, but by the 1930s they came to be called Akita.

17. Saitō, *Nihon no inu to ōkami,* viii.

18. In 1988 journalist Suzuki Takurō (1924–94) published an article in which he claimed that the idea for the Hachikō story originated with *Asahi* reporter Watanabe Shin'ichirō (1900–88), but it seems most likely that the article was suggested by Saitō and written by Watanabe. Suzuki Takurō, "Asahi shinbun ga tsukutta 'Chūken Hachikō' shinwa," *Bungei shunjū* 66, no. 10 (August 1988): 94. Saitō's leading role in the popularization of Hachikō was recognized by the *Mainichi shinbun,* which called him "The Parent Who Gave Birth to the 'Loyal Dog Hachikō' " in the title of his obituary in 1964. "Inu o ai shi kenkyū hitosuji, 'Chūken Hachikō' umi no oya, dōbutsu aigo shūkan o mae ni, Saitō-san no shi," *Mainichi shinbun,* 20 September 1964.

19. "Itoshi ya rōken monogatari: Ima wa yo ni naki shujin no kaeri o machikaneru nana nenkan," *Asahi shinbun,* 4 October 1932, 8.

20. Tokyo Imperial Hotel holiday card, personal collection, Christine Kim, Washington, D.C. The selection of dogs is not surprising. The following year, 1934, was the Year of the Dog according to the Chinese astrological calendar, and in Japan New Year's greeting cards often feature one of the twelve animals of the appointed zodiac.

21. For the most in-depth treatment of Keller's visit, see Nicholas C. Rhoden, *Pawprints in Japan: Dogs in Myth and History* (Richmond, CA: Fire Lake Press, 2002), 33–54.

22. Saitō, "Nihon inu to wa donna inu ka," in *Nihon no inu to ōkami,* 271.

23. Takada Susumu, "Aikenka retsuden," *Bungei shunjū* 82, no. 5 (March 2004): 188.

24. Saitō Hiroshi, "Nihon inu no hanashi, danseiteki na utsukushii kata, yūkan de seishitsu, subete no ten de sekai muhi," *Yomiuri shinbun,* 29 April 1929, 3; Shinzo Kobayashi, "The Pure Japanese-Breed of Dog: Westernizing of Japan Has Had Its Effect upon the *Canis Familiaris Japonicus,*" *American Kennel Gazette* 47, no. 5 (1 May 1930): 19–21, 113–15. Kobayashi noted that Saitō supplied him with advice and materials for his piece.

25. "Nihon inu hozon kai kaiin meibo," *Nihon inu* 1, no. 1 (April 1932): 74–78.

26. Baba Kazuo, ed., *Senjika Nihon bunka dantai jiten,* 4 vols. (Tokyo: Ōzora sha, 1990), 2:824–25.

27. Julia Adeney Thomas, *Reconfiguring Modernity: Concepts of Nature in Japanese Political Ideology* (Berkeley: University of California Press, 2001), 179–208.

28. Mariko Shinoda, "Scientists as Preservationists: Natural Monuments in Japan, 1906–1931," *Historia Scientiarum* 8, no. 2 (1998): 143–46.

29. Department of Education, *Preservation of Natural Monuments in Japan II* (Tokyo: Monbushō, 1933), 19. The Ministry of Home Affairs administered the law from its passage until 1928, when jurisdiction was transferred to the Ministry of Education. From 1920 to 1926, twenty-four zoological items were designated as natural monuments. Most of these were areas inhabited by wild animals, but they also included a number of wild species, such as the Mikado pheasant and the Japanese spoonbill, as well as domesticated animals such as the long-tailed

chicken and the diminutive Mishima cattle. Shinoda, "Scientists as Preservationists," 148; Department of Education, *Preservation of Natural Monuments*, 20.

30. Watase Shōzaburō, "Nihonken ni tsuite," *Inu no zasshi* 31 (January 1921): 5; "Inu to Nihon bunka," *Inu no zasshi* 34 (August 1921): 11–14; "Nihonken no kigen ni tsuite," *Rigaku kai* 20, no. 2 (1922): 26–26. Watase used the terms *Nihonken* and *waken* interchangeably to refer to native dogs.

31. *Shiseki meishō tennen ki'nenbutsu shitei*, no. 82, D531 (1933–1941), unpaginated, Bureau of Cultural Affairs, Ministry of Education Archive, Tokyo, Japan.

32. "Wakentō yorokobe: Shiba inu ga tennen ki'nenbutsu ni," *Asahi shinbun*, 11 October 1936, 13.

33. Kishi Kazutoshi, *Chūken Hachikō monogatari* (Tokyo: Monasu, 1934), 463–64.

34. Stephanitz, *The German Shepherd in Word and Picture*, 196–97.

35. Kishi, *Chūken Hachikō monogatari*, 21.

36. Hayashi Masaharu, ed., *Hachikō bunken shū* (Tokyo: Hayashi Masaharu, 1991), 210–11.

37. Ibid.

38. Saitō, *Nihon no inu to ōkami*, 269–70.

39. Hata Ichirō, "Nihon inu kaigai shinshutsu," *Nihon inu* 3, no. 7 (July 1934): 147–48.

40. Ibid., 134–40.

41. Yanagita contributed several articles to the Society's magazine and assisted Saitō in the discovery of a Meiji-era natural history archive in Yamagata Prefecture that included some rare illustrations of indigenous canines. The text probably confirmed Saitō's dislike for Westernizing trends of the second half of the nineteenth century. As mentioned in chapter 2, it described how foreign dogs were spreading rapidly while local dogs were disappearing. For more on Yanagita's early fascination with Japan's mountain regions, which he abandoned in the late 1920s for the rice-yielding plains, see Gerald Figal, *Civilization and Monsters: Spirits of Modernity in Meiji Japan* (Durham: Duke University Press, 1999), 138–39; Eiji Oguma, *A Genealogy of "Japanese" Self-Images*, trans. David Askew (Melbourne: Trans Pacific Press, 2002), 175–80.

42. Saitō, *Nihon no inu to ōkami*, 269.

43. Takahisa, *Nihon inu no kaikata*, 219.

44. Stephanitz, *German Shepherd*, 18, 22–23. As part of his effort to effectively link the Roman Empire with his fascist regime, Mussolini, actively incorporated wolf and eagle iconography to inspire national passion. The former symbol was based on a myth of a she-wolf who was said to have raised the future founders of the city of Rome, Romulus and Remus, after the twins were abandoned on the shores of the Tiber Sea by their parents, Mars, the god of war, and Rhea Silvia, a princess. See Piero Melograni, "The Cult of the Duce in Mussolini's Italy," *Journal of Contemporary History* 11, no. 4 (October 1976): 229–30; Richard J. Samuels, *Machiavelli's Children: Leaders and Their Legacies in Italy and Japan* (Ithaca: Cornell University Press, 2003), 160. I put "German" shepherd in quotation marks because the breed, just as the Akita, Shiba, and other "Japanese" dogs later were, was created, codified, nationalized, and imagined to be German.

45. Sax, *Animals in the Third Reich*, 75–76.

46. Ibid., 84.

47. See Yanagita, "Ōkami no yukue" and "Ōkami shi zatsudan," in *Yanagita Kunio zenshū*, 32 vols. (Tokyo: Chikuma shobō, 1990), 24:584–630. The second article was originally published in *Nihon inu* in two parts in September 1932 and January 1933.

48. Tsukamoto, *Edo jidaijin to dōbutsu*, 163.

49. Arnold Arluke and Borio Sax, "Understanding Nazi Animal Protection and the Holocaust," *Anthrozoös* 5, no. 1 (1992): 6–31.

50. Wippermann and Berentzen, *Die Deutschen und ihre Hunde*, 69. See also Enrique Ucelay Da Cal, "The Influence of Animal Breeding on Political Racism," *History of European Ideas* 15, no. 4–6 (1992): 717–25.

51. Wippermann and Berentzen, *Die Deutschen und ihre Hunde*, 75.

52. Although stalwart Japanese eugenicists failed to convince government bureaucrats to implement policies like those of Hitler, historian Christopher W. A. Szpilman argues that their popular writings and speeches "created a kind of social consensus in favor of such ideas." Szpilman, "Fascist and Quasi-Fascist Ideas in Interwar Japan, 1918–1914," in *Japan in the Fascist Era*, 81.

53. Tessa Morris-Suzuki, *Reinventing Japan: Time, Space, Nation* (Armonk, NY: M. E. Sharpe, 1998), 87.

54. For an excellent treatment of these issues, see Oguma, *Genealogy of "Japanese" Self-Images*.

55. "Nihon to Manshū wa inu ni oite mo kyōdai," *Yomiuri shinbun*, 25 September 1935, 5. In 1936 Hasebe moved to Tokyo Imperial University, where three years later he became the founding member of the first anthropology department in Japan. Around that time, he embraced the myth of Japanese ethnic homogeneity, which was closely connected to his famous postwar theory that a population of Paleolithic humans, known as Akashi Man, had lived on the archipelago. Oguma, *Genealogy of "Japanese" Self-images*, 226–36, 265–66, 305–14. For more on Hasebe, see the introduction by Holger Frank, ed., *Kotondo Hasebe: On the Skulls and Lower Japanese Stone Age Dog Races* (Paderborn, DEU: Lykos Press, 2008).

56. "Nichiman no chi ni musubu koinu," *Yomiuri shinbun*, 19 June 1941, 3.

57. "Doitsu he 'daihyō Hachikō': Kaigai ni takamaru Nihon inu kenkyū," *Asahi shinbun*, 29 November 1935, 13.

58. "Kore wa chin hakken da: Chōsen ni 'Nihonken,'" *Asahi shinbun*, 29 March 1937, 15.

59. Mori published his research in the 1 April 1937 issue of *Chōsen hakubutsugaku kai kaihō*. I obtained a copy of the cover of this journal with a photograph of a Jindo dog, but I have been unable to find an extant copy of the entire journal and the article in question anywhere in Japan, Korea, or the United States. According to the 1919 Law for Preserving Scenery and Historic and Natural Monuments, the preservation of natural monuments in Sakhalin; Korea; Taiwan; and the Mariana, Marshall, and Caroline Islands was under the control of local governments. The Jindo dog appears to have been placed under this designation by the colonial government on 3 May 1938. I have been unable to precisely pinpoint when the Poongsan was selected, but it may have been in 1942. Thanks to Ann Kim and Jaeoh Park, who assisted me in locating valuable information related to this issue.

60. Saitō, *Nihon no inu to ōkami*, 271. The breeding standards for shepherd dogs also stipulate that a dog's ears must stand erect, a requirement that created considerable anxiety for breeders.

61. Saitō Hirokichi, "Aiken monogatari," republished in *Zenshū Nihon dōbutsu shi*, 26 vols. (Tokyo: Kōdansha, 1983), 12:60–61. Ishikawa is credited with spreading Darwinian evolutionary theory in Japan by publishing his notes of lectures delivered by Edward S. Morse, the American zoologist who taught at Tokyo University from 1877 to 1879 (see chaps. 1 and 2).

62. Saitō, *Nihon no inu to ōkami*, 334–35. Some people claimed that Hachikō's ear flopped because of wounds sustained during fights with other dogs.

63. Ibid., 332.

64. Shiina Noritaka, *Taishō hakubutsukan hiwa* (Tokyo: Ronzōsha, 2002), 262–68. Ueno's widow, Yaeko, apparently joined Saitō in insisting that Hachikō's ear stand erect.

65. Samuel J. M. M. Alberti, "Constructing Nature behind Glass," *Museum and Society* 6, no. 2 (July 2008): 79–81.

66. Thomas, *Man and the Natural World*, 106–7; Kete, *Beast in the Boudoir*, 22–37.

67. For more on Greyfriars Bobby, see Kean, *Animal Rights*, 86–88.

68. Wippermann and Berentzen, *Die Deutschen und ihre Hunde*, 69. This translation is by Manuel Metzner, who translated several chapters of this book on my behalf.

69. Arluke and Sanders, *Regarding Animals*, 148–49; Wippermann and Berentzen, *Die Deutschen und ihre Hunde*, 76.

70. For a translation of some of the early chapters of *Hakken-den*, see Haruo Shrine, ed., *Early Modern Japanese Literature: An Anthology* (New York: Columbia University Press, 2002), 887–909. For another Meiji-era popular children's story featuring faithful dogs, which was influenced by *Nansō Satomi hakken-den*, see L. Halliday Piel, "Loyal Dogs and Meiji Boys: The Controversy over Japan's First Children's Story, *Koganemaru* (1891)," *Children's Literature* 38 (2010): 207–22.

71. See "Inu sae" and "On o mukui shi inu," in Kaigo Tokiomi, Ishikawa Ken, and Ishikawa Matsutarō, eds., *Nihon kyōkasho taikei: Kindai hen, dai-2-kan: Shūshin 2* (Tokyo: Kōdansha, 1962), 353, 361–62.

72. Thanks to John Mertz for explaining the relevance of Bakin's text. I have adopted some of his language from our e-mail exchange. John Mertz, e-mail to author, 21 May 2009.

73. Chiba Yū, "Hachikō zanshō: Sono shirarezaru koto nado," *Hokuroku shinbun*, 11 November 1999.

74. Maekawa Senpan, "Ima ni Hachikō no mainichi wa konna koto ni naru darō," *Yomiuri shinbun*, 18 March 1935, 7.

75. In addition to Saitō, the fund-raising group included Dr. Itagaki Shirō, a university colleague of the late Ueno and Hachikō's veterinarian; Koga Tadamichi, director of the Ueno Zoological Gardens; Kataoka Ken, chief of the Arable Land Section of the Ministry of Agriculture, where the professor had been a consultant; Yoshikawa Chūichi, the station chief; and Sasaki Hideichi, an elementary school administrator. Rhoden, *Pawprints in Japan*, 11–12.

76. Saitō, *Nihon no inu to ōkami*, 337; Nihon inu hozon kai, ed., *Shadan hōjin Nihon inu hozon kai sōritsu gojū shūnen shi* (Tokyo: Nihon inu hozon kai, 1978), 55–57.

77. I have, unfortunately, been unable to locate an extant copy of this footage.

78. The Movement for the Clarification of the National Polity emerged as part of a widespread right-wing backlash to a theory advanced by the liberal constitutional scholar Minobe Tatsukichi (1873–1948), who asserted that sovereign power rested with the state and that the emperor exercised power only as the highest organ of the state under the constitution. In 1935 conservative and patriotic groups in academic, military, and bureaucratic circles publicly denounced Minobe, and the movement thoroughly purged the theory from all aspects of public life.

79. Hiraiwa Yonekichi, "Hachikō no shōgai," *Dōbutsu bungaku* 154 (June 1988): 3–4. Hiraiwa includes the entire poem in the article.

80. Miyawaki Shunzō, *Shōwa hachi nen: Shibuya eki* (Tokyo: PHP Kenkyūjo, 1995), 110.

81. "Chūken Hachikō monogatari," *Asahi shinbun*, 23 April 1934, Hachikō shinbun kiji album, unpaginated, Tōkyō-to Shibuya-ku Shirane Ki'nen Kyōdo Bunkakan Archive, Tokyo, Japan.

82. Hayashi, *Hachikō bunken shū*, 245–47.

83. Noguchi Ujō, "Chūgi o tataeru uta," in Kume Gen'ichi, *Dōbutsu bidan* (Tokyo: Kinnohoshisha, 1934), 1–3.

84. *Chūken Hachikō kiroku: Shōten hen, gekan*, unpaginated, Eastern Japan Railways Shibuya Station Archive, Tokyo; Nihon Kokuyū Tetsudō Shibuya Eki, ed., *Shibuya eki 100 nen shi, Chūken Hachikō 50 nen shi* (Tokyo: Nihon Kokuyū Tetsudō Shibuya Eki, 1985), 176–221.

85. Imagawa, *Inu no gendai shi*, 163.

86. Kaigo Tokitomi, Ishikawa Ken, and Ishikawa Matsutarō, eds., *Nihon kyōkasho taikei, kindai-hen, dai-2-kan: Shūshin 3* (Tokyo: Kōdansha, 1962), 245.

87. A story with the precisely the same title was featured in the third-year ethics primer. In that tale, Nagata Sakichi, a Tokugawa-era historical figure, continues to demonstrate his fidelity to his former employer even after being unfairly dismissed when falsely accused of an offense by a jealous co-worker. Ibid., 254.

88. Monbushō, *Jinjō shōgaku shūshin sho, maki ni kyōshi yō* (Tokyo: Monbushō, 1935), 134–45.

89. Kobayashi Gen, "Sangatsu no kakka gakushū shiryō," *Gakushū kenkyū* 15 (1936): 115–16.

90. Ono Susumi, *Chūkon ode: Chūken Hachikō* (Ōdate, Akita Prefecture: Ono Susumi chosaku hankōkai, 1937), 155.

91. Ōdate-shi shi hensan iinkai, ed., *Ōdate-shi shi*, 5 vols. (Ōdate: Ōdate-shi, 1986), 3*ge*: 335–36; Ono, *Chūkon ode*, inside front cover page; Chiba Yū, *Chūken Hachikō monogatari: Hachikō wa hontō ni chūken datta* (Ōdate: Chiba Yū, 2009).

92. Suzuki, "Asahi shinbun ga tsukutta 'Chūken Hachikō' shinwa," 95.

93. *Chūken Hachikō kiroku*, unpaginated. For more on the valorization of Tōgō, see Tanaka Hiromi, "Kyozō no gunshin Tōgō Heihachirō," *This Is Yomiuri* (September 1993): 220–47.

94. Hiraiwa Yonekichi, "On o wasereru na," *Zenshū Nihon dōbutsu shi*, 26 vols. (Tokyo: Kōdansha, 1983), 9:69–70. For an in-depth look at Hiraiwa, see Katano Yuka, *Aiken'ō: Hiraiwa Yonekichi den* (Tokyo: Shōgakkan, 2006).

95. Saitō, *Nihon no inu to ōkami*, 338–39.

96. Hasegawa Nyozekan, "Hachikō o chūshin to shite," *Bungei shunjū* 13, no. 4 (April 1935): 144–46.

97. Mary L. Hanneman, "Dissent from Within: Hasegawa Nyozekan, Liberal Critic of Fascism," *Monumenta Nipponica* 52, no. 1 (Spring 1997): 42. See also Richard Torrance, "*The People's Library:* The Spirit of Prose Literature versus Fascism," in *The Culture of Japanese Fascism*, ed. Alan Tansman (Durham: Duke University Press, 2009), 58–59.

98. After these events, Hasegawa turned to investigating Japan's unique character and participated in the Shōwa Research Association (Shōwa kenkyūkai), a quasi-governmental group of some three hundred intellectuals who in the late 1930s urged the government to adopt national-mobilization measures. The historian Andrew Barshay has argued that, through his involvement with the association and focus on Japanese national character, Hasegawa came to be mobilized by government authorities and increasingly unable to criticize the state effectively. Indeed, even in his analysis of the Hachikō phenomenon, Hasegawa's concern with Japanese character is evident in his use of the term "national tendencies." Andrew Barshay, *State and Intellectual in Imperial Japan: The Public Man in Crisis* (Berkeley: University of California Press, 1988), 189. For a more sympathetic view of Hasegawa, see Hanneman, "Dissent from Within," 35–58.

99. Saitō, "Chūken Hachikō no hakusei," in *Shadan hōjin Nihon inu hozon kai*, 108.

100. See, for example, Ben Markland, "Native and Immigrant Dogs," *Chicago Daily Tribune*, 26 March 1942, 16.

101. Shimizu Yoshitarō, "Hachikō," *Kyūshū nippō*, 26 March 1935, Hachikō shinbun kiji album, unpaginated.

102. Seidensticker, *Tokyo Rising*, 124.

103. Hayashi, *Hachikō bunken shū*, 300. Reports about the discovery of the skewers prompted numerous counterclaims. One of the most detailed accounts issued from an author writing under the pseudonym Hikari Kazeo, who asserted that he was a party to the postmortem while a student at Tokyo Agricultural University where Hachikō's autopsy and dissection were performed. The author conceded that five skewers of about five centimeters were lodged inside of Hachikō's gut, but he contended that they had not caused any damage to the stomach lining and that the cause of death, as Saitō and others maintained, was filariasis. Hikari Kazeo [pseud.], "Chūken Hachikō no kaibō," *Kotori to inu*, (1 August 1947): 4. Speculation about Hachikō's cause of death continues to this day. In 2011, seventy-six years after his demise, scientists at Tokyo University announced that an analysis of Hachikō's preserved internal organs revealed a malignant tumor and that cancer and filaria, not skewers, were probably the major factors in his death. "Hachikō no shiin, gan datta? Hozon no zōki o MRI satsuei," *Asahi shinbun*, 1 March 2011.

104. Wippermann and Berentzen, *Die Deutschen und ihre Hunde*, 70.

105. "The Standards Points of the 'Nippon Inu' Adopted by the Nippon-Inu Hozonkai," *Nihon inu* 3, no. 7 (July 1934): 149.

106. Saitō, "Nihonken no hanashi," *Yomiuri shinbun*, 29 April 1929, 3.

107. "Nihonken monogatari: Yōken ni sugureta shotokuchō," *Asahi shinbun*, 14 September 1932, 10. Though the article is unsigned, it is likely that Saitō wrote it. It was published about two months before the first article about Hachikō appeared in the *Asahi*.

108. "Mamore Nihonken, hokoru beki tokushitsu no kazukazu, noridashita Monbushō," *Yomiuri shinbun*, 7 July 1936, 7. See also "Nihonken o minaosu," *Mainichi shinbun*, 8 February 1937, 7, Osaka edition.

109. Yamada Shunryō, "'Kihaku' to iu koto ni tsuite," *Nihon inu 9, no. 7* (July 1938), in *Shadan hōjin Nihon inu hozon kai*, 212–14.

110. Utsumi Hantarō, "Nihonjin to Nihon inu," *Nihon inu 8*, no. 10 (October 1939), in *Shadan hōjin Nihon inu hozon kai*, 226

111. Stephanitz, *German Shepherd*, 280.

112. Imagawa, *Inu no gendai shi*, 60.

113. Araki Sadao, "Hōken jidai no gun'yōken, Nihonken no seinō o kenkyū shitai," in *Shadan hōjin Nihon inu hozon kai*, 109–10; Saitō Hiroshi, "Nihonken no chōkyō," *Nihon inu* 1, no. 1 (April 1932): 34–39. Araki's article was originally published in the Osaka edition of the *Mainichi* newspaper.

114. "Akita-ken no shussei," *Yomiuri shinbun*, 21 January 1939, 7.

115. Utsumi, "Nihonjin to Nihonken," 226.

116. Kogire-kai, ed., *Kogire-kai Auction Catalogue* (Kyoto: Kogire-kai, 2002). The dog is probably a male, but it is impossible to be certain. Thanks to Jack Stoneman for bringing this painting to my attention.

117. Uezawa Kenji, *Shōhei o nakaseta gunba inu hato bukun monogatari* (Tokyo: Jitsugyō no Nihon sha, 1938), 196–208. Uezawa states in the preface that his intended audience is teenage boys and girls.

118. Ibid., 208.

119. Rikugun tsuwamono henshūbu, ed., *Senjin sōwa shū* (Tokyo: Rikugun Zaigō Gunjinkai Honbu Tsuwamono Hakkōsho, 1934), 6–7.

120. John Dower, *War without Mercy: Race and Power in the Pacific War* (New York: Pantheon, 1986), 253. See also, Klaus Antoni, "Momotarō (The Peach Boy) and the Spirit of Japan: Concerning the Function of a Fairy Tale in Japanese Nationalism of the Early Shōwa Age," *Asian Folklore Studies* 50 (1991): 155–88.

121. The image comes from Monbushō, *Shogakkō kokugo yomihon* (Tokyo: Monbushō, 1933), 61. For a view of how images of Momotarō's dog were "Japanized" over time in official and private media, see Karazawa Tomitarō, *Zusetsu Meiji hyaku nen no jidō shi*, 2 vols. (Tokyo: Kōdansha, 1968), 1:539–50.

122. Saitō, "Honkai no shimei narabi ni jigyō to Nihon inu no shōrai," in *Shadan hōjin Nihon inu hozon kai*, 240–41. Emphasis is in the original.

123. Kishi, *Chūken Hachikō monogatari*, 46.

124. Hayashi, *Hachikō bunken shū*, 309–10. Sympathy for Hachikō was far from uniform. Saitō recalled that, even before the requisition, some people furtively placed placards around the statue's neck urging that that dog, too, be "called up." Saitō, *Nihon no inu to ōkami*, 340–41. The Ōdate statue of Hachikō was also melted down in the spring of 1945 and was reconstructed in a different form in 1987. In 2004 a statue nearly identical to the original one in Ōdate and the one at Shibuya, except with both ears standing erect, was constructed outside of the Ōdate railway station.

125. "Saiken sareru Hachikō no dōzō," *Asahi shinbun*, 18 July 1947, 2.

126. Sassa's grandfather, Tomofusa (1854–1906), was a progovernment politician, zealous nationalist, and pan-Asianist. His father Hirō (1897–1948), a left-leaning political science professor, was dismissed along with other faculty members at Kyushu University for their liberal

views. In the early thirties, Hirō, like the liberal critic Hasegawa, wrote disapprovingly about the growth of fascism, which he regarded as an oppressive form of government. Sassa Hirō, *Seiji no hinkon* (Tokyo: Chikura shobō, 1931), 54–55; Sassa, *Nihon fashizumu no hatten katei* (Tokyo: Asano shoten, 1933), 1–17, 97–113. From the mid-1930s, once again like Hasegawa, he became involved in quasi-government projects such as the Shōwa Research Association, which weakened his earlier critical stance. He also worked as an editor for the *Kumamoto nichinichi* and *Asahi* newspapers. In a successful effort to avoid being purged by SCAP for support of the wartime regime, Sassa resigned from his *Asahi* editorship in 1946, and the following year he was elected a member of the national Diet in the first postwar election. An illness killed him in late 1948 and prevented him from seeing his son follow him in a successful career in the worlds of politics and publishing.

127. Like Nakasone, Sassa became an outspoken proponent of revising Article Nine, the "no war, no arms" clause of the 1947 Constitution, and for a "normalized," or less restricted, role for the country's postwar military, the Self-Defense Force.

128. Sassa Atsuyuki, "Koe: Chūken Hachikō," *Asahi shinbun*, 19 January 1948, 2; Sassa, e-mail to author, 17 November 2003.

129. Andō Takeshi, "Shibuya no Chūken Hachikō," *Asahi shinbun*, 28 May 2009, 26.

130. Mainichi shinbunsha, ed., *Shōwa shi zen-kiroku: Chronicle 1926–1989* (Tokyo: Mainichi shinbunsha, 1989), 426.

131. See, for example, Kitano Michihiko, *Meiken monogatari* (Tokyo: Jitsugyō no Nihon sha, 1950), 11–25. Jitsugyō no Nihon sha, it may be noted, is the same company that published the jingoistic *War Horses, Dogs, and Pigeons that Caused Soldiers to Weep* twelve years earlier. Every few years or so, once the occupation ended, publishers resurrected the Hachikō tale to take advantage of a new generation of youngsters, but any political connotations were almost nil. In the Gordon W. Prange Collection at the University of Maryland and in archives in Japan, including the International Library of Children's Literature in Ueno and the Tachikawa Prefectural Tama Library, I could only find a single children's book that mentioned Hachikō during the first five years of the occupation, and even that reference only alluded to the dog in passing.

132. *Hachikō monogatari* (advertisement), *Asahi shinbun*, 31 August 1987, 14. The former movie gets some of the basic facts of history and even of Hachikō's life story wrong. It closes with images of soldiers marching past Hachikō's dead body outside Shibuya station and leaves the impression, like many other accounts, that the Hachikō phenomenon was a final heart-warming episode before the advent of militarism, rather than being itself thoroughly saturated by and contributing to the culture of fascism. Not surprisingly, most retellings of the story, such as the 1971 picture book (which is based on a 1934 version) simply sidestep such issues and any sort of context. One exception, though, is Ayano Masaru, *Hontō no Hachikō monogatari—mo ichido aitai*, illustrated by Hidaka Yasushi (Tokyo: Hāto shuppan, 1998).

133. See, for example, Iwagō Mitsuaki and, Iwagō Hideko, *Nippon no inu* (Tokyo: Shinchōsha, 1998).

134. Abe Kōbō, *Suichū toshi; dendorokakariya* (Tokyo: Shinchōsha, 1973), 36–44.

135. For a personal, but historically flawed, account of a local aficionado's postwar efforts to breed and show Akita dogs, see Martha Sherrill, *Dog Man: An Uncommon Life on a Faraway Mountain* (New York: Penguin Press, 2008). Sherrill asserts that her book's protagonist, Morie Sawataishi, was an extraordinary pioneer in the movement to preserve the Akita. She ignores or is simply unaware of the movement's two-decade history and the advantages that the breed enjoyed that allowed many dogs to escape some of the worst depredations of the final years of the war.

136. Fujiwara Eiji, "Kaisetsu" of "Aiken monogatari," in *Zenshū Nihon dōbutsu shi* 12:375.

137. Obara Iwao, interview with author, Tokyo, 2 July 2001. Obara is the former section chief of zoology at the National Science Museum.

4. Dogs of War

1. Eric Hobsbawm, *The Age of Extremes: A History of the World, 1914–1991* (New York: Vintage, 1996), 44.

2. Yamamoto Kajirō, "Uma, inu, kokeshi," *Kaizō* 23 (May 1941): 111. Yamamoto wrote this article just after the release of his movie, *Uma* (Horse), the only film produced by the Tōei motion picture studio that year. Despite the militarism of the day, Yamamoto largely avoided making the film into a propaganda piece for the government. The film told of a young girl and her family raising a horse in northern Japan. The family planned to contribute the horse to the military, but this theme was apparently so subtle that in order to guarantee the film's release Tōei officials added a written message before the opening credits from Army Minister Tōjō Hideki reminding people that the military relied on the public to produce strong, healthy horses.

3. The U.S. military even experimented with a macabre plan to equip bats with tiny incendiary bombs to be air-dropped over Japan. The scheme was only scrapped after several costly mishaps in the New Mexico desert, including the destruction of a general's automobile and an airplane hanger. Robert E. Lubow, *The War Animals: The Training and Use of Animals as Weapons of War* (New York: Doubleday, 1977), 32–33.

4. See, for example, Thomas R. Buecker, "The Fort Robinson War Dog Reception and Training Center, 1942–1946," *Military History of the West* 27, no. 1 (1997): 33–58; Steven J. Corvi, "Men of Mercy: The Evolution of the Royal Army Veterinary Corps and the Soldier-Horse Bond During the Great War," *Journal of the Society for Army Historical Research* 76, no. 308 (1998): 272–84; R. L. DiNardo and Austin Bay, "Horse-drawn Transport in the German Army," *Journal of Contemporary History* 23, no. 1 (1988): 129–42; Imagawa, *Inu no gendai shi*, 7–78; Kuroiwa Hisako, *Densho bato: Mōhitotsu no IT* (Tokyo: Bungei shunjū, 2000); Ōe Shinobu, *Nichiro sensō no gunji shiteki kenkyū* (Tokyo: Iwanami shoten, 1976), 449–60; Sugimoto Ryū, "Nihon rikugun to bahitsu mondai—gunba shigen hogo hō no seiritsu ni kanshite," *Ritsumeikan daigaku jinbun kagaku kenkyūsho kiyō* 82 (December 2003): 83–115; and Takeuchi Ginjirō, *Fukoku kyōba* (Tokyo: Kōdansha, 1999).

5. See, for example, Jilly Cooper, *Animals in War: Valiant Horses, Courageous Dogs, and Other Unsung Animal Heroes* (London: William Heinmann, 1983; Guilford, CT: Lyons Press, 2002); Charles L. Dean, *Soldiers and Sled Dogs: A History of Military Dog Mushing* (Lincoln: University of Nebraska Press, 2005); Juliet Gardiner, *The Animals' War: Animals in Wartime from the First World War to the Present Day* (London: Portrait, 2006); Blythe Hamer, *Dogs at War: True Stories of Canine Courage under Fire* (London: Carleton, 2001); Michael G. Lemish, *War Dogs: A History of Loyalty and Heroism* (Washington, DC: Brassey's, 1996); William W. Putney, *Always Faithful: A Memoir of the Marine Dogs of WW II* (New York: Free Press, 2001); and Tanabe Yukio, "Inpāru sakusen de zenmetsu shita dai 15 gun no gunba 12,000 tō no higeki," *Jūi chikusan shinpō* 671 (June 1977): 361–64.

6. Notable exceptions include Wippermann and Berentzen, *Die Deutschen und ihre Hunde;* Sax, *Animals in the Third Reich;* and Kean, *Animal Rights.* In addition, a few historians, such as John Dower in *War without Mercy,* have explored the use of animal imagery within the wider sphere of wartime propaganda, though with little or no attention to animals employed by the military.

7. Tactically, there is no question that horses fulfilled the most important role during the two world wars. In numerical terms, if the millions of germs nurtured by and used on a limited scale by military organizations such as Japan's infamous Unit 731 are excluded, horses were by far the most widely deployed nonhuman creatures.

8. As noted in chapter 2, communists in Japan and elsewhere associated certain canines, such as guard and pet dogs, with capitalist wealth and bourgeois luxury. Mao, in particular, seems to have been quite fond of the phrase "running dogs" (*zou gou*). He and others used it most frequently to refer to the "running dogs of imperialism" and the "running dogs of capitalism."

Many communists regarded pet dogs as decadent—as an extra mouth for the wealthy to feed at the expense of the people. The running dog also represents viciousness and servility. See, for example, Mao Tse-tung, "Revolutionary Forces of the World Unite, Fight against Imperialist Aggression!" (November 1948), *Selected Works of Mao Tse-tung*, 5 vols. (Oxford: Pergamon Press, 1961), 4:284. Thanks to Alex Cook for information about Mao's rhetorical use of dogs. I have adopted some of his language from our e-mail exchange.

9. J. Jupin, *Les chiens militaires dans l'armée française* (Paris: Berger-Leurault, 1887).

10. "The Dogs of War," *New York Times*, 29 January 1888, 4.

11. "The Use of Dogs in War: A Frenchman's Notion of Them as Soldiers," *New York Times*, 7 April 1889, 17. Although the two articles are unsigned, it is likely that the same reporter wrote both. His advocacy of the adoption of dogs for war did not come without some misgivings. In the former article, he expressed concern that it was degrading for humans to delegate warfare to canines. Perhaps he feared that the beasts, once trained, might turn on their masters. In the final sentence of the first article, he seems to express precisely that reservation: "The attack of a disciplined army of curs will be far more formidable than the guerrilla warfare to which it has hitherto been exposed. Nay, should not proud man himself hesitate thus to put the means of conquest in the paws of his ancient servant?"

12. See his review of the *Animals' War* exhibition held at the Imperial War Museum in London from 2006 to 2007 and the "Review" of Juliet Gardiner's exhibition catalogue, *The Animals' War*, by Jonathan Burt in *History Today* (October 2006): 70–71.

13. Lemish, *War Dogs*, 11–29. Many dogs and other animals became mascots during the Second World War, too. See Dorothea St. Hill Bourne, *They Also Serve* (London: Winchester Publications, 1947).

14. Arthur F. Jones, "Prince Enlists for a 'Dog' War," *New York Times*, 30 January 1927, XX14.

15. "Keisatsu-ken," *Taiwan nichinichi shinpō*, 15 December 1911, 7; "Kōdō-gun to sasoku-inu," *Taiwan nichinichi shinpō*, 3 February 1912, 1.

16. "Keisatsu-ken," *Taiwan nichinichi shinpō*, 15 December 1911, 7.

17. Ishikawa Yasumasa, "Washinton inuten monogatari," *Shinra* (February 1994): 44; Sawabe Shōzō, interview by author, Chōfu, Japan, 6 March 2003.

18. Imagawa, *Inu no gendai shi*, 30.

19. Ibid., 15.

20. Issei Kin'ya, "Omoide 'zeikan kanshi-ken,'" in *JSV sōritsu 60 nenshi*, ed. Shadan hōjin Nihon shepādo inu tōroku kyōkai (Tokyo: Shadan hōjin Nihon shepādo inu tōroku kyōkai, 1993), 565.

21. Takahashi Masato, *Nagano-ken Manshū kaitaku shi: Giyūtai kaitakudan*, 2 vols. (Matsumoto: Kyōdo shuppansha, 1981), 2:141; Takahashi, *Nagano-ken Manshū kaitaku shi*, 1:79.

22. "The Joy of Breeding," *Ie no hikari* (October 1939): 1. The "shepherd" refers to the occupation of the homeowner and not to the dog. An accompanying photo shows a mother, her children, and a dog, but it is impossible to determine the animal's breed.

23. Brian Vesey-Fitzgerald, *The Domestic Dog: An Introduction to its History* (London: Routledge, 1957), 138–39.

24. Fairfax Downey, *Dogs for Defense: American Dogs in the Second World War, 1941–45* (New York: Daniel P. McDonald, 1955); Anna M. Waller, *Dogs and National Defense* (Washington, DC: Department of the Army, Office of the Quartermaster General, 1958); Thomas Young, *Dogs for Democracy: The Story of America's Canine Heroes in the Global War* (New York: Bernard Ackerman, 1944), 20.

25. Baba, *Senjika Nihon bunka dantai jiten*, 3:43–44.

26. Imagawa, *Inu no gendai shi*, 38–54.

27. William J. Kelch, "Canine Soldiers," *Military Review* 62, no. 10 (October 1982): 2.

28. The War Office, *The Training of War Dogs* (London: War Office, 1962), 2.

29. Hara Takeshi and Yasuoka Akio, eds., *Nihon riku-kaigun jiten* (Tokyo: Ōraisha, 1997), 403. By comparison, Hara and Yasuoka estimate that the Imperial Army employed nearly half a million horses and approximately three thousand pigeons during the early 1940s.

30. Lemish, *War Dogs*, 117–41; Putney, *Always Faithful*, 113–201; John M. Behan, *Dogs of War* (New York: Charles Scribner's Sons, 1946).

31. Kojima Munekichi, *Shokyū kanbu no tai-jissen chakugan* (Tokyo: Buyōdō, 1936), 235.

32. Imagawa, *Inu no gendai shi*, 60–66. For more on U.S. training procedures, see Buecker, "Fort Robinson Dog Reception and Training Center." During the First World War, a London *Times* correspondent on the Western front reported that "it is the dogs who enlist the men's sympathies more than anything else. Like frightened children they join the ranks, nestling down by the side of the men for warmth and protection." Kean, *Animal Rights*, 173.

33. See, for example, J. Robert Lilly and Michael B. Puckett, "Social Control and Dogs: A Sociohistorical Analysis," *Crime and Delinquency* 43, no. 2 (April 1997): 123–47.

34. Wippermann and Berentzen, *Die Deutschen und ihre Hunde*, 74–87.

35. Philip Snow, *The Fall of Hong Kong: Britain, China, and the Japanese Occupation* (New Haven: Yale University Press, 2003), 167, 214.

36. Mark R. Peattie, "Japanese Treaty Port Settlements in China, 1895–1937," in *The Japanese Informal Empire in China, 1895–1937*, ed. Peter Duus, Ramon H. Myers, and Mark R. Peattie (Princeton: Princeton University Press, 1989), 186.

37. Ton Shan-yan, *Shokuminchi Taiwan no genjūmin to Nihonjin keisatsukan no kazokutachi*, trans. Uezumi Etsuko (Tokyo: Nihon kikan shuppan sentā, 2000), 96–97. Wu-she was the site of an uprising by Taiwanese Atayal tribespeople and its brutal suppression by colonial police in 1930.

38. Shashin kurabu (1901), Japanese Colonial Government Archives, National Library, Taiwan Branch, Taipei; Joseph R. Allen, "Taipei Park: Signs of Occupation," *Journal of Asian Studies*, 66, no. 1 (February 2007): 180. Thanks to Allen and Jon Renner for their cooperation. This dog appears to have a docked tail, which would indicate it was used primarily for hunting.

39. See, for example, "Tenhare gunyōken," *Tairiku shinbun*, 14 April 1941, 3.

40. "Manshū kara kikan shita gunken han'in ni Manshū ni okeru gunyōken katsudō jitsujō o kiku," *Inu no kenkyū* 4, no. 2 (1935): 20.

41. For more about how the *Donga ilbo*, which was founded by wealthy intelligentsia from a former Yanban family in 1920, thrived during and after the colonial era, see Kimura Kan, *Kankoku ni okeru "ken'ishugi" taisei no seiritsu* (Tokyo: Mineruva, 2003).

42. "P'ihaeja rŭl yŏkbanghaya sagwa kkŭt e hwahae yo'gu kunma poch'ungbu puwŏn i kakch'ŏ ro tora Najin kun'gyŏn munje kihu," *Tonga ilbo* [*Dong-a ilbo*], 15 December, 1933; "Yŏlmyŏng sinŭmjung kunmabu kŏrō kosojunbijung Najin kun'gyŏngyoin sakŏn," *Tonga ilbo* [*Dong-a ilbo*], 20 December 1933; "P'ihaeja siryo kun'gyŏnsakŏn ildallak," *Tonga ilbo* [*Dong-a ilbo*], 28 December 1933, 2.

43. "Suwŏnji nakyōb chuptaga pŏn'gyŏn sonyŏ e ge kyosang pudanggukja ŭi piindojŏk ŏnsa e ildanbumin ŭn pinanjaja," *Tonga ilbo* [*Dong-a ilbo*], 19 December 1933, 3; "Pan'gyŏn e ge kyosangdanghan sonyŏ saengmyŏng ŭn widok Pusanbu Suwŏllim sahyŏng sakŏn ŭi kihu pu ŭi t'aedo rŭl ildanbinan," *Tonga ilbo* [*Dong-a ilbo*], 21 December 1933.

44. "Suwŏllim e pan'gyŏn sayongje nŭn Chosŏnin puminjŏnch'e ŭi moyok 29 il e ch'ŏlp'ech'ianŭmyŏn Chosŏnin ŭiwŏn chongsajik," *Tonga ilbo* [*Dong-a ilbo*], 30 March 1934, 3. Thanks to Naomi Chi for translating this material.

45. "Yuhaemuikhan Suwŏllim chosokmaegak ŭl tongnon buyun ŭn maegakhal su ŏbtago tappyŏn pan'gyŏn sayongdo ŭiryŏn kyesok," *Tonga ilbo* [*Dong-a ilbo*], 3 April 1934, 5.

46. "Munje ŭi pan'gyŏn sayong ŭl p'yeji, Pusanbumin ŭi kangkyŏnghan pandaero indosang munje suhaegyŏl," *Tonga ilbo* [*Dong-a ilbo*], 14 April 1935, 3.

47. "Sallimgamsu ŭi pan'gyŏn i Ubok-tongmin ŭl kyosang p'ihaeja kajokdŭl sapdŭl koswego Suwŏn Yi Wang-sik sangam ŭi sowi," *Tonga ilbo* [*Dong-a ilbo*], 24 June 1934, 3.

48. Incidents involving dogs owned by elite Koreans may have occurred after the colonial era ended, but perhaps wealthy Koreans may have become less inclined to keep dogs, such as the shepherd, that were closely associated with Japanese rule.

49. Haruyo Taya Cook and Theodore F. Cook, *Japan at War: An Oral History* (New York: New Press, 1992), 59–60.

50. See, for example, Snow, *Fall of Hong Kong*, 263.

51. Kaigo Tokiomi, Ishikawa Ken, and Ishikawa Matsutarō, eds., *Nihon kyōkasho taikei, kindai-hen, dai-7-kan: Kokugo 4*, 27 vols. (Tokyo: Kōdansha, 1964), 7:559.

52. Katherine C. Grier, "'The Eden of Home': Changing Understanding of Cruelty and Kindness to Animals in Middle-Class American Households, 1820–1900," in *Animals in Human Histories: The Mirror of Nature and Culture*, ed. Mary Henninger-Voss (Rochester, NY: University of Rochester Press, 2002), 344–47; Kathleen Kete, "Animals in Human Empire," in *A Cultural History of Animals in the Age of Empire*, ed. Kathleen Kete (Oxford: Berg, 2007), 7–8.

53. Chiba Haruo, *Shōgaku kokugo tokuhon no shidō to sono riron*, 2 vols. (Tokyo: Kōseikaku shoten, 1933), 1:49–50.

54. Tanaka Toyotarō, *Shōgaku kokugo tokuhon no jissaiteki toriatsukai, jinjōka dai ichi* (Tokyo: Meguro shoten, 1933), 72. See also Harada Naoshige and Tagami Shinkichi, *Shōgaku kokugo tokuhon mohan shidō sho, jinjōka, dai ichi gakunen, zenki yō* (Tokyo: Meguro shoten, 1933), 64–80.

55. Kaigo Tokiomi, Ishikawa Ken, and Ishikawa Matsutarō, eds., *Nihon kyōkasho taikei, kindai-hen, dai-25-kan: Shōka 5* (Tokyo: Kōdansha, 1964), 295.

56. Nihon hōsō kyōkai, ed., *Hōsō gojū nen shi, shiryō-hen* (Tokyo: Nihon hōsō shuppan kyōkai, 1977), 285–86.

57. For an example of a story-card play, see Fukushima Ujirō, *Sensen ni hoero gunken*, 4th ed. (Kobe: Kōbe Gunken Gakkō, 1939), Don Cohn collections, New York City. For one such board game, see "Gunken denrei gēmu," *Shōnen kurabu*, April 1934, fold-out page. For a well-known song, "Bokura no gun'yōken," broadcast by NHK radio, see Akiyama Masami, ed., *Rajio ga kataru kodomotachi Shōwa shi* (Tokyo: Ōzorasha, 1992), 164–65. For a sample of wartime paintings with military-animal themes, see Rikugun bijutsu kyōkai, ed., *Seisen bijutsu* (Tokyo: Rikugun Bijutsu Kyōkai, 1939); Rikugun bijutsu kyōkai, ed., *Seisen bijutsu*, vol. 2 (Tokyo: Rikugun Bijutsu Kyōkai, 1942). For more on the soft propaganda of textiles during the Second World War, see Jacqueline Marx Atkins, ed., *Wearing Propaganda: Textiles on the Home Front in Japan, Britain, and the United States, 1931–1945* (New Haven: Yale University Press, 2005), 350–55; Inui Yoshiko, ed., *Zusetsu: Kimonogara ni miru sensō* (Tokyo: Inpakuto shuppankai, 2007).

58. Probably the best-known story of this former genre was "The Invisible Airplane" (Mienai hikōki), written by Yamanaka Minetarō (1885–1966) and illustrated by Ise Yoshio (1905–87), which ran in the monthly boys' magazine *Shōnen kurabu* from April 1935 until March 1936 and chronicled the adventures of Takeru, a shepherd army dog, and his nine-year-old master, Ōishi Masao, who together prevent enemy spies from stealing a technology that will make Japanese airplanes invisible and therefore invincible.

59. Imagawa, *Inu no gendai shi*, 21–22; "Meiyo no senshi o togeta Itakura taii no san aiken," *Asahi shinbun*, 29 November 1931, 29.

60. Louise Young, *Japan's Total Empire: Manchuria and the Culture of Wartime Imperialism* (Berkeley: University of California Press, 1998), 72.

61. Minami Masaya, "Chūken no hi wa ima narinu," *Yasukuni* (1 March 1992): 5. The Japanese is: Chūken no ishibumi no ima narinu; Kongō Nachi no senkō to; Jurī no isao eikyū ni; Warewa wa tataen morotomo ni.

62. Kaigo, Ishikawa, and Ishikawa, eds., *Nihon kyōkasho taikei, kindai-hen, dai-7-kan: Kokugo 4*, 679–80. The Order of the Golden Kite, established in 1890, was the highest honor that a

member of the military could receive. According to the eighth-century imperial chronicle *Nihon shoki*, a golden kite appeared out of nowhere during a crucial battle in Emperor Jimmu's eastward advance and landed on the tip of Jimmu's bow. The kite was so brilliant that it startled the enemy soldiers and allowed the imperial army to achieve victory.

63. Imagawa, *Inu no gendai shi*, 21–22.

64. Kofudera Tatsumi, "Kagayaku gunken no tegara: Kongō, Nachi no ireisai," *Shūkan shōkokumin* (4 October 1942): 18.

65. Tanaka Toyotarō, *Shōgaku kokugo tokuhon no jissaiteki toriatsukai, jinjōka kan go* (Tokyo: Meguro shoten, 1935), 298–99.

66. Miyagawa Kikuyoshi, ed., *Shōgaku kokugo tokuhon kaisetsu: Junjōka yō*, 12 vols. (Tokyo: Meiji tosho, 1935), 5:495–96. See also Harada Naoshige and Tagami Shinkichi, *Shōgaku kokugo tokuhon mohan shidō sho, jinjōka, dai san gakunen, zenki yō* (Tokyo: Meguro shoten, 1935), 350–77.

67. Ibid., 485–86. In the same commentary, Miyagawa vehemently derided critics who protested with "dreamlike pacifism" that war stories and other tales, such as the legend of the peach boy Momotarō, were jingoistic and inappropriate for children. Tales of war heroism, he countered, were vital in raising the spirits and fortitude of all national subjects. 495–96.

68. *Kindābukku*, (November 1939): 7–8, Don Cohn collection, New York City. This special issue, whose cover showed a massive shepherd dog licking the cheek of a beaming child against the background of the Rising Sun flag, was dedicated exclusively to dogs. It had several pages featuring the use of dogs by Japanese samurai and soldiers and an explanation of dog breeds, as well as the story of Balto, an Alaskan malamute who led his sled team to deliver antitoxin serum from Anchorage to the stricken town of Nome in Alaska in January 1925. That same year, the sculptor Frederick George Richard Roth (1872–1944) designed a statue of the dog that stands in Central Park in New York City. A more lifelike version of Balto, who like Hachikō was preserved by taxidermy after his death in 1933, is housed at the Cleveland Museum of Natural History.

69. Uezawa, *Shōhei o nakaseta gunba inu hato bukun monogatari*, 196–208. For a tale with a similar theme, see Iguchi Seiha, "Nomonhan sensen bidan: Gunken 'Nana' no tegara," in *Manga to dōbutsu bidan* (Tokyo: Dai Nihon yūbenkai kōdansha, 1939), 66–71.

70. Yoshino Yumisuke, *Koinu to heitai-san* (Tokyo: Tankaidō shuppan, 1943), 63, 89. See also Kamo Kyōsuke, *Koinu no jūgun* (Tokyo: Nakamura shoten, 1943).

71. Christa Kamenetsky, *Children's Literature in Hitler's Germany: The Cultural Policy of National Socialism* (Athens: Ohio University Press, 1984), 183.

72. See Helena Pycior, "The Making of the 'First Dog': President Warren G. Harding and Laddie Boy," *Society and Animals* 13, no. 2 (2005): 109–38; Helena Pycior, "The Public and Private Lives of 'First Dogs': Warren G. Harding's Laddie Boy and Franklin D. Roosevelt's Fala," in *Beastly Natures: Animals, Humans, and the Study of History*, ed. Dorothee Brantz (Charlottesville: University of Virginia Press, 2010), 176–203.

73. John H. Crider, "Fala, Never in the Doghouse," *New York Times Magazine* (15 October 1944): 26. See also Derr, *A Dog's History of America*, 305–10.

74. Elisabeth Bumiller, "White House Monday, Except for End," *New York Times*, 18 March 2003, 1, 26.

75. For illustrated accounts of this phenomenon, see L. Douglas Keeney, *Buddies: Men, Dogs, and World War II* (Osceola, WI: MBI, 2001); Kawamura Kiyoko, *Senba no inutachi: Okāsan, boku mo kaeritakatta* (Tokyo: Wārudo foto puresu, 2006).

76. "Sensen senshi no nasake ni 'inu to saru' mo nakanaori," *Yomiuri shinbun*, 25 May 1939, 1; "'Sora no Momotarō' o tomo ni inu to saru," *Yomiuri shinbun*, 20 August 1941, 3; "Sensen ni nakayoshi inu to saru," *Yomiuri shinbun*, 13 December 1942, 4.

77. Norakuro is an abbreviated name that combines the first part of *norainu* ("stray dog") with "kuro" from the personal name Kurokichi.

78. Ministry of Finance, Printing Bureau, *20-seiki dezain kitte*, 9 February 2000, no. 6.

79. Yamaguchi Masao, "Norakuro wa warera no dōjidai jin," *Chūō kōron* 91, no. 3 (March 1976): 97–100.

80. Katō Ken'ichi, *Shōnen kurabu jidai* (Tokyo: Kōdansha, 1968), 109. For a brief examination of how children responded to messages directed at them in Japanese print media during the final months of the war, see Owen Griffiths, "Japanese Children and the Culture of Death, January–August 1945," in *Children and War: A Historical Anthology*, ed. James Marten (New York: New York University Press, 2002), 160–71.

81. For the similar guiding principles of each organization, see Ozaki Hotsuki, *Omoide no shōnen kurabu jidai: Natsukashi no meisaku hakurankai* (Tokyo: Kōdansha, 1997), 97; Wm. Theodore de Bary, ed., *Sources of Japanese Tradition* (New York: Columbia University Press, 1958), 705–7.

82. For an analysis of *Tintin in the Congo* and its influence on French imperialist attitudes, see Philip Dine, "The French Colonial Empire in Juvenile Fiction: From Jules Verne to Tintin," *Historical Reflections* 23, no. 2 (1997): 197–201.

83. Hideto Tanaka, "National Ideals of Japanese Boys in Shōnen kurabu during the Early 1930s" (master's thesis, Columbia University, 2000), 10.

84. Tagawa Suihō, *Norakuro manga zenshū* (Tokyo: Kōdansha, 1967), 4. The Japanese is: Moto no yado nashi, norainu; ima de wa mōken rentai de; oto ni kikoeta ninkimono.

85. Ozaki, *Omoide no shōnen kurabu jidai*, 97.

86. Ibid., 94.

87. Franklin P. Adams, Forward to Young, *Dogs for Democracy*, 5.

88. Wippermann and Berentzen, *Die Deutschen und ihre Hunde*, 76; Downey, *Dogs for Defense*, 6.

89. "Gun'yōken no daikōshin," *Kōen* 367 (3 July 1933): 9.

90. Film footage of shepherd dogs being consecrated for duty at Sensōji can be found in the digitized archives of the Istituto Luce in Rome. Thanks to Reto Hofmann for alerting me to this material.

91. Sawabe, interview with author, 6 March 2003. The Japanese is: Katte kuru zo to, isamashiku chigatte kuni o deta kara wa; tegara tatezu ni shi naryō ka; shingun rappa kiku tabi ni; mabuta ni ukabu hata no nami.

92. Undated letter to "Sir or Madam" and certificate number 248, Drawer F, *Dogs in War* Exhibition (25 January–15 April 2005), The Kennel Club, London.

93. For more on the ceremonies at Ueno, see Ian J. Miller, *The Nature of the Beast: Empire and Exhibition at the Tokyo Imperial Zoo* (Berkeley: University of California Press, forthcoming), chapter 4. For a recent study of the memorialization of canine war dead, see Elmer Veldkamp, "Eiyū ni natta inutachi: Gun'yōken irei to dōbutsu kuyō no hen'yō," in *Hito to dōbutsu no Nihon shi*, ed. Suga Yutaka (Tokyo: Yoshikawa kōbunkan, 2009), 3:44–68.

94. William M. Tuttle, Jr., *"Daddy's Gone to War": The Second World War in the Lives of America's Children* (Oxford: Oxford University Press, 1993), 112–33.

95. For example, see "Gunken shussei," *Shōjo kurabu*, (March 1940): 1; Lemish, *War Dogs*, 35; *Gun'yōken* 7, no. 5 (July 1938): viii (photograph).

96. "P.S. 66 Pupils Give Dog to Serve with K-9 Corps," in Downey, *Dogs for Defense*, 155.

97. Helen Orr Watson, *Trooper, U.S. Army Dog* (Boston: Houghton Mifflin, 1943).

98. Jō Hideo, "Masao to gunken," *Aikoku fujin* (April 1932): 5.

99. In addition to the tale of Kongō and Nachi, there are parallels between the film and a story about military dogs that was taught in primary schools in Manchukuo beginning in 1935. In the textbook account, three dogs, Doru, Esu, and Jon (John) put an end to sabotage of a communications line by killing two "bandits" and chasing away two others. "Gunken

no hanashi," in *Zaiman Nihonjin yō kyōkasho shūsei*, 10 vols., ed. Isoda Kazuo (Tokyo: Kashiwa shobō, 2000), 2:162–63.

100. "Sensen ni hoeyu," *Kinema junpō* 588 (21 September 1936): 107. Reports of the heroics of Japanese army dogs even appeared in overseas newspapers, such as a 1938 account in the weekly "Dogs" column in the *Washington Post*. The story told of Sergeant, a powerful German shepherd dog, who purportedly dragged himself thirty miles, after his leg was shattered by an enemy bullet, to deliver a message that led to the rescue of a besieged Japanese outpost in China. "Dogs," *Washington Post*, 5 June 1938, PY6.

101. "Sensen ni hoeyu," *Gun'yōken* 5, no. 7 (1 April 1936): 246–47. See also Katō Jirō, "Sensen ni hoeyu: sepādo eiga o miru," *Shepādo* (January 1938): 66.

102. "Gunken Aren no shi," *Tōkyō shinbun*, 1939; Teshima Tamie Album, unpaginated, Yūshūkan Military and War Memorial Museum, Yasukuni Shrine, Tokyo, Japan.

103. Teshima Tamie, "Komogomo no kokoro," *Teikoku gun'yōken kyōkai Tōkyō shibu hō* (September 1938), Teshima Tamie Album, Yūshūkan Military and War Memorial Museum. "Homare" is an affectionate appellation often added to the end of an animal's given name.

104. "Gunken Aren no shi."

105. Monbushō, *Shotōka kokugo ichi*, kyōshiyō (Tokyo: Monbushō, 1942), 144–45.

106. Kaigo Tokiomi, Ishikawa Ken, and Ishikawa Matsutarō, eds., *Nihon kyōkasho taikei, kindai-hen, dai-8-kan: Kokugo 5* (Tokyo: Kōdansha, 1964), 452–55.

107. Kaigo Tokiomi, Ishikawa Ken, and Ishikawa Matsutarō eds., *Nihon kyōkasho taikei, kin-dai-hen, dai-25-kan: Shōka 5* (Tokyo: Kōdansha, 1964), 439. Thanks to Elizabeth Kenney for introducing this song to me. The Japanese is: Ike tono meirei, masshigura; Kawaii gunken, masshigura; Katakata, katakata, katakata; Dan, dan, dan, tama no naka. Ano inu, ute ute, uchimakure; Nogasu na, nogasu na, uchimakure; Katakata, katakata, katakata; Teki no tama. Yoshi koi, yoshi koi, Tone koi koi; Watashi da, watashi da, Tone koi koi; Katakata, katakata, katakata; Dan, dan, dan, tama no naka. Although only fifth-year students read the story as a part of their Japanese studies, all primary students sang the song. For more on school music, see Ury Eppstein, "School Songs before and after the War. From 'Children Tank Soldiers' to 'Everyone a Good Child,'" *Monumenta Nipponica* 42, no. 4 (Winter 1987): 431–47.

108. Inui, *Zusetsu*, 111–13.

109. The U.S. military's policy during the Second World War was an exception to the tendency of national armies to not return canines to their owners or other civilians. Following the war, about three thousand of the eight thousand dogs still in service returned to civilian life. Derr, *A Dog's History of America*, 304.

110. "Dog Admirals" (reprinted from *Newsweek*, 15 February 1943), in Downey, *Dogs for Defense*, 154–55.

111. "Girl Scouts Aid War Dog Fund," *New York Times*, 22 July 1943, 16.

112. Hachiōji-shi kyōdo shiryō kan, ed., *Sensō to hitobito no kurashi* (Hachiōji: Hachiōji-shi kyōiku iinkai, 1995), 44.

113. Gardiner, *Animals' War*, 174–75.

114. *Teikoku gikai shūgiin iinkai kiroku 114, Shōwa hen*, 75th sess., Yosan iinkai giroku, dai 9 kai (13 February 1940), 349.

115. Ikeda, "Fuyō inu: Kōban he watasu," *Yomiuri shinbun*, 27 March 1941, 4.

116. See, for example, Tsukamoto, *Shōrui o meguru seiji*, 181; Matsui Akira, "Kōkogaku kara mita inu," *Buraku kaihō nara* 11 (1999): 7–25.

117. Imagawa, *Inu no gendai shi*, 120.

118. Hachiōji shi kyōdo shiryō kan, *Sensō to hitobito no kurashi*, 44.

119. Iwagawa, *Inu no gendai shi*, 124.

120. Tōkyō-to ed., *Senjika "tochō" no kōhō katsudō* (Tokyo: Tōkyō-to, 1996), 177–78; "Tōkyō dai kūshū, sensai shi" henshū iinkai ed., *Tōkyō dai kūshū, sensai shi*, 5 vols. (Tokyo: Tōkyō kūshū o kiroku suru kai, 1974), 5:39–40.

121. Imagawa, *Inu no gendai shi*, 120–24. The British government attempted to ban dogs from cities during the First World War, but the plan failed because of public resistance. Kean, *Animal Rights*, 176–77.

122. See, for an example from Asahikawa in north central Hokkaido, the personal recollections of Tanabe Yasuichi, "Inu mo sensō he," *Dōyū* 434 (10 January 1997): 18.

123. "Directions to Dog Owners" (1918), British Dogs' Wool Association, item 3, Drawer D, *Dogs in War* Exhibition (25 January–15 April 2005), The Kennel Club, London.

124. Imagawa, *Inu no gendai shi*, 121.

125. Kiyosawa Kiyoshi, *A Diary of Darkness: The Wartime Diary of Kiyosawa Kiyoshi*, trans. Eugene Soviak and Kamiyama Tamie (Princeton: Princeton University Press, 1999), 42.

126. Nakashima Satoru, *Kanagawa-ken kyōkenbyō yobō gaishi* (Yokohama: Nakashima Satoru, 1973), 32.

127. Hachiōji-shi kyōdo shiryō kan, ed., *Hachiōji no kūgeki to sensai no kiroku* (Hachiōji: Hachiōji-shi kyōiku iinkai, 1985), 508. For similar initiatives aimed at British rabbit breeders during the Second World War, see Gardiner, *Animals' War*, 179–81.

128. Teshima Tamie, "Komogomo no kokoro."

129. Imagawa, *Inu no gendai shi*, 128.

130. Kazuko Tsurumi, *Social Change and the Individual: Japan before and after Defeat in World War II* (Princeton: Princeton University Press, 1970), 99–137.

131. Ōe Kenzaburō, *Okurete kita seinen* (Tokyo: Shinchōsha, 1970), 33–41.

132. Inoue Komichi, "Senjichū dōbutsu mo gisei ni natta," Nihon sei kō kai (Anglican Episcopal Church in Japan). http://www.nskk.org/tokyo/data/9511sengo/0018. htm (accessed 30 July 2004).

133. Taking advantage of the ever-growing enthusiasm for dogs, Self-Defense Force public relations specialists deployed dogs for recruiting purposes in the late 1990s to create an image of the SDF as an inoffensive and pleasant organization. See Sabine Frühstück and Eyal Ben-Ari, "'Now We Show It All!' Normalization and the Management of Violence in Japan's Armed Forces," *Journal of Japanese Studies* 28 (Winter 2002): 23. The Japanese government asserted that Samawah, where the SDF was stationed in southern Iraq, was peaceful and that the goal of deployment was to provide humanitarian relief and reconstruction. After conducting tasks such as water purification and the rebuilding of schools, the SDF withdrew in 2006.

134. Uemura Hideaki, *Wan nyan tantei dan: Sensō de shinda inu ya neko no hanashi* (Tokyo: Popurasha, 1984); Inoue Komichi, *Inu no kieta hi* (Tokyo: Kinnohoshisha, 1986); Matsui Hiroshi, "Senjichū no chikken kennō no undō," *Sekai* 465 (August 1984): 304–17.

135. Minami, "Chūken no hi wa ima narinu," 5.

136. George Kerr, "Formosa's Return to China," *Far Eastern Survey* 16, no. 18 (15 October 1947): 205; Jack Belden, *China Shakes the World* (New York: Harpers and Bros., 1949); Ō Ikutoku, *Taiwan: Kūmon suru sono rekishi* (Tokyo: Kōbundō, 1970), 141. Thanks to Kawashima Shin for bringing this expression to my attention.

137. See, for example, *Didaozhan* (Tunnel warfare), 1965.

5. A Dog's World

1. Pet Food Manufacturers Association, Japan, http://www.jppfma.org/ (accessed 24 April 2006). According to the American Pet Products Manufacturers Association, an estimated 43.5% of U.S. households owned a pet dog for a total of approximately 74 million dogs in 2005. http://www.appma.org/ (accessed 24 April 2006). The European Pet Food Industry Federation

calculated that the dog population of the European Union in 2005 was around 56 million. http://www.fediaf.org/ ggentree.htm (accessed 24 April 2006).

2. Thorstein Veblen, *The Theory of the Leisure Class: An Economic Study of Institutions* (1899; New York: Mentor 1963), 103. For a broader treatment of human use and abuse of animals as pets, see Yi-Fu Tuan, *Dominance and Affection: The Making of Pets* (New Haven: Yale University Press, 1984).

3. Tanizaki Jun'ichirō, *Some Prefer Nettles*, trans. Edward Seidensticker (Tokyo: Tuttle, 2001). For several examples of the interwar link between wealth and purebred foreign dogs from the world of painting, see Kendall H. Brown and Sharon Minichiello, *Taishō Chic: Japanese Modernity, Nostalgia, and Deco* (Honolulu: Honolulu Academy of Arts, 2001), 54–55.

4. For more about department stores as spaces of consumption during the 1920s and 1930s, see Louise Young, "Marketing the Modern: Department Stores, Consumer Culture, and the New Middle Class in Interwar Japan," *International Labor and Working-Class History* 55 (Spring 1999): 52–70.

5. The deployment of other canine metaphors in reference to the U.S.-Japan relationship has been far less complimentary. In the 1970s, artist Ogawara Shū (1911–2002) painted at least two paintings, *Gunka shakai* (A herded society) and *Mure* (A herd), that used groups of dogs as symbols to criticize the "group mentality that existed among Japanese people, not only during the war when they supported the military government without question, but also after the war when they began uncritically embracing U.S. policies." Asato Ikeda, "Twentieth-Century Japanese Art and the Wartime State: Reassessing the Art of Ogawara Shū and Fujita Tsuguharu," *Asia-Pacific Journal* 43–2–10, 25 October 2010, http://www.japanfocus.org/-Asato-Ikeda/3432 (accessed 3 March 2011). More recently, both left-wing and right-wing critics of the government's decision to send Self-Defense Force troops to Iraq in 2003 as a show of support to the George W. Bush administration's "war on terror," routinely referred to Japanese prime minister Koizumi Jun'ichirō as Bush's "pooch" (*pochi*). For an example from the Right, see Kobayashi Yoshinori, "Shin gomanizumu," *Sapio* (14 April 2004): 57. Likewise, critics of British prime minister Tony Blair often referred to him as Bush's poodle, which sharply contrasted with another canine, the bulldog, which was strongly associated with an earlier British wartime leader, Winston Churchill.

6. Yoshida Shigeru, "Ōiso hōdan," *Nihon keizai shinbun*, 1 January 1958, 8.

7. Sawabe, interview 6 March 2003.

8. "Kaiyasui Shiba-ken," *Nihon keizai shinbun*, 13 March 1952, 8.

9. "Shadan hōjin Japan keneru kurabu, *JKC 40 nen shi*, 180.

10. See Kawamoto Saburō, *Eiga no Shōwa zakkaten, zokuzoku* (Tokyo: Shōgakkan, 1996), 120–23.

11. Kawamoto Saburō, *Eiga no Shōwa zakkaten, kankatsu hen* (Tokyo: Shōgakkan, 1999), 121.

12. Ishii Momoko, *Nonchan kumo ni noru* (1947; Tokyo: Kakugawa shoten, 1973).

13. William Manchester, *American Caesar: Douglas MacArthur, 1880–1964* (Boston: Little, Brown, and Company, 1978), 517.

14. Inoue Hisashi, *Aoba shigereru* (Tokyo: Bungei shunjū, 1973), 51–54. Thanks to Christopher Robins for directing me to this novel.

15. A very different perspective of U.S. military bases and dogs can be seen in the grainy black-and-white images of photographer Moriyama Daidō (1938–). Reflecting a much darker view of America's foreign policies in Asia and the U.S. military's presence in Japan in the late 1960s and early 1970s, Moriyama's photos capture the underside of life in the base town of Misawa on the northern tip of the main island of Honshu—youth motorcycle gangs, prostitutes, and several haunting impressions of stray dogs roaming the outskirts of the base. See Sandra S. Phillips, Alexandra Munroe, and Daido Moriyama, *Daido Moriyama: Stray Dog* (San Francisco: San Francisco Museum of Modern Art, 1999).

16. Jack Baird, "Akita Brought from Japan," *New York World-Telegram and Sun*, 29 January 1960; John Rendel, "Akitas Whelped First Time in State," *New York Times*, 3 February 1966.

17. "Goering's Dog Now Lives in Altadena," *Los Angeles Times*, 12 November 1951, A2.

18. Shadan hōjin Japan keneru kurabu, *JKC 40 nen shi*, 178–79.

19. Ibid.

20. "Nihon no inuten no kusawake, Washinton inuten," *Nihonbashi* (February 2000): 13.

21. Sawabe Shōzō, interview by author, Chōfu, Japan, 22 June 2004.

22. Burt, *Animals in Film*.

23. "Nankyoku Karafuto-ken ki'nen dōzō kensetsu ni tsuite," *Dōbutsu no tomo* 22 (March–April 1933): 1.

24. Ministry of Finance, Printing Bureau, *20-seiki dezain kitte*, 21 July 2000, no. 12.

25. For more on Laika, see Amy Nelson, "The Legacy of Laika: Celebrity, Sacrifice, and the Soviet Space Dog," in Brantz, *Beastly Natures*, 204–24.

26. For a history of the postwar Japanese electrical-goods industry and the creation of domestic consumers for these products, see Simon Partner, *Assembled in Japan: Electrical Goods and the Making of the Japanese Consumer* (Berkeley: University of California Press, 1999). For a contemporary portrait, see Ezra F. Vogel, *Japan's New Middle Class: The Salary Man and His Family in a Tokyo Suburb* (Berkeley: University of California Press, 1963).

27. Marilyn Ivy, "Formations of Mass Culture," in *Postwar Japan as History*, ed. Andrew Gordon (Berkeley: University of California Press, 1993), 249.

28. "Jintan—Kōfuku no rēru o shiku," *Mainichi shinbun*, 3 January 1958, 10. The advertisement appeared in other major daily newspapers as well. The advertiser's inclusion of the dog can partially be explained by the fact that 1958 was a Year of the Dog, but their subtle placement of the dog in the staged photograph and the popularity of Lassie and other real and fictional dogs certainly contributed to their decision.

29. See, for example, David Pilling, "Every Dog Has Its Day in Japan," *Financial Times*, 8 June 2004, 11; Hiroko Kimura, "Creature Comforts Fuel Business Boom," *Japan Times*, 1 March 2004; Wohn Dong-hee, "Canines No Longer Lead a Dog's Life," *International Herald Tribune-JoongAng Daily*, 1 July 2005, W1.

30. For an overview of dog keeping in Germany and the United States, respectively, see Wippermann and Berentzen, *Die Deutschen und ihre Hunde*, 113–30; Katherine C. Grier, *Pets in America: A History* (Chapel Hill: University of North Carolina Press, 2006).

31. Miyata Katsushige, "Nihon no keizai seichō to petto ni taisuru ishiki no henka," *Hito to dōbutsu no kankei gakkai shi* 9, no. 10 (August 2001): 41.

32. Ōhira Ken, *Yutakasa no seishin byōri*, 40th ed. (Tokyo: Iwanami shoten, 1990), 157–58.

33. See, for example, "Kettōsho mo kamikuzu dōzen," *Asahi shinbun*, 27 June 1970, 22.

34. Ken Gardner, "This Is How They Die," *The People*, 13 April 1969, 1–4. For Japanese responses to accusations in 1968 and 1969, see "Gyakutai da nante tondemo nai," *Mainichi shinbun*, 16 May 1968; "Nihonjin ha hontō no aikenka ka," *Asahi shinbun*, 17 June 1969, 21.

35. "Nihon de ha inu ga gyakutai sarete iru," *Asahi shinbun*, 14 April 1969 (evening edition), 10.

36. Shadan hōjin Japan keneru kurabu, *JKC 50 nen shi* (Tokyo: Japan keneru kurabu, 2000), 89.

37. Kase Toshikazu, "'Sesshō sezu' no kairitsu," *Asahi shinbun*, 17 June 1969, 21.

38. Mark Derr, *Dog's Best Friend: Annals of the Dog-Human Relationship* (1997; Chicago: University of Chicago Press, 2004), 214; James Serpell, *In the Company of Animals: A Study of Human-Animal Relationships* (London: Basil Blackwell, 1986), 15. Derr's book expands his investigation of the systemic and ongoing exploitation of dogs in the United States by puppy mills and leading dog-fancying organizations such as the AKC. Mark Derr, "The Politics of Dogs," *Atlantic Monthly* (March 1990): 49–72.

39. Sabata Toyoyuki, "Nihonjin to Seiyōjin to inu," *Yomiuri shinbun*, 6 June 1969.

40. See, for example, "Tsuki ni zatto ichiman biki," *Asahi shinbun*, 5 November 1965, 16; "Inugai jidai," *Asahi shinbun*, 27 October 1970, 27.

41. Akiko Kondo, "How Much Do You Want that Dog in the Window?" *Japan Times*, 13 March 2004.

42. "Shiyakusho waki ni 'suteinu bako,'" *Asahi shinbun*, 10 September 1986, 15; "Wanwan bokkusu o Kitami-shi ga tekkyo," *Asahi shinbun*, 12 September 1986, 22.

43. Sankei Shinbun, ed., *Wanchan paradaisu 2000: Petto yōhin gaido* (Tokyo: Sankei shinbun, 2000), 10–13.

44. The CM Research Center reported that the Kū-chan spots were viewers' favorite commercials in 2004 and 2005. Kaho Shimizu and Mayumi Negishi, "Aggressive TV Commercials Paid Off—Perhaps too Much," *Japan Times*, 18 May 2006.

45. Disney has taken advantage of and probably further fueled the enthusiasm for the breed with its release of *Beverly Hills Chihuahua* in 2008.

46. Takahashi Yūri, Ishii Yōhei, and Fukuda Keitsuke, "Petto bijinesu no shinjitsu," *Shūkan Tōyō Keizai* (15 March 2003): 106–7; Hiroko Kimura, "Pooch Paradise," *Japan Times*, 29 February 2004. Kū-chan could only help Aiful so much. In April 2006, the company's shady reputation returned when government regulators penalized the firm for illegal loan-collection practices.

47. For an example of the association between women and felines from early modern France, see Robert Darnton, "Workers Revolt: The Great Cat Massacre of the Rue Saint-Séverin," in *The Great Cat Massacre and Other Episodes in French Cultural History* (New York: Vintage, 1985), 75–104.

48. Konpanion-animaru risāchi (Companion animal information and research center), "Data on Dog and Cat Ownership." On Konpanion-animaru risāchi website, http://www.cairc.org/e/ apartment_pet/data/data1.html (accessed 5 July 2004). "Akita-ken mamore: Kogata-inu būmu, kainushi kōreika de genshō," *Nihon keizai shinbun*, 28 February 2005.

49. See, for example, "Onna no petto de kono mōkekata," *Shūkan bunshun* (5 February 1986): 126. For recent trends in the United States, see Jon Mooallem, "The Modern Kennel Conundrum," *New York Times*, 4 February 2007.

50. McHugh, *Dog*, 79–91.

51. John Clammer, *Contemporary Urban Japan: A Sociology of Consumption* (Oxford: Blackwell, 1997), 4.

52. For more on this phenomenon, see Sharon Kinsella, "Cuties in Japan," in *Women, Media, and Consumption in Japan*, ed. Lise Skov and Brian Moeran (Honolulu: University of Hawaii Press, 1996), 220–54.

53. Ruth La Ferla, "Woman's Best Friend, or Accessory?" *New York Times*, 7 December 2006.

54. Takahashi, Ishii, and Fukuda, "Petto bijinesu no shinjitsu," 107–10; Derr, *Dog's Best Friend*.

55. Pierre Bourdieu, *Distinction: A Social Critique of the Judgement of Taste*, trans. Richard Nice (Cambridge: Harvard University Press, 1984).

56. For a discussion of the relationship between social change and pets and other animals in the West, see Adrian Franklin, *Animals and Modern Cultures: A Sociology of Human-Animal Relations in Modernity* (London: Sage, 1999). For a contrary and more global view, see Richard W. Bulliet, *Hunters, Herders, and Hamburgers: The Past and Future of Human-Animal Relationships* (New York: Columbia University Press, 2005).

57. Sophie Hardach, "In Dog We Trust: Japan's Childless Turn to Canines," *Boston Globe*, 26 August 2007.

58. Peggy Orenstein, "Parasites in Prēt-à-Porter Are Threatening Japan's Economy," *New York Times*, 1 July 2001.

59. *Asahi shinbun* (Nagoya edition), 25 March 2006, 16–17; "Asahi kōkoku shō gekkan shō happyō," *Asahi shinbun*, 27 April 2006, 9.

60. Because the most popular and numerous small dogs are of foreign breed, the inclusion of the Shiba is probably not an accurate representation of these burgeoning numbers of "children," but in Japan it is still probably unthinkable to represent the country's offspring as partially or non-Japanese, even if the "child" is a canine.

61. The extent of the Shiba's popularity and continuing nationalist connotations of indigenous dogs is aptly illustrated by the fact that the store at the Yūshūkan Military and War Memorial Museum on the grounds of Yasukuni Shrine sells no fewer than three different versions of stuffed toy Shibas.

62. "Petto wa kazoku da to omou?" *Asahi shinbun*, 3 July 2010; Martin Fackler, "Japan, Home of the Cute and Inbred Dog," *New York Times*, 28 December 2006; Hardach, "In Dog We Trust." In the United States, too, the number of households with one or more dogs (38%) outnumbers those with children (35%). Derr, *Dog's Best Friend*, 4.

63. See, for example, the analysis by sociologist Yamada Masahiro, *Kazoku petto: Danna yori mo petto ga taisetsu?!* (Tokyo: Bunshun bunko, 2007).

64. Harriet Ritvo, "Animal Planet," *Environmental History* 9, no. 2 (April 2004): 204–20.

65. See, for example, Michael Wines, "Once Banned but Now Pampered, Dogs Reflect China's Rise," *New York Times*, 25 August 2010, A7; Lydia Polgreen, "Matchmaking in India: Canine Division," *New York Times*, 18 August 2009, A5.

66. Donna Haraway, *The Companion Species Manifesto: Dogs, People, and Significant Otherness* (Chicago: Prickly Paradigm Press, 2003).

67. Fujimura Kaori, "Gakkō ni wan-chan ga yatte kuru! Inu kara kodamotachi ga manabu 'inochi no omosa,'" *Shūkan Asahi* (3 March 2006): 130–34.

68. Fackler, "Japan, Home of the Cute and Inbred Dog."

69. James Vlahos, "Pill-Popping Pets," *New York Times Magazine*, 13 July 2008.

70. Kim Chung-ho, "The Chindo Dog: A Proud Korean Breed," *Koreana* 1, no. 1 (1994): 77.

71. Han'guk Minjok munhwa yŏngu wŏn, ed., *Han'guk minjok munhwa tae paekkwa sajŏn*, 27 vols. (Kyŏnggi-do Sŏndgnam-si, ROK: Academy of Korean Studies, 1991), 21:247–48. Thanks to Joy Kim for translating these and other passages. The dogs still figure in diplomatic relations, albeit of a different sort. During his historic visit to Pyongyang in 2000, South Korean president Kim Dae-jung received two Poongsan puppies from North Korean leader Kim Jong-il.

72. "Korea's Native Dog Makes Debut in D.C.," PR Web Press Release Newswire website, http://www.prweb.com/releases/2006/8/prweb420367. htm (accessed 20 August 2008).

73. Ha Ji-hong, "Sapsaree: Guardians of the East Sea," *Koreana* 12, no. 12 (Summer 1998): 73.

74. Limb Jae-un, "Saving a Loyal Breed from Near-Extinction," *JoongAng Daily*, 2 December 2005, http://service.joins.com/asp/print_article_english.asp?aid=2650638&esectcode=e_life&title=Saving+a+loyal+breed+from+near-extinction (accessed 3 March 2010).

75. "Korea's Native Dog Makes Debut in D.C.," PR Web Press Release Newswire, http://www.prweb.com/releases/2006/08/prweb420367.htm (accessed 17 May 2010).

76. Myrna Shiboleth, *The Israel Canaan Dog*, 2nd ed. (Loveland, CO: Alpine, 1994), 1–6.

77. Some other examples of attempts to transform local pariah dogs into legitimate breeds deserving of national and middle-class respect in postcolonial societies include the basenji from the Congo, the Xoloitzcuintle or Mexican Hairless Dog, the Thai ridgeback, the Australian dingo, the Rajapalayam and the Mudhol hound in India, the Phu Quoc dog in Vietnam, and the Africanis in South Africa after apartheid came to an end in 1994.

78. Coppinger and Coppinger, *Dogs*, 252.

79. Donna J. Haraway, *Simians, Cyborgs, and Women: The Reinvention of Nature* (New York: Routledge, 1991), 21. See also Molly H. Mullin, "Mirrors and Windows: Sociocultural Studies of Human-Animal Relationships," *Annual Review of Anthropology* 28 (1999): 201–24.

80. Tanabe Yūichi and Yamazaki Kaori, "Hyōtei irai chōsa ni motozuku inu hinshu ni yoru kōdō tokusei no chigai—katei inu he no tekisei o chūshin ni," *Jūi chikusan shinpō* 54, no. 1 (2001): 9–14.

BIBLIOGRAPHY

Abe Kōbō. "Te." In *Suichū toshi; dendorokakariya*, 36–44. Tokyo: Shinchōsha, 1973.

Abe Yoshio. "On the Corean and Japanese Wolves." *Journal of Science of the Hiroshima University* 1 (1930): 1–32.

Akiyama Masami, ed. *Rajio ga kataru kodomotachi Shōwa shi*. Tokyo: Ōzorasha, 1992.

Alberti, Samuel J. M. M. "Constructing Nature behind Glass." *Museum and Society* 6, no. 2 (July 2008): 73–97.

Alcock, Rutherford. *Capital of the Tycoon: A Narrative of a Three Years' Residence in Japan*. 2 vols. London: Longman, 1863.

Allen, Charles, ed. *Plain Tales from the Raj: Images of British India in the Twentieth Century*. London: André Deutsch, 1975.

Allen, Joseph R. "Taipei Park: Signs of Occupation." *Journal of Asian Studies* 66, no. 1 (February 2007): 159–99.

American Pet Products Manufacturers Association. "Industry Statistics and Trends." http://www.appma.org/ (accessed 24 April 2006).

Amino Yoshihiko. *Nihon no rekishi o yominaosu*. Tokyo: Chikuma gakugei bunko, 2005.

Anderson, Benedict. *Imagined Communities*. London: Verso, 1983.

Anderson, Virginia De John. *Creatures of Empire: How Domestic Animals Transformed Early America*. Oxford: Oxford University Press, 2004.

Antoni, Klaus. "Momotarō (The Peach Boy) and the Spirit of Japan: Concerning the Function of a Fairy Tale in Japanese Nationalism of the Early Shōwa Age." *Asian Folklore Studies* 50 (1991): 155–88.

Arluke, Arnold, and Clifton Sanders. *Regarding Animals*. Philadelphia: Temple University Press, 1996.

Arluke, Arnold, and Borio Sax. "Understanding Nazi Animal Protection and the Holocaust." *Anthrozoös* 5, no. 1 (1992): 6–31.

Atkins, Jacqueline Marx, ed. *Wearing Propaganda: Textiles on the Home Front in Japan, Britain, and the United States, 1931–1945*. New Haven: Yale University Press, 2005.

Ayano Masaru. *Hontō no Hachikō monogatari—mo ichido aitai*. Illustrated by Hidaka Yasushi. Tokyo: Hāto Shuppan, 1998.

Baba Kazuo, ed. *Senjika Nihon bunka dantai jiten*. 4 vols. Tokyo: Ōzorasha, 1990.

Bain, Read. "The Culture of Canines: A Note on Subhuman Sociology." *Sociology and Social Research* (July–August 1928): 545–56.

Baird, Jack. "Akita Brought from Japan." *New York World-Telegram and Sun*, 29 January 1960.

Baker, Steve. *Picturing the Beast: Animals, Identity, and Representation*. 1993. Reprint, Champaign: University of Illinois Press, 2001.

———. *The Postmodern Animal*. London: Reaktion, 2000.

Bankoff, Greg, and Sandra Swart, *Breeds of Empire: The "Invention" of the Horse in Southeast Asia and Southern Africa 1500–1950*. Copenhagen: NIAS Press, 2007.

Barshay, Andrew. *State and Intellectual in Imperial Japan: The Public Man in Crisis*. Berkeley: University of California Press, 1988.

Batchelor, John. "Findings after 62 Years in Japan." *Hokkaidō shakai jigyō* 18 (1939): 30–33.

Baur, John E. *Dogs on the Frontier*. 1964. Reprint, Fairfax, VA: Delinger's, 1982.

Beck, Alan M. *The Ecology of Stray Dogs: A Study of Free-Ranging Urban Animals*. Baltimore: York Press, 1973.

Behan, John M. *Dogs of War*. New York: Charles Scribner's Sons, 1946.

Belden, Jack. *China Shakes the World*. New York: Harpers and Brothers, 1949.

Berger, John. *About Looking*. New York: Pantheon, 1980.

Bickers, Robert A., and Jeffrey N. Wasserstrom. "Shanghai's 'Dogs and Chinese Not Admitted' Sign: Legend, History, and Memory." *China Quarterly* 142 (June 1995): 444–66.

Bigot, S. *Le Japon en 1897*. Tokyo: publisher unknown, 1897. Paul C. Blum Collection, Yokohama Archives of History, Yokohama.

Bird, Isabella L. *Korea and Her Neighbors: A Narrative of Travel, with an Account of the Recent Vicissitudes and Present Position of the Country*. 1897. Reprint, Rutland, VT: Charles E. Tuttle, 1986.

———. *Unbeaten Tracks in Japan*. 1880. Reprint, London: Murray, 1885.

Bodart-Bailey, Beatrice M. *The Dog Shogun: The Personality and Policies of Tokugawa Tsunayoshi*. Honolulu: University of Hawaii Press, 2006.

———. "The Laws of Compassion." *Monumenta Nipponica* 40, no. 2 (Summer 1985): 163–89.

Bolitho, Harold. "The Dog Shogun." In *Self and Biography: Essays on the Individual and Society in Asia*, edited by Gungwu Wang, 123–39. Sydney: Sydney University Press for the Australian Academy of the Humanities, 1975.

Borneman, John. "Race, Ethnicity, Species, Breed: Totemism and Horse-Breed Classification in America." *Comparative Studies in Society and History* 30, no. 1 (January 1988): 25–51.

Bourdieu, Pierre. *Distinction: A Social Critique of the Judgement of Taste*, translated by Richard Nice. Cambridge: Harvard University Press, 1984.

Bourne, Dorothea St. Hill. *They Also Serve*. London: Winchester Publications, 1947.

Bousquet, George Hilaire. *Le Japon de nos jours*. Paris: Hachette, 1877.

Boyce, James. "Canine Revolution: The Social and Environmental Impact of the Introduction of the Dog to Tasmania." *Environmental History* 11, no. 1 (2006): 102–29.

Boyd, James. "Horse Power: The Japanese Army, Mongolia, and the Horse." *Japan Forum* 22, no. 1–2 (2010): 23–42.

Brantz, Dorothee, ed. *Beastly Natures: Animals, Humans, and the Study of History*. Charlottesville: University of Virginia Press, 2010.

Brehm, Alfred Edmund. *Brehm's Life of Animals: A Complete Natural History for Popular Home Instruction and for the Use of Schools*. 7 vols. Chicago: Marquis, 1896.

Brown, Kendall H., and Sharon Minichiello. *Taisho Chic: Japanese Modernity, Nostalgia, and Deco*. Honolulu: Honolulu Academy of Arts, 2001.

Brummet, Palmira. *Image and Imperialism in the Ottoman Revolutionary Press, 1908–1911*. Albany: State University of New York Press, 2000.

Budiansky, Stephen. *The Truth about Dogs: An Inquiry into the Ancestry, Social Conventions, Mental Habits, and Moral Fiber of* Canis Familiaris. New York: Penguin, 2000.

Buecker, Thomas R. "The Fort Robinson War Dog Reception and Training Center, 1942–1946." *Military History of the West* 27, no. 1 (1997): 33–58.

Bulliet, Richard W. *Hunters, Herders, and Hamburgers: The Past and Future of Human-Animal Relationships*. New York: Columbia University Press, 2005.

Burt, Jonathan. *Animals in Film*. London: Reaktion, 2002.

——. "Review of *The Animals' War* Exhibition and *The Animals' War: Animals in Wartime from the First World War to the Present Day*." *History Today* (October 2006): 70–71.

Campbell, John. "The Seminoles, Bloodhounds, and Abolitionism." *Journal of Southern History* 72, no. 2 (May 2006): 259–302.

Chamberlain, Basil Hall. *Japanese Things; Being Notes on Various Subjects Connected with Japan, For the Use of Travelers and Others*. 1890. Reprint, Tokyo: Tuttle, 1971.

Cheang, Sarah. "Women, Pets, and Imperialism: The British Pekingese Dog and Nostalgia for Old China." *Journal of British Studies* 45 (April 2006): 359–87.

Chiba Haruo. *Shōgakkō kokugo tokuhon no shidō to sono riron*. 2 vols. Tokyo: Kōseikaku shoten, 1933.

Chiba Michiko, Yuichi Tanabe, Takashi Tojo, and Tsutomu Muraoka. *Japanese Dogs: Akita, Shiba and Other Breeds*, translated by Lucy North. Tokyo: odansha International, 2003.

Chiba Yū. *Chūken Hachikō monogatari: Hachikō wa hontō ni chūken data*. Ōdate: Chiba Yū, 2009.

——. "Hachikō zanshō: Sono shirarezaru koto nado." *Hokuroku shinbun*, 11 November 1999.

"Chikukenhyō no nai inu ya kyōken wa bokusatsu." *Tōkyō koshinbun*, 1 July 1880. In *Meiji nyūsu jiten*, edited by Edamatsu Shigeyuki, Sugiura Tadashi, and Yagi Kyōsuke. 9 vols. Tokyo: Mainichi komyunikēshonzu, 1983–86.

Chrystan, Julie. *Hachiko: The True Story of the Royal Dogs of Japan and One Faithful Akita*. Beverly Hills: Dove Books, 2009.

Chūken Hachikō kiroku: Shōten hen, gekan. Eastern Japan Railways Shibuya Station Archive, Tokyo.

"Chūken Hachikō monogatari." *Asahi shinbun*, 23 April 1934. Hachikō shinbun kiji album, Tokyo-to Shibuya-ku Shirane Kinen Kyōdo Bunkakan Archive, Tokyo.

Clammer, John. *Contemporary Urban Japan: A Sociology of Consumption*. Oxford: Blackwell, 1997.

Coetzee, J. M. *Disgrace*. New York: Viking, 1999.

Coleman, Jon T. *Vicious: Wolves and Men in America*. New Haven: Yale University Press, 2004.

Collier, V. W. *Dogs of China and Japan, in Nature and Art*. London: Heinemann, 1921.

Cook, Haruyo Taya, and Theodore F. Cook, *Japan at War: An Oral History*. New York: New Press, 1992.

Cooper, Jilly. *Animals in War: Valiant Horses, Courageous Dogs, and Other Unsung Animal Heroes*. 1983. Reprint, Guilford, CT: Lyons Press, 2002.

Coppinger, Raymond, and Lorna Coppinger. *Dogs: A New Understanding of Canine Origin, Behavior, and Evolution*. Chicago: University of Chicago Press, 2001.

Coren, Stanley. *How to Speak Dog*. New York: Fireside, 2001.

Cortazzi, Hugh, "Sir Rutherford Alcock: Minister at Edo, 1859–62." In *British Envoys in Japan, 1859–1972*, edited by Hugh Cortazzi, 9–21. Folkestone, UK: Global Orient, 2004.

——. *Victorians in Japan: In and around the Treaty Ports*. London: Athlone, 1987.

Corvi, Steven J. "Men of Mercy: The Evolution of the Royal Army Veterinary Corps and the Soldier-Horse Bond during the Great War." *Journal of the Society for Army Historical Research* 76, no. 308 (1998): 272–84.

Crosby, Alfred W. *Ecological Imperialism: The Biological Expansion of Europe, 900–1900*. Cambridge: Cambridge University Press, 1986.

Cumming, R. Gordon. *Five Years of a Hunter's Life in the Far Interior of South Africa*. 2 vols. New York: Harper and Brothers, 1850.

Daily Press. *The Chronicle and Directory for China, Japan, and the Philippines, for the Year 1869*. Hong Kong: Daily Press, 1869.

Darnton, Robert. *The Great Cat Massacre and Other Episodes in French Cultural History*. New York: Vintage, 1985.

Darwin, Charles. *On the Origin of Species by Means of Natural Selection; The Descent of Man and Selection in Relation to Sex*. Vol. 49 of *Great Books of the Western World*. Chicago: Encyclopedia Britannica, 1955.

Davis, Henry P., ed. *The New Dog Encyclopedia*. Harrisburg, PA: Stackpole, 1970.

Dean, Charles L. *Soldiers and Sled Dogs: A History of Military Dog Mushing*. Lincoln: University of Nebraska Press, 2005.

De Bary, William Theodore, ed. *Sources of Japanese Tradition*. New York: Columbia University Press, 1958.

Department of Education. *Preservation of Natural Monuments in Japan II*. Tokyo: Monbushō, 1933.

Derr, Mark. *Dog's Best Friend: Annals of the Dog-Human Relationship*. 1997. Reprint, Chicago: University of Chicago Press, 2004.

——. *A Dog's History of America: How Our Best Friend Explored, Conquered, and Settled a Continent*. New York: North Point Press, 2004.

——. "The Politics of Dogs." *Atlantic Monthly* (March 1990): 49–72.

De Vos, George, and Hiroshi Wagatsuma. *Japan's Invisible Race*. Berkeley: University of California Press, 1967.

Dickens, Frederick Victor. *The Life of Sir Harry Parkes II*. 1894. Reprint, Wilmington, DE: Scholarly Resources, 1973.

DiNardo, R. L., and Austin Bay. "Horse-drawn Transport in the German Army." *Journal of Contemporary History* 23, no. 1 (1988): 129–42.

Dine, Philip. "The French Colonial Empire in Juvenile Fiction: From Jules Verne to Tintin." *Historical Reflections* 23, no. 2 (1997): 197–201.

"The Dog, Described and Illustrated." *Harper's New Monthly Magazine* 10, no. 59 (April 1855): 615–28.

Dower, John. *War without Mercy: Race and Power in the Pacific War*. New York: Pantheon, 1986.

Downey, Fairfax. *Dogs for Defense: American Dogs in the Second World War, 1941–45*. New York: Daniel P. McDonald, 1955.

Dubois, Laurent. *Avengers of the New World: The Story of the Haitian Revolution*. Cambridge: Belknap Press, 2004.

Dun, Edwin. "Edwin Dun Photo Album." Unpaginated. Dun and Machimura Memorial Museum, Sapporo.

——. *Reminiscences of Nearly a Half Century in Japan* [n.d.]. Resource Collection for Northern Studies, Hokkaido University Library, Sapporo.

Duus, Peter. "Presidential Address: Weapons of the Weak, Weapons of the Strong—The Development of the Japanese Political Cartoon." *Journal of Asian Studies* 60 (2001): 965–97.

Edamatsu Shigeyuki, Sugiura Tadashi, and Yagi Kyōsuke, eds. *Meiji nyūsu jiten.* 9 vols. Tokyo: Mainichi komyunikēshonzu, 1983–86.

Elias, Norbert. *The Civilizing Process.* Oxford: Blackwell, 1994.

Emi Chizuko. "Saigō Takamori dōzō kō: Sono kensetsu katei o chūshin ni." *Bunka shigengaku* 3 (31 March 2005): 69–82.

Eppstein, Ury. "School Songs before and after the War: From 'Children Tank Soldiers' to 'Everyone a Good Child.'" *Monumenta Nipponica* 42, no. 4 (Winter 1987): 431–47.

European Pet Food Industry Federation. "Facts and Figures." http://www.fediaf.org/ (accessed 24 April 2006).

Falasca-Zamponi, Simonetta. *Fascist Spectacle: The Aesthetics of Power in Mussolini's Italy.* Berkeley: University of California Press, 1997.

Figal, Gerald. *Civilizations and Monsters: Spirits of Modernity in Meiji Japan.* Durham: Duke University Press, 1999.

Fleming, George. *Travels on Horseback in Mantchu Tartary: Being a Summer's Ride beyond the Great Wall of China.* London: Hurst and Blackett, 1863.

Fortune, Robert. *A Journey to the Tea Countries of China.* London: John Murray, 1852.

——. *Yedo and Peking: A Narrative of a Journey to the Capitals of Japan and China.* London: Murray, 1863.

Frank, Hogler, ed. *Kotondo Hasebe: On the Skulls and Lower Japanese Stone Age Dog Races.* Paderborn, DEU: Lykos Press, 2008.

Franklin, Adrian. *Animals and Modern Cultures: A Sociology of Human-Animal Relations in Modernity.* London: Sage, 1999.

Fraser, Mary Crawford. *A Diplomat's Wife in Japan: Sketches at the Turn of the Century,* edited by Hugh Cortazzi. New York: Weatherhill, 1982.

Fraser, Mrs. Hugh [Mary Crawford]. *Letters from Japan: A Record of Modern Life in the Island Empire.* London: MacMillan, 1905.

Frühstück, Sabine, and Eyal Ben-Ari. "'Now We Show It All!' Normalization and the Management of Violence in Japan's Armed Forces." *Journal of Japanese Studies* 28 (Winter 2002): 1–39.

Frykman, Jonas, and Orvar Löfgren. *Culture Builders: A Historical Anthropology of the Middle-Class Life.* New Brunswick, NJ: Rutgers University Press, 1987.

Fudge, Erica. "A Left-Handed Blow: Writing the History of Animals." In *Representing Animals,* edited by Nigel Rothfels, 3–18. Bloomington: Indiana University Press, 2002.

——. *Pets.* Stocksfield, UK: Acumen, 2008.

Fujimura Kaori. "Gakkō ni wan-chan ga yatte kuru! Inu kara kodamotachi ga manabu 'inochi no omosa.'" *Shūkan Asahi* (3 March 2006): 130–34.

Fujita, Fumiko. *American Pioneers and the Japanese Frontier: American Experts in Nineteenth-Century Japan.* Westport, CT: Greenwood Press, 1994.

Fujitani, Takashi. *Splendid Monarchy: Power and Pageantry in Modern Japan.* Berkeley: University of California Press, 1998.

Fujiwara Eiji. "Kaisetsu." In *Zenshū Nihon dōbutsu shi* 12:374–82.

Fukushima Ujirō. *Sensen ni hoero gunken.* 4th ed. Kobe: Kōbe gunken gakkō, 1939. Don Cohn Collection, New York City.

Fukuzawa Yukichi. "Refuting Nishi's Discussion on Travel by Foreigners in the Country." In *Meiroku Zasshi: Journal of the Japanese Enlightenment,* translated by William Reynolds Braisted. Cambridge: Harvard University Press, 1976.

Gardiner, Juliet. *The Animals' War: Animals in Wartime from the First World War to the Present Day.* London: Portrait, 2006.

Gardner, Ken. "This Is How They Die." *The People,* 13 April 1969, 1–4.

Gillmore, Parker. *The Hunter's Arcadia.* London: Chapman and Hall, 1886.

Gluck, Carol. *Japan's Modern Myths: Ideology in the Late Meiji Period.* Princeton: Princeton University Press, 1985.

"Goering's Dog Now Lives in Altadena." *Los Angeles Times,* 12 November 1951, A2.

Gordon, Andrew. *Labor and Imperial Democracy in Prewar Japan.* Berkeley: University of California Press, 1991.

Gordon, Mrs. Will. "Glimpses of Old Korea." *Transactions and Proceedings of Japan Society, London* 16 (1918): 97–113.

Gordon, Robert J. "Fido: Dog Tales of Colonialism in Namibia." In *African Environments: Past and Present,* edited by JoAnne McGregor and William Beinart, 240–54. Oxford: Curry, 2003.

Grier, Katherine C. *Pets in America: A History.* Chapel Hill: University of North Carolina Press, 2006.

Griffis, William Elliot. *The Mikado's Empire.* 7th ed. New York: Harper and Brothers, 1894.

Griffiths, Owen. "Japanese Children and the Culture of Death, January–August 1945." In *Children and War: A Historical Anthology,* edited by James Marten. New York: New York University Press, 2002.

"Gunken Aren no shi." *Tōkyō shinbun,* 1939. Teshima Tamie Album, Yūshūkan War Memorial Museum, Yasukuni Shrine, Tokyo.

"Gunken shussei." *Shōjo Kurabu* (March 1940): 1.

"Gun'yōken no daikōshin." *Kōen* 367 (3 July 1933): 9.

Ha Ji-hong. "Sapsaree: Guardians of the East Sea." *Koreana* 12, no. 12 (Summer 1998): 70–73.

Hachiōji-shi kyōdo shiryō kan, ed. *Hachiōji no kūgeki to senzai no kiroku.* Hachiōji: Hachiōji-shi kyōiku iinkai, 1985.

——. *Sensō to hitobito no kurashi.* Hachiōji: Hachiōji-shi kyōiku iinkai, 1995.

Haga Tōru et al. *Bigō sobyō korekushon.* Vol. 2, *Meiji no seisō.* Tokyo: Iwanami shoten, 1989.

Hamer, Blythe. *Dogs at War: True Stories of Canine Courage under Fire.* London: Carleton, 2001.

Hane, Mikiso. *Peasants, Rebels, and Outcastes: The Underside of Modern Japan.* New York: Pantheon, 1982.

Han'guk Minjok munhwa yŏngu wŏn, ed. *Han'guk minjok munhwa tae paekkwa sajŏn.* 27 vols. Kyŏnggi-do Sŏndgnam-si, ROK: Academy of Korean Studies, 1991.

Hanneman, Mary L. "Dissent from Within: Hasegawa Nyozekan, Liberal Critic of Fascism." *Monumenta Nipponica* 52, no. 1 (Spring 1997): 35–58.

Hara Takeshi, and Yasuoka Akio, eds. *Nihon riku-kaigun jiten.* Tokyo: Ōraisha, 1997.

Harada Naoshige, and Tagami Shinkichi. *Shōgaku kokugo tokuhon mohan shidō sho, jinjōka, dai ichi gakunen, zenki yō.* Tokyo: Meguro shoten, 1933.

Haraway, Donna. *Simians, Cyborgs, and Women: The Reinvention of Nature.* New York: Routledge, 1991.

——. "Teddy Bear Patriarchy: Taxidermy in the Garden of Eden, New York City, 1908–1936." *Social Text* 11 (Winter 1984–85): 20–64.

Haraway, Donna J. *The Companion Species Manifesto: Dogs, People, and Significant Otherness.* Chicago: Prickly Paradigm Press, 2003.

Hardach, Sophie. "In Dog We Trust: Japan's Childless Turn to Canines." *Boston Globe*, 26 August 2007.

Harootunian, Harry. *Overcome by Modernity: History, Culture, and Community in Interwar Japan.* Princeton: Princeton University Press, 2000.

Harris, Townsend. *The Complete Journal of Townsend Harris, First American Consul and Minister to Japan.* Rutland, VT.: Charles E. Tuttle, 1959.

Hasegawa Nyozekan. "Hachikō o chūshin toshite." *Bungei shunjū* 13, no. 4 (April 1935): 144–46.

Hashimoto Gyokuransai [Utagawa Sadahide]. *Yokohama kaikō kenmonshi.* 1862. Reprint, Tokyo: Meicho kankōkai, 1967.

Hayashi Masaharu, ed. *Hachikō bunken shū.* Tokyo: Hayashi Masaharu, 1991.

Hawes, A. G. S., and Ernest Mason Satow. *A Handbook for Travellers in Central and Northern Japan.* Yokohama: Kelly, 1881.

Hawks, Francis L. *Narrative of the Expedition of an American Squadron to the China Seas and Japan.* 1856. Reprint, Mineola, NY: Dover, 2000.

Helft, Claude, and Jiang Hong Chen. *Hatchiko, chien de Tokyo.* Paris: Picquier Jeunesse, 2005.

Hikari Kazeo [pseud.]. "Chūken Hachikō no kaibō." *Kotori to inu.* (1 August 1947): 4.

Hiraiwa Yonekichi. "Hachikō no shōgai." *Dōbutsu bungaku* 154 (June 1988): 2–5.

———. "On o wasereru na." In vol. 9, *Zenshū Nihon dōbutsu shi.* 26 vols. Tokyo: Kōdansha, 1983.

Hirata Atsutane. *Hirata Atsutane zenshū.* 15 vols. Tokyo: Meicho shuppan, 1976–81.

Hoare, J. E. *Japan's Treaty Ports and Foreign Settlements: The Uninvited Guests, 1859–1899.* Folkestone, UK: Japan Library, 1994.

Hobsbawm, Eric. *The Age of Extremes: A History of the World, 1914–1991.* New York: Vintage, 1996.

Hobsbawm, Eric J., and Terence Ranger, eds. *The Invention of Tradition.* Cambridge: Cambridge University Press, 1983.

Hokkaidō Keisatsu Henshu Iinkai, ed. *Hokkaidō keisatsu shi.* Sapporo: Hokkaidō keisatsu honbu, 1968.

Honda Kinkichirō. "Kenhei o kizuite minken o fusegu." *Marumaru chinbun* (3 April 1880): 2456–57.

Howell, David. *Capitalism from Within: Economy, Society, and the State in a Japanese Fishery.* Berkeley: University of California Press, 1995.

Iguchi Seiha. "Nomonhan sensen bidan: Gunken 'Nana' no tegara." In *Manga to dōbutsu bidan.* Tokyo: Dai Nihon yūbenkai kōdansha, 1939.

Ikeda, Asato. "Twentieth Century Japanese Art and the Wartime State: Reassessing the Art of Ogawara Shū and Fujita Tsuguharu." *Asia-Pacific Journal* 43, no. 2 (25 October 2010): 10. http://www.japanfocus.org/-Asato-Ikeda/3432 (accessed 3 March 2011).

Ikegami, Eiko. *The Taming of the Samurai: Honorific Individualism and the Making of Modern Japan.* Cambridge: Harvard University Press, 1995.

Imagawa Isao. *Inu no gendai shi.* Tokyo: Gendai shokan, 1996.

Inokuma Ken'ichirō. *Tekketsu.* Tokyo: Meiji shuppansha, 1911.

Inoue Hisashi. *Aoba shigereru.* Tokyo: Bungei shunjū, 1973.

Inoue Komichi. *Inu no kieta hi.* Tokyo: Kinnohoshisha, 1986.

———. "Senjichū dōbutsu mo gisei ni natta." Nihon sei kō kai (Anglican Episcopal Church in Japan). http://www.nskk.org/tokyo/data/9511sengo/0018.htm (accessed 28 June 2004).

Inui Yoshiko, ed. *Zusetsu: Kimonogara ni miru sensō.* Tokyo: Inpakuto shuppankai, 2007.

Ishii Momoko. *Nonchan kumo ni noru.* Tokyo: Kakugawa shoten, 1973.

Ishikawa Yasumasa. "Washinton inuten monogatari." *Shinra* (February 1994): 44–47.

Isoda Kazuo, ed. *Zaiman Nihonjin yō kyōkasho shūsei.* 10 vols. Tokyo: Kashiwa shobō, 2000.

Issei Kin'ya, "Omoide 'zeikan kanshi-ken'." In *JSV sōritsu 60 nenshi,* edited by Shadan hōjin Nihon shepādo inu tōroku kyōkai. Tokyo: Shadan hōjin Nihon shepādo inu tōroku kyōkai, 1993.

Ivy, Marilyn. "Formations of Mass Culture." In *Postwar Japan as History,* edited by Andrew Gordon, 239–58. Berkeley: University of California Press, 1993.

Iwagō Mitsuaki, and Iwagō Hideko. *Nippon no inu.* Tokyo: Shinchōsha, 1998.

Jackson, A. V. Williams. *From Constantinople to the Home of Omar Khayyam.* 1911. Reprint, Piscataway, NJ: Gorgias Press, 2002.

Jacobs, Nancy J. "The Great Bophuthatswana Donkey Massacre: Discourse on the Ass and the Politics of Class and Grass." *American Historical Review* 106 (2001): 485–507.

Jenkins, A. P., ed. *The Journal and Official Correspondence of Bernard Jean Bettelheim 1845–54, Part 1 (1845–51).* Haebaru, Okinawa: Okniawa-ken kyōikuinkai, 2005.

"Jiu-Yiba" Lishi Bowuguan (September 18 Incident Historical Museum). "Xuexing baoxing zhongzhong." "Jiu-Yiba" Lishi Bowuguan. http://www.918 museum.org.cn/918mmapp/info _describe.asp?code=ev19310041 (accessed 30 July 2004).

Jō Hideo. "Masao to gunken." *Aikoku fujin* (April 1932): 5.

Johnson, Sara E. "'You Should Give Them Blacks to Eat': Waging Inter-American Wars of Torture and Terror." *American Quarterly* 61, no. 1 (March 2009): 65–92.

Jones, Hazel J. *Live Machines: Hired Foreigners and Meiji Japan.* Vancouver: University of British Columbia Press, 1980.

Joyce, Barry Alan. "'As the Wolf from the Dog'; American Overseas Exploration and the Compartmentalization of Humankind: 1838–1859." PhD diss., University of California–Riverside, 1995.

———. *The Shaping of American Enthnography: The Wilkes Exploring Expedition, 1838–1842.* Lincoln: University of Nebraska Press, 2001.

Jupin, J. *Les chiens militaires dans l'armée française.* Paris: Berger-Leurault, 1887.

Kaigo Tokiomi, Ishikawa Ken, and Ishikawa Matsutarō, eds. *Nihon kyōkasho taikei, kindai hen, dai-2-kan: Shūshin 2.* Tokyo: Kōdansha, 1962.

———. *Nihon kyōkasho taikei, kindai-hen, dai-2-kan: Shūshin 3.* Tokyo: Kōdansha, 1962.

———. *Nihon kyōkasho taikei, kindai-hen, dai-7-kan: Kokugo 4.* Tokyo: Kōdansha, 1964.

———. *Nihon kyōkasho taikei, kindai-hen, dai-8-kan: Kokugo 5.* Tokyo: Kōdansha, 1964.

———. *Nihon kyōkasho taikei, kindai-hen, dai-25-kan: Shōka 5.* Tokyo: Kōdansha, 1965.

Kakizaki Hakyō. *Ishū Retsuzō.* 1790. Reprint, Hakodate: Tosho Rikai, 1988.

Kamenetsky, Christa. *Children's Literature in Hitler's Germany: The Cultural Policy of National Socialism.* Athens: Ohio University Press, 1984.

Kamo Kyōsuke. *Koinu no jūgun.* Tokyo: Nakamura shoten, 1943.

Kanagaki Robun, Ochiai Yoshiiku, and Kan Fusao. *Seiyō dōchū hizakurige.* Tokyo: Bankyūkaku, 1870.

Kanagawa kenritsu rekishi hakubutsukan, ed. *Yokohama ukiyoe to sora tobu eishi Gountei Sadahide.* Yokohama: Kanagawa Kenritsu Rekishi Hakubutsukan, 1997.

Karazawa Tomitarō. *Zusetsu Meiji hyaku nen no jidō shi.* 2 vols. Tokyo: Kōdansha, 1968.

Katano Yuka. *Aiken'ō: Hiraiwa Yonekichi den.* Tokyo: Shōgakkan, 2006.

Katō Jirō. "Sensen ni hoeyu: sepādo eiga o miru." *Shepādo* (January 1938): 66.

Katō Ken'ichi. *Shōnen Kurabu jidai*. Tokyo: Kōdansha, 1968.

Kawamoto Saburō. *Eiga no Shōwa zakkaten, kankatsu hen*. Tokyo: Shōgakkan, 1999.

——. *Eiga no Shōwa zakkaten, zokuzoku*. Tokyo: Shōgakkan, 1996.

Kawamura Kiyoko. *Senba no inutachi: Okāsan, boku mo kaeritakatta*. Tokyo: Wōrudo foto puresu, 2006.

Kawano Mitsunaga, ed. *Ōita-ken keisatsu shi*. Ōita: Ōita-ken keisatsu-bu, 1943.

Kean, Hilda. *Animal Rights: Political and Social Change in Britain since 1800*. London: Reaktion, 1998.

Keene, Donald, ed. *Anthology of Japanese Literature: Earliest Era to Mid-Nineteenth Century*. Rutland, VT.: Tuttle, 1975.

——. *The Japanese Discovery of Europe, 1720–1830*. Stanford: Stanford University Press, 1969.

Keeney, L. Douglas. *Buddies: Men, Dogs, and World War II*. Osceola, WI: MBI, 2001.

Kei Shoran. *Kodai Chūgoku no inu bunka: Shokuyō to saishi o chūshin ni*. Osaka: Osaka Daigaku Shuppankai, 2005.

Kelch, William J. "Canine Soldiers." *Military Review* 62, no. 10 (October 1982): 32–41.

Kerr, George. "Formosa's Return to China." *Far Eastern Survey* 16, no. 18 (15 October 1947): 205.

Kete, Kathleen. "Animals and Human Empire." In *A Cultural History of Animals in the Age of Empire*, edited by Kathleen Kete, 1–24. Oxford: Berg, 2007.

——. *The Beast in the Boudoir: Petkeeping in Nineteenth-Century Paris*. Berkeley: University of California Press, 1994.

Kim Chung-ho. "The Chindo Dog: A Proud Korean Breed." *Koreana* 1, no. 1 (1994): 74–77.

Kimura Kan. *Kankoku ni okeru "ken'ishugi" taisei no seiritsu*. Tokyo: Mineruva, 2003.

Kindābukku 11, no. 11, November 1939. Don Cohn Collection, New York City.

Kinsella, Sharon. "Cuties in Japan." In *Women, Media, and Consumption in Japan*, edited by Lise Skov and Brian Moeran, 220–54. Honolulu: University of Hawaii Press, 1996.

Kipling, John Lockwood. *Beast and Man in India: A Popular Sketch of Indian Animals in Their Relations with the People*. London: MacMillan, 1891.

Kipling, Rudyard. *Collected Dog Stories*. Garden City, NY: Doubleday, 1934.

Kishi Kazutoshi. *Chūken Hachikō monogatari*. Tokyo: Monasu, 1934.

Kitano Michihiko. *Meiken monogatari*. Tokyo: Jitsugyō no Nihon sha, 1950.

Kiyosawa Kiyoshi. *A Diary of Darkness: The Wartime Diary of Kiyosawa Kiyoshi*, translated by Eugene Soviak and Kamiyama Tamie. Princeton: Princeton University Press, 1999.

"Kizoku fugō no jūni jikan rōdō." *Aka* (1 October 1919): 6.

Knollys, Henry. *Sketches of Life in Japan*. London: Chapman and Hall, 1887.

Kobayashi Gen. "Sangatsu no kakka gakushū shiryō." *Gakushū kenkyū* 15 (1936): 115–16.

Kobayashi Takiji. *"The Factory Ship" and "The Absentee Landlord,"* translated by Frank Motofuji. Tokyo: University of Tokyo Press, 1973.

Kobayashi Yoshinori. "Shin gomanizumu." *Sapio* (14 April 2004): 57–70.

Kofudera Tatsumi. "Kagayaku gunken no tegara: Kongō, Nachi no ireisai." *Shūkan shōkokumin* (4 October 1942): 18–19.

Kogire-kai, ed. *Kogire-kai Auction Catalogue*. Kyoto: Kogire-kai, 2002.

Kōhō-shitsu. "Ueno no mori no Saigō no inu." *Katei-ken* (January 1985): 12–14.

Kojima Munekichi. *Shokyū kanbu no tai-jissen chakugan*. Tokyo: Buyōdō, 1936.

Konpanion-animaru risāchi (Companion Animal Information and Research Center). "Data on Dog and Cat Ownership." Konpanion-animaru risāchi. http://www. cairc.org/e/apartment_pet/ data/data1.html (accessed 5 July 2004).

Koster, Shizuko O. *Hachi-ko: The Samurai Dog.* Baltimore: PublishAmerica, 2007.

Kouwenhoven, Arlette, and Matthi Forrer. *Siebold and Japan: His Life and Work.* Leiden, NLD: Hotei, 2000.

Kuga Kōun. "Shīboruto to Nihon no inu." *Shīboruto kenkyū* (November 1985): 93–112.

Kume Gen'ichi. *Dōbutsu bidan.* Tokyo: Kinnohoshisha, 1934.

——. *Hachikō.* Tokyo: Kinnohoshisha, 1971.

Kunaichō, ed. *Shimōsa goryō bokujō shi.* Tokyo: Kunaichō, 1974.

Kuroiwa Hisako. *Densho bato: Mōhitotsu no IT.* Tokyo: Bungei shunjū, 2000.

Lambert, E. N. "E. N. Lambert Photo Album, No. 11" (Ac1–211c). Yokohama Archives of History, Yokohama.

Lawson, Lady Kate. *Highways and Homes of Japan.* London: Adelphi Terrace, 1920.

Lee, R. *Acecdotes of the Habits and Instincts of Animals.* Philadelphia: Lindsay, 1854.

Leighton, Robert. *The New Book of the Dog: A Comprehensive Natural History of British Dogs and Their Foreign Relatives, with Chapters on Law, Breeding, Kennel Management, and Veterinary Treatment.* London: Cassell, 1907.

Lekan, Thomas M. *Imagining the Nation in Nature: Landscape Preservation and German Identity, 1885–1945.* Cambridge: Harvard University Press, 2004.

Lemish, Michael G. *War Dogs: A History of Loyalty and Heroism.* Washington, DC: Brassey's, 1996.

Lévi-Strauss, Claude. *Totemism,* translated by Rodney Needham. Boston: Beacon Press, 1964.

Lilly, J. Robert, and Michael B. Puckett. "Social Control and Dogs: A Sociohistorical Analysis." *Crime and Delinquency* 43, no. 2 (April 1997): 123–47.

Limb Jae-un. "Saving a Loyal Breed from Near-Extinction." *JoongAng Daily,* 2 December 2005.

Little, Archibald John. *Through the Yang-tse Gorges, or Trade and Travel in Western China.* London: Samson Low, Marston, and Company, 1898.

Little, Mrs. Archibald [Alicia]. *Intimate China.* London: Hutchinson and Co., 1899.

Lockhart, James, ed. *We People Here: Nahuatl Accounts of the Conquest of Mexico.* Berkeley: University of California Press, 1993.

Lowell, Percival. *Chosön: The Land of the Morning Calm; A Sketch of Korea.* Boston: Ticknor, 1886.

Lubow, Robert E. *The War Animals: The Training and Use of Animals as Weapons of War.* New York: Doubleday, 1977.

Lydekker, Richard, ed. *The Royal Natural History.* 6 vols. London: F. Warne, 1893.

MacKenzie, John M. *Empire of Hunting: Hunting, Conservation, and British Imperialism.* Manchester, UK: Manchester University Press, 1988.

——. "The Imperial Pioneer and Hunter and the British Masculine Stereotype in Late Victorian and Edwardian Times." In *Manliness and Morality: Middle-Class Masculinity in Britain and America, 1800–1940,* edited by J. A. Mangan and James Walvin, 178–98. New York: St. Martin's Press, 1987.

Maeda Ai, Haga Toru, and Ogi Shinzō, eds. *Meiji Taishō zu shi.* 17 vols. Tokyo: Chikuma shobō, 1978.

Mainichi shinbunsha, ed. *Shōwa shi zen-kiroku: Chronicle 1926–1989.* Tokyo: Mainichi shinbunsha, 1989.

Malcolmson, Robert, and Stephanos Mastoris. *The English Pig: A History*. London: Hambledon Press, 1998.

Manchester, William. *American Caesar: Douglas MacArthur, 1880–1964*. Boston: Little, Brown, and Company, 1978.

Mangan, J. A., and Callum McKenzie. "'Pig-Sticking Is the Greatest Fun': Martial Conditioning on the Hunting Fields of Empire." In *Militarism, Sport, Europe: War without Weapons,* edited by J. A. Mangum, 97–119. London: Routledge, 2003.

"Manshū kara kikan shita gunken han'in ni Manshū ni okeru gunyōken katsudō jitsujō o kiku." *Inu no kenkyū* 4, no. 2 (1935): 20–23.

Mao Tse-tung. *Selected Works of Mao Tse-tung*. 5 vols. Oxford: Pergamon Press, 1961.

Markland, Ben. "Native and Immigrant Dogs." *Chicago Daily Tribune*, 26 March 1942, 16.

Marvin, John T. *The Book of All Terriers*. New York: Howell Book House, 1976.

Mastromarino, Mark A. "Teaching Old Dogs New Tricks: The English Mastiff and the Anglo-American Experience." *The Historian: A Journal of History* 49 (1986): 10–25.

Matsui Akira. "Kōkogaku kara mita inu." *Buraku kaiho Nara* 11 (1999): 7–25.

Matsui Hiroshi. "Senjichū no chikuken kennō no undo." *Sekai* 465 (August 1984): 304–17.

McHugh, Susan. *Dog*. London: Reaktion Books, 2004.

Meech-Pekarik, Julia. *The World of the Meiji Print: Impressions of a New Civilization*. New York: Weatherhill, 1987.

Meiji bunka kenkyūkai, ed. *Meiji bunka zenshū*. 28 vols. Tokyo: Nihon hyōronsha, 1967–68.

———. *Meiji bunka zenshū: Meiji jibutsu kigen*. Tokyo: Nihon hyōronsha, 1984.

Meinertzhagen, Colonel R. *Kenya Diary, 1902–1906*. Edinburgh: Oliver and Boyd, 1957.

Melograni, Piero. "The Cult of the Duce in Mussolini's Italy." *Journal of Contemporary History* 11, no. 4 (October 1976): 221–37.

Melville, Elinor G. K. *A Plague of Sheep: Environmental Consequences of the Conquest of Mexico*. Cambridge: Cambridge University Press, 1994.

Mertz, John Pierre. "Internalizing Social Difference: Kanagaki Robun's *Shanks' Mare to Western Seas*." In *New Directions in the Study of Meiji Japan,* edited by Helen Hardacre and Adam L. Kern, 219–28. Leiden, NLD: Brill, 1997.

Miller, Ian. *The Nature of the Beast: Empire and Exhibition at the Tokyo Imperial Zoo*. Berkeley: University of California Press, forthcoming.

Minami Masaya. "Chūken no hi wa ima narinu." *Yasukuni* (1 March 1992): 4–5.

Ministry of Finance, Printing Bureau, *20-seiki dezain kitte,* 9, 23 February, and 21 July 2000.

Miyagawa Kikuyoshi, ed. *Shōgaku kokugo tokuhon kaisetsu: Junjōka yō*. 12 vols. Tokyo: Meiji tosho, 1935.

Miyata Katsushige. "Nihon no keizai seichō to petto ni taisuru ishiki no henka." *Hito to dōbutsu no kankei gakkai shi* 9, no. 10 (August 2001): 40–44.

Miyawaki Shunzō. *Shōwa hachi nen: Shibuya eki*. Tokyo: PHP kenkyūsho, 1995.

Miyoshi, Masao. *As We Saw Them: The First Japanese Embassy to the United States*. New York: Kodansha, 1994.

Monbushō. *Jinjō shōgaku shūshin sho, maki ni kyōshi yō*. Tokyo: Monbushō, 1935.

———. *Shogakkō kokugo yomihon*. Tokyo: Monbushō, 1933.

———. *Shotōka kokugo ichi, kyōshiyō*. Tokyo: Monbushō, 1942.

Morris-Suzuki, Tessa. *Reinventing Japan: Time, Space, Nation*. Armonk, NY: M. E. Sharpe, 1998.

Morse, Edward S. *Japan Day by Day, 1877, 1878–79, 1882–83.* 2 vols. Boston: Houghton Mifflin, 1917.

Muir, Edward. *Mad Blood Stirring: Vendetta and Factions in Friuli during the Renaissance.* Baltimore: Johns Hopkins University Press, 1993.

Mullin, Molly H. "Mirrors and Windows: Sociocultural Studies of Human-Animal Relationships." *Annual Review of Anthropology* 28 (1999): 201–24.

"Mushu no yaken bokusatsusha he teate kin shikyū no ken" (8 April 1878). In *Shusai roku* (A4–54, no. 51), Hokkaido Prefectural Archives, Sapporo.

Myers, Ramon H., and Mark R. Peattic. *The Japanese Colonial Empire, 1895–1945.* Princeton: Princeton University Press, 1984.

Najita, Tetsuo, and H. D. Harootunian. "Japanese Revolt against the West: Political and Cultural Criticism in the Twentieth Century." In *Cambridge History of Japan.* Vol. 6, *The Twentieth Century,* edited by Peter Duus, 711–74. Cambridge: Cambridge University Press, 1988.

Nakashima Satoru. *Kanagawa-ken kyōkenbyō yobō gai shi.* Yokohama: Nakashima Satoru, 1973.

"Nankyoku Karafuto-ken ki'nen dōzō kensetsu ni tsuite." *Dōbutsu no tomo* 22 (March–April 1933): 1.

"Nanshū dōzō no aiken ga mondai," *Hōchi shinbun,* 18 August 1898. In *Meiji nyūsu jiten,* edited by Edamatsu Shigeyuki, Sugiura Tadashi, and Yagi Kyōsuke, 6:274. 9 vols. Tokyo: Mainichi komyunikēshonzu, 1983–86.

Nemoto Kanta. "Kateiken toshite no korī." *Kaitei-ken* 72 (April 1960): 1–3.

Newman, Lesléa. *Hachiko Waits.* New York: Henry Holt, 2004.

Nihon hōsō kyōkai, ed. *Hōsō gojū nen shi, shiryō-hen.* Tokyo: Nihon hōsō shuppan kyōkai, 1977.

Nihon inu hozon kai, ed. *Shadan hōjin Nihon inu hozon kai sōritsu gojū shūnen shi.* Tokyo: Nihon inu hozon kai, 1978.

Nihon Kokuyū Tetsudō Shibuya Eki, ed. *Shibuya eki 100 nen shi, Chūken Hachikō 50 nen shi.* Tokyo: Nihon Kokuyū Tetsudō Shibuya Eki, 1985.

"Nihon no inuten no kusawake, Washinton inuten." *Nihonbashi* (February 2000): 13.

"Niikappu bokujo uma oyobi hatachi o songai suru yaken sakkaku hō no ken" (25 January 1878). In *Honchōbu katatsu shorui* (02422, no. 6), Hokkaido Prefectural Archives, Sapporo.

Nishi Amane. "Travel by Foreigners within the Country (Naichi Ryokō)." In *Meiroku Zasshi: Journal of the Japanese Enlightenment,* translated by William Reynolds Braisted, 287–93. Cambridge: Harvard University Press, 1976.

Notehelfer, F. G., ed. *Japan through American Eyes: The Journal of Francis Hall, Kangawa and Yokohama, 1859–1866.* Princeton: Princeton University Press, 1992.

Nunobiki Toshio. "Hashika inu." *Nihon rekishi* 331 (December 1975): 75–81.

Ō Ikutoku. *Taiwan: Kūmon suru sono rekishi.* Tokyo: Kōbundō, 1970.

Ōdate-shi shi hensan iinkai, ed. *Ōdate-shi shi.* 5 vols. Ōdate: Ōdate-shi, 1986.

Ōe Kenzaburo. *Okurete kita seinen.* Tokyo: Shinchōsha, 1970.

Ōe Shinobu. *Nichiro sensō no gunji shiteki kenkyū.* Tokyo: Iwanami shoten, 1976.

Oguma, Eiji. *A Genealogy of "Japanese" Self-images,* translated by David Askew. Melbourne: Trans Pacific Press, 2002.

Ōhira Ken. *Yutakasa no seishin byōri.* 40th ed. Tokyo: Iwanami shinsho, 1990.

Okada Akio. *Inu to neko.* Tokyo: Mainichi shinbunsha, 1980.

Oliphant, Laurence. *Elgin's Mission to China and Japan.* 1859. Reprint, Hong Kong: Oxford University Press, 1970.

———. *Episodes in a Life of Adventure, or Moss from a Rolling Stone*. 1887. Reprint, Richmond, UK: Curzon Press, 2000.

"Onna no petto de kono mōkekata." *Shūkan bunshun* (5 February 1986): 126–29.

Ono Susumi. *Chūkon ode: Chūken Hachikō*. Ōdate-chō, Akita Prefecture: Ono Susumi chosaku hankōkai, 1932.

Ono Yoshirō. *"Seiketsu" no kindai*. Tokyo: Kōdansha, 1997.

Ownby, Ted. *Subduing Satan: Religion, Recreation, and Manhood in the Rural South, 1865–1920*. Chapel Hill: University of North Carolina Press, 1990.

Ozaki Hozuki. *Omoide no Shōnen Kurabu jidai: Natsukashi no meisaku hakurankai*. Tokyo: Kōdansha, 1997.

Palsetia, Jesse S. "Mad Dogs and Parsis: The Bombay Dog Riots of 1832." *Journal of the Royal Asiatic Society* 11, no. 1 (2001): 13–30.

Parker, Heidi G., et al. "Genetic Structure of the Purebred Domestic Dog." *Science* 304 (21 May 2004): 1163.

Parker, Merryl. "The Cunning Dingo." *Society and Animals* 15, no. 1 (2007): 69–78.

Partner, Simon. *Assembled in Japan: Electrical Goods and the Making of the Japanese Consumer*. Berkeley: University of California Press, 1999.

Paxton, Robert O. "The Five Stages of Fascism." *Journal of Modern History* 70 (March 1998): 1–23.

Peattie, Mark R. "Japanese Treaty Port Settlements in China, 1895–1937." In *The Japanese Informal Empire in China, 1895–1937*, edited by Peter Duus, Ramon H. Myers, and Mark R. Peattie, 166–209. Princeton: Princeton University Press, 1989.

Pemberton, Neil, and Michael Worboys. *Mad Dogs and Englishmen: Rabies in Britain, 1830–2000*. London: Palgrave Macmillan, 2007.

Perry, Matthew Calbraith. *The Japan Expedition, 1852–1854: The Personal Journal of Commodore Matthew C. Perry*, edited by Roger Pineau. Washington, DC: Smithsonian Institution Press, 1968.

Pet Food Manufacturers Association, Japan. "Inu neko shiiku ritsu, zenkoku chōsa." http://www.jppfma.org (accessed 24 April 2006).

Phillips, Sandra S., Alexandra Munroe, and Daido Moriyama. *Daido Moriyama: Stray Dog*. San Francisco: San Francisco Museum of Modern Art, 1999.

Piel, L. Halliday. "Loyal Dogs and Meiji Boys: The Controversy over Japan's First Children's Story, *Koganemaru* (1891)." *Children's Literature* 38 (2010): 207–22.

Pilling, David. "Every Dog Has its Day in Japan." *Financial Times*, 8 June 2004, 11.

Pincus, Leslie. *Authenticating Culture in Imperial Japan: Kuki Shūzō and the Rise of National Aesthetics*. Berkeley: University of California Press, 1995.

Pollan, Michael. *The Botony of Desire: A Plant's-Eye View of the World*. New York: Random House, 2001.

Povish, Shirley. "Ali Declares War, Then Takes Wing, Foreman Dogs It." *Washington Post*, 28 October 1974, D1.

PR Web Press Release Newswire website. "Korea's Native Dog Makes Debut in D.C." http://www.prweb.com/releases/2006/8/prweb420367.htm (accessed 20 August 2008).

Pycior, Helena. "The Making of the 'First Dog': President Warren G. Harding and Laddie Boy." *Society and Animals* 13, no. 2: 109–38.

Putney, William W. *Always Faithful: A Memoir of the Marine Dogs of WWII*. New York: Free Press, 2001.

Ravina, Mark. *The Last Samurai: The Life and Battles of Saigō Takamori*. Hoboken, NJ: John Wiley and Sons, 2004.

Reynolds, E. Bruce, ed. *Japan in the Fascist Era*. New York: Palgrave Macmillan, 2004.

Rhoden, Nicholas C. *Pawprints in Japan: Dogs in Myth and History*. Richmond, CA: Fire Lake Press, 2002.

Rikugun bijutsu kyōkai, ed. *Seisen bijutsu*. Tokyo: Rikugun Bijutsu Kyōkai, 1939.

——. *Seisen bijutsu*. Vol. 2. Tokyo: Rikugun Bijutsu Kyōkai, 1942.

Rikugun tsuwamono henshūbu, ed. *Senjin sōwa shū*. Tokyo: Rikugun Zaigō Gunjinkai Honbu Tsuwamono Hakkōsho, 1934.

Ritvo, Harriet. *The Animal Estate: The English and Other Creatures in the Victorian Age*. Cambridge: Harvard University Press, 1987.

——. "Animal Planet." *Environmental History* 9, no. 2 (April 2004): 204–20.

——. *The Platypus and the Mermaid and Other Figments of the Classifying Imagination*. Cambridge: Harvard University Press, 1997.

——. "Pride and Pedigree: The Evolution of the Victorian Dog Fancy." *Victorian Studies* 29, no. 2 (Winter 1986): 227–53.

Rosenblum, Robert. *The Dog in Art from Rococo to Post-Modernism*. New York: H. N. Abrams, 1988.

Rusling, James F. *Across America; or, The Great West and the Pacific Coast*. New York: Sheldon and Company, 1874.

Russell, Edmund. "Evolutionary History: Prospectus for a New Field." *Environmental History* 8, no. 2 (April 2003): 204–28.

Ryūkyū Ōkoku Hyōjoshomonjo, ed. Ryūkyū Ōkoku Hyōjoshomonjo henshū iinkai. 20 vols. Urasoe, Okinawa: Urasoe-shi kyōiku iinkai, 1989.

Saitō Hirokichi. "Aiken monogatari." In *Zenshū Nihon dōbutsu shi*, 12:5–102. 26 vols. Tokyo: Kōdansha, 1983.

——. *Nihon no inu to ōkami*. Tokyo: Sekkaisha, 1964.

Sakanishi, Shio, ed. *Some Unpublished Letters of Townsend Harris*. New York: Japan Reference Library, 1941.

Samuels, Richard J. *Machiavelli's Children: Leaders and Their Legacies in Italy and Japan*. Ithaca: Cornell University Press, 2003.

Sankei Shinbun, ed. *Wanchan paradaisu 2000: Petto yōhin gaido*. Tokyo: Sankei shinbun, 2000.

Sasaki Toshikazu. "Inu wa senzo nari ya—Ainu no sōsei setsuwa to Wazo dōsō ron" In *Kita kara no Nihon shi*, edited by Hokkaidō-Tōhoku Kenkyūkai, 189–225. 2 vols. Tokyo: Sanseidō, 1990.

Sassa Hirō. *Nihon fasshizumu no hatten katei*. Tokyo: Asano shoten, 1932.

——. *Seiji no hinkon*. Tokyo: Chikura shobō, 1931.

Satow, Ernest Mason, and A. G. S. Hawes. *A Handbook for Travellers in Central and Northern Japan*. Yokohama: Kelly, 1881.

Sax, Borio. *Animals in the Third Reich: Pets, Scapegoats, and the Holocaust*. New York: Continuum, 2000.

Schwarz, Marion. *A History of Dogs in the Early Americas*. New Haven: Yale University Press, 1977.

Scott, James C. *Domination and the Arts of Resistance: Hidden Transcripts*. New Haven: Yale University Press, 1990.

——. *Weapons of the Weak: Everyday Forms of Peasant Resistance*. New Haven: Yale University Press, 1985.

Seidensticker, Edwin. *Tokyo Rising: The City since the Great Earthquake*. New York: Knopf, 1990.

Selous, Frederick Courtney. *A Hunter's Wanderings in Africa*. London: MacMillan, 1907.

"Sensen ni hoeyu." *Kinema junpō* 588 (21 September 1936): 107.

Serpell, James, ed. *The Domestic Dog: Its Evolution, Behaviour, and Interactions with People*. Cambridge: Cambridge University Press, 1995.

———. *In the Company of Animals: A Study of Human-Animal Relationships*. London: Basil Blackwell, 1986.

Shadan hōjin Japan Keneru Kurabu, ed. *JKC 40 nen shi*. Tokyo: Japan Keneru Kurabu, 1990.

———. *JKC 50 nen shi*. Tokyo: Japan Keneru Kurabu, 2000.

Shashin Kurabu (1901), Japanese Colonial Government Archives, National Library, Taiwan Branch, Taipei.

Sherrill, Martha. *Dog Man: An Uncommon Life on a Faraway Mountain*. New York: Penguin Press, 2008.

Shiboleth, Myrna. *The Israel Canaan Dog*. 2nd ed. Loveland, CO: Alpine, 1994.

Shiga Shigetaka. *Shiga Jūkō zenshū*. 8 vols. Tokyo: Shiga Jūkō zenshū hankō kai, 1927–29.

Shiina Noritaka, *Taishō hakubutsukan hiwa*. Tokyo: Ronzōsha, 2002.

Shimizu Isao, *Bigō ga mita Nihonjin*. Tokyo: Kōdansha, 2001.

———, ed. *Meiji mangakan*. Tokyo: Kōdansha, 1979.

Shimizu Yoshitarō. "Hachikō." *Kyūshū nippō*, 26 March 1935. Hachikō shinbun kiji album, Tōkyō-to Shibuya-ku Shirane Kinen Kyōdo Bunkakan Archive, Tokyo.

Shinoda, Mariko. "Scientists as Preservationists: Natural Monuments in Japan, 1906–1931." *Historia Scientiarum* 8, no. 2 (1998): 141–55.

Shirane, Haruo, ed. *Early Modern Japanese Literature: An Anthology*. New York: Columbia University Press, 2002.

Shiseki meishō tennen ki'nenbutsu shitei, no. 82, D531 (1933–1941). Bureau of Cultural Affairs, Ministry of Education Archive, Tokyo.

Siddle, Richard. *Race, Resistance, and the Ainu of Japan*. London: Routledge, 1996.

Siebold, Philipp Franz von, with Conrad Jacob Temminck. *Fauna Japonica*. 1842–44; Tokyo: Shokubutsu Bunken Hankō kai, 1934.

Sims, Joseph Patterson. "Dog Map of the World: The Countries of Origin of Some Seventy Breeds of Domesticated Dogs, Half of Them Evolved in the British Isles!" London: Illustrated London News, 1933.

Skabelund, Aaron. "Breeding Racism: The Imperial Battlefields of the 'German' Shepherd." *Society and Animals* 16, no. 4 (Winter 2008): 354–71.

Smith, Anthony D. *The Ethnic Origins of Nations*. New York: Basil Backwell, 1986.

Snow, Philip. *The Fall of Hong Kong: Britain, China, and the Japanese Occupation*. New Haven: Yale University Press, 2003.

Soeda Tomomichi. *Enka no Meiji Taishō shi*. Tokyo: Tōsui shobo, 1982.

Spivak, Gayatri Chakravorty. "Can the Subaltern Speak?" In *Marxism and the Interpretation of Culture*, edited by Cary Nelson and Lawrence Grossberg, 271–313. Urbana: University of Illinois Press, 1998.

Sramek, Joseph. "'Face Him Like a Briton': Tiger Hunting, Imperialism, and British Masculinity in Colonial India, 1800–1875." *Victorian Studies* 47, no. 4 (2006): 659–80.

Steinhart, Edward I. "The Imperial Hunt in Colonial Kenya, c. 1880–1909." In *Animals in Human Histories*, edited by Mary Henninger-Voss, 144–81. Rochester, NY: University of Rochester Press, 2002.

Stephanitz, Max von. *Doitsu shepādo inu: Kaisetsu to shashin*, translated by Arisaka Mitsutaka and Karita Hideo. 5 vols. Tokyo: Teikoku gun'yōken kyōkai, 1934–36.

——. *The German Shepherd in Word and Picture*, translated by Carrington Charke and revised by Joseph Schwabacher. Jena, DEU: Anton Kämfe, 1923.

Stern, Pamela Cross, and Tom Mather. *The Complete Japanese Chin*. New York: Howell Book House, 1997.

Sterry, Lorraine. *Victorian Women Travelers in Meiji Japan: Discovering a "New" Land*. London: Global Oriental, 2009.

Storey, William K. "Big Cats and Imperialism: Lion and Tiger Hunting in Kenya and Northern India, 1898–1930." *Journal of World History* 2, no. 2 (1991): 135–73.

Sugimoto Ryū. "Nihon rikugun to bahitsu mondai—gunba shigen hogo hō no seiritsu ni kanshite." *Ritsumeikan daigaku jinbun kagaku kenkyūsho kiyō* 82 (December 2003): 83–115.

Suzuki Takurō. "Asahi shinbun ga tsukutta 'Chūken Hachikō' shinwa." *Bungei shunjū* 66, no. 10 (August 1988): 94

Tagawa Suihō. *Norakuro manga zenshū*. Tokyo: Kōdansha, 1967.

Takada Susumu. "Aikenka retsuden." *Bungei shunjū* 82, no. 5 (March 2004): 182–89.

Takahashi Masato. *Nagano-ken Manshū kaitaku shi: Giyūtai kaitakudan*. 2 vols. Matsumoto: Kyōdo shuppansha, 1981.

Takahashi Yūri, Ishii Yōhei, and Fukuda Keitsuke. "Petto bijinesu no shinjitsu." *Shūkan Tōyō Keizai* (15 March 2003): 106–7.

Takahisa Heishirō. *Nihon inu no kaikata*. Tokyo: Shunyōdō, 1933.

Takeuchi Ginjirō. *Fukoku kyōba*. Tokyo: Kōdansha, 1999.

Tanabe Yasuichi. "Inu mo sensō he." *Dōyū* 434 (10 January 1998): 18.

Tanabe Yūichi and Yamazaki Kaori. "Hyōtei irai chōsa ni motozuku inu hinshu ni yoru kōdō tokusei no chigai—katei inu he no tekisei o chūshin ni." *Jūi chikusan shinpō* 54, no. 1 (2001): 9–14.

Tanabe Yukio. "Inpāru sakusen de zenmetsu shita dai 15 gun no gunba 12,000 tō no higeki." *Jūi chikusan shinpō* 671 (June 1977): 361–64.

Tanaka, Hideto. "National Ideals of Japanese Boys in *Shōnen Kurabu* during the Early 1930s." Master's thesis, Columbia University, 2000.

Tanaka Hiromi. "Kyozō no gunshin Tōgō Heihachirō." *This is Yomiuri* (September 1993): 220–47.

Tanaka Toyotarō. *Shōgaku kokugo tokuhon no jissaiteki toriatsukai, jinjōka dai ichi*. Tokyo: Meguro shoten, 1933.

Taniguchi Kengo. *Inu no Nihon shi: Ningen to tomo ni ayunda ichiman nen no monogatari*. Tokyo: PHP kenkyūjo, 2000.

Tanazaki Jun'ichirō. *Some Prefer Nettles*, translated by Edward Seidensticker. Tokyo: Tuttle, 2001.

Taylor, George. *Man's Friend, the Dog*. New York: Stokes, 1891.

Teikoku gikai shūgiin iinkai kiroku 114, Shōwa hen.

Teshima Tamie. "Komogomo no kokoro." *Teikoku gun'yōken kyōkai Tōkyō shibu hō* (September 1938). Teshima Tamie Album, Yūshūkan Military and War Memorial Museum, Yasukuni Shrine, Tokyo.

Thiong'o, Ngũgĩ wa. *A Grain of Wheat*. Oxford: Heinemann, 1967.

Thomas, Elizabeth Marshall. *The Hidden Life of Dogs*. New York: Houghton Mifflin, 1993.

Thomas, Julia Adeney. *Reconfiguring Modernity: Concepts of Nature in Japanese Political Ideology*. Berkeley: University of California Press, 2001.

Thomas, Keith. *Man and the Natural World: Changing Attitudes in England, 1500–1800*. Oxford: Oxford University Press, 1983.

Thurston, Mary E. *The Lost History of the Canine Race: Our 15,000-Year Love Affair with Dogs*. Kansas City: Andrews and McMeel, 1996.

"Tokushū: Tokugawa Yoshinobu." *Taiyō* 449 (April 1998): cover page.

Tōkyō-to. *Senjika "tochō" no kōhō katsudō*. Tokyo: Tōkyō-to, 1996.

"Tōkyō dai kūshū, sensai shi" henshū iinkai. *Tōkyō dai kūshū, sensai shi*. 5 vols. Tokyo: Tōkyō kūshū o kiroku suru kai, 1974.

Ton Shan-yan. *Shokuminchi Taiwan no genjūmin to Nihonjin keisatsukan no kazokutachi*, translated by Uezumi Etsuko. Tokyo: Nihon kikan shuppan sentā, 2000.

Torrance, Richard. "*The People's Library:* The Spirit of Prose Literature versus Fascism." In *The Culture of Japanese Fascism*, edited by Alan Tansman, 56–79. Durham: Duke University Press, 2009.

Tropp, Jacob. "Dogs, Poison, and the Meaning of Colonial Intervention in the Transkei, South Africa." *Journal of African History* 43 (2002): 451–72.

Tsukamoto Akira. "Jingū kōgō densetsu to kinsei Nihon to Chōsen-kan." *Shinrin* 76, no. 6 (1996): 1–33.

Tsukamoto Manabu. *Edo jidaijin to dōbutsu*. Tokyo: Nihon editā sukūru shuppan, 1995.

——. "Inu." In *Nihon minzoku daijiten*, edited by Fukuda Ajio et al. 2 vols. Tokyo: Yoshikawa kōbunkan, 1999.

——. *Shōrui o meguru seiji: Genroku no fōkuroa*. Tokyo: Heibonsha, 1993.

Tsunoyama Yukihiro. "O-yatoi gaikokujin Appu Jonzu (hoi)." *Kansai daigaku keizai ronshū* 38 (1987): 38–39.

——. "O-yatoi gaikokujin Appu Jonzu: Shimōsa bokuyōjō ni okeru men'yō kaiiku." *Kansai daigaku keizai ronshū* 37, no. 6 (1986): 585–618.

Tsurumi, Kazuko. *Social Change and the Individual: Japan Before and After Defeat in World War II*. Princeton: Princeton University Press, 1970.

Tuan, Yi-Fu. *Dominance and Affection: The Making of Pets*. New Haven: Yale University Press, 1984.

Turner, Pamela S. *Hachiko: The True Story of a Loyal Dog*. Boston: Houghton Mifflin, 2004.

Tuttle, William M., Jr. *"Daddy's Gone to War": The Second World War in the Lives of America's Children*. Oxford: Oxford University Press, 1993.

Ucelay Da Cal, Enrique. "The Influence of Animal Breeding on Political Racism." *History of European Ideas* 15, no. 4–6 (1992): 717–25.

Uchida Roan. "Inu monogatari." In *Uchida Roan zenshū*, edited by Nomura Takashi, 383–405. 13 vols. Tokyo: Yumani shobō, 1986.

Uchimura, Kanzō. *The Diary of a Japanese Convert*. New York: Fleming H. Revell, 1895.

Uemura Hideaki. *Wan nyan tantei dan: Sensō de shinda inu ya neko no hanashi*. Tokyo: Popurasha, 1984.

Uezawa Kenji. *Shōhei o nakaseta gunba inu hato bukan monogatari*. Tokyo: Jitsugyō no Nihon sha, 1938.

Utsunomiya bijutsukan. *Bigot: Retrospective*. Utsunomiya: Utsunomiya bijutsukan, 1998.

Van Sittert, Lance. "'Keeping the Enemy at Bay': The Extermination of Wild Carnivora in the Cape Colony, 1889–1910." *Environmental History* 3, no. 3 (July 1998): 311–32.

Van Sittert, Lance, and Sandra Swart. *Canis Africanis: A Dog History of Southern Africa*. Leiden, NLD: Brill, 2008.

Varner, Jeannette Johnson, and John Grier Varner. *Dogs of the Conquest*. Norman: University of Oklahoma Press, 1983.

Veblen, Thorstein. *The Theory of the Leisure Class: An Economic Study of Institutions.* 1899. Reprint, New York: Mentor, 1963.

Velde, Paul van der, and Rudolf Bachofner, eds. *The Deshima Diaries: Marginalia, 1700–1740.* Tokyo: Japan-Netherlands Institute, 1992.

Veldkamp, Elmer. "Eiyū to natta inutachi: Gunyōken irei to dōbutsu kuyō no henyō." In *Hito to dōbutsu no Nihon shi,* edited by Suga Yutaka, 44–68. 3 vols. Tokyo: Yoshikawa kōbunkan, 2009.

Vesey-Fitzgerald, Brian. *The Domestic Dog: An Introduction to Its History.* London: Routledge, 1957.

Vogel, Ezra F. *Japan's New Middle Class: The Salary Man and His Family in a Tokyo Suburb.* Berkeley: University of California Press, 1963.

Walker, Brett L. *The Conquest of Ainu Lands: Ecology and Culture in Japanese Expansion, 1590–1800.* Berkeley: University of California Press, 2001.

———. *The Lost Wolves of Japan: Reflections on the History of Science, Culture, and the Environment.* Seattle: Weyerhaeuser Series, University of Washington Press, 2005.

Waller, Anna M. *Dogs and National Defense.* Washington, DC: Department of the Army, Office of the Quartermaster General, 1958.

Walton, John K. "Mad Dogs and Englishman: The Conflict over Rabies in Late Victorian England." *Journal of Social History* 13 (1979): 219–39.

War Office. *The Training of War Dogs.* London: The War Office, 1962.

Watanabe Kyōji. *Yukishi yo no omokage.* Fukuoka: Ashi shobō, 1998.

Watase Shōzaburō. "Inu to Nihon bunka." *Inu no zasshi* 34 (August 1922): 11–14.

———. "Nihonken ni tsuite." *Inu no zasshi* 31 (January 1921): 5.

———. "Nihonken no kigen ni tsuite." *Rigaku kai* 20, no. 2 (1922): 26–26.

Watson, Helen Orr. *Trooper, U.S. Army Dog.* Boston: Houghton Mifflin, 1943.

Wedde, Ian. "Walking the Dog." In *Knowing Animals,* edited by Laurence Simmons and Philip Armstrong, 266–88. Leiden, NLD: Brill, 2007.

White, David Gordon. *Myths of the Dog-Man.* Chicago: University of Chicago Press, 1991.

Wippermann, Wolfgang, and Detlef Berentzen. *Die Deutschen und ihre Hunde: Ein Sonderweg der Mentalitätsgeschichte?* Berlin: Siedler, 1999.

Wohn Dong-hee. "Canines No Longer Lead a Dog's Life." *International Herald Tribune-JoongAng Daily,* 1 July 2005, W1.

Wood, Frances. *No Dogs and Not Many Chinese: Treaty Port Life in China, 1843–1943.* London: John Murray, 1998.

"Yaken bokusatsu ni tsuite no teiji bun." Yokota Masao Papers, Sanrizuka Museum of the Imperial Household Ranch, Narita, Japan.

Yamada Kazuyuki. "'Hokkaidō ijū kaiko roku' to Iwane Seichi." *Shizunai bungei* 11 (1991): 45–68.

Yamada Masahiro. *Kazoku petto: Danna yori mo petto ga taisetsu?!* Tokyo: Bunshun bunko, 2007.

Yamada Takako. *Ainu no sekaikan.* Tokyo: Kōdansha, 1994.

Yamaguchi Masao. "Norakuro wa warera no dōjidai jin." *Chūō kōron* 91, no. 3 (March 1976): 84–100

Yamamoto Kajirō. "Uma, inu, kokeshi." *Kaizō* 23 (May 1941): 110–13.

Yanagita Kunio. *Yanagita Kunio zenshū.* 32 vols. Tokyo: Chikuma shobō, 1989.

Yasumaru Yoshio. "Minshū undo ni okeru 'kindai.'" In Minushū undō, edited by Yasumaru Yoshio and Fukaya Katsumi, 447–504. Vol. 21 of "*Nihon kindai shisō taikei.*" 23 vols. Tokyo: Iwanami shoten, 1989.

Yokota Masao Papers, Sanrizuka Museum of the Imperial Household Ranch, Narita, Japan.

Yonemura, Ann. *Yokohama: Prints from Nineteenth-Century Japan.* Washington, DC: Smithsonian Institution Press, 1990.

Yoshida Chizuko. "Saigō-san no aiken." *Ueno* 417 (January 1994): 16–17.

Yoshino Yumisuke. *Koinu to heitai-san.* Tokyo: Tankaidō shuppan, 1943.

Young, Louise. "Marketing the Modern: Department Stores, Consumer Culture, and the New Middle Class in Interwar Japan." *International Labor and Working-Class History* 55 (Spring 1999): 52–70.

——. *Total Empire: Manchuria and the Culture of Wartime Imperialism.* Berkeley: University of California Press, 1998.

Young, Thomas. *Dogs for Democracy: The Story of America's Canine Heroes in the Global War.* New York: Bernard Ackerman, 1944.

INDEX

Italic page numbers refer to illustrations. Color figures and captions are not referenced in this index.

Abe Kōbō, 127

Abu Ghraib, 170

Adventures of Tintin, The (Hergé), 153

Africa, 2, 29, 50, 68, 134; colonial dogs in, 28, 118, 169; dog extermination campaigns in, 55, 69; on "Dog Map of the World," 23–24; hunting dogs in, 22–23; indigenous dogs in, 18–19; racial anxieties in, 46; scavenger dogs in, 3, 19, 48. *See also* kaffir; "rumble in the jungle;" South Africa

African Americans, 48, 79

Aibo, 184

Aiful consumer credit company, 187, 230n46

Ainu: bounty hunters, 66; creation legends of, 67; discrimination against, 65–66, 67, 68, 70

Ainu dogs, 65–66, 67, 69

Aka, 34–35, *36*, 77

Aka (Red), 81

Akasaka, 73

Akita, 114, 119–20, 126–28, 187, 194, 213n16, 219n135; designation as national treasure, 91, 99, 101; and Hachikō, 87–88, 94, 177; and Keller, 95–96, 124, 177; and MacArthur, 176; recognition of breed abroad, 91, 172, 177, 192

Akita Prefecture, 87, 93, 95

Akiyama, 27

Alaska, 134, 138, 224n68

Alberti, Samuel, 107

Alcock, Sir Rutherford, 28, 41–42, 63, 75, 205n30, 205n66

Alexandra, Princess of Wales, 26

Ali, Muhammad, 51

All Japan Guard Dog Association (Zen nihon keibi ken kyōkai), 174

"American dog," 19–20, 21, 26, 27, 71

American Indians, 29, 134; denigration of, 18, 30, 48, 67–69; and Lewis and Clark, 67

American Kennel Club, 23–24, 26, 134, 176, 177, 191, 201–2n14, 202n23

American Kennel Gazette, 27, 97

Americas, 29–30, 50

Anderson, Virgina DeJohn, 13

Andō Hiroshige II, 31, *32*

Andō Shō, 110, 114, 126

Andō Takeshi, 126, 180

Animal Estate: The English and Other Creatures in the Victorian Age, The (Ritvo), 15

animal welfare, 61, 77–79, 113, 127, 179, 188. *See also* Japan Society for Prevention of Cruelty to Animals; Royal Society for Prevention of Cruelty to Animals

Animal Welfare Day, 168
animals (nonhuman): and Buddhism, 61;
   and imperialism, 1–4, 11–13
Antarctica, 179
Aoba shigereru (Inoue), 176
Aoyama Cemetery, 109
Aren Homare, 158–60, 162, 163
Army Dog Memorial Statue (Gunken irei
   zō), 168
army dogs. *See* military dogs
Army Infantry School, 135
Arupusu taishō (Alpine victory), 109
Asanuma Inejirō, 128
Asia-Pacific War. *See* World War II
Atami, 28, 34, *35*
Australia, 24, 50, 67; dingo (*see* dingo);
   extermination campaigns in, 55, 69
Austria, 191

Baker, Steve, 200n23
Bakin (Takizawa Bakin), 108
bald eagle, American, 89
Baltimore, 79
Balto, 224n68
Barney, 151
Baron von Zeiglerhoff, 177
Barrow, Mr. C., 36–37, 39, 41
Barshay, Andrew, 217n98
Barton, Benjamin Smith, 69
bats, 220n3
bear, Russian, 89, 153
Beasts and Man in India (John Lockwood
   Kipling), 28
Beck, Alan, 79
Bedouin society, 194
Belgium, 51, 191
Belmont, August, Jr., 202n23
Berentzen, Detlef, 104
Bergen-Belsen POW and concentration
   camp, 177
Bettelheim, Bernard Jean, 41
Bigot, Georges, 34–35, *36, 74–75,* 76–78,
   204n35, 210n71
Bird, Isabella, 18–20, 21, 28, 40, 49, 200n1
birds, 59–60, 61, 62, 76–77, 98, 127
Blackie, 176
Blair, Tony, 228n5
Blondie, 89

Blondie (comic strip), 178
Borneman, John, 8–9
bounty system, 65, 66, 71
Bourdieu, Pierre, 188
Bousquet, George Hilaire, 47
breed: conflation with race, 8–9; continuing influence of, 195; definition of, 3,
   8–9; relationship to class, 10
Britain, 101, 108, 163; animal welfare in,
   77; class anxieties in, 3, 21–22; concerns about rabies in, 81; dog-breeding
   practices in, 2–3, 22–23; on "Dog Map
   of the World," 23–24, 25; fascism in,
   90; imperialism of, 22–23; and Japanese puppy-mills, 184–86; and military
   dogs, 134, 137, 138, 155, 156; and
   shepherd dogs, 134. *See also* bulldog,
   English; Kennel Club (English)
British army, 134, 137, 156
British Dogs' Wool Association, 165
Buddhism, 61
Budiansky, Stephen, 12
bulldog, English, 23–24, 27, 45, 57, 100,
   152, 194; as symbol of Britain, 24, 889,
   228n5
Bungei shunjū, 116
bunmei kaika. See "civilization and enlightenment"
Bunmei kaika (pamphlet), 57–59
burakumin, 72–73, 164
Burt, Jonathan, 15, 134, 179
Bush, George W., 150–51, 228n5
bushidō (way of the warrior) 109, 118

Cairo, 19
Cambridge University, 141
"Can the Subaltern Speak?" (Spivak), 13
canine imperialism: and class, 56–62;
   definition of, 2–4; legacies of, 50–52,
   169–70, 191–97; organizing principles
   of, 23–25; precedents of, 29–30; rhetoric
   of, 4, 8–11, 18, 20, 68; types of, 11–13
Cape Colony, 69
Cape Jackal, 24
capitalism, 4
cats, 12, 25, 49, 77, 79, 163, 165, 190,
   212n94; and femininity, 187
Chamberlain, Basil Hall, 25–26

Chiba Haruo, 144–45, 154

Chiba Prefecture: Army Infantry School in, 135–36, 146; elimination of canines in, 62–63, 65, 66, 69, 71, 73

chickens, 77; Japanese long-tailed, 213–14n29

chien de chasse (hunting dogs), 37

chien de rue (street dogs), 37

children: and Hachikō, 108–17; and Norakuro, 152–53; and pet dogs, 157–64, 166, 175, 178, 181, 188–90

chin (Japanese spaniel), 31, 38–39, 84, 102, 165, 191–92, 202n20; on "Dog Map of the World," 25; and Orientalism, 27; popularity in Europe and the United States, 26–27; presented as gifts, 26, 202n22; as representative canine of Japan, 25–27, 91, 191

China, 2, 5, 6, 28, 41, 44, 165; and *chin*, 25, 102; denigration of ethnic minorities in, 50–51; on "Dog Map of the World," 27; indigenous dogs of, 19, 21, 40, 43; Japanese imperialism in, 85, 95, 134, 140–41, 151–53; Liaodong Peninsula, 82, 84; memories of colonial dogs in, 50, 169–70, 206–7n93, 207n97; military dogs in, 132, *140*, 153–55, 161; rabies in, 49; Shangdong Peninsula, 134; Western imperialism in, 2, 6, 28; wild dogs in, 121. *See also* Chinese; Chinese Nationalists; Mao Tse-tung

Chinese: collaborators, 169–70; comparisons to docile canines, 149–50; dog eating by, 140; films, 169–70; Han, 170; portrayal as pigs, 154, 169; boar, 70. *See also* China; Chinese Nationalists; Mao Tse-tung

Chinese Nationalists, 149, 169

Chūken Hachikō monogatari (The story of the "Loyal Dog" Hachikō) (Kishi), *88*, 99, 110–11, 115, 123

Chūō kōron, 119

Churchill, Winston, 228n5

Cisco, 174

civilization: and colonial dogs, 20–23, 39–40, 57, 61, 121; definition of, 9, 40; and dog eating, 140, 185; and domestication, 10; and elimination of canines, 53–56, 61–66, 82, 86, 185; and imperialism, 5, 12–13; lingering influence of, 185; and native dogs, 19–24, 39–40, 44–50, 68–69, 121; relationship to loyalty and race, 8–12; "The Story of Enlightened and Unenlightened Dogs," 57–59

"civilization and enlightenment" (*bunmei kaika*), 5, 58–59, 71, 74

Clark, William, 67

class: and dog keeping in Britain, 21–24; and dog keeping in Japan, 56–62, 71–73, 76, 79, 92, 172–75, 180–82, 185; and hunting dogs, 51, 61; and rabies, 62–63, 81; relationship to breed, 8–11; and welfare in Japan, 79. *See also* lower class; middle class; upper class

colonial dog: bravery of, 18; cultural supremacy of, 55; defined, 19–20; fears about degeneration of, 46; identification with human colonizers, 20, 27–37, 141; intelligence of, 41; "Japanese" dogs as, 91, 123; loyalty of, 18, 28, 41, 43–45; pairing with native dog, 19–21, 29, 39–40, 44–45, 47, 50, 89; physical disorders of, 194–95; physical size and power of, 28–29, 31–34, 43–44; privileging of, 24–25, 57–60, 72–73, 85, 99, 179; purity of, 45–46, 49. *See also* native dog

Colonization Agency. *See* Kaitakushi

Colorado, 68

Columbia University, 49

Columbus, Christopher, 29

communists: in China, 50, 132, 170, 207n97, 220n8; in Japan, 81, 116, 220n8

concentration camps, 139, 177, 185

Confucianism, 9, 108

Confucius, 41

Congo, 51, 153

conquistadores, 29–30

coolies, 43, *74*, *75*, 76

Coppinger, Lorna, 12, 19

Coppinger, Raymond, 12, 19

Coren, Stanley, 14

coyotes, 55

Crider, John H., 151

Cuba, 203n38
cultural imperialism, 11, 172–82, 184

Dalian (Darien), 136
Darwin, Charles, 38, 45, 49; Darwinian science, 16, 45, 47, 48–49; *The Descent of Man,* 45; *Origin of Species,* 45. *See also* social Darwinism
deer, 66, 70, 103, 206n85
Deshima, 37
dhole, 85
dingo, 49, 55, 231n77
Dinky, 187
Disney, Walt, 152
Disney Company, 178, 180, 230n45
Dōbutsu gyakutai bōshi kai (Society for the Prevention of Abuse to Animals), 78
dog behavior, 7, 12–13, 17, 38–39, 47, 59, 196–97
dog breeding, 1, 4, 8–10; development of, 2, 12, 191, 194–95; relationship to class, 21–23; standards of, 101–3, 106, 118, 129
dog breeds and types: Afghan hound, 25; Africanis, 231n77; Akita (*see* Akita); Australian dingo, 231n77; Basenji, 231n77; beagle, 34, 76; borzoi, 31; bull terrier, 43, 173; cairn terrier, 174; Canaan dog, 193–94; Chihuahua, 7, 24, 187; cocker spaniel, 176, 178, 187; collie, 18, 157, 173, 178–79, 187; dachshund, 28, 92, 117; dandie dinmont terrier, 28; Doberman pinscher, 92, 102, 119; English Airedale terrier, 118–19; English bulldog (*see* bulldog, English); English foxhound, 28; English greyhound, 23; English setter, 24, 59; Eskimo dog, 85; fox terrier, 153, 162; French poodle, 24; German pointer, 59; German shepherd (*see* "German" shepherd); Great Dane, 28; greyhound, 28, 29, 31, 173; Hokkaido, 99; Japanese spaniel (see *chin*); Jindo, 106, 192–93, 215n59; Kai, 99, 105, 118; Kishū, 99, 118; Koshino, 99; Maltese, 28, 188; mastiff, 28–30; Mudol hound, 231n77; Old English sheepdog, 193; Pekingese, 25, 27, 205n74; Phu Quoc dog, 231n77; Pomeranian, 188;
Poongsan, 106, 193, 215n59, 231n71; Rajapalayam, 231n77; retrievers, 28; Rhodesian Ridgehound, 25; Sakhalin husky (*Karafuto-ken*), 179–80; Sapsaree (Sapsal), 193, 196; Satsuma, 211n92; schnauzer, 92; Shantung (Tibetan) terrier, 36, 59, 204n52, 205n74; Shiba, 99, 120, 176, 187, 190, 231nn60–61; Shikoku, 99; Siberian husky, 85; Skye terrier, 28–29, 36, 108, 203n34; Spitz, 60, 175–76, 178; St. Bernard, 7; Thai ridgeback, 231n77; Tosa, 102; Xoloitzcuintle, 231n77; Yankee terrier, 24; Yorkshire terrier, 188;
dog keeping: early modern forms of, 3; modern forms of, 2–4, 191
"Dog Map of the World," 21, 23–25, 27, 92, 191, 192
dog meat, consumption of: in China, 140; in Germany, 164; in Japan, 126, 164, 167; in Korea, 140, 185, 193
dog pounds, 73, 81, 113, 186, 195
Dog Shogun. *See* Tokugawa Tsunayoshi
dog shows, 23–24, 26, 101
dog taxes, 47, 81–82, 165
dogcatchers, 71–73, 79, 81, 92, 113, 186
dog-fancying clubs. *See names of individual organizations*
Doggo, 51
dogs: agency of, 12, 196; cemeteries for, 180, 183; clinics, 179, 184; costuming of, 60; as creole, 46; dog-care books, 92; dog fighting, 30, 102; fidelity of, 108; human's special relationship with, 6, 90, 155; infantilization of, 188; intelligence of, 6; licensing of, 47, 53, 66, 71–72, 73, 81; training of, 12–13, 131, 196. *See also* dog breeds and types
Dogs for Defense, 138, 155, 157, 162, 164
domestication, 10–12
Donga ilbo, 142–43, 222n41
Doru (Doll), 158
Dower, John, 121
Dreams (Yume), 168–69
Dun, Edwin, 62–66, 67
Dutch, 30, 37, 70–71
Dutch East Asia Company, 30
Duus, Peter, 80

eastern Europe, 21, 48
Echizen domain, 19–20
Edinburgh, 108
Edo, 26, 28, 37, 42, 44. *See also* Tokyo
education: ethics, 113–14, 127, 147,
216n87; textbooks, 108, 113– 15, 122,
127, 144–45, 147–49, 153–54, 161
Egypt, 19
Eight Below, 180
Eisenhower, Dwight, 179
Elder, Gwen, 162–63
Elgin, Lord, 36
Emishi, 63
England. *See* Britain
Enmei Temple, 147
Esashi, 66
Esu (dog in Manchuria), 143
Esu (dog in *Sensen ni hoeyu*), 157–58, 160
Esu (dog in *Umarete wa mita keredo*), 173, 175
eugenics, 8, 103–5, 107, 194
European Union, 172, 227–28n1
extraterritoriality, 28, 73, 82, 208n24
Ezo, 5, 56, 67. *See also* Hokkaido
Prefecture

Fala, 150–51, 162
farming, 55
fascism, 89–90, 95; criticism of, 116,
218–19n126; emergence of, 90; and
Hachikō, 1, 88, 91; language of, 89, 91;
and loyalty, 90–91, 108; non-canine
animals as symbols of, 90; and purity
of blood, 101–7; use and meaning of
the term, 90–91; and violence, 90–91,
117–23; and wolves, 103–4
Fauna Japonica (Siebold), 37
Federation Cynologique Internationale,
191–92, 194
Felix the Cat, 152
femininity: of lapdogs, 25, 27, 187
feral and semiferal dogs, 7, 19, 47, 53–55,
69, 103, 144, 164
Fifteen-Year War. *See* World War II
Fijians, 48
Fleming, George, 19–21, 206–7n93
Foreman, George, 51
Fortune, Robert, 44
foxes, 28, 47–48

France, 63, 76, 82, 108, 177, 191, 203n37;
on "Dog Map of the World," 24; fascist
influence in, 90; French expatriates in
Japan, 34–35, 47, 76; and imperialism,
11, 29; and military dogs, 133–34
Franco-Prussian War, 133
Fraser, Mary Crawford, 59
Frisbee, 190
frogs, 76, 164
Fudge, Erica, 14
Fuji, Mount, 28, 114, 127
Fujihara, 18
fukoku kyōhei. See "rich country, strong
army"
Fukui Prefecture, 19
Fukushima Yoshie, 143–44
Fukuzawa Yukichi, 75
Futabatei Shimei, 146

Gere, Richard, 88
"German" shepherd, 27, 99–100, 174,
194, 207n98, 214n44; as archetype of
colonial dog, 51, 194; Baron von Zeiglerhoff, 177; development of breed,
92; fidelity of, 108–9; in *Hogan's Heroes,*
177–78; identification with German
people, 24, 92, 95, 99; and "Japanese"
dogs, 91, 106, 118; Japanization of,
148; Japan Shepherd Association,
138; Japan Shepherd Club, 138, 148;
memories of, 51, 168–69, 177–78; as
military dog, 109, 118–19, 131, 135–36,
146–49, 154–58, 161; and Kongō
and Nachi, 136, 146–49, *150,* 157–58,
160–61, 168; and Nazis, 89, 104, 108,
139–40, 150; popularity in Britain, 117,
134; popularity in the United States,
117, 134, 177; Rin Tin Tin, 134; and
Stephanitz, 92, 95, 97, 99, 103–4, 106,
108, 118–19, 121, 136–37, 194; use by
colonial regimes, 118, 131, 136–37, 140,
142–44; use as police dogs, 118, 131;
and wolves, 103–4
German Southwest Africa, 188
Germany, 98, 109, 135, 177, 191; dog
eating in, 164; on "Dog Map of the
World," 24, 92; and fascism, 90–91;
and imperialism, 82; and Japan, 91,

Germany *(cont.)*
135; National Socialism, 103–4, 108; use of military dogs in, 134, 137–38, 155; Wehrmacht, 137; and wolves, 103–4. *See also* "German" shepherd; Hitler, Adolf; Stephanitz, Max von
germs, 130, 220n7
Gestapo, 139
Gidget, 187
Ginza, 101
Girl Scouts, 162
globalization, 7, 55
goats, 154, 204n42
Goering, Hermann, 177
Gordon, Andrew, 90
Gordon, Mrs. Will, 43
Gordon, Robert J., 47
gorillas, 153
gozoku kyōwa (harmony of five peoples), 154
Greyfriars Bobby, 108
Grier, Katherine C., 144
Griffis, William Elliot, 19–21, 26, 27, 71, 201n5
guard dogs, 12, 131, 133, 144, 175; in China, 169–70; in colonial Korea, 142–43; in German POW and concentration camps, 139, 177; Japan Guard Dog Association, 174; in Manchuria, 136
Gunjingō, 121, 149
"Gunken Tone" (Tone, the army dog), 161–62
Gurkha people, 25

Hachi: A Dog's Tale, 88
Hachikō, 1–2, 5, 87–89, 91, 94; and children, 108–17; commemorative stamps of, 88; Exit, 87; and Keller, 95–96, 124, 177; and motion pictures, 80, 109, 127, 219n132; Ōdate statue, 114, 218n124; photographs of, 87, *88*, 94, *100*, 106–7, 110; and questions about purity, 94; Shibuya statue, 110–12, 114–15, 124–27, 135, 218n124; Shop, 109; Square, 109; stories in ethics textbooks, 113–14; taxidermic mount of, 87, *100*, 101, 107

Hachikō monogatari (The story of Hachikō), 88, 127, 219n132
Hachiōji, 163–64, 166
Haitian Revolution, 203n38
Hakodate, 35, 43, 65–66
Hale, Horatio, 48
Hall, Francis, 35, 43
Hamamatsu, 124
Hara Takeshi, 138
Haraway, Donna, 15, 195
Harootunian, Harry, 93
Harper's New Monthly Magazine, 18, 20–21
Harris, Townsend, 28, 202n22
Hasebe Kotondo, 105–6, 215n55
Hasegawa Nyozekan, 116–17, 217n98
Hashimoto Gyokuransai (Utagawa Sadahide), 39, 204n46; *Yokohama kaikō kenmonshi,* 31, *33,* 34
Hata Ichirō, 102
Hata Shunroku, 163
hawks, 3
Hergé (Georges Remi), 153
Hershey chocolate company, 178
Hideyoshi Toyotomi, 193
Hiraiwa Yonekichi, 69–70, 115–16, 117, 128
Hirata Atsutane, 70–71
Hitler, Adolf, 89, 103–4, 150, 194
Hobsbawm, Eric, 130
Hogan's Heroes, 177–78
Hokkaido Prefecture, 5, 106; Edwin Dunn in, 63–65; Kitami, 186; native dogs in, 35–36, 48–49, 63–69, 71; rabies outbreaks in, 56, 65–66; ranching in, 64
Hollström, Lasse, 88
Honda Kinkichirō, 80–81
Hong Kong, 140
horses, 28, 35, 58, 63, 83, 152, 205n66; horse ranching, 65; military, 29, 78, 121, 130–33, 168, 220n2, 220n7, 222n29
Hume, David, 24
hunting, 21–22, 25, 28, 30, 55, 64, 99; and Ainu, 66; for birds and small game, 59, 61, 62, 83, 84; as imperial symbol, 141; with indigenous "Japanese" dogs, 70, 91, 103
hunting dogs, 34–35, 37–39, 67, 70, 165; as imperial symbols, 25, 141;

"Japanese" dogs as, 117, 119; on safari, 22–23, 25, 201n12; as symbol of urban and foreign extravagance, 61
Hussein, Saddam, 151
hyenas, 55
Hyōgo Prefecture, 72

Ichang, 43
Ichihashi Toshio, 168
Imagawa Isao, 139
Imai Takako, 178
Imperial Military Dog Association, 138, 141, 147, 155–56, *159*, 160, 165
imperialism: age of exploration and conquest, 29–30; age of "New Imperialism," 4, 18, 54–55, 67, 192; internal colonization, 67; types, 11–12. *See also* canine imperialism; unequal treaties
India, 6, 20–21, 55; indigenous dogs in, 19, 21, 40, 44, 48, 69, 85; Western dogs in, 28, 43–44, 46, 56–57
indigenous dog. *See* native dog
Inokuma Ken'ichirō, 85–86
Inoue Hisashi, 176
Inoue Tankei (Inoue Yasuji), 60
internal colonization, 67
"*Inu monogatari*" (Uchida), 85
Inu no kaikata (How to raise a dog), 178
"*Inu no tegara*" (The exploits of dogs), 147–49
inujini (dying like a dog), 162, 166–67, 169
Inukai Tsuyoshi, 95
inukoroshiya (dog killer), 72, 81, 167
Inumaru Tetsuzō, 95
Ise Yoshio, 223n58
Ishibashi Tanzan, 174
Ishii Kendō, 59
Ishikawa Chiyomatsu, 107–8, 215n61
Israel, 192–94
Istanbul, 19, 49, 79
Itagaki Shirō, 216n75
Itakura Itaru, 146–49
Itakura Yasuyuki, 147
Italy, 90, 214n44
Itō Hirobumi, 60
Ivy, Marilyn, 180
Iwane Seiichi, 65
Izu Peninsula, 34, 36–37

Jack, 37, 39, 41
jackals, 24, 40, 48, 55, 69, 85; jackal-like dogs, 43, 47
Jackson, A. V. Williams, 49
Japan Gazette, 37
Japan Humane Society (Nihon jindō kai), 79
Japan Kennel Club (Japan keneru kurabu), 174, 176, 178, 183, 185
Japan Shepherd Association (Nihon shepādo kyōkai), 138
Japan Shepherd Club (Nihon shepādo kurabu), 138, 148
Japan Society for the Prevention of Cruelty to Animals (Nihon dōbutsu aigo kyōkai), 128, 179, *181*
Japan Society of London, 43
Japan Weekly Mail, 49, 62, 76, 78
Japanese Communist Party, 116
Japanese Dog Association (Nihon inu kyōkai), 102
"Japanese" dogs: nationalization of, 91–101; official recognition of, 99. *See also* Hachikō; Society for the Preservation of the Japanese Dog
Japanese Imperial military, 91, 95–97, 105, 119; and military dogs, 132–41, 147; and Norakuro, 152–53. *See also* Kwantung Army; Self-Defense Force
"Japanese Rose," 26
Japanese spaniel. *See chin*
Japanese spoonbill, 213n29
japonisme, 25, 27
Jesuit missionaries, 30
Jimmu (emperor), 100, 223–24n62
Jindo Island, 106
jinshū (race), 105
Jirō, *100*, 179–80, *181*
jiyū minken undō (people's rights movement), 79–81
Johns Hopkins University, 98
Jones, D. W. Ap, 62–63, 65–67, 73, 208n24
Joyce, Barry Alan, 48
Jupin, Lieutenant J., 133, 221n11

"K-9 Corps," 157
Kaburagi Tokio, 98, 118

kaffir, 20–21, 23, 46

"*Kaika to fukaika no inu no hanashi*," 57–59

Kaikōsha, 168

Kaikōsha kiji, 134

Kaitakushi (Colonization Agency), *64*, 65, 66

Kakizaki Hakyō, 67

kame, 60, 61, 73, 79, 81

Kamikaze-gō, 96

kamishibai (picture-story shows), 146

Kanagaki Robun, 57, *58*

Kanagawa Prefecture, 35, 43, 73, 147, 166

Kase Toshikazu, 185

Kataoka Ken, 216n75

Kateiken (Family Dog magazine), 183

Kawakami Otojirō, 81

Keane, Hilda, 15

Keijō Imperial University, 106

Keller, Helen, 95–96, 124, 177

Kennel Club (English), 23, 176, 191–92, 201n14

Kenpeitai military police, 135, 140

Kenward, Mrs. William, 177

Kete, Kathleen, 21, 93, 108, 144

Kim Dae-jung, 231n71

Kim In Hwa, 143

Kim Jong-il, 231n71

Kip, W. Ruloff, 27

Kipling, John Lockwood, 28, 40, 46, 51, 56–57, 203n29

Kipling, Rudyard, 28, 43–44

Kirigaoka Shrine, 141

Kishi Kazutoshi, *88*, 99–100, 111, 115

Kita Reikichi, 163

Kitakyūshū, 164

Kitami, 136

Kiyosawa Kiyoshi, 166

Knollys, Henry, 77

Kobayashi Gen, 114

Kobayashi Kikuzaburō, 112–13

Kobayashi Takiji, 81

Kobe, *74*, 76, 210n71

Kōdansha publishing house, 151–53

Kodomo no shi kenkyū, 115

Koga Tadamichi, 216n75

Koinu to heitai-san (Yoshino), 149

Koizumi Jun'ichirō, 228n5

Kokkai kisei dōmeikai (League to Establish a National Assembly), 80

Kokken (National Dog magazine), 102

Kōkoku seishin kai (Imperial Spirit Society), 112

Kokutai meichō undō (Movement for the Clarification of the National Polity), 111

Kokutai no hongi (Fundamentals of our national polity), 103

kokutai (national political essence), 91

Koma-go, 101

Kongō, 136, 146–49, *150*, 157, 158, 160–61, 168

Korea, 2, 70, 85, 112, 135, 152, 154; elimination of indigenous dogs in, 141, 211n89; guard dogs in, 143, 223n48; indigenous dogs of, 40, 43, 49, 106; Japanese colonial dogs in, 131, 134–35, 138, 141–43; North Korea, 193, 231n71; postcolonial memories of colonial dogs in, 51, 164, 169; recognition of Korean dogs, 106, 192–94, 196; South Korea, 192–93, 231n71. *See also* Koreans

Koreana, 193

Koreans: dog eating by, 140, 185, 193

Kowongyeon, 143

Kū-chan, 187, 230n44

Kuki Ryūichi, 83

Kurahara Koreyoshi, 180

Kuroda Kiyotaka, 61

Kurosawa Akira, 168–69

Kusunoki Masashige, 83

Kwantung Army, 95, 136, 146–47

Lady and the Tramp (*Wanwan monogatari*), 178

Lahore Museum, 28

Laika, 180

lapdogs, 22, 26, 35, 39, 163, 188, 205n74; and Orientalism, 25–27; and popularity among wealthy women, 60. See also *chin;* toy dogs

Lassie (*Meiken Rasshī*), 178, 188

Law for Preserving Scenery and Historic and Natural Monuments (Shiseki meisho tennen kinenbutsu hozon hō), 97

Lawson, Lady Kate, 42–43

Lee, Ang, 169–70

Legally Blonde, 187
Legally Blonde II, 187
Leiden, 37–38
Leighton, Robert, 46
Lewis, Meriwether, 67
Liaodong Peninsula, 82, 84
Liberal Democratic Party, 127
Lindy, 173
lion, British, 89
Little, Alicia, 205n74
Little, Archibald John, 43, 205n74
livestock, 13, 55, 62, 65–66, 71, 163
Lowell, Percival, 40, 43
lower class, 22–24, 76
loyalty: and colonial dogs, 29, 54; definition of, 9; and Hachikō, 1, 108–16; of "Japanese" dogs, 123; lingering influence of, 195; of military dogs, 132, 146–49; and native dogs, 54–55; and Norakuro, 153–54; relationship to civilization and race, 8–12
Lust, Caution, 169–70
Lydekker, Richard, 48

MacArthur, Douglas, 176
MacKenzie, John M., 25, 201n133
Madame Yeddo, 26
Maekawa Senpan, 109
Manchukuo, 95, 105, 112, 136, 147, 154, 175. *See also* Manchuria
Manchuria, 106; and canine links to Japan, 105; Japanese intrusion into, 95; memories of colonial dogs in, 170; military, police, and guard dogs in, 131, 136–38, 142–44, 146–50, 153–54, 158–60; native dogs in, 85. *See also* Kongō; Manchurian Incident; Nachi
Manchurian Incident, 94–95, 116, 132, 135–36, 155, 157, 168, 170; and Kongō and Nachi, 136, 146–47
Manchurian Military-Dog Association (Manshū gun'yōken kyōkai), 136, 141
Manet, Édouard, 26
Mao Tse-tung, 220—21n8
Marumaru chinbun, 80
masculinity, 153, 187; of colonial dog, 25, 39; of "Japanese" dogs, 117–18, 120; of military dogs, 157

Master Sam Spooner, 26
Mastromarino, Mark A., 29
Matsumae clan, 67
Matsumori Taneyasu, 62
Matsuo, 82
Matsushita Corporation, 190
Matsuya department store, 101
McHugh, Susan, 188
Meguro, 158
Meiji emperor, 59, 101, 205n69
Meiji empress, 114
Meiji Restoration, 62, 82–84
Meiji Seika confectionary company, 178
Meiji Shrine, 112
Meiroku zasshi, 75
Meirokusha, 74
Merī, 146, 148
Messmer, Otto, 152
Miako, 26
Mickey Mouse, 152
middle class, 3, 39, 144, 188, 192, 231n77; American, 176; British, 3, 24; Japanese, 59–60, 79, 91–92, 95, 146, 172–75, 180–82, 185
Middle East, 19, 21, 23–24, 170, 193
Mikado Kennel, 110, *111*, 135, 155, 171, 173. *See also* Sawabe Kenjirō; Sawabe Shōzō; Washington Dog Shop
Mikado's Empire, The (Griffis), 19
military dogs: American, 133–34, 138–39, 155; and boys, 144–57; British, 134, 137–38, 156; Chinese, 132; as companions, 139; in education, 144–54; in Franco-Prussian War, 133; French, 133–34; gendering of, 117, 157; German, 134; and girls, 157–62; Japanese, 135–39, 146–50, 155–62; "Japanese" dogs as, 105, 118, 128; as mascots, 134, 139; memories of, 143–44, 167–70; and Mussolini, 90; practical value of, 134, 139; Soviet, 138; use by samurai, 133; use by Spanish conquestidors, 29
Minami Jirō, 147
Ministry of Education, 145–46, 213–14n29; and Hachikō, 108–11, 114–15, 127; and military dogs, 144, 147–48, 161; and Norakuro, 152; preservation of

Ministry of Education (cont.)
  indigenous "Japanese" dogs, 91, 97, 99,
  117, 196; preservation of native Korean
  dogs, 106
Ministry of the Environment, 186
Ministry of Foreign Affairs, 96, 111
Ministry of Home Affairs, 62, 213n29
Ministry of Munitions, 163
Ministry of Welfare, 163
Minoru, 176
minzoku (national people), 105
Misawa, 228n15
Mishima cattle, 213–14n29
missionaries, 30–31, 41
Miyagawa Kikuyoshi, 148–49, 224n67
Miyanoshita, 36
Miyoshi Manabu, 98
Mobutu Sese Seko, 51
Mollison, J. P., 37
Momotarō, 121–22, 151, 224n67
Monbetsu, 65
Mongolia, 120, 154
mongrel, 11
"mongrel" dogs, 3, 8, 25, 26, 45–46, 55,
  195; in Africa, 23, 46–47; in Britain,
  22–23, 25, 49; in Israel, 194; in Japan,
  47, 49, 85, 93, 152; in North America, 68
monkeys: "aping" Japanese as, 76; as mili-
  tary pets, 151; as Momotarō's vassal,
  121; and Norakuro, 152–53
Monument to the Loyal Dogs, 147
Mori Tamezō, 106
Moriyama Daidō, 228n15
Morris-Suzuki, Tessa, 105
Morse, Edward S., 39, 47–48, 60, 77,
  205n84, 215n61
Most, Konrad, 137
Mukden Incident. See Manchurian
  Incident
Museum of Japanese Occupation of
  Manchuria (Dongbei lunxian shi
  chenglieguan), 170
Mussolini, Benito, 90
My Life as a Dog, 85

Nachi, 136, 146–49, 150, 157–58, 160–61,
  168
Nagano Prefecture, 137, 166

Nagasaki, 37, 81
naichi ryokō (traveling within the country),
  74. See also unequal treaties
naichi zakkyo (mixed residences within the
  country), 74. See also unequal treaties
Naisen ittai (Japan and Korea as one
  body), 154
Najin, 142–43
Najita, Tetsuo, 93
Nakashima Satoru, 166
Nakasone Yasuhiro, 125
Nanba Shinshichirō, 60–61
Nankyoku de hataraita Karafuto-ken no
  kinenzō (Memorial statue to the Sakha-
  lin huskies who worked in Antarctica),
  179–80, 181
Nankyoku monogatari (Antarctica), 180
Nansō Satomi hakken-den (Bakin), 108
National Mobilization Law, 138
National Museum of Modern Art, 93
National Park Law, 98
National Science Museum, 87, 100, 101,
  107, 180
National Science Museum of Natural His-
  tory, 37
National Socialism (Nazism). See Germany.
nationalism: British, 21; Chinese, 170,
  207n97; Israeli, 193–94; Japanese, 1,
  51, 89, 93, 98, 105, 124, 127, 145–46;
  Korean, 192
Native Americans. See American Indians
native dog: belligerence of, 18–19, 40, 43;
  cowardliness of, 18, 40, 44; defined,
  18, 20–21; degeneration of, 18, 45–46;
  dislike for foreigners, 43; elimination
  of, 55, 62–66; filthiness of, 19, 49–50;
  identification with lower class people,
  75–77; as mongrels, 46–49, 55; pairing
  with colonial dog, 20, 39; and rabies,
  49–50, 55, 63–66; racialization of,
  46–47; savagery of, 18, 40, 68; stupidity of, 40; transformation into colonial
  dog, 2, 86, 91–92, 123, 192–94; treachery of, 69; wolfishness of, 18, 40, 43,
  47–49, 55, 63, 68
Nazis. See Germany
Nemuro, 66
Nepal, 25

Netherlands, 37, 191
New World. *See* Americas
New York City, 26, 157
New Zealand, 55, 69
NHK (Nihon hōsō kyōkai), 96, 112, 146
Nihon fashizumu hihan (Hasegawa), 116
Nihon inu kyōkai (Japanese Dog Association), 102
Nihon jindō kai (Japan Humane Society), 79
Nihon Television, 178
Nihon University, 102, 179
Nihonbashi, 135, 155, 171
Niigata Prefecture, 94
Niikappu ranch, 65
Nishi Amane, 74–75
Nitta Yoshisada, 112
Nogi Maresuke, 112
Noguchi Ujō, 112
Non-chan kumo ni noru (Non-chan riding on the clouds), 175
Norakuro (Tagawa), 151–54, 180
North America, 2, 24, 55, 67–69

Odajima Jirō (Odajima Jujin), 114
Ōdate, 87, 114, 213n16, 218n124
Ōdo rakudo (realm of peace and prosperity), 154
Ōe Kenzaburō, 167
Ogawara Shū, 228n5
Ōhira Ken, 184
Okakura Tenshin, 83
Okinawa, 5, 69. *See also* Ryukyu Islands
Oliphant, Laurence: 36, 38, 41, 42
"On o wasureru na" ("Don't forget your debts of gratitude"), 113–14
Ono Susumi, 114
Opium War, First, 28
"Oppekepē Song," 81
Orientalism, 25–27, 42
Ozu Yasujirō, 173

"parasite singles," 189
pariah, 20
pariah dogs, 18–20, 46, 48, 192; in China, 19; in eastern Europe, 48; in India, 19–20, 44; in Istanbul, 19, 49; in Japan, 50, 77; in the Middle East, 19, 21

Park Chung Hee, 192
Parkes, Sir Harry, 42, 205n69
Pearl Harbor, 132
Peony, 173
People, The (newspaper), 185
people's-rights movement (*jiyū minken undō*), 79–81
Perry, Jane, 26
Perry, Matthew C., 26, 28, 30, 34, 85, 202nn21–22
pet(s), 7, 10, 21–22, 29, 42, 49, 54, 77; definition of, 183; as products, 172, 182–91; during World War II, 163–64, 165–66
pet dogs, 17, 22, 44–45, 53, 108, 121, 189; and children, 151, 166, 189–90; commoditization of, 183–89; as companions, 6, 37, 173, 183, 188, 190, 195; cyberpets, 184, 186; disposal of, 164–65, 186; donation to military of, 154–57, 162, 165–66; as family members, 39, 180–81, 183, 190; and health problems, 191, 194–95; identification with colonizers and upper class, 28, 34, 73–75, 220—21n8; and middle class, 95, 172; military dogs as, 139; popularity of, 2–3, 144, 171–72, 182; and social ills, 189–90; as status symbol, 64, 172
pet stores, 171–73, 182–83, 187–88. *See also* Mikado Kennel; Washington Dog Shop
Peters, W. T., 26
pheasants: Mikado, 213n29; as Momotarō's vassal, 121
photography, 15–16, 87, 107, 158–60, 179, 190, 196
pie dog. *See* pariah dogs
pigeons, 77, 121, 127, 130, 152, 222n29
pigs: as symbol of Chinese, 153–54, 169
Pochi kurabu (Pooch Club), 113
police dogs, 131, 133–36, 138–41, 143–44, 165
Pollan, Michael, 12
Port Arthur, 105
Port-au-Prince, 203n38
puppy mills, 184, 186
purebred dogs: as companions of colonizers, 19–21, 28, 47, 49; definition of, 8;

purebred dogs *(cont.)*
  on "Dog Map of the World," 24; health disorders of, 191, 194–95; "Japanese" dogs, 93–94, 101–3, 106–7, 120, 128, 165; popularity of, 3, 6, 59, 81, 170; and rabies, 49–50; as representative of nations, 23–24, 129, 192–94; as status symbol, 140, 172–73, 188
Pusan, 143
Pyongyang, 231n71

Qing Empire, 5, 82, 199n6
Qingdao, 135–36, 148

rabbits, 76, 83, 166
rabies, 7, 54–55, 75–76; causes of, 49, 207n95; and class issues, 81; control and prevention of, 62–66, 71–73; and imperialism, 56; incidence of during nineteenth century, 49, 63, 65–66; Tokugawa-era outbreaks of, 69–70; during World War II, 164–65
race: and breed, 8–9, 194; definition of, 8; and domestication, 10; Japanese discourses about, 101–8; National Socialist notions of, 104–5; relationship to civilization and loyalty, 8–11; and Social Darwinian thought, 45
racism, scientific, 18, 40, 45–49, 53, 63, 67
Rags, 28
ranching, 55, 61, 64, 86
Reader's Digest, 174
Red Cross Society of Japan, 42
Renoir, Pierre-Auguste, 26
"rich country, strong army" (*fukoku kyōhei*), 5, 71
Richardson, E. H., 137
Rin Tin Tin, 134, 177
risshin shusse (advancement), 153
Ritvo, Harriet, 15, 21–23, 190
Roei no uta (Bivouac ballad), 155
Rokumeikan (Deer-cry Pavilion), 60, 76
rōnin, 42, 75; forty-seven Akō samurai, 112
Roosevelt, Franklin D., 150–51, 162
Roth, Frederick George Richard, 224n68
Rothschild family, 26
Royal Air Force, 156

Royal Army Veterinary Corps, 137
Royal Society for the Prevention of Cruelty to Animals, 137
"rumble in the jungle," 51
Rusling, James F., 68
Russo-Japanese War, 85, 115, 136
Rutgers College, 19
Ryukyu Islands, 5, 41, 106, 202n22. *See also* Okinawa
Ryukyu, Kingdom of, 41

Sabata Toyoyuki, 186
Sada Masashi, 181
Saigō Takamori, 83–84, 86, 155, 211n91
Saitō Hirokichi (Saitō Hiroshi): and breed standards, 95–99, 102–6, 117–19; correspondence with Stephanitz, 106; and Hachikō, 94, 106–7, 110–11, 113, 115–17, 124, 126–29; and Jirō and Tarō, 179–80; and the Society for the Preservation of the Japanese Dog, 93, 95, 122–23, 128; and the Society for the Prevention of Cruelty to Animals, 128, 179
Sakano Hisako, 111
Sakura, 37–38
samurai, 9, 25, 57, 59, 63, 108; attacks on Westerners, 42, 205n66, 205n69; comparisons to "Japanese" dogs, 109, 118; and dog eating, 164; and military dogs, 133. *See also* rōnin
San Fran, 174
Sandy, 162
Sapporo, 65–66
Sapporo Agricultural College, 66
Sasaki Hideichi, 216n75
Sassa Atsuyuki, 125–26, 218–19n126
Sassa Hirō, 218–19n126
Sassa Tomofusa, 218–19n126
Satsuma, 84
Sawabe Kenjirō, 135, 155, 171, 174, 176, 178–79
Sawabe Shōzō, 155–56, 178–79
Sax, Boria, 91
Seaman, 67
Seidensticker, Edwin, 88
Seiyō dōchū hizakurige (Kanagaki), 57
Sekai, 168

Self-Defense Force, 168, 219n127, 227n133
Sensen ni hoeyu (Barks at the battlefront), 157, 160
September 18 Incident Historical Museum ("Jin Yiba" lishi bowuguan), 170
Sergeant Okamoto, 151
Serpell, James, 6
Shah, 42
Shandong Peninsula, 134–35
Shanghai, 135, 141, 173
sheep, 62–65, 154, 200–201n1, 210n55
sheepdogs, 64,
shepherd dog. *See* "German" shepherd
Shibuya railway station, 87, 94, 109, *111*, 112–14, 124, 126, 128
Shidehara Kijūrō, 174
Shiga Shigetaka, 61
Shimizu Yoshitarō, 117
Shimoda (dog), 26
Shimoda (village), 36, 41
Shimōsa ranch, 62–63
Shinoda Mariko, 98
Shizunai experimental farm, 65
Shizuoka Prefecture, 34
Shōchiku-Fuji movie studio, 88
Shōhei o nakaseta gunba inu hato bukun monogatari (Stories of Gallant War Horses, Dogs, and Pigeons that Caused Soldiers to Weep), 121, 149
Shōnen kurabu (Boys' club), 59, 151–54, 223n58
Shōwa kenkyūkai (Shōwa Research Association), 217n98, 218–19n126
Shūzenji Temple, 34
Siddle, Richard, 67
Siebold, Philipp Franz von, 37–38
SieboldHuis Museum, 38
Sims, Joseph Patterson, 201–2n14
Sino-Japanese War, First, 82, 84
Sittert, Lance van, 69
slavery, 29, 48, 67
sled dogs, *100*, 179–80
Snowy, 153
social Darwinism, 8, 16, 45, 47, 68, 89
Society for the German Shepherd Dog (Verein für deutsche Schäferhunde), 92, 136

Society for the Preservation of the Japanese Dog (Nihon ken hozon kai), *94, 94*–95, 97–99, 103–5, 118–20, 122, 165, 196; branches in the colonies, 106, 141; breeding standards, 101–2; establishment of, 93; and Hachikō, 94, 101, 109, 112–13, 115, 124; membership, 97; reestablishment of, 128. *See also* Saitō Hirokichi
Society for the Prevention of Abuse to Animals (Dōbutsu gyakutai bōshi kai), 78
Soeda Juichi, 141, *142*
South Africa, 46–47
South America, 23
South American Wolf, 24
South Manchurian Railway, 136, 138
South Pole, 179
Southern Barbarian (*Nanbanjin*), 30
Soviet Union, 138, 153
Spivak, Gayatri, 13–14, 16
Spot, 151
SS (Schutzstaffel), 139
stamps, commemorative: Hachikō, 88; Jirō and Tarō, 180; Norakurō, 151
Stephanitz, Max von, 95, 97, 106, 118–19, 121, 136–37, 194; *Der deutsche Schäferhund in Wort und Bild*, 92, 99, 103–4, 108, 119
Stirling, Admiral Sir James, 26
stray dog(s), 42, 75, 88, 99, 112, 151–53; adopted as pets, 134, 175; attacks by, 186; elimination of, 77–78, 81, 164, 166, 186; Hachikō as, 113, 117; policing of, 79; regulations against, 71–73; around U.S. military bases, 228n15. *See also* dogcatchers
strychnine, 65
Stubby, 134
Sullivan, Pat, 152
Supreme Commander for the Allied Powers (SCAP), 124
Suzuki Takurō, 213n18
Syria, 19

Tade kuu mushi (*Some Prefer Nettles*) (Tanizaki), 173
Tagawa Suihō (Takamizawa Nakatarō), 152–54
Tahitians, 48

Taiwan, 64, 79, 106, 112; campaigns against native dogs in, 82, 141; colonial dogs in, 134–35, 138, 141, *142;* colonization of, 5, 82, 84; memories of colonial dogs in, 169

Takahisa Heishirō, 103

Takamura Kōun, 83

Takashimaya department store, 171, 173

Takayama Takao, 114–15

Tamagotchi, 184

Tani Kanjō, 79

Tanizaki Jun'ichirō, 173

Tarō, 179–80, *181*

"Tarō's dog," 85

taxidermy, 15–16, 127, 180, 196, 224n68; and Hachikō, 87–88, *100*, 101, 107

Temminck, Conrad Jacob, 37, *38*

Terashima Munenori, 63

Teshima Tamie, 158–60, 162–63, 166

Tetsu, 126

Third Reich. *See* Germany

Thomas, Julia Adeney, 98

Thomas, Keith, 2, 54, 108

Tierra Del Fuego, 45

Timber Wolf, 24

Tintin, 153

Toba-e, 34, 76–77

Toby, 28

Tōei movie studio, 220n2

Tōgō Heihachirō, 115

Tōhoku Imperial University, 105

Tōjō Hideki, 220n2

Tokaidō railway line, 124

Tokibō, 61–62

Tokugawa Period, 9, 26, 30–31, 38, 42, 67, 102, 108; canine ecology during, 25, 37, 54; consumption of dog meat during, 164; Dog Shogun, 61, 70; elimination of dogs during, 70–72; rabies outbreaks during, 70

Tokugawa Tsunayoshi (Dog Shogun), 61, 70

Tokugawa Yoshinobu, 59

Tokyo, 42, 56, 60, 62–64, 83, 87–88, 93–96, 112; and dog regulations, 71–73, 81, 165; and Hachikō, 1, 94, *100*, 114, 124–25; and military dogs, 155, 166;

police, 78, 134; and rabies, 63. *See also* Edo; Meguro; Nihonbashi

Tokyo Agricultural University, 217n103

Tokyo bijutsu gakkō (Tokyo Fine Arts Academy), 93

Tokyo Chamber of Commerce, 124

Tokyo Chikuken, 184–86

Tokyo Imperial Hotel, 95, *96*

Tokyo Imperial University, 39, 87, 98, 118, 125, 215n55, 217n103

Tōkyō kaika hanjō shi, 56

Tokyo Military Dog Training Research Group, *159*

Tokyo Tower, 180, *181*

tonarigumi (neighborhood associations), 163

total war, 4, 130–31, 133, 167

toy dogs, 25, 70. *See also* lapdogs

Tōzenji Temple, 42, 205n68

treaty revision, 74–77, 84

treaty-port system, 5

Trooper, U.S. Army Dog (Watson), 157

Tsukamoto Manabu, 3, 35

Tsurumi, Kazuko, 167

Tuttle, William M., Jr., 157

Uchida Roan, 84–85

Uchimura Kanzō, 66

Ueno Eizaburō, 87, 111–12, 114, 117

Ueno Park, 83, 87, 155

Ueno Yaeko, 112, 114, 215n64

Ueno Zoological Gardens, 157

Ugaki Kazushige, 141

Uma (Horse), 220n2

Umarete wa mita keredo (I Was Born, But...), 173, 175

umeyo fuyaseyo (be fruitful and multiply), 164

unequal treaties, 30, 54, 71, 74, 77, 82

Unit 731, 220n7

United States, 21, 26, 64, 90, 96, 98, 122, 165; and Akita, 177; alliance with Japan, 174; bombing of Japan by, 126, 128, 171; on "Dog Map of the World," 23–25; dog keeping in, 144, 171, 173, 178, 183; dog population of, 172, 187; elimination of canines in, 3, 55, 69, 186; and "German" dogs, 117, 177–78;

and Hachikō, 112; imperialism of, 4–5, 11, 19, 30, 62, 67–68; and lapdogs, 26–27, 165; military, 133–34, 138–39, 155, 174, 176, 220n3, 226n109, 228n15; and military dogs, 134, 137–38, 151, 155, 157, 162, 164, 167; occupation of Japan by, 3, 171, 175–76; postwar influence of, 127, 171–72, 179, 187

University of Pennsylvania, 179

upper class, 172; and dog keeping, 22, 62, 76, 81; middle class influenced by, 60

Utagawa Yoshifuji, 53

Veblen, Thorstein, 172, 188

Victoria, Queen, 26

waken. *See* "Japanese" dogs

Walker, Brett L., 47

war dogs. *See* military dogs

Washington Dog Shop (Washinton inuten), 171, 174, 178–79. *See also* Mikado Kennel

Waste of Food Order, 163

Watanabe Shin'ichirō, 213n18

Watase Shōzaburō, 98

Watson, Helen Orr, 157

West Bank, 94

Western dogs: privileging of, 24–25, 57–60, 72–73, 85, 99, 179

Western imperialism: age of exploration and conquest, 29–30; nineteenth and early twentieth century, 1–4, 6, 10, 25, 47, 50, 53–55, 86, 184, 191

Westminster Kennel Club, 26

whiteness, 39

Wild Dog of East Africa, 24

wild dogs (*yaken*), 7, 47–49, 53–56, 63–71, 75, 103, 164; in China, 121, 142, 149; on "Dog Map of the World," 24; in Taiwan, 82

Wipperman, Wolfgang, 104

wolves, 7, 87, 93, *100*, 120, 149; extermination of, 48, 54–55, 62, 65–67; as fascist symbol, 91, 103–4; relationship to canines, 47–48, 68–70, 85, 103–4, 118;

Romulus and Remus, 214n44; wolfish and wolf-like dogs, 18–20, 43, 47–48, 55, 68, 103–4, 118, 206n84

working class. *See* lower class

World War I (First World War), 130, 152, 177, 222n32, 227n121; canine mobilization during, 132, 134–35, 137

World War II (Second World War), 91, 93, 96, 167, 171–72, 185, 187; canine and human mobilization during, 130, 132–33, 138–39, 144, 151–54, 226n109

Wright, Frank Lloyd, 95

Yaegaki, 60

Yamada Shunryō, 119

Yamagata Prefecture, 62, 93, 214n41

Yamaguchi Masao, 152

Yamaguchi Otaya, 128

Yamamoto Kajirō, 109, 130, 168, 220n2

Yamamoto Teijirō, 111, 126–27

Yamanaka Minetarō, 223n58

Yamato damashii (Japanese spirit), 121, 145, 149

Yamato state, 63

Yanagita Kunio, 72, 103–4, 214n41

Yasukuni Shrine, *160*, 168, 231n61

Yasuoka Akio, 138

Yiddo, 26

yōken. See Western dogs

Yokohama, 20, 31, *33*, 34–38, 42–43, 50, 73, 84, 178

Yokohama kaikō kenmonshi (Hashimoto), 31, *33*

Yokohama-e (Yokohama pictures), 31–34

Yoshida Shigeru, 174

Yoshikawa Chūichi, 114, 216n75

Yoshino Yumisuke, 149

Young, Louise, 147

Yoyogi, 123

Yume (*Dreams*), 168–69

Yume Inu DX (Dream Inu DX), 184

Yūshūkan (Yūshūkan Military and War Memorial Museum), 168, 231n61

zodiac (Chinese), 61, 152, 213n20, 229n28

Zushi, 147, 168

STUDIES OF THE WEATHERHEAD
EAST ASIAN INSTITUTE

COLUMBIA UNIVERSITY

Selected Titles

Complete list at: http://www.columbia.edu/cu/weai/weatherhead-studies.html.

Planning for Empire: Reform Bureaucrats and the Japanese Wartime State, by Janis Mimura. Cornell University Press, 2011.

Passage to Manhood: Youth Migration, Heroin, and AIDS in Southwest China, by Shao-hua Liu. Stanford University Press, 2010.

Imperial Japan at Its Zenith: The Wartime Celebration of the Empire's 2,600th Anniversary, by Kenneth J. Ruoff. Cornell University Press, 2010.

Behind the Gate: Inventing Students in Beijing, by Fabio Lanza. Columbia University Press, 2010.

Postwar History Education in Japan and the Germanys: Guilty Lessons, by Julian Dierkes. Routledge, 2010.

The Aesthetics of Japanese Fascism, by Alan Tansman. University of California Press, 2009.

The Growth Idea: Purpose and Prosperity in Postwar Japan, by Scott O'Bryan. University of Hawai'i Press, 2009.

National History and the World of Nations: Capital, State, and the Rhetoric of History in Japan, France, and the United States, by Christopher Hill. Duke University Press, 2008.

Leprosy in China: A History, by Angela Ki Che Leung. Columbia University Press, 2008.

Kingdom of Beauty: Mingei and the Politics of Folk Art in Imperial Japan, by Kim Brandt. Duke University Press, 2007.

Mediasphere Shanghai: The Aesthetics of Cultural Production, by Alexander Des Forges. University of Hawai'i Press, 2007.

Modern Passings: Death Rites, Politics, and Social Change in Imperial Japan, by Andrew Bernstein. University of Hawai'i Press, 2006.

The Making of the "Rape of Nanjing": The History and Memory of the Nanjing Massacre in Japan, China, and the United States, by Takashi Yoshida. Oxford University Press, 2006.

Bad Youth: Juvenile Delinquency and the Politics of Everyday Life in Modern Japan, 1895–1945, by David Ambaras. University of California Press, 2005.

Rearranging the Landscape of the Gods: The Politics of a Pilgrimage Site in Japan, 1573–1912, by Sarah Thal. University of Chicago Press, 2005.

The Merchants of Zigong: Industrial Entrepreneurship in Early Modern China, by Madeleine Zelin. Columbia University Press, 2005.

Science and the Building of a Modern Japan, by Morris Low. Palgrave Macmillan, 2005.

Kinship, Contract, Community, and State: Anthropological Perspectives on China, by Myron L. Cohen. Stanford University Press, 2005.

Reluctant Pioneers: China's Expansion Northward, 1644–1937, by James Reardon-Anderson. Stanford University Press, 2005.

Takeuchi Yoshimi: Displacing the West, by Richard Calichman. Cornell East Asia Program, 2004.

Gutenberg in Shanghai: Chinese Print Capitalism, 1876–1937, by Christopher A. Reed. UBC Press, 2004.

Japan's Colonization of Korea: Discourse and Power, by Alexis Dudden. University of Hawai'i Press, 2004.

Divorce in Japan: Family, Gender, and the State, 1600–2000, by Harald Fuess. Stanford University Press 2004.